Empire Builder Extraordinary, Sir George Goldie

Sir George Goldie painted in 1898 by Hubert von Herkomer, R.A. (1849-1914). *Courtesy The National Portrait Gallery, London.*

EMPIRE
BUILDER
EXTRAORDINARY

SIR GEORGE GOLDIE

His Philosophy of Government and Empire

D. J. M. Muffett

L'oeuvre c'est tout; L'homme c'est rien.

*It is what is accomplished that matters; not the man who
accomplishes it.*

SHEARWATER PRESS
DOUGLAS . ISLE OF MAN

For A.D.E.M.

". . . . . it is not the beginning or the continuing,
but the carrying on until it is utterly finished that
yieldeth the true glory."

From a prayer written by Sir Francis Drake
before Cadiz, April 19, 1587.

© D. J. M. Muffett

First Published 1978

ISBN 0 904980 18 9

Printed in the Isle of Man
by Bridson & Horrox Limited,
for Shearwater Press Limited,
Welch House, Church Road,
Onchan, Isle of Man.

A note on the Motto which Sir George Goldie adopted as his guiding principle.

In frequent correspondence with his friends, Goldie alluded to the motto reproduced on the title page, *L'oeuvre c'est tout; L'homme c'est rien.* This is actually a misquotation—or perhaps, rather, a reformulation—of a line which Gustave Flaubert (1821-1880) wrote to George Sand (Amandine-Aurore-Lucille Dudevant, née Dupin, 1804-1876) in December, 1875, *L'homme n'est rien, l'oeuvre tout.* It is recorded in *Lettres de Gustave Flaubert à George Sand*, Charpentier, Paris, 1889.

Goldie's modification of it is curiously reflected in a remark that Sherlock Holmes is made to say to Dr. Watson in the closing sentence of "The Adventure of the Red Headed League", which appeared in the *Strand Magazine* of August, 1891, where he employs the phrase as *L'homme c'est rien—l'oeuvre c'est tout,* thus using the correct order of Flaubert as well as the inaccurate wording of Goldie.

It is interesting to speculate, in view of the close similarity of attitude on Imperial affairs to which they both adhered, whether Doyle acquired the quote from Goldie, and thus whether there was not, therefore, something of Goldie in Holmes!

The full translation of the quotation in its context is:—

"But, in the ideal vision that I have of art, I believe that it is not right to show anything of *self,* and that an artist ought no more to appear in his work than does God appear in nature. The man is nothing, the work is everything! This discipline, which can sometimes originate from a misconception, is not easy to follow."

"Mais dans l'idéal que j'ai de l'art, je crois qu'on ne doit rien montrer des siennes, et que l'artiste ne doit pas plus apparaître dans son oeuvre que Dieu dans la nature. L'homme n'est rien, l'oeuvre tout! Cette discipline, qui peut partir d'un point de vue faux, n'est pas facile à observer."

Crossing the Asa River after leaving Ilorin. *Courtesy U.A.C. International.*

Table of Contents

Preface

Only two biographies of Sir George Goldie exist. They are, first, that by Lady Gerald Wellesley (née Dorothy Ashton), [1] step-daughter of the Earl of Scarbrough. The work is a warm and human memoir, *Sir George Goldie: Founder of Nigeria,* based primarily on her adolescent memories of him, and it was published by Macmillan and Company within a decade of his death. It also contains, by way of an introduction, an interesting historical essay by Stephen Gwynn. [2] The book reflects, in a manner that a more sophisticated and structured study never could, the magnetism and charisma of the subject and the sheer integrity of his massive intellect.

The second work is that of Dr. J. E. Flint, *Sir George Goldie and the making of Nigeria,* published by the Oxford University Press in 1960. This book is a meticulous and valuable analysis of the period during which he was most closely associated with the political and commercial development of areas of the Niger Basin, and it contains, in addition, some interesting details of his life both before and after that particular episode. It also leaves a number of fascinating questions unanswered.

There is a Hausa proverb—of which Sir George would probably have disapproved mightily had he heard it, as well he might have done—*Wak'a a bakin mai ita ta fi dad'i.* A song sounds sweetest from the lips of its composer. Goldie's reservations would have stemmed however from his whole-hearted rejection and condemnation of self-advertisement, and this is not the issue here.

For years it has been the conventional wisdom that with the exception of his introduction to one book—C. F. S. Vandeleur's *Campaigning on the Upper Nile and Niger* [3] (Methuen, 1898)—Goldie left nothing of his original writing behind him. It is true that sometime shortly after the outbreak of the First World War he did destroy all personal papers, though why he did so, even though made public for decades, has been largely misconstrued. [4] Nothing will ever be able to obscure the loss to students of either Africa or Empire that this destruction represents, ranking as it does with the incendiarist orgy of Lady Burton who burned a mass of her husband's unpublished manuscripts and diaries immediately upon his death in 1890. Biographers

9

like Wellesley and Flint, the fortunate ones, were thus compelled to have recourse to those private collections of papers in which his correspondence was preserved, such as the Scarbrough Papers or the John Holt Papers, or in the case of Dame Margery Perham, the Lugard Papers. But it is not only in such restricted intercourse that the image of a *public man* emerges. Private relationships of this nature tell only half the story, for such a man has always two aspects to his character, the private and the public, and they are complimentary.

It came as a pleasing revelation, therefore, during research on a much broader analysis of the interactions of the mercantile community on the Middle Niger with the various components of the Sokoto Caliphate between 1870 and 1900—research that began in 1963 and is still incomplete—to discover that there *was* to be found a number of items for which Goldie had been responsible.

In fact, as the research developed, it become clear that far from there being a paucity, there was a veritable plethora of them—one, moreover, which needed to be handled with a certain amount of rigour if it was to be kept within reasonable bounds and under satisfactory discipline.

A simple, but logical, set of criteria was therefore applied by which to assess the value of each piece for reproduction. It was as follows:—

(i) All articles, monographs or addresses written or delivered by Goldie have been reproduced in full if a third party saw fit to publish them for public dissemination, it being argued that it (and therefore contemporary thought) must thereby have regarded his views on the subject to have been of relevance to the issue being examined.

(ii) All letters which Goldie wrote to the *Times* and such items appearing in that organ headed "Sir George Goldie on . . .", as well as verbatim interviews with correspondents, where they could be located, have also been fully reprinted, on the grounds that if Goldie thought sufficient of a matter to write to the *Times* about it, it must have seemed important to *him,* while if the Editor, or Reuters' Agency, sought his views on any matter, what he said about it must have appeared worthwhile to *them.*

(iii) Those obituary notices that Goldie composed on others, and which were not reproduced in the "commercial" Press, are reprinted on the grounds that if he thought enough of a person so to write about him, then their relationship must have been one of importance.

(iv) Scholarly articles or presentations by him appearing in the journals or periodicals of learned societies etc., have been fully reproduced, where they can be traced, though it is freely accepted that others may yet come to light if the search is sufficiently diligent, as indeed may also be the case in respect of any other of the classifications.

(v) Addresses and speeches made in a presidential or other capacity in a public forum have been fully reprinted, as have those of sufficient importance before learned societies etc., but some others, e.g. those of a "housekeeping" nature such as "Reviews of the year's activities'' etc. have been edited to eliminate merely parochial concerns.

The result has been the accumulation of:—

(a) Seven articles, monographs or reviews.
(b) Twenty-eight letters to the *Times,* three exclusive interviews and four expressions of opinion.
(c) Three obituaries.
(d) Five scholarly presentations, and
(e) Seven addresses to learned and philanthropic societies.

The following study therefore reproduces, it is believed, almost all— or at least a great deal—of the public writing or speaking of Sir George Goldie on a variety of important contemporary issues that has survived the indifference of his fellows or his set determination to eradicate as much of his own memorial as he could.

To this there are two exceptions. The first is that his Report to the shareholders of the Royal Niger Company, Chartered and Limited on the conduct of the 1897 Bida and Ilorin Campaign has not been included because its specialised nature demands a closer and more detailed examination than a study of this sort could afford it and because such is, in fact, now well advanced. The second is that the observations made at the Annual General Meeting of the Royal Niger Company (or of its predecessors) have been omitted, whether Goldie was in the chair or not, because it is impossible to say at what point or to what extent Goldie alone was speaking, or the degree to which, for example, Lord Aberdare was enunciating Goldie's views, or Goldie was reflecting the views of others. Frequent quotations have been employed, however, as necessary.

Many fascinating insights into Goldie's mind and character follow from what he said or wrote in public. From it too, may be drawn some interesting conclusions as to his philosophy of Government and Empire, which the monograph incorporated also seeks to amplify. For the same reasons, the relevant sections of the 1898 Selborne Committee Report on the future of the Niger Territories, Lagos and the Niger Coast—a Committee on which Goldie played a dominant role—have also been included.

1975 marked the fiftieth anniversary of Sir George Goldie's death which occurred on 20th August, 1925. By his contemporaries his contribution to Africa and Empire was recognised as being gigantic and both he and it were applauded, though, admittedly more by the cognoscente than by officialdom. But after his virtually complete withdrawal from public life, which occurred about the time of the outbreak of the First World War, the remembrance of his achievement began to be obscured. It is not without its significance and its poignancy that Lady Wellesley felt compelled to reproduce on the fly-leaf of her memoir the quotation: ''Herostratus lives that burnt the Temple of Diana: He is almost lost that built it.'' (Sir Thomas Browne, 1605-82).

11

History has a habit of redressing the swings of its analytical pendulum. Reputations do not always survive pristine and others are often refurbished. It may be that fifty years after his death, it is not too soon to reconsider that of George Dashwood Taubman Goldie.

It would be remiss indeed to fail to acknowledge that without the dedicated enthusiasm of Mrs. Erica Strasser, Mr. Harry Hutchinson and Mr. William Spinelli, all of the Reference Department of the Duquesne University Library, the many sources which have been drawn upon could never have been tapped, or that without the generous assistance of Mr. Bernard Cheeseman and the Staff of the Library and Records Department of the Foreign and Commonwealth Office, London, who served as a sort of court of last resort, some of the most interesting items of all would not have been forthcoming. A very special debt is owed to Miss K. Brooks of the United Africa Company for her help in tracing documents in the Public Records Office and to Dr. Emma Kirk of Duquesne University for her help in tracing Goldie's classical allusions.

All faults and shortcomings are my own.

D. J. M. MUFFETT.

Institute of African Affairs,
Duquesne University,
Pittsburgh,
Pennyslvania.
20th August, 1975.

(1) Wellesley, Dorothy Violet, Duchess of Wellington, 1889-1956. Daughter of Robert Ashton of Croughton, Cheshire. After her father's death, her mother married the 10th Earl of Scarbrough in 1899. In 1914, Dorothy Ashton married Lord Gerald Wellesley who succeeded his nephew as seventh Duke in 1943. Poet, romantic, natural rebel (Victoria Sackville-West in D.N.B.), she was befriended both by Goldie and W. B. Yeats, who greatly admired her work.

(2) Gwynn, Stephen Lucius, 1864-1950. Author and Irish Nationalist; educated at St. Columbia's College, Dublin and Brasenose College, Oxford; First Class *lit hum.* 1886, Nationalist M.P. Galway City; Published *Lives* of Goldsmith, Mary Kingsley, Scott, R. L. Stevenson and Swift, and co-author of a *Life of Sir Charles Wentworth Dilke.*

(3) See page 113 *et seq.*

(4) As it appears, Goldie felt that the War deprived his work of value, made him outdated, and that the peace, when it came, would be cause for fear. See Wellesley, *op cit.,* p. 145. See also p. 30 ff.

I

Sir George Goldie:
Visionary, Statesman, Adventurer

Sir George Goldie in private life. *Courtesy The Manx Museum, Douglas, Isle of Man.*

CHAPTER I

"Ah! did you once see Shelly plain,
And did he stop and speak to you?"

Robert Browning. *Memorabilia I*

"All achievement" he said "begins with a dream. My dream, as a child, was to colour the map red." [1] He did so.

Yet it was also this same man who extracted a most solemn promise from both his son and his daughter not only that they would never write anything about him themselves, but that they would not even assist, directly or indirectly, any one else to do so either. "All that I wish to be recorded of myself can be read under the articles headed 'Nigeria' and 'Goldie' in the *Encyclopaedia Britannica*. If you break this promise to me I swear I will rise and haunt you." [2]

Somewhere between these two extremes, the one a burning childhood ambition—which, be it added, he accomplished in good measure—maturing into an urge for achievement, the other a reticence that inspired an ever-present ache to go unrecognised, lies the enigma that was George Dashwood Taubman Goldie, for such was the name of his own choosing.

He was born on Wednesday the twentieth of May, 1846 and his real name then was Goldie-Taubman. His father, Lieutenant-Colonel Sir John Taubman Goldie-Taubman, formerly of the Scots Guards, was Speaker of the House of Keys in the Isle of Man. His mother was Caroline Hoveden of Hemingford in Cambridgeshire. She was her husband's second wife and there was a step-brother and sister by the former marriage and two brothers by the second.

The family was well to do but not wealthy, at least not by nineteenth century standards. It sprang from the same stock—the Squirearchy—that had provided very many of the soldiers, sailors and statesmen who, between the seventeenth and twentieth centuries, graced the English scene. Wellington and the elder Pitt are but two of the kind. Wolfe was another. Washington was also of the same breed, albeit transplanted across the Atlantic.

Very little indeed is known about Goldie's childhood. "I had the good fortune" he once remarked, "to lose both my parents before they could have any influence on me."[3] Perhaps this was part of the extraordinary empathy that existed between the Goldie of the later years and the young Dorothy Ashton, step-daughter of his dear friend and admirer, Lord Scarbrough.

There is some evidence that later in life Goldie realised that as a younger man he had in fact sought to find surrogates for the lost relationship. When Lord Aberdare, who had been the first Chairman both of the National African Company and of the Royal Niger Company, died in 1895, Goldie wrote to Scarbrough:-"I certainly felt for him all the affection and respect that a son has for a noble father [and he] . . . wrote me once that he looked on me as a younger brother."[4]

People other than his parents however did have a most profound influence upon the formation of his character. Darwin was one, and Huxley was another. In fact, his friendship with Leonard Darwin, the great man's fourth surviving son, endured throughout both of their lives and it is to Major Darwin (of whom more later) that some of the most intimate insights into Goldie's character are due.

One of the great passions of his life was reading, and he read omnivorously. "I never travelled [in Egypt] without an extra camel to carry my books alone."[5] Towards the end of his life he derived a great deal of comfort from this interest. His last letter to Dorothy Ashton, dated 12th June, 1924, contains the following passage:—" . . . I read most of the day and night, and am quite content and peaceful, taking if possible more interest than before in life and thought. I could do with more than 24 hours in the day, and am never bored."[6] Almost his last words were:—"I am spending my last twenty-four hours of life in my favourite occupation: reading."[7]

To some extent therefore, Goldie's education was highly selective and in this respect it mirrors the same pattern that another near-contemporary—though a full generation his junior and one who has impinged much more positively upon our own times—adopted for his own—Winston Churchill, an equally scatterbrain subaltern who came to realise his need for the intellectual stimulation of books relatively late in life.

The evidence indeed—though it is all indirect—is that, as a child, George was self-willed, somewhat precocious,[8] and give to fits of almost ungovernable temper as well as to dark spells of introspection. These at any rate are the characteristics that Dorothy Ashton identifies most critically with episodes of her own youthful development and which, it appears, most evoked his sympathy. "How you remind me of my youth," he would say on such occasions, assuring her whilst comforting her that he had been just like she was, only "far more so."[9]

Second to his reading came his love of Wagner's music, which had been with him since his boyhood and which in no way diminished in spite of a somewhat bizarre chance encounter with the composer in a German railway carriage a few years later.[10]

As in most similar cases, the family holdings were entailed. The house on the Isle of Man, near Douglas, was known as "The Nunnery" and it is no coincidence that the old Royal Niger Company house in Lokoja, from whence Goldie embarked upon his finest hour in 1897, is still known by this name. But the system left little in prospect for a younger son. The Army, probably, perhaps the Church, or as a far-out last resort, the Law; but in 1862, the time when George had to make his choice, *Commerce* was unthinkable!

The only surprise, therefore, in the choice he did make, was the choice itself—the Royal Engineers,. Every self-respecting officer of the Cavalry or of the Line or of the "Brigade" knew that *all* "Sappers" were either "Mad, Married or Methodist." Mad, because who but a lunatic would opt for such an Arm; Married, because they were paid a pittance more than the others and could afford to marry as subalterns (which nobody else could), and Methodist because they were essentially "not quite", being drawn from the emergent technological elite of the burgeoning middle class.

Nevertheless, it was with this very group that George Taubman Goldie, with a family tradition firmly allied to the Brigade of Guards, chose to associate himself, and accordingly he entered Woolwich in 1863. He was commissioned in 1865. He was not a studious or even particularly motivated cadet!

"I was like a gun-powder magazine. I was blind drunk when I passed my final examination for the Engineers. Two years later a relation died leaving me his fortune. I was so excited by the freedom that this gave me, that I bolted without sending in my papers, and leaving all my belongings behind. I went straight to Egypt. There I fell in love with an Arab girl. We lived in the desert for three years. Garden of Allah! She died of consumption. I came home to lead a life of idleness and dissipation." (11)

That these three years, spent as some claim, and as Goldie himself often implies, in a Bedouin encampment along the Upper Nile and in the Sudan, had a profound effect on the formation of Goldie's perceptions as to the character, longings and aspirations of the native peoples of Africa goes without saying. Few indeed are the colonial pro-consuls who can draw upon the experience of three years spent in the bosom of a tribal society and the understanding that this inevitably must bring. Moreover, the very existence of this episode presupposes a materially different attitude towards the native populations than, for example, that of Lugard, whose "Secret Circular B", issued in 1914 when he had become Governor-General of an amalgamated northern and southern Nigeria, had to be so hastily withdrawn because of its impracticality and the sense of outrage which some of its more pungent observations engendered. (12)

From this Egyptian experience, also, undoubtedly stemmed Goldie's perception—as he described it—of "the essential homogeneity of this great belt of Africa which is called the Sudan—extending from Senegambia to the Red Sea." (13) This was the concept that fired his enthusiasm and was to bring him to Africa for a second time to begin his life's work.

He returned from the desert broken-hearted. It is almost certainly to

this period that he refers when he confided in Dorothy Ashton that when he was "a young man he had himself considered the question of suicide, and had decided once and for ever against it. 'I always carry, however,' he added, 'a tube of poison in my pocket in case of accident. I would not live if mutilated or incurably ill.' "(14)

But he was not a man to mourn too long—"I am never sorry for the dead."(15) Employed in the Nunnery at that time was a governess, Matilda Catherine Elliot, a Yorkshire girl, and the two fell head over heels in romantic love. There then followed an elopement, in the best tradition of the times, to Paris—the Paris, precisely, of *Nana* and the then epitome of "Sin City." How permanent the liaison had been intended in the first place is not clear. George "was very fond of women, and no man admitted it more frankly." Much later in life, reports of his personal relationships did him damage in Court circles and are said to have affected the attitude of Queen Victoria towards him. (16)

If, as appears to be most likely, the association was regarded as the mere satisfaction of a passing fancy however, both parties miscalculated. For they reached Paris only a short time before the Prussian Army, and did not get out until the siege was lifted on 28th January, 1871. By then the couple were irrevocably compromised.

On the scandal that was created, the record is silent. The pressures, both on Goldie and the girl (she was twenty-three to Goldie's twenty-four), the horrified family conferences, the tears and the recriminations, the accusations and the anger can therefore only be guessed at. The upshot, however was that on 8th July, 1871, the two were quietly married at St. Marylebone Church in London. Throughout his life, Goldie always insisted that his marriage dated from 1870. In Common Law in fact it did, since merely living together can establish the relationship. The conclusion is thus inescapable that he regarded the ceremony in the church merely as a sop to the families.

Having the predilections that he did, it was hardly to be expected that Goldie would be the most faithful of spouses and he clearly was not. It is interesting to speculate whether a reference to the strains and stresses of those early years of matrimony can be read into his remark to Dorothy Ashton "When I was years older than you I left England, to escape from the sound of church bells."(17) On the other hand, it is only fair to say that a deep mutual understanding and affection seems to have grown between the two and that later on, especially, the marriage had all the appearances of being normally satisfactory and happy. Two children were born to it, a son Valentine and a daughter Alice. When Lady Goldie (whom he called by the pet-name "Maude") died in April of 1898, at a moment, it so happened, when Goldie was going through one of the most critical periods of his life, he wrote to his friend Leonard Darwin ". . . a sad letter, showing deep feeling at the death of his wife. 'I am trying your prescription of work; but all interest has gone out of it, for the time . . .' "(18)

That he too, as well as being attracted by, was attractive to women is borne out by the fact that immediately after his wife's death "an intimate woman friend had written to him proposing marriage." Asked by Lady Wellesley what his reaction had been, Goldie replied, "I sent her a copy of [Ibsen's] *Rosmersholm!*" (19)

Attracted and attractive or not, however, there is no question at all but that Goldie would have fallen nowadays straight into the classification of "male chauvinist." He had a deep rooted aversion, apparently, to all questions of Women's Suffrage, a not uncommon reaction on the part of those who put their women on pedestals and romanticise them. Why he should have had the same sort of antipathy to the Daylight Saving Bill is not clear, practical administrator and pragmatist that he was, but both subjects were likely to make him "flare like a straw bonfire." (20)

He combined in his character "uncontrollable passions, ruthlessness, indifference to individuals, contempt for sentimentality in any form, with the excitability and sensitiveness of a child; and a child's peculiar capacity for anger and pain." (21) "He was, moreover, a violent and uncompromising man. He had a good deal of uncontrolled temper and was lashed into frenzies of impatience by stupidity, or incompetence. Never did man suffer fools less gladly." (22)

But there is another side to this picture, "Why do we follow this man blindly, only to get hit?" a subordinate once asked. (23) Another subordinate provided the answer.

In January, 1880 (on Friday 3rd to be precise) Goldie took on the first officeboy ever to be employed by the United African Company. He was a Joseph Trigge, who rose to be a prosperous London merchant, with offices in Mowbray House, Norfolk Street. Shortly after Goldie's death he was reported as follows in the journal *West Africa*. (24)

" . . . I may say that those who were associated with him had to work early and late, in season and out of season . . . To be in his service was to realise you were with a masterful man, whose instructions had to be obeyed. Yet one learned to love him; some to fear him also. Those who did not carry out his instructions, or showed slackness, were severly dealt with . . . Sir George, when he gave a man special work to do would close the door on him, and tell him privately why he wanted it done. This was to get the man personally interested. Not only did he see that his orders were carried out, but he grasped every detail of the work himself. Naturally, in a few years, those associated with him in administrative work and trading in Nigeria, and at London headquarters began to realise that they were fellow empire-builders with him . . . he had round him a very small though devoted staff."

Yet for all his powers of leadership and "his determination to dominate those who came into contact with him for any purpose connected with his work" (25) there was an incredible vulnerability only just beneath the surface.

"Believing himself to be, at all times, calm as Diogenes before Alexander, he was in reality the most easily ruffled of human beings. He was highly inflammable. The slightest contretemps (provided it was slight enough) would cause him to lose his detachment instantly. Had, however the town been overwhelmed by an earthquake, had the Martians descended suddenly from the sky, he would have remained unmoved and immensely interested." (26)

For all that, however, he knew both how and when to control himself. When Dorothy Ashton, in a tantrum, slammed the door, Goldie rebuked her.

"I have only slammed the door once in my life. I reserved that satisfaction for a great occasion. If you do it once, it may be effective. (My occasion was) when I was informed by Her Majesty's Government that Queen Victoria had refused to grant me a Charter for my work in Nigeria. I had worked five years to obtain it. I got up, I went out, and I slammed the door. I got my Charter." (27)

The conclusion seems to be inescapable however that on the one issue of "self effacement," Goldie was not normal. Dorothy Ashton states quite bluntly that "his wish to remain unrecognised amounted almost to a mania." (28)

Exactly how he himself felt on the subject is clear from a letter which he wrote in 1898 to his friend Leonard Darwin, then Secretary of the Royal Geographical Society, agreeing to accept nomination if the then President (Markham) decided not to stand:—

"I have always been ready to accept work and responsibility; but I cannot remember having ever felt, during my 52 years of life, the slightest symptoms of that curious disease—ambition—which craves for leadership, honour, money or notoriety, and I believe I am absolutely germ proof. On the other hand I am weakly sensitive to ill-will, jealousies and calumny . . ." (29)

Again, in·1904, he wrote:—"Perhaps I am too indifferent in life to these questions of individuals. With me 'L'oeuvre c'est tout, l'homme c'est rien.' But I hold tightly to principles."

Still again, this time in February, 1911, when by most accounts his life's work was done, but when the African Society, of which he was the retiring President, was making arrangements to entertain H.R.H. The Duke of Connaught to dinner and Goldie was writing to ask Darwin to propose the toast to "The Chairman":—"I never want to be spoken of—the less you say about *me* the happier I shall be; but I cannot bear being misrepresented. You are one of the few who remember the past and know the facts." (30)

Realist that he was, he showed that he was fully aware that it was no use denying the magnitude of his achievements. He did sometimes try to shrug them off though, as in this jocund reference which he made to Darwin, this time in 1893. "I shall not mention the Niger Company in my remarks. I always get bored when I hear a parent talking of his or her child." (31)

Given this hyper-sensitivity, it is certainly fair to speculate how he could have been induced in 1897 to accept a K.C.M.G. Dorothy Wellesley states categorically that he refused a peerage and she moved in circles where such things are common knowledge. (32) Why, therefore, accept the lesser award? The reason is probably quite simple and involves his driving principle, quoted to Darwin above. If Goldie felt that·

20

"L'oeuvre" would be forwarded by *"L'homme"* following a course of action that was permissible, then he would follow it. The honour of 1887 came to him after the work done at Berlin, after the grant of the Charter, after the Company had acquired what he perceived to be its own appropriate "stature." This Company he still intended to guide and if, to do so, he could operate more efficiently if his peers perceived his own personal status to be one of acknowledgement and approva: by "The Establishment," then by all means accept the outward trappings of such approval. The same could probably be said of his creation as a Privy Councillor in 1898, at a time when the most crucial negotiations were being pursued with France and when his position on the Selborne Committee would permit him to leave, as he believed, a permanent mark on future British policy.

His acceptance of an Honorary Doctorate from both Oxford and Cambridge in 1898, however, falls into another pattern, as probably also does his election as a Fellow of the Royal Society. Goldie's appreciation of the advantages that education could bring to administration was both enduring and acute. H. R. Mill, when Vice-President of the Royal Geographical Society, recognised it quite clearly. Goldie, he states, had joined the Society in 1877. He served on the Council from 1891,

"winning the confidence of Sir Clements Markham, who was helped more than once by his prudent and far-seeing advice . . . [Goldie had then succeeded Sir Clements as President of the Society and during his Presidency] his advocacy had been influential in placing Geography for the first time in its proper place in the competitive examinations of the Civil Service. In the University of Cambridge the Geography School had been strengthened . . . and in Oxford [there was an up-grading of Faculty and there was also] begun the reorganization of Geography in the . . . University of London. The subsidies to the old Universities were maintained and small grants were also made . . . [to] new Geography Schools in the Universities of Edinburgh and of Wales."(33)

A prime reason for refusing the peerage, however, can probably be found in his deep anger, expressed to Scarbrough in a letter, over the way his subordinates had been treated by the Government:—

"The anniversary of Bida,
January 26, 1900
S.S. *Clyde.* Nearing Penang.

. . . I have given up all idea of the Government ever utilising my services for the Empire. My eyes were opened by Flint's name not appearing among the C.M.G's on the 1st January;(34)

He adds, perhaps significantly,

"I asked nothing for myself; as I prefer to feel that the country *owes* me something; but it is clear that Lord Salisbury has forgotten the services of the United African, National African, and Royal Niger Companies."(35)

Physically, Goldie must have been rather like a tensed spring. He worked for years, sixteen hours out of twenty-four. (36) Most people who saw him were struck by an appearance of height, but Dorothy Ashton, when he was about fifty-five, describes him as being only " . . . five-foot-nine in height, ill-made, spare to the point of emaciation, rapid and violent in his movements, his nervous force extraordinary, the nose the beak of an eagle, the eyes blue rapiers." [37]

Mr. Trigge perceived him as follows:—"Sir George was then [1880] a tall, slim, fair, blue-eyed man, with piercing eyes, which seemed to bore holes into one. That piercing glance was characteristic of him to the end of his life." [38]

This was the description, strangely enough, which Lord Scarbrough quoted in his assessment of Goldie in the Dictionary of National Biography and therefore it must be assumed that he preferred it to his step-daughter's. Much of both descriptions, however, can be discerned in the Von Herkomer portrait.

The complexity of his character matches the differing perceptions of his physique.

To Dorothy Ashton, who certainly knew him as well as anyone, he was "a creature peculiarly interesting, eccentric and loveable . . . interesting, in fact, not only nor even chiefly, on account of his work . . . but on account of his strange personality." [39] He had, she says, no literary ambition, no desire to be popular, and absolutely no urge to make money. [40]

But there was also a darker, more secretive side.

"One great reason we have for reticence about ourselves (for which we have been censured) is that I hold that a man going to steal a march on his neighbour ought not to blow trumpets to show how fast he is advancing. Before France is alive to the work we are doing, that work will be done—securely." [41]

This, however, was not without its own element of idealism. As Wellesley observes, "rightly or wrongly, he believed in British Government for African peoples, and he gave it to them. He believed in his own country . . ." [42] How he came to this belief is also related.

"When I was a little older than you, I acquired a settled gloom that nothing could shake . . . I sat down on the sea shore, placing a large black pebble beside me . . . [whilst pretending that] by touching that pebble [I could] wipe out . . . all . . . life on earth . . . so that [it] had never existed. I sat for hours staring at the sea. After a long time . . . I touched the pebble . . . [Then] I started my work in Africa." [43]

(1) *Sir George Goldie: Founder of Nigeria* by Dorothy Wellesley; MacMillan & Co., London, 1934; p. 93.
(2) *Ibid.* p. ix.
(3) *Ibid.* p. 103.
(4) *Ibid.* p. 76. Henry Austin Bruce, first Baron Aberdare, 1815-1895. Home Secretary, 1868-73. See page 213 for Goldie's Obituary of him, published in the *Geographical Journal* in 1895.
(5) *Ibid.* p. 105. According to J. E. Flint in *Sir George Goldie and the Making of Nigeria*, O.U.P. 1960; Goldie ordered books which he collected at Suakin. His reading at this time included all five volumes of Barth's *Travels in Africa*.

(6) *Ibid.* p. 134.

(7) *Ibid.* p. 159.

(8) According to Flint, *op cit.,* p. 4, he was a near genius at mental arithmetic as a child. For Goldie's own view of some aspect of his school-days, see p. 261.

(9) *Ibid.* p. 108.

(10) *Ibid.* pp. 111-112.

(11) *Ibid.* p. 94. It must be remarked also that some of the best Colonial Governors began their careers as Royal Engineers. Amongst them must be listed Sir William Guggisberg, Sir William MacGregor and Sir Percy Girouard, but three of the outstanding examples that spring immediately to mind.

(12) The Author feels bound to state that he never personally examined "Secret Circular 'B' ''. The last existing copy was destroyed, it is believed, about 1945. Several officers of undoubted probity have claimed that they did receive it however and that it was withdrawn in a hurry. Goldie's activities in Egypt would have fallen directly under its ban and one of its allegedly more objectionable features was supposed to be an equation of miscegenation with bestiality. The existence of the Secret Circular passed into common knowledge and even into Service folklore. q.v. *The A.D.O. Bende.*

(13) Wellesley *op cit.* p. 22; "Historical Essay" by Stephen Gwynn. Goldie himself, in 1899, when the Niger Company Directors presented him with his portrait (see Frontispiece), described his vision of empire on the Niger as "only the revival of an earlier dream of mine in another part of Africa.''; the *Times* 28 October, 1899. He also refers to this period several times as the occasion when he first encountered Hausas. See page 166.

(14) *Ibid.* p. 128.

(15) *Ibid.*

(16) *Ibid.* p.113. The legend of Goldie's promiscuity persisted however, and has frequently been invoked to detract from his achievements. For an example, see pages 55 and 56. Some recent studies, however, have tended to show that it was not the fact of the promiscuity itself that was frowned on at this period as much as it becoming a matter of open scandal. See Leslie A.; *The Marlbrough House Set,* Doubleday, New York, 1972.

(17) *Ibid.* p. 106. Alternatively, of course, the reference may have been to an entanglement associated with his earlier departure when he went to Egypt.

(18) Darwin, Major Leonard. "Transcript of an interview given by Sir George Goldie in March, 1899." *Journal of the Royal African Society;* Vol. 35, p. 142.

(19) Wellesley; *op cit.* p. 120. *Rosmersholm* was Ibsen's last social drama and is thus a prelude to his later psychological studies. Rosmer's unhappy marriage to his neurotic and unsympathetic wife Beata ends in her drowning herself in a millpond. Rebecca West, a friend of both Rosmer and Beata, with whom he had been suspected of 'living in sin', is, after typically Ibsen complications, invited by him to prove her loyalty by jumping into the millpond too. This she promptly proceeds to do, being joined at the last minute by Rosmer so that the two lovers perish together in a final embrace. Goldie's action is thus a somewhat back-handed compliment to Lady Goldie, and how the other lady took it all is not recorded by Wellesley, though, if, as is argued later, the lady concerned was Flora Shaw, this episode had profound repercussions.

(20) *Ibid.* p. 115.

(21) *Ibid.* p.113.

(22) *Ibid.* p. 114.

(23) *Ibid.* *

(24) *West Africa;* 29 August, 1925; p. 1097.

(25) Gwynn in Wellesley *op cit.* p. 30.

(26) *Ibid.* p. 114-5.

(27) *Ibid.* p. 94. Perham also claims that Goldie added another threat, namely that he would sell the Company's rights to "a foreign power." This she regards as being in some way improper, though it is not easy to discern where any impropriety would lie. See the *Spectator,* 18 January, 1935.

(28) *Ibid.* p. vii.

(29) Darwin *op cit.* p. 142. For a note on the motto see page V.

(30) *Ibid.* p. 143. For details of this dinner see pages 290-305. For possible reasons for Goldie's concern, see page 32 *et seq.* In responding to Darwin's toast—Darwin was then President of the R.G.S.—Goldie also referred to him "as the son of one of the greatest men the world has ever produced."

(31) *Ibid.* p. 141.
(32) Wellesley *op cit.* p. 157.
(33) H. R. Mill: *The Record of the Royal Geographical Society 1830-1930,* R.G.S., London, 1930. pp. 171-2. Mill also credits Goldie and Darwin with rescuing Scott's first Antarctic Expedition, financed jointly by the Royal Society and the R.G.S., from almost certain abortion.
(34) Wellesley, *op cit.,* p. 79.
(35) *Ibid.*
(36) *Ibid.* p. 116.
(37) *Ibid.* p. 91.
(38) *West Africa,* 29 August, 1925, p. 1005.
(39) Wellesley, *op cit.* p. vi.
(40) *Ibid.* p. viii.
(41) *Ibid.* p. 42. Goldie to Scarbrough, 11 June, 1890.
(42) *Ibid.* p. 151.
(43) *Ibid.* p. 109.

CHAPTER II

"Elevate my earth-bound nature, to a nobler, loftier aim;
Aid the struggling love of duty, crush the selfish love of fame;"

Roche Abbey by Sir George Goldie
(undated)

It would be quite impossible, in the little space here available, to attempt to explore in any detail exactly what Goldie's achievements in the Niger Valley really were. Such an examination must await another time.

To establish the continuity between his *personality* and his *philosophy* however, it is necessary to refer at least to an outline of his activities. Fortunately, there are two authoritative synopses readily available. It will be recalled that when forbidding his children to assist in the writing of any biographies, he said that the only memorials he wished for were those contained in the *Encyclopaedia Britannica.* [1]

The first of the two passages following contaihs all that is relevant in the article headed "Goldie" in the 11th Edition of that work. There is some internal evidence that the article came from Leonard Darwin's pen. If so, then it is doubly authoritative in that not only would Darwin have had access to all the data, but Goldie would have been in constant consultation with him also. [2]

" . . . Sir George Goldie travelled in all parts of Africa, gaining an extensive knowledge of the continent, and first visited the country of the Niger in 1877. He conceived the idea of adding to the British Empire the then little known regions of the lower and middle Niger, and for over twenty years his efforts were devoted to the realisation of this conception. The method by which he determined to work was the revival of government by chartered company within the empire—a method suppose to be buried with the East India Company. The first step was to combine all British commercial interests in the Niger, and this he accomplished in 1879 when the United African Company was formed. In 1881 Goldie sought a charter from the imperial government (the 2nd Gladstone ministry). Objections of various kinds were raised. To meet them the capital of the company (renamed the National African Company) was increased from £125,000 to £1,000,000, and great energy was displayed in founding stations on the Niger. At this time French traders, encouraged by Gambetta, established themselves on

25

the lower river, thus rendering it difficult for the company to obtain territorial rights: but the Frenchmen were bought out in 1884, so that at the Berlin conference on West Africa in 1885, Mr. Goldie, present as an expert on matters relating to the river, was able to announce that on the lower Niger the British flag alone flew. Meantime the Niger coastline had been placed under British protection. Through Joseph Thomson, David McIntosh, D. W. Sargent, J. Flint, William Wallace, E. Dangerfield and numerous other agents, over 400 political treaties—drawn up by Goldie—were made with the chiefs of the lower Niger and the Hausa states. The scruples of the British government being overcome, a charter was at length granted (July, 1886), the National African Company becoming the Royal Niger Company, with Lord Aberdare as governor and Goldie as vice-governor. In 1895, on Lord Aberdare's death, Goldie became governor of the company, whose destinies he had guided throughout.

The building up of Nigeria as a British state had to be carried on in face of further difficulties raised by French travellers with political missions, and also in face of German opposition. From 1884 to 1890, Prince Bismarck was a persistent antagonist, and the strenuous efforts he made to secure for Germany the basin of the lower Niger and Lake Chad were even more dangerous to Goldie's schemes of empire than the ambitions of France. Herr E. R. Flegel, who had travelled in Nigeria during 1882-1884 under the auspices of the British company, was sent out in 1885 by the newly-formed German Colonial Society to secure treaties for Germany, which had established itself at Cameroon. After Flegel's death in 1886 his work was continued by his companion Dr. Staudinger, while Herr Hoenigsberg was despatched to stir up trouble in the occupied portions of the Company's territory—or, as he expressed it, "to burst up the charter." He was finally arrested at Onitsha, and, after trial by the company's supreme court at Asaba, was expelled from the country. Prince Bismarck then sent out his nephew, Herr von Puttkamer, as German consul-general to Nigeria, with orders to report on this affair, and when this report was published in a White Book, Bismarck demanded heavy damages from the company. Meanwhile Bismarck maintained constant pressure on the British government to compel the Royal Niger Company to a division of spheres of influence, whereby Great Britain would have lost a third, and the most valuable part, of the company's territory. But he fell from power in March 1890, and in July following Lord Salisbury concluded the famous "Heligoland" agreement (3) with Germany. After this event the aggressive action of Germany in Nigeria entirely ceased, and the door was opened for a final settlement of the Nigeria-Cameroon frontiers. These negotiations, which resulted in an agreement in 1893, were initiated by Goldie as a means of arresting the advance of France into Nigeria from the direction of the Congo. By conceding to Germany a long but narrow strip of territory between Adamawa and Lake Chad, to which she had no treaty claims, a barrier was raised against French expeditions, semi-military and semi-exploratory, which sought to enter Nigeria from the east. Later French efforts at aggression were made from the western or Dahomeyan side, despite an agreement concluded with France in 1890 respecting the northern frontier.

The hostility of certain Fula princes led the company to despatch in 1897, an expedition against the Mohammedan states of Nupe and Illorin. This expedition was organized and personally directed by Goldie and was completely successful. Internal peace was thus secured, but in the following year the differences with France in regard to the frontier line became acute, and compelled the intervention of the British government. In the negotiations which ensued Goldie was instrumental in preserving for Great Britain the whole of the navigable stretch of the lower Niger. It was, however, evidently impossible for a chartered company to hold its own against the state-supported protectorates of France and Germany, and in consequence, on the 1st of January, 1900, the Royal Niger Company transferred its territories to the British government for the sum of £865,000. The ceded territory together with the small Niger Coast Protectorate, already under imperial control, was formed into the two protectorates of northern and southern Nigeria.

The article in the *Encyclopaedia* headed "Nigeria" was written by Flora (Shaw) Lugard, then and still a reputedly formidable authority in her own right, even if she was also an outspoken and dedicated promoter of her husband's career and reputation. The section of it dealing with Goldie is necessarily comparatively brief but there are nuances of certain as yet unexplained discrepancies of view between, for example, her own and those of Lord Scarbrough and Goldie as to the machinery of government which the Chartered Company bequeathed to the High Commissioner.

The relevant portion of the article reads:—

" . . . The Consulate at Lokoja was re-established a few years later to meet the still steadily growing requirements of British trade upon the river. In 1880 the influence of the international 'scramble for Africa' made itself felt by the establishment under the recognized protection of the French government of two French firms which opened upwards of thirty trading stations on the Lower Niger. The establishment of these firms was admittedly a political move which coincided with the extension of French influence from Senegal into the interior. Nearly at the same time a young Englishman, George Goldie-Taubman, afterwards better known as Sir George Goldie (q.v.), having some private interests on the Niger, conceived the idea of amalgamating all local British interests and creating a British province on the Niger. To effect this end the United African Company was formed in1879, and trade was pushed upon the river with an energy which convinced the French firms of the futility of their less united efforts. They yielded the field and allowed themselves to be bought out by the United African Company in 1884. At the Berlin Conference held in 1884-1885 the British representative was able to state that Great Britain alone possessed trading interests on the Lower Niger, and in June, 1885, a British protectorate was notified over the coast lands known as the Oil Rivers. Germany had in the meantime established itself in Cameroon, and the new British protectorate extended along the Gulf of Guinea from the British colony of Lagos on the west to the new German colony on the east, where the Rio del Rey marked the frontier. In the following year, 1886, the United African Company received a royal charter under the title of the Royal Niger Company. The territories which were placed by the charter under the control of the company were those immediately bordering the Lower Niger in its course from the confluence at Lokoja to the sea. On the coast they extended from the Forcados to the Nun mouth of the river. Beyond the confluence European trade had not at that time penetrated to the interior.

The interior was held by powerful Mohammedan rulers who had imposed a military domination upon the indigenous races and were not prepared to open their territories to European intercourse. To secure British political influence, and to preserve a possible field for future development, the Niger Company had negotiated treaties with some of the most important of these rulers, and the nominal extension of the company's territories was carried over the whole sphere of influence thus secured. The movements of Germany from the south-east, and of France from the west and north, were thus held in check, and by securing international agreements the mutual limits of the three European powers concerned were definitely fixed. The principal treaties relating to the German frontiers were negotiated in 1886 and 1893; the Anglo-French treaties were more numerous, those of 1890 and 1898, which laid down the main lines of division between French and British possessions on the northern and western frontiers of Nigeria, having been supplemented by many lesser rectifications of frontier. (See Africa, para. 5). It was not until 1909 that the whole of the frontier between Nigeria and the French and German possessions had been definitely demarcated. Thus, mainly by the action of the Royal Niger Company, a territory of vast extent, into which the chartered company itself was not able to carry either administrative or trading operations, was secured for Great Britain. In 1897, at a time when disputes with France upon the western frontier had reached a very active stage, the company entered upon a campaign against the Mohammedan sovereign of Nupe. This campaign would, no doubt, have led to important results had the company retained its administrative powers. In the expedition a force of 500 Hausa, drilled and trained by the company, and led by thirty white officers—of whom some were lent for the occasion by the War Office—decisively defeated a force of some thousands of native troops, led by the emir of Nupe himself. The capital town of Bida was taken and the emir deposed. From Bida the expedition marched to Illorin *(sic)*, where again the whole district submitted to the authority of the company. In Illorin the campaign had some lasting effect. In Nupe, on the northern side of the river, as the company was unable to occupy the territory conquered, (4) things shortly reverted to their previous condition. When the company's troops were withdrawn the deposed emir returned and reoccupied the throne, leaving the situation to be dealt with after the territories of the company had been transferred to the crown.

The complications to which the pressure of foreign nations, and especially of France, on the frontiers of the territories gave rise, became at this period so acute that the resources of a private company were manifestly inadequate to meet the possible necessities of the position. Relations with France on the western border became so strained that in 1897 Mr. Chamberlain, who was then secretary of state for the colonies, thought it necessary to raise a local force, afterwards known as the West African Frontier Force, for the special defence of the frontiers of the West African dependencies. In these circumstances it was judged advisable to place the territories of the Royal Niger Company, to which the general name of Nigeria had been given, under the direct control of the crown. It was therefore arranged that in consideration of compensation for private rights the company should surrender its charter and transfer all political rights in the territories to the Crown. The transfer took place on the 1st January, 1900, from which date the company, which dropped the name of 'royal,' became a purely trading corporation. The southern portion of the territories was amalgamated with the Niger Coast Protectorate, the whole district taking the name of the Protectorate of Southern Nigeria, while the northern portion, extending from a line drawn slightly above 7°N to the frontier of the French possessions on the north and including the confluence of the Niger and the Benue at Lokoja, was proclaimed a protectorate under the name of Northern Nigeria.

The company, during its tenure of administrative power under the charter, had organized its territories south of the confluence, into trading districts, over each of which there was placed a European agent. The executive powers in Africa were entrusted to an agent general with three provincial and twelve district superintendents. There was a small judicial staff directed by a chief justice, and there was a native constabulary of about 1,000 men, trained and drilled by white officers. The company kept also upon the river a fleet of about thirty steamers. The entire direction of the proceedings of the company was, however, in the hands of the council in London, and the administrative control of the territories was practically from first to last vested in the person of Sir George Goldie. The local work of the representatives of the company was mainly commercial. When, on the surrender of the charter, Sir George Goldie withdrew from the company, the administrative element disappeared. No administrative records were handed over, and very little machinery remained. Two enactments, however, bore testimony to the legislation of the company. One, which by force of circumstances remained inoperative, was the abolition of the legal status of slavery, proclaimed in the year of Queen Victoria's jubilee (1897). The other, more practical, which has remained in operation to the present day, confirmed and enforced by the succeeding administration, was the absolute prohibition of the trade in spirits beyond the parallel of 7°."

Exactly what weight can be placed on the claim that Lugard was left without either adequate administrative machinery or continuity in the setting up of the Imperial Administration is not entirely clear. Certainly, it has always been accepted up to date, again as the conventional wisdom (based largely on Lugard's own statements as formalised in his Annual Reports) that he received no transmission of administrative data from the R.N.C. and that all the Company's records were deliberately destroyed. Some of them have, however, come to light quite recently and there is certainly a mass of them, now to be found in the Public Record Office, which at the time was in continuous use in both the Foreign and Colonial Offices—any sweeping claim such as Lugard made must therefore be liable to the subsequent correction of the record, and the record from the earliest time is quite clearly stated.

On 27 October, 1899, an Extraordinary General Meeting of the Royal Niger Company shareholders was convened to consider the notification received from the government of an intention to revoke the Charter on the 1st of January following. At this meeting, Lord Scarbrough stated that he had been deeply impressed, on the occasion of his quite frequent visits to the territories over a number of years, at seeing something of the "remarkable organisation" which existed there, and which was due to the administrative genius of Goldie alone. So much was this so that:—"directly one enters the [Niger], enterprise and energy are evident on all sides and everywhere one is struck with the perfection of the organization which has been designed to meet constantly changing and abnormal conditions." [5]

Goldie responded to this praise by proposing the passage of a resolution expressing the gratitude of the Shareholders for the " . . . loyal and able services of the officials, officers and others both living and deceased, in Africa and in Europe, who have served the company during the 13 years of its administration of the Niger territories . . ." He added:—

"On January 1 next the company will lay down its powers, duties and responsibilities of government . . . The Imperial Government, both in order to secure continuity in Nigeria and also to prevent a waste of money are taking over a considerable proportion of the company's staff. They are taking over some of the leading members of the executive department, as well as the judicial department, the whole of the company's troops, with their officers, the greater portion of the medical staff, and, of course, the whole staff connected with the engineering workshops and repairing yard at Akassa.''(6)

Frankness and honesty, however, compel the observation that the one single person most responsible for all the questioning and confusion is Goldie himself. It is one thing to be reluctant, as he was, to permit a biographer to write up even the comparatively brief and modest biographical note that Mrs. Stopford Greene (7) proposed, or refuse, as he also did, the offer of several publishers to put out his own autobiography. Such can, indeed, be put down to a perfectly acceptable level of distaste for what he described as the legions of "self-advertisers, from Caesar to Napoleon" whom he regarded as the "worst enemies of human progress," and, under those circumstances, his refusal to "forswear my principles and join the army of notoriety hunters—poor things," can be applauded. (8) But it is quite another thing, deliberately to destroy a priceless archive as he did, and it is a wonder that he, with his bent for classical analogy, did not see in this the same mindless urge for destruction that robbed the world of the treasures of Alexandria!

This wanton waste—and it was all of that and quite indefensible—has often been attributed to pique. Brief reference has already been made to the much more rational explanation that Wellesley gives. In the early 1930's she wrote to Mr. Ronald Norman (9) who had been a colleague of Goldie's on the L.C.C., as well as being a friend. She was seeking papers of public interest and, as anticipated, she got none. Mr. Norman did inform her, however, that Goldie told him that he had burnt his papers "shortly after the outbreak of War in 1914, feeling [as he said] that [his life-work] 'was deprived of value.' He . . .said: 'Since the War I feel that I am out of date.' ''(10)

Another remark of the same bent reveals how much the War affected him. Asked by a friend whom he met in the street if he was afraid of the War, he answered "No . . . I am afraid of the Peace." (11) It is all too easy for the modern generation, reared as it has been in an aura of permanent insecurity, to fail to appreciate the absolutely devastating effect that the course taken by the Great War had on "the Edwardians." It shattered their world; it ruined their social structure; and it played havoc with their convictions.

The casualties which they suffered as a class were out of all proportion and were something which they had never contemplated. In 1918, Lady Cynthia Elcho, who had married Herbert Asquith's second son, wrote: "I think [peace] will require more courage than anything that has gone before . . . and one will at last fully recognise that the dead are not only dead for the duration of the war." (12)

Goldie's remarks would seem to show that he understood what was afoot rather earlier than did most of his contemporaries.

(1) See p. 15.
(2) If Darwin did not write the article, then someone is guilty of plagiarism. Compare its text with that of Darwin's article in the *National Review* of 1899, pp. 968-979. "British Expansion in West Africa."

(3) Under this agreement Britain ceded to Germany the island of Heligoland in return for a recognition of British interest in Zanzibar etc.

(4) Because of the danger of a confrontation with France, the Company undertook, in an agreement with the Colonial Office, not to employ its troops north of Jebba. From the Company's point of view it was a disastrous arrangement, from which stems almost all of the subsequent accusations of its administrative incapacity. (See page 40 ff.)

(5) The *Times* October 28, 1899.

(6) *Ibid.* Some of the staff which Lugard *did* inherit, Burdon, Cargill, Hewby, Wallace, for example, rank as the best of Lugard's early administrators. Lugard moreover, as Commandant of the Frontier Force since 1898, had a long period of adjustment "cheek by jowl" with the Company's Administration, though as will be shown this was hardly a happy one.

(7) Alice Sophia Amelia Stopford Green, 1848-1929. The person who conceived of the African Society as a memorial to Mary Kingsley and a competent historian in her own right, as well as in co-operation with her husband. See Wellesley, *op cit*, p. 146 *et seq.*

(8) *Ibid*, p. 148.

(9) Norman, Ronald Collett, 1873-1964, Chairman, L.C.C., 1907-22. Vice-Chairman, B.B.C., 1933-35; Chairman, 1935-39. See also p. 9.

(10) Wellesley, *op cit.*, p. 145.

(11) *Ibid,* p. 133. The story of this encounter was written by Goldie to Dorothy Ashton in a letter dated 19 November, 1916.

(12) Leslie, *op cit,* p. 264.

CHAPTER III

"Herostratus lives that burnt the Temple of Diana:
He is almost lost that built it." [1]
Sir Thomas Browne. *Urn-Burial or Hyariotaphia* (1658)

To a large extent, Goldie was unable totally to achieve that anonymity for which his soul craved, and this inability stemmed directly from the magnitude of what he succeeded in doing, which, in the first decade of the century, was much more widely appreciated than it later became to be.

The Victorian and Edwardian ages—and Goldie was always more Edwardian than Victorian in his relatively free thinking—were both periods characterised by intrepidity and innovation. Thus measured against most of his contemporaries Goldie was, in all respects, a giant. Among other things, according to Markham, he spoke eight languages [2] —though Goldie himself had reservations about his degree of competence in some of them. [3]

Nevertheless, his intensely private nature, allied to his forbiddingly patrician exterior and his flaring temper, would, in a lesser man, have been enough to ensure for him that oblivion he was seeking. But Goldie was too big a man to be obliterated in such a self-immolation, whether or not—as some hold—he did lend himself, almost willingly as it were, to a sort of "Establishment" inspired *auto-da-fé* to placate the French.

The question therefore that remains to be answered is whether there has been a due and sufficient recognition not of Goldie's contribution to the building of the Empire in territorial or geographical terms—and few men can have matched it—but in terms rather of the ideological impact that his thinking had on the developing theories of Colonialism itself, and especially on the direction which British colonial policy was to take in the twentieth century, first in the Niger Valley, but later in most parts of Africa as well.

It is here especially that Goldie's yearning for anonymity, his extremely *private* nature, withdrawn and aloof as he often was, has given most scope for his contribution not only to be overlooked, but even to be mis-attributed. For it is at the very point that Goldie's star appears to begin to dim that its light is further outshone by the incandescence of that of the rising Lugard.

Dominating any objective analysis of Goldie's philosophy of government, is the fact that from the turn of the century until Goldie's death in 1925, and even, indeed, beyond it, relations between him and Sir Frederick Lugard deteriorated from affection and friendship to hostility and open enmity. It is clear also, that for the most part, the determination that this was to be so was Lugard's and that up to 1912, at least, Goldie was reluctant to recognise the pass to which their affairs had come and did what he could to put things back more on their old footing. The analysis which follows, however, is based on twin hypotheses:—

(1) That it was Flora Shaw who, on the death of Lady Goldie in 1898, was the recipient of the copy of *Rosmersholm* [3]

(2) That it was not until after 1912 that Goldie was at last prepared to acquiesce in the broadening of the breach, whereupon it promptly became unbridgeable.

The continued inaccessability of Lugard's personal diaries to a broader scholarship, freed as they now would be from the zealous oversight of his brother Edward, [4] makes it difficult indeed to assess the true degree of the deterioration in relations between him and the man who made him. Nicolson, [5] following Perham, [6] believes that the breach occurred irreparably as early as 1903, and that it arose directly from an attempt by Lugard to discredit Goldie in front of a meeting of the Royal Geographical Society in November of that year.

If this was ever Lugard's intention—and he may well have been a tool rather than a prime-mover, although, as will be shown, on his first exposure to it he had formed a uniformly low opinion of the value of the Company's system of government—then the forum he chose was an unfortunate one. Goldie had been a member of that Society since 1877 and a member of its Council since 1891. He was now one of its Vice-Presidents and in only eighteen months would be elected to succeed the then President, the redoubtable ex-East India Company official, Sir Clements Markham, [7] the man who, next to Murchison, had made the Society what is was and of whom Goldie was an intimate and trusted advisor. [8] To attack him there would be at least ill-advised, for this was indeed Goldie's home ground.

More to the point, the paper which Lugard read that Wednesday night (4th November, 1903), before an audience that included Sir Harry Johnston, [9] *as delivered* contained nothing to excite the ire of a man like Goldie. Perhaps it is a little brash, even ill-mannered, and it does give a general impression that nothing much happened in Nigeria until Lugard arrived there. But that was fully in keeping, and Goldie could hardly have expected otherwise, for he had seen this facet of Lugard's character in their official relationships nearly ten years before, and even more clearly in the last days of the Company's administration when he had had to support Wallace against Lugard and Watts against his deputy, Willcocks. [10]

It is, in fact, now almost certain that it was this last episode which provided the true genesis of the later disagreement in 1903 and as there are also other aspects of importance in connection with it, it is worthwhile digressing slightly to examine it in some detail.

In August of 1898, Lugard had gone home for consultations with the Colonial and War Offices, leaving his old friend of Indian days, Colonel James Willcocks, as Acting Commandant of the Frontier Force. Willcocks, as his own writings show, was a typical Army officer of the period. He was nothing like as experienced as Lugard, and was certainly not a theoretician of either Administration or Government. [11]

Early in September, Willcocks received a complaint by telegram, apparently from the Lagos Government, alleging that war-parties from Ilorin had raided villages inside the Lagos Protectorate and requesting him to send and remonstrate. Any request for such action ought, of course, to have been addressed to the Royal Niger Company, which was still the only lawful Government in the Niger Territories, and the whole incident must therefore be regarded as part of the on-going feud that had raged between the Lagos Protectorate and the R.N.C. since before Governor Carter's day. [12] Willcocks, however, fell for it!

A corporal and one private soldier were accordingly despatched to Ilorin bearing a letter from Willcock's which the Emir promptly rejected. As a result, it was claimed, the men were "hustled and knocked about, food denied them, and finally kicked out of the town."

Willcocks' next step was to send an officer, Captain the Hon. Richard Fitzroy Somerset, Grenadier Guards, [13] and an escort of fifty men to Ilorin with another communication from him to the Emir. This second action only underlines the fundamental misconception of his role and status that must have existed in Willcocks' mind—a situation for which Lugard must be held primarily responsible. If such is not accepted, then the only other explanation is that an "incident" was being deliberately "manufactured." [14]

The party arrived in Ilorin on 28th September, where the Emir "after a lot of havering" received Somerset, but was "not particularly civil (and his court very much the reverse) [and] refused to supply [him] with food . . . and was altogether very off hand." The next day, the Emir tried to return the letter unopened!

Matters then went form bad to worse, with Somerset obdurate and the Emir uncompromising on the letter, but otherwise offering traditional hospitality, whilst, of course, Somerset kept Willcocks fully informed. The result therefore was that Willcocks began telegraphing details to the Colonial Office in London. He clearly did not get the support he was hoping for.

Goldie, apprised of the situation, immediately sided with the Emir against the soldiers, and with Watts against Willcocks. So, it appears, did the Secretary of State. On 17th October, 1898, in response to a further cable from Willcocks, Goldie wrote a letter, in his own inimitable scrawl—nothing else describes his handwriting—to Antrobus, the Assistant Under Secretary of State, in the following terms:—

My dear Antrobus,

Events are moving just as I foresaw they would move, and as I told the Chancellor of the Exchequer they would move. The whole question is whether the Secretary of State is to control his officers or to be controlled by them.

In the Company's day, the corresponding question never arose.

I do not think that that *excellent soldier,* Colonel Willcocks, raises any new questions in his last cablegram. He persists, as before, that Ilorin has "insulted H.M. Government."

I hold he has done nothing of the kind. In rejecting Willcocks' letter, he has believed himself to be showing fidelity to the Company—the only representative of the Empire that he knows. He is a fine fellow.

If a reign of the sword is to supersede statesmanship, if England can spare the force and money to smash the Central Sudan into an amorphous condition and then reorganise it on a new basis, I raise no objection. It may be the best policy. But it must be deliberately planned and systematically carried out and not by spasmodic efforts.

I hope today's cablegram has gone [?promptly?]

George Taubman Goldie[15]

This is a most important document, not least because of the very serious mis-interpretations of it which have been applied to matters entirely out of context.[16] Enclosed with it, Goldie also sent his own suggested draft for a further telegram which he felt ought to be sent to Colonel Willcocks. It reads as follows:—

Suggested cablegram to Colonel Willcocks—to be sent in *addition* to that arranged this morning.
[?Throw?] responsibility on Agent General for maintenance order Illorin. Send all communications Illorin through Agent General.

The letter puts in a nutshell the dilemma that was to face successive Secretaries of State from Chamberlain onwards in their dealings with Lugard. Was the dog to wag the tail, or was the tail to wag the dog? Goldie's defence of the Emir's actions, moreover, was a classic response on the part of a protagonist of indirect rule!

The cable that was sent to Willcocks the next day (18th), read:—

[Your No. 62 of 16th October]. Goldie is telegraphing to Agent General to go if possible himself to Ilorin, or in default to send competent representative, to insist on respectful reception of your letter. In the meantime leave officer and escort where they are and telegraph result of visit of Company's Officer.

Its draft was approved by Lord Salisbury in person.

But, this was not to be the end of the matter. Somerset, in Ilorin, had his own contacts within the departments of Whitehall, and promptly proceeded to use them in a personal, pencil-written, letter to a friend running over eight foolscap pages and accompanied by the exhortation "of which please make as much use as you like." Very quickly, the letter found its way (in typescript) into the Colonial Office files.

From a Service point of view, Somerset's action was utterly improper. He proceeded to attack not only the Company's local representatives behind their backs, but also "Goldie & Co." as well, whom he accused of deliberate misrepresentation. Highlights from this communciations are as follows:— [17]

. . . First of all I must tell you that from the very outset of our arrival at Jebba the Niger Company have thwarted us in every possible way and have even gone so far as to stop the people selling to us so that we should be obliged to deal with them for everything. This they accomplished by what is known in strikes as "Picquets" and so serious did it become not only to the Europeans but even to our men that we could not get enough fresh meat and stuff to eat, naturally it culminated in a row between Watts (acting Agent General) and Colonel Willcocks and led to intense ill-feeling between the Imperial troops and the Niger Company. Watts, as you may perhaps know, has no pretensions to be a gentleman and was mate on some merchant tramp. I want you to remember this so as to understand as I go on what the feelings of Officers in Col. Willcocks' position, or even in mine must be to find ourselves at the beck and call of a man of this description and to find the Secretary of State backing him up against the *Imperial Officers.*

He then continued:—

Now we've all heard a great deal about Ilorin but I don't suppose any one at home knows that it has *never been* subjugated and that it is a byword in all Yorubaland and the surrounding countries for all that is cruel and all that is meant by slavery . . . Of course you can buy slaves by the dozen in the open market; that you can do on a smaller scale in a good many places (the advent of the British flag, especially when carried by a trading company, does *not,* my dear Oliver, as we all thought in our happy childhood, abolish slavery!) but also they practise the most horrible cruelties. Only 2½ months ago an Officer of my Battalion coming through Ilorin saw a man lying in the market place in front of the Emir's "palace" with his head cut off and with various unmentionable parts of his body displayed on his stomach. He asked the Emir about it, upon which the old scoundrel with roars of laughter, said the man had committed suicide! And when told it was rather impossible to completely cut off one's own head etc., he only roared the more . . . I have told you enough to show, I hope, that the Niger Company's stories mayn't all (!) be true, but I should just like to tell you that the Bishop and Mr. *(sic)* Tugwell [18] were coming through from Oyo to Jebba and (I met them at the Oyo River) were treated by the Emir with great civility and saw no sign of a slave! Now I have had information brought me two months ago that Watts had warned the Emir of the Bishop's probable arrival and had told him not to let his Lordship see anything he had better not! The Emir thought this such a good joke that he told everybody—and it got to me through our interpreter whose wife is a "Princess" of Ilorin. How's that for high!

Now to the main affair.

Just about the beginning of August, Watts who has just become Acting Agent General paid a visit to Ilorin—from that moment there has been trouble. The first intimation I had of it was day after day people coming in from the Ilorin farms to complain that Watts had authorised the Emir to collect tribute and that dozens of people were being put into prison and chains and some being killed for being friendly with the white men. Why I heard all this was being Adjutant the people were all brought to me when they arrived.

Somerset then detailed the steps which he had taken, as the

representative of Colonel Willcocks, to persuade the Emir to accept his communication and then continued:—

Now isn't that sufficient? And you can imagine what it is to an Officer of the Imperial forces to sit down and see the British flag insulted, and the British prestige suffering (as it is for they all say in the town that we are afraid of them!) to please a rotten, cheating trading company, with a man of Watts' stamp *over* me! In addition to all this my interpreter was attacked and so were some of my carriers and when I remonstrated with the Emir he said it shouldn't happen again and had warned his people and begged my pardon etc., and then yesterday there was a big meeting at the "Palace" when it was decided:

1. To have nothing to do with us at all.
2. That no food should be brought to us.
3. That any soldiers or carriers found in the town were to be killed.

In addition they have comfortably discussed how to poison our drinking water! The above resolutions were given out in the Mosques yesterday (the Mahommedan Sunday) with the result that one of my carriers was attacked and very roughly handled! Now my dear Oliver does the Secretary of State think that he is going to get a good class of officer out here if dirty niggers are to be allowed to do as they like and to treat the Imperial Flag and Imperial Force just as they please? We are all fairly disgusted with it and I, for one, will not soldier in a country where I am not allowed to make my flag—to say nothing of myself—respected. If we are withdrawn now the last state of Ilorin will be worse than the first.

Warming to his subject, he now proceeded to attack the Company's administration at its most vulnerable spot:— (19)

What is the state of Bida now? Do you know that this winter he slave raided up to half a day's sail from Jebba!! You must, if you are going to rule this country (which mind you the Niger Company have never even *attempted* to do) do so with a firm hand, there must be no double dealing or doubtful policy with a native—they are not to be trusted for a moment and the great thing with them is to strike home and strike *quickly* otherwise they think you are afraid of them and if that once gets into their heads, you are in for a big thing I can tell you. No doubt the initial mistake was ever sending out Imperial Forces with Imperial Officers to act under the orders of a few traders. It does not do—the Niger Company naturally (and I don't blame them) want to make out a fine case (for valuation) for themselves, and they therefore pretend they have ruled this country. Believe me, beyond the walls of their warehouses, they haven't got nor ever have had a single bit of power. It is easy enough to keep in with a Native ruler if you wink the other eye at slavery etc. and that is exactly what they have done—this I had from Watts himself!

I suppose Watts will make out the deuce of a case of mismanagement and misrepresentation against me, but as my reports are all in order 'I don't care a—little bit!' I suppose when we have Majuba'd enough to satisfy (20) Watts I shall go back to Jebba and resume my multifarious duties . . .

One must sympathise with Somerset to some extent, however extreme his notions may seem to be nowadays. Nevertheless, he does go a long way towards destroying his own case and giving complete (though unwitting) confirmation to Goldie's interpretation of events by writing:—

[On 29 September], I again saw [the Emir], when he tried to return the letter to me *unopened* saying he and his people would have nothing to do with it. To give him every chance I refused to take it, went very carefully through the events which brought me here and even through the contents of the letter. The only result was that neither he nor his "council" took the least notice of what I was saying and so after having *twice* warned him personally and his Baloguns that if he persisted in this course he would meet with severe punishment, I withdrew. Now today is October 22nd, so I have been here 27 days, during that time he has approached me with presents as have also his Baloguns (which I naturally have refused) but they one and all have studiously and steadfastly refused to accept the letter (even after the Emir opened it which he did last week) or to take any notice of it—this in spite of the fact that I have warned him that I could hold no communciation with him until he informed me that he would answer the letter . . . Our men are awfully sick at not having a go at the enemy[!] and seriously I do hope Mr. Chamberlain won't be led by Sir G. Goldie. I've no doubt the latter is a very honest and delightful gentleman but he *can't* know what is going on here—the absolute robbery of the native and the brutes most of the Niger Company's employees are . . .I can tell you honestly that I came out with the greatest possible admiration for the Niger Company, but that changed very quickly indeed.

There is also a sense of real pathos when reading the last few lines of his letter and in realising that by the time his leave came round, he was dead and buried:—

I must stop now so I can't tell you my impressions of the country. It ain't a healthy one but up to date I have been awfully lucky, only four little goes of fever and mostly as fit as a flea, but it runs you down fearfully especially in the rains. Of course I have been lucky in being a lot on the move and having lots to do. Those two things are the great secret of health in this country. My best love to Margaret and many thanks for her letter, which I hope to answer in the distant future. I *hope* to come home in April.

But to return to the matter of Lugard's lecture to the Royal Geographical Society in 1903, one, indeed, in which the Somerset episode now assumes an especial relevance. It is true that Goldie absented himself from the meeting in spite of a previously declared intention to be present, but the excuse that he gave, namely the death of an aunt whose executor he was, was a legitimate one. In addition, he had specifically requested the President, Markham, to read out his letter of apology for his absence, one in which he praised Lugard highly and extolled his "splendid career" in Northern Nigeria which "has not to my mind received the full attention it deserves."

This he ascribed partly to a "want of public interest in West African affairs, but partly also to [Lugard's] having a weakness shared by many other great men—excessive modesty." (21) This may have been a barbed shaft in view of Lugard's fascination with the "self-advertisement" which Goldie abhorred, but on the other hand, Goldie might then sincerely have believed it! Unless, therefore, there is additional unpublished information on this point, it is not easy to see the basis for Perham's positive ascription of the feud to this instance. She certainly establishes beyond question that Goldie did object to certain observations that Lugard proposed to make according to the draft he had sent to the Society's Secretary, Scott Keltie, and to which Keltie had drawn Goldie's attention, but Lugard had cut them out, and it is quite certain that prudence as well as anything else had dictated this course, for if the two *had* clashed, Lugard would have been just as bloodied—if not more so—than Goldie, who had written to him:—" . . . I do not want to stand up and *flatly* contradict your main point—in a score of words." (22)

As will be shown, the real crux of the argument was to centre on Lugard's determination to "resurrect" the Somerset story of the impotence of the Company's agents. To do this *ex post facto* of the settlement which had been arrived at between the Company (that is, really, between Goldie) and the Government, would be to strike at Goldie's personal integrity as well as boost Lugard's own achievements.

It must be remembered that it was only a scant three months before that the death of the Sultan Ahmadu Atthiru at Burmi had put the final and irrevocable seal of success on Lugard's endeavours in the Kano/Sokoto campaign—a campaign which, had he been less than totally successful, might have cost him dearly, for he had been close indeed to flaunting a direct instruction from the Secretary of State's deputy, the Earl of Onslow, to avoid a confrontation.

What it was that Goldie objected to is, however, relatively unimportant, for he won his point anyway. What *is* important, is that the contretemps occurred at all, and as to the reason for this, there are some very firm indications indeed.

Perham makes it abundantly clear, (23) although Bell gives no hint of it, (24) that, say sometime from around 1892, Flora Shaw had been deeply in love with Goldie. She also establishes that, on the death of Lady Goldie on 26 April, 1898, Flora had "not only seemed to expect that, in proper course, she and Goldie would marry but [she also] wanted this to happen [with all the force of her nature]."

What Perham rejects, however, and the grounds for her so doing are not entirely convincing ones, is the suggestion that Flora Shaw was the un-named "intimate woman friend" of Goldie's who had written to him, according to Lady Wellesley (25) "immediately after Lady's Goldie's death . . . proposing marriage," and who had been so decisively rebuffed with the receipt of a copy of *Romersholm*. (26)

Perham's indignation at Goldie (27) justified though to some extent it may be—does not seem to support the grounds on which she makes so positive a statement that the Rosmersholm rebuff "could not possibly apply to the eminent.and dignified woman described by Miss Moberly Bell and further revealed in the Lugard papers." It did not, and for two good reasons. First, it applied to the forty-seven year old spinster, Flora Shaw, who had been in love with a married man for some six or seven years, and secondly, the Moberly Bell work, shallow as it is, was the "official life" for which both Lugard and his brother helped to "prepare the material." (28)

Goldie, also, was not without his sensibilities, and it can hardly have been welcome to him, deeply affected as Darwin has made clear he was, [29] to receive a proposal to remarry under such circumstances. If Goldie was careless of Flora's feelings, she was certainly no less insensitive to his.

That it *was* Flora who made this approach and that it was she who suffered the rebuff, fits perfectly into the framework of the scanty evidence available. And the pattern emerging thereafter fits equally well into the subsequent deterioration of relationship between the two men in her life.

Her reaction was almost classically predictable in the terms of a romantic novel. She "fell into a sadness; then into a fast; thence to a watch; thence into a weakness," only avoiding the fate that befell Hamlet by the onset of a fully fledged nervous breakdown, the effects of which lasted for over two years. She resigned from the *Times*, whose Colonial Editor she was; she became morose and introspective; and as such, she was identified by Lugard as a kindred soul. "He saw the successful, self-reliant Flora struck down just as he had been many years before [by Celia]." [30]

When they married, Flora was fifty-one and Lugard forty-four. She was therefore a couple of years older in respect to him than she herself was younger than Goldie. And, irrespective of what they came to mean to each other later on (and the proof of the depth of that relationship is positive), initially she saw their marriage only as the public manifestation of a "loyal friendship made absolute for life." [31] On another occasion, she wrote:—"You once said you would win my *love*. I, too, hope to win yours . . . We can not force it. Let us not try on either side; but let us be content to marry as friends." [32]

Her wedding night, and the night after, was spent in a state of nervous collapse with Lugard "nursing her as an invalid," and with him "each [evening taking] an hour's violent walk to the top of some hill . . ."

The conclusion that Flora Shaw married Lugard "on the rebound" from her rejection by Goldie is difficult to avoid, as also is the conclusion that from this time she determined to make Goldie pay for it!

Perham observes:—"From the time of Flora's breakdown and her engagement to Lugard, his friendship for Goldie came to an end." [33] This might be the case for Lugard, but, as noted, it seems premature to regard it as being so for Goldie. In Part VI there is reproduced Goldie's 1912 eulogy of Lugard which would seem to deny that he accepted that their relationship was lost at that time. But from her marriage onwards, it is Flora who begins to orchestrate the recurrent theme of the "inadequacy" of the Company as an administrative organisation, and it is from this time also that Goldie takes occasions, as they arise, to rebut the claim. The examples of Flora reverting to this theme are legion, but one of the clearest, as well as one of the earliest, is that in her letter to Chamberlain, dated as being written from "Moreji *(sic)* on the Niger, [34] 16 August, 1902"—a station where the Company had had a trading hulk moored for decades. She wrote:—

"The progress which has been made in the annexation and organisation of the inland territories lying back from the highway of the river *and untouched except in theory by the Niger Co.,* seems to me almost incredible . . . ." (35)

It was the repetition of this sentiment by Lugard a year later in the draft of his R.G.S. address (and in terms peculiarly reminiscent of Somerset's letter) that was one of the things to which Goldie objected. This we know for sure, because in his correspondence with Lugard on the subject he had written:—

"I *could* not have spoken after you without flatly contradicting the statement that 'it was not safe for their agents to travel far from their warehouses.' Hewby—who is, I suppose, still with you—could, I am sure, give you a very different account of the "Company's work in the Bakundi and Donga regions, between 1890 and 1900. Nor could I admit that the diplomatic relations of the Company with Nassarawa, Muri and Bauchi (which effectually checked the slave-raiding across the Benue which existed up to 1890) were not a form of administration, although of course not comparable with the effective occupation that you have established.

But most of my fear of misconception falls to the ground if you cut out the passage to which you refer." (36)

Flora's harping on the theme recurs, however, implicitly or stated, in her *Brittanica* articles and in her address on 18 March, 1904, to the Royal Society of Arts (37) and in May to the Royal Colonial Institute, (38) and is continually pressed thereafter.

As to the true reason for the utter failure in communication which developed between Goldie and Lugard—a failure which, as Perham notes, ultimately rendered Lugard hardly to be brought in later life to mention Goldie's name—there is also a certain amount of evidence at hand.

Before Lugard's marriage to Flora Shaw the relationship between the two men had been warm, even intimate, but there was no possible question as to which of the two was the real *pezzo novanti.* Goldie called the shots even when Lugard was taking his first steps towards his High Commissionership as Commandant of the Frontier Force. Goldie, in fact, clearly used his influence to get Lugard the post in the first place and backed him for the later appointment too.

But how much of Goldie's conceptual and ideological perceptions also rubbed off on his erstwhile subordinate? Any examination of *that* question, for whatever reasons, has almost entirely escaped the attention of scholars up to date.

In any attempt to evaluate Lugard's work, whether one tries to do so by-viewing his contribution enthusiastically and positively, or more critically and negatively, (39) one fact must be admitted, and that is that his apologists, beginning with Flora, who after their marriage became the nonpareil of such, have been extraordinarily successful in presenting such a picture of political, administrative and intellectual omniscience that it is difficult indeed for an objective observer to suggest even the slightest modification of this myth-perception without running an imminent risk of being pilloried for allowing personal or other extraneous considerations to intrude to colour his analysis. Hero worship may be a delightful and satisfying destination at which scholarship may with propriety arrive, but it is surely an execrable point of departure!

One thing, however, is absolutely certain, and that is that, with regard to Lugard, no-one who has spent long hours spread over many years reading and re-reading, in the dusty files of Provincial and Divisional Offices scattered as diversely as from Yola to Borgu or from Lokoja to Kano (with intermediate stops at Kaduna, Lagos, Sokoto, Zaria or Maidugari, among others), the narrow, petty, carping, picayune and self-serving minutes, notes and instructions to his subordinates, written often in his own hand and frequently couched in such terms of open and patronising contempt that it seems almost miraculous that men such as Burdon and Temple tolerated them, is ever likely to come away from that experience with any need to counter a bias induced by an excessive adulation. Far more likely is it, indeed, that he will find himself concurring with the assessment of Joyce Cary, namely that "Lugard is a mean man and a spiteful man. He will take a great deal of trouble to put an enemy or a critic out of the way." [40]

Such indeed the files make him, and they (unlike even a diary) were not written with any eye to future publication or to image-building, save as they represent the writer's perception of the proper relationship between himself as the superior being, and his sevitors in the field.

The fact that Lugard had these characteristics, however, obviously in no way ought to obscure the contributions that he did make, or indeed to detract in any way from his achievements. Nor, therefore, should Goldie's peculiar quirks and foibles obscure his achievements either, though it is pertinent to observe that these same eccentricities went far towards contributing to the ease with which Lugard—aided mightily by the decade or so of difference in their respective ages, a difference which allowed him to project his own reputation into tne very era of decolonisation itself—was enabled to pre-empt the philosophical and ideological field of early Administration Theory almost exclusively.

Some things, however, Goldie could not conceal or destroy. One such corpus was the bulk of his public speaking and writing, now reproduced in sequence for the first time. Another was (and this definitively) the opinion of his professional contemporaries. In this respect, Goldie differed materially from Lugard, who, however brilliant he may have been in other fields, was clearly a lamentably poor judge of men, a thing at which Goldie was consummately expert.

Lugard, moreover, was congenitally incapable of delegating authority, whilst Goldie was always giving the impression of being generously assured that his subordinates would serve him well, which, of course, made certain that they did! Lugard, too, was prone to favourites, and, in respect to his younger brother Edward, was positively nepotistic. The result of both these foibles not infrequently was that, with this "inner circle" as a filter, much of the information that Lugard received was sychophantic and, of course, many of the favourites were later well to the forefront in the creation of the legend.

42

For scholars of later decades, moreover, it is possible that the repetition of quotations somewhat out of context may have seriously distorted their perceptions as to the single-mindedness with which Lugard's immediate administrative successors in Northern Nigeria executed "his" policy. It may be the case that their actions were undertaken not in a spirit of automatic and unquestioned reverence at the magnificence of "his" conceptions, as has sometimes been represented to have been the case, but, rather, that they were acting in obedience to a larger, Colonial Office inspired masterplan, and one which Goldie had been instrumental in initiating. [41]

But Goldie's contemporaries were somewhat more forthright than most of Lugard's were and perhaps, therefore, they were the more accurate—and this includes even those who were avowedly his commercial and entrepreneurial rivals and opponents, even perhaps his enemies.

That he had some powerful partisans as well, goes without saying, for to Mary Kingsley he was " . . . one of those great men, who, from time to time, rise up in England and go down quietly into the world and give her dominion therein . . ." [42] and she classed him with Clive and Nicholson and Raffles and Brooke.

But it was not as a merchant adventurer—the role in which Mary most romantically and consistently cast not only Goldie, but also John Holt and Alfred Jones, the driving force behind the shipping line of Elder Dempster—that Goldie was to achieve that grasp of history that would make him truly great and stamp his mark on the next sixty-five years. Huge as his achievements were in that field, they pale into insignificance alongside the influence he was to have on the philosophy of colonial rule by Britain—for it is to Goldie that must be given the credit for the modern enunciation of the Doctrine of Indirect Rule within the West African context.

To say that anyone "invented" the system of Indirect Rule is, of course, unmitigated nonsense. In the gigantic sweep of its relativity to political hegemony, Caesar Augustus was one of its more recent practitioners in his governance of Herod the Great. It was ancient when Ghana ruled two hundred vassal princes in accordance with it or when King Charibael of Mapharites ruled Rhapta. [43] The principle itself is as old as man's dominion over man. It is probable, however that the first "colonial" European to realise its potential in West Africa was Sir George Maclean, of the Royal African Colonial Corps, Governor of Cape Coast in 1830, and, in effect, the man who set up the Gold Coast Protectorate. In 1842, he was commended by the Select Parliamentary Committee as having:—

"acquired a very wholesome influence over a coast not much less than 150 miles in extent to a considerable distance inland . . . and exercising a useful though irregular jurisdiction among the neighbouring tribes." [44]

On the Gold Coast having eventually materialised, Maclean was appointed its "Judicial Assessor,"—

"his duty being to administer justice among the natives and try, in concert with native Chiefs, cases in which natives alone were concerned, according to native law as far as it could be applied in harmony with civilised ideas of justice—a thing that Maclean himself during his government founded and which has done infinite good since in West Africa and made the name of England beloved and powerful."(45)

But as to who it was who refined the doctrine and articulated it and then formally enunciated it, there can no longer be any doubt or prevarication. It was Sir George Goldie. And the effects which were to result from this doctrine of his were far-reaching indeed.

It is true, as has been noted, that not everyone, in trying to reach a fair assessment of Goldie's work, has had the unrivalled opportunities which Flint enjoyed of total access to the Scarbrough or John Holt Papers. Those that do not, for amplification must be content with the additional small but highly pertinent selection which Stephen Gwynn preserved in the historical essay which forms the first section of Lady Wellesley's work. It is true too, that it appears remarkable that, given the promise of this sample, more of Goldie's political philosophy was not developed from the greater corpus itself and it would be interesting indeed to know whether data which would throw light upon this aspect of Goldie's intellectualism were in fact, for whatever reason, disregarded.

It would also be interesting, after such a passage of time, to learn whether Lugard's own voluminous correspondence, not only with Goldie but with others, throws any light upon his own perceptions of how his attitudes towards indigenous institutions changed and an enhanced appreciation of "native" culture, mores and aspirations developed.

When Lugard first came to West Africa, as Goldie's entry for the race to Nikki, his contempt for the principles of "indirectness" was almost blistering. The King of Bussa was playing hard to get, and Lugard was distinctly unappreciative.

" . . . on his whim the representative of the Company has to stand in the sun and wait, with a fever on him etc. At Rome we must do as the Romans do, but my heart sinks at the thought that I must submit to such customs and indignities for another year! . . . I don't see my way clearly in this business I have undertaken. I am altogether the wrong man . . . A man used to *trading*, arguing, haggling, and *not* to ruling or asserting himself might succeed, but I could hardly have been chosen on those grounds . . . a subsidised third-class savage inside the Company's territory—what am I to expect when I get entirely beyond their influence? . . . About 9 a.m. got a message from this beast of a 'King' at last . . .(46)

Something must have happened to change his mind between then and 1906 when he wrote his first Political Memorandum!

Even as late as 1898, Lugard, by supporting the somewhat intemperate tantrums of Somerset and the ham-handed excursions of Willcocks into the Company's domain of diplomacy as already described showed but little appreciation of the principles which he was to advocate so successfully in later years. (47)

How, therefore, was the miraculous conversion to be effected? By what means was a new St. Paul to be transformed on the road to Damascus?

Authority for so categorical an attribution of the "Doctrine" to Goldie as has now been made did not, however, emerge immediately, or even soon. Nor does it appear in modern analyses. To Flint—and to Perham—Goldie slips lower and lower down the slope of either policy-making activity or of interest from the moment that the decision was made by the government to opt for a revocation of the Charter. To them, Goldie's apogee of either power or influence was the campaign of 1897, and in a sense, this is true.

But in 1909, close enough to know, but twelve years later and distant enough to be objective, the assertion that it was Goldie who fathered the "Doctrine of Indirect Rule" and thus left his stamp indelibly on Nigeria, receives a startling and incontrovertible confirmation from none other than Hesketh Bell, [48] Lugard's successor once removed.

Bell had only just been appointed Governor of Northern Nigeria. At that time it was the custom for Residents in charge of each Province to submit to His Excellency a semi-annual report, setting out in great detail the progress of their administration from every January to June and from each July to December. Burdon was then the Resident in charge of Sokoto.

Whether as a means of "conditioning" the new Governor, of presenting, as it were a policy *fait accompli,* a fixed procedure from which it would be almost impossible for a new broom—then an unknown quantity—to depart, Burdon had used the latest of these reports as a vehicle for a somewhat fulsome panegyric on his staff's competence and performance, cast firmly under the mantle of that "indirectness" to which he was personally indubitably completely wedded.

In paragraph 2 of that report, dated 2 October, 1909, reference 1084/1909, (and acknowledged by the Secretary of the Government, together with His Excellency's comments on 28 October, 1909) [49] Burdon wrote:

"Speaking generally, I am exceedingly pleased at the progress of the Province in the past three years [i.e. since 1906, the year of the Satiru Rebellion], due I believe first and foremost to the endeavor of all Residents to secure continuity of Policy.

The principle on which the policy of this province has always been based has been "Indirect Administration." This has been the aim of [successive political officers, named and listed], altered in no essential from my original basis which I believe met with the approval of His Excellency Sir. F. D. Lugard. I feel justified in claiming that the present condition of the Province is proof of the soundness of the principle of rule through Native Chiefs . . ."

In making his reference to Lugard, it must be remembered that Burdon was merely acknowledging the extent to which the former had "pre-empted" Indirect Rule as his own philosophy, a pre-emption indeed, going right back to his assumption of office in 1900.

In his Annual Report to the Colonial Office, 1900-1901, Lugard had written: [50]

45

"The policy which I am endeavouring to carry out as regards the natives of the Protectorate may, perhaps, be usefully summarised here. The Government utilises and works through the native chiefs, and avails itself of the intelligence and powers of governing of the Fulani caste in particular, but insists upon their observance of the fundamental laws of humanity and justice. Residents are appointed whose primary duty it is to promote this policy by the establishment of native courts, in which bribery and extortion and inhuman punishments shall be gradually abolished . . . If an Emir proves unamenable to persuasion or to threats, and will not desist from such actions (as in the case of Kontagora and Bida) he is deposed, and in each case a Fulani or other successor recognised by the people has been installed in his place. The traditional tribute (except that in slaves) paid by the villages to their chiefs, is insisted upon, and its incidence and collection are being regularised so as to prevent extortion or an undue burden on the agricultural or trading classes. I recognise the obligation of the chiefs to contribute to the revenue in return for the enhancement of their dues resulting from this system, and, in return for the protection of the roads from the robbers which used to infest them, and for the improvement of communications, etc. But I have not as yet formulated any definite line of action in this connection, since it is one which needs the utmost tact, and I should prefer to discuss it with the chiefs themselves on my return to the Protectorate before forming any definite conclusions . . ."

In the above there is no hint that the philosophy which underlies the policy as enumerated was that of any person other than Lugard or that it was anything but an innovative experiment on his part. In fact, the concluding sentences of the same paragraph appear deliberately designed to convey the impression that the policy was his alone and that it was only by constant vigilance and encouragement that it could be maintained in the conceptual purity with which he had endowed it.

"Among the wholly uncivilised pagan tribes, who owe no allegiance to a paramount chief, it is often difficult to apply these principles of rule, and the political officers have to undertake a more direct responsibility owing to the difficulty, and often impossibility, of establishing native courts, and to the lawless habits of the people. Among these tribes it is my policy to centralise authority, as far as may be, in a recognised chief, and to introduce the civilising agency of trade, while repressing all intertribal quarrels.

In the first year, some small progress along these lines has been made, and I look for increasing results in the coming year with a somewhat more adequate and more fully organised staff of capable and zealous political officers."(51)

This, however, was only the beginning. In 1906, Lugard published the first edition of his *Political Memoranda*—a work which was duly revised and amended in 1911 and 1918 and which was still required reading for all Administrative Officers in Northern Nigeria as late as 1947. It contained a number of his essays on policy, written separately and now collected together in one volume. In May, 1905, revised September, 1906, Lugard had composed a memorandum on *Native Chiefs*. He numbered it No. 9.

"I am anxious in every possible way to conteract any tendency that may develop on the part of the people to throw off the rule of their Chiefs and to support the authority of the Native Chiefs, though I consider that it is necessary to retain the

Military and Police Forces solely under government at present and probably for some time to come." (52)

He continued, elaborating on the theme somewhat,

"The prestige and influence of the Chiefs can best be upheld by letting the peasantry see that government itself treats them as an integral part of the machinery of the Administration . . . in which the Native Chiefs have clearly defined duties and an acknowledged *status* equally with British officials." (53)

This was a far cry from his former attitude to the "beast of a King" of Boussa!

In his foreword to the volume of collected Memoranda, dated 12 February, 1905, Government House, Northern Nigeria, Lugard wrote:—

"They [the memoranda] have no legal value . . . but they will serve to explain the views of the High Commissioner, and the methods by which, in actual practice, the Proclamations can, in his opinion, best be enforced and Administrative problems solved."

He had written to them and he claimed "to promote continuity and uniformity of policy and to act as a guide on the application of the proclamations and in other matters."

Burdon's diffident, (and almost word for word) echoes of these sentiments and his gentle reminder that he believed that the principles on which he was working "met with the approval" of Lugard, can only be taken as an attempt to signal to the new arrival that there was a set and approved policy in being with which it might be best not to meddle too extensively.

His shock, therefore must have been doubly acute when His Excellency's observations on his Report were communicated to him by the Secretary. (54)

Para 2. Surely this was the policy outlined by Mr. Chamberlain in 1898 on the advice of Sir. G. Goldie and others, *including myself.* Sir F. Lugard *adopted this policy on transfer in 1900,* and it has been carried out ever since in a more or less thorough manner according to the ideas of the various Residents." (55) [italics added]

One must, however, sympathise with Burdon somewhat. He clearly did not know exactly which horse to back in his dealings with Hesketh Bell; was it to be Goldie or Lugard? In fact he did make a serious effort to hedge his bets in paragraph 49 of the same report (56) when he observed:—"I hold very strongly to the opinion expressed by Sir George Goldie in his preface to Vandeleur's *Campaigning on the Upper Nile and Niger."* (57) In respect, that is, to the administration of justice and the Native Court system. Even earlier, however, (58) Burdon had written:—

"Sir George Goldie has taught us that the British aim in the country should be to teach existing rulers to govern their own people . . . and not try to force direct British rule on the Africans . . . I quickly realised the greatness of this ideal and preached it in and out of season against strong opposition . . . I carried my policy to its logical conclusion and supported my chiefs to the utmost, sometimes to an extent which exceeded the intentions of the Governor.''

It may be, therefore, that Hesketh Bell's ready appreciation of Goldie's determining role was not unwelcome to Burdon!

At the time when Hesketh Bell and Burdon were getting the "feel" of each other administratively, Lugard was safely out of sight and, as the above correspondence would seem to indicate, was in a fair way to being put out of mind as well. In view of the frictions that had developed since the new Liberal Government under Campbell-Bannerman had taken office at the end of December in that year, culminating in the oppostion which Lugard's suppression of the Satiru rising, (59) and especially of its aftermath at Hadejia, had evoked in the new Parliamentary Under Secretary of State—a brash young man whom Flora cordially detested named Winston Churchill—it seemed hardly conceivable that Lugard would ever return to Africa. In fact, so certain was he that his years of authority were over, that he was most pleasantly surprised when, in the late spring of the following year (1907), he was offered the Governorship of Hong Kong. He arrived in that Colony almost exactly one year after having given up his post in Northern Nigeria—and after having been brought to realise that unemployment was neither to his nor Flora's taste. (60)

As far as Goldie was concerned, however, it would be ridiculous to assume that he had shut himself off from the affairs of Northern Nigeria as absolutely as some of his public utterances would seem to indicate. (61) In fact, there is both direct and indirect evidence to establish the contrary.

In the first place, he had supported the Lugard's in their "Scheme" [for Continuous Administration]. It would have been odd if he had not done so, because the idea had been his to begin with, (62) and it fitted in well with his insistence that extraordinary situations require extraordinary solutions. It is, however, worth noting that it was Flora and Lugard who sought his help in this matter, a thing which they would hardly have done if either of them had perceived him, on his part, to be as personally hostile to them as has been suggested. (63)

In the second place, the murder of Captain Maloney at Keffi in 1902, (64) and, even more so, the slaughter of the Assistant Residents Hillary and Scott and of Lieutenant Blackwood of the Mounted Infantry at Satiru, to say nothing of the rank and file killed with them, together with the unusual ferocity and barbarity that accompanied the end of the two Administrative Officers, (65) had gone far to justify Goldie's worst forebodings which he has expressed in the Selborne Committee's Report as to the danger of adopting a too "forward" policy. (66)

In fact, the whole opposition to this policy—the one which Lugard had adopted after 1900, often in the face of objection from the permanent officials—which the new administration was again articulating, did not necessarily stem, as Flora believed, from the "Manchester mob" mentality of the new Government. It had been rationally and cogently argued nearly eight years before it came to be espoused, by no less an expert than Goldie. It was now being advanced by Churchill once again, and he was echoing Goldie's own sentiments that wholesale attempts at the administrative incorporation of the whole territory should be slowed. (67)

One can also be certain that Goldie was kept well informed as to the minutiae of how matters were proceeding administratively under the new regime. Burdon (Sokoto), Cargill (Kano), Festing (Kano), and Hewby (Bornu), to say nothing of Wallace, Lugard's Deputy (and Girouard's and Bell's), were all ex-R.N.C. men with whom it is not to be conceived that Goldie did not meet and keep in contact during their annual leaves. Scarborough too, with whom Goldie was in very frequent social communication, had his own sources of information through the Agents General, Flint or Watts. All of these would have talked with absolute frankness (and with no impropriety) to their former Chief, and Goldie can confidently be regarded as being perpetually as well briefed as the Colonial Office—if not better!

Thus, the clear absence of any indications, prior to 1912, that Goldie had any reservations about what Lugard was attempting to do in Nigeria, or that he was in any way opposed either to his policies or to his administrative direction—with the exception, that is, of Lugard's "forward policy" which he was, Satiru notwithstanding, successful in accomplishing—must therefore be taken as evidence of Goldie's tacit overall approval.

There is the undoubted fact, moreover, that Goldie would have been even more appreciative, *as were the permanent officials of the Colonial Office,* of the degree to which Lugard's subordinates *extended* the principles of Indirect Rule after Lugard's 1907 departure. The emergence of the Native Treasury system, the development of the philosophy which C. L. Temple set forth in his extraordinary book, (68) and the open acceptance by Lugard's successors of a very high degree of decentralisation indeed, were not merely fully in accord with what Goldie believed, but were what he had, in fact, consistently advocated or were inherent in it as being desirable and inevitable projections.

Up to 1912, therefore, Goldie had good reason to be content; he could look with a certain satisfaction at the way he knew things were developing in the country he had created. His only concern, throughout this period, was to see that the Company had a reasonable share of acknowledgement for its achievements, and his determination so to do is readily seen to be reflected in many of the examples of his public speaking or writing which follow.

It is also, of course, totally false to assume—as has so often been the case—that during this period between 1900 and 1912 Goldie was little more than a broken reed. Such is far from being the truth. He was appointed to sit on two Royal Commissions, the *Royal Commission on the Conduct of the South African War* and the *Royal Commission on War Stores in Africa,* (69) and both of them were "blue ribbon" affairs, the questions they were investigating being matters of the highest public policy and of deep popular concern. Of the two, the first was perhaps the more important and the more prestigious.

The relationship between the Army and the politicians throughout the whole of the Edwardian era (and, indeed, somewhat before and after the era itself began or ended) was an especially tense and difficult one. Strain had begun to show itself as early as the Ashanti and Zulu Wars, as well as in connection with the Gordon episode and the relief of Khartoum. The Boer War underlined it starkly, and its really serious manifestation erupted in the Curragh Incident of 1914, an event which many authorities believe constituted an embryonic military *coup d'etat.* Others, whilst not taking this view, nonetheless regard the incident as being seminal in the subsequent development of civil oversight of military affairs. [70]

The Chairman of the *Royal Commission on the Conduct of the South African War* was the Earl of Elgin, [71] a former Viceroy of India and the man who in 1905 was to become Campbell-Bannerman's Colonial Secretary. With him was Lord Esher; [72] Field Marshal Sir H. W. Norman; [73] Admiral Sir J. Ommanney Hopkins; [74] Sir John Edge, formerly Chief Justice of the North West Provinces of India, [75] and "Sir John Jackson, the eminent contractor." [76]

But, when Balfour rose in the House to announce those names, he was unable to add that of the seventh member and the Prime Minister was kept in that state of suspension "for some weeks", during which time he could do no more than express the hope that he would be able to secure the services of the gentleman in question. [77]

When the announcement was finally made on 10 September, 1902, it was Goldie for whom everybody had been waiting. Next day, the *Times* very nearly "went overboard" in its enthusiasm.

"[the name] is that of Sir George Goldie, whose admirable work in the conquest, government and administration of Nigeria constitutes a lasting claim on the gratitude of all who have the interests of the Empire at heart [and who] . . . in circumstances of no small difficulty, and with very necessarily limited resources at his command . . . showed how foresight, judgement, and firmness of purpose could secure a rare combination of efficiency with economy." [78]

This, it was clear, was no random appointment of an elder colonial administrator. Goldie was being sought for his knowledge and experience, and could afford to keep the Prime Minister waiting for his answer, for as long as was needed for him to satisfy himself that what was being asked of him was genuinely worthwhile and something he could support.

When it came to the pinch, the members of the Commission were a mixed lot. Esher, a brilliant courtier, and Goldie, were clearly the dominant faction. Esher and Goldie, moreover, were something of kindred spirits, in that Lord Esher shunned public acclaim as much as he did.

An intimate of the King, Esher wielded enormous power behind the scenes. Sir Frederick Ponsonby, the King's Private Secretary, wrote of him:—"[Esher's strongest point] was that he never minded who got credit for any measure he devised so long as it was adopted by the authorities." [79]

Anita Leslie notes:—"[Esher] wanted to do a great deal—but without being noticed. His ambition was the reverse of ordinary ambition. He wished to attain power without recognition, without applause—his enemies said without responsibility." [80]

Given such a congruence of outlook, it is hardly to be wondered at if the two were drawn together intellectually, and there is clear evidence that this was so.

Lord Esher was in the habit of writing a personal letter to the King practically every night during the Commission's sessions, describing the evidence that they had heard, and sometimes giving an inkling as to the way in which its collective mind was moving. These letters, as befitted the status of the correspondents, were always strictly formal, couched in the third person, and never exceeding the bounds of strict propriety. One Commissioner only is singled out for any show of approbation, and that one is Goldie.

Writing his final letter on the subject, Esher tells the King:—

"Lord Esher presents his humble duty and begs to inform Your Majesty that the Report of the S.A. War Commission was signed by all Your Majesty's Commissioners on Thursday last.

The document has been considerably strengthened in its final stages [but] Lord Esher will not conceal from Your Majesty that he would have preferred [it if] a clearer judgement had been formed by the Commissioners, but reluctance to do this was so great that it was not to be overcome . . . [Accordingly] Lord Esher has found it necessary to write a separate note, appended to the Report, dealing with the [need for a re-organisation of the War Office and] the question of the position of a Commander in Chief in the future, his views upon which are known to Your Majesty.

To this note Sir George Goldie and Sir John Jackson have subscribed.

Sir George Goldie has also appended a note upon a most interesting point, that of 'compulsory national military education,' and has expressed views with which Lord Esher is in cordial agreement." [81]

To have the "cordial agreement" of a man like Esher was of no little value. He was undoubtedly one of the half dozen most influential men in the nation, and he knew how to use his power at that! A man who would turn down not only the appointment of Secretary of War but also the Viceroyalty of India, preferring to operate behind the scenes as the King's most trusted confidant, and who delivered a judgement in those terms, was someone who's opinion was not lightly to be disdained.

Far from Goldie's opportunities for the exercise of quiet but effective influence waning during this period, therefore, they were immeasurably extended, especially after Elgin took over the Colonial Office; for, Esher's view apart, Goldie's contribution to the success and reception of the Elgin Commission was certainly not minor, in that it attracted considerable public attention, most of which was favourable. [82]

His image as a thinker and a scholar was further enhanced at this time by his active and highly successful Presidencies of the Royal Geographical Society and of the African Society, and by his involvement in the affairs of the British Association, the Royal Society and the Colonial Institute. As President of the R.G.S., he hosted the only meeting in its history at which the Sovereign Patron was present in person.(83) Whilst President of the African Society, he entertained H.R.H. The Duke of Connaught on his return from South Africa in 1911. (84)

Even without these special circumstances, office in all or any of these bodies carried with it its own specialised avenues of influence, and an indication of their strength and value can be seen in the assiduous avidity with which the industrious Flora (and Lugard) courted an appearance before some of them, fulfilling as they did in the context of the times much the same function as the modern television interview and thus being greatly sought after.

From 1908, also, Goldie had another role, this time as an Alderman on the London County Council, a position which gave him still further opportunities to broaden and enlarge his contacts with business and the City.

Then, late in 1911, as far as Nigeria was concerned, the bombshell burst. Lewis Harcourt,(85) the Colonial Secretary from 1910-1915, in succession to Elgin, persuaded Lugard to accept the task of fusing the two administrations of Northern and Southern Nigeria into one and of amalgamating the territories. The emoluments were, by the standards of the time, princely (£7,500 in all) and the opportunity dazzling. In effect, Harcourt had made Lugard "an offer that he couldn't refuse."

He returned to Britain on 19 April, 1912. Less than a month later, on 16 May, the African Society hosted the dinner in his honour at the "Troc." But it was not only in his honour, but in that of all his predecessors in the North as well, and of Sir Walter Egerton too, from Southern Nigeria, the man whom Lugard would be shortly replacing there.(86) Added for good measure was the Rt. Hon. John Elliot Burns,(87) the Minister of Health who was undoubtedly intended to be representative of that lost legion of the rank and file employees of the Royal Niger Company.

The word "all" is used advisedly above, for the gathering included every single person who had held the substantive appointment giving control over Northern Nigeria since 1895 (when Lord Aberdare died), and the only person who had exercised the same authority over Southern Nigeria.

Nicolson's view that the dinner was arranged with the premeditated determination of reminding Lugard that others besides himself had had a hand in the making of Nigeria has a more than innate validity. The fact that Goldie, so lately retired as President of the Society—a post that had been taken over by Sir Clement Hill, formerly of the Foreign Office and then a Member of Parliament—was the principal speaker, is also not without its special significance. But it must be stressed also, that at this dinner Goldie went out of his way to give a resounding endorsement of the warmth of his personal friendship for Lugard. (88)

Something happened therefore *after* that date to destroy their relationship and it appears indeed, that it was at that same point that Goldie finally gave up, washing his hands of the whole business. Nothing else will explain the abruptness with which *all* his interests (except for the L.C.C.) were abandoned.

What that something was is not easy to identify, but the clue can probably be found in a report by Major Darwin (89) on the interview that he had with Goldie in 1899. It concerned Goldie's views on the governance of Africa and it in some ways amplifies what he had written in his introduction to Vandeleur. (90)

In 1899, Darwin had been asked to contribute an article on Nigeria to that extremely prestigious organ the *National Review,* (91) and he still had available his shorthand notes.

"From shorthand notes of an interview with Sir George Goldie in March, 1899.

'In regions where Europeans can colonise, in the proper sense of the word, there can be little doubt that the proper system is to establish a European system of law and administration with due regard to Native customs and Native prejudices . . . Such a system, however, is quite inapplicable to densely populated regions where the whiteman must always be in an absolute considerable minority, where he can never hope to rule by force alone, and where his ideas, if they could be enforced upon the Native populations, would create endless discomfort and misery . . . In such regions the only true policy of government is to adopt the local Native governments already existing, and to be content with controlling their excesses and with maintaining peace amongst themselves . . .

I think [that the phrase *sphere of influence*] exactly expresses the idea of European rule over Africa, namely, each colonising nation should have its own sphere within which no other civilised nation should interfere, but that colonising nations shall not be bound or inclined to exercise in their sphere more than the general influence which is necessary for the gradual progress of civilisation.' ''

Goldie then went on to argue that the difficulties of recruiting and maintaining staff of the necessary high quality in such regions, coupled with the inevitable dis-continuity of policy occasioned by the long and frequent periods of absence which such staff required to remain healthy, re-inforced his recommendations, and added:—

"Moreover, however it may be in other parts of the world, it is certain that the population of Nigeria, whether Mohammedan or Pagan, entertains entirely different views of life from those entertained in this country, and they would rather be misgoverned by their own people than be governed by the very best of our officials."(92)

It was this basic principle, in Goldie's view the *sine qua non* of good colonial government, that Lugard, now at the zenith of his power and opportunity, was about to subject to an intrusion that amounted to a rape.

It was also, no doubt, the perception of this fact that created in the minds both of the permanent officials at the middle levels of the Colonial Office, like Strachey,[93] and of the Northern officers, like Temple, with whom they were in touch, the foreboding which they did not hesitate to express[94] either on the news of Lugard's reappointment being received, or later.

There is no intention here to engage in a critical analysis of Lugard's administrative policy during his term of office from 1912 on. It is sufficient to say merely that Goldie must have found the following aspects of it alien to his whole philosophy and utterly distasteful.

(a) Lugard's opposition to the embryonic "independent states" of Governors MacGregor, Egerton and others[95] and especially, his Abeokuta policy up to 1914, [96]

(b) His determination to sweep away the "constitutional litter"[97] which he detected in the existence of such polities, and his intention to "streamline" their relationship with the new Central Government.

(c) The policy of the imposition of Direct Taxation, against which Goldie had so firmly set his face from the days of the Selborne Committee, [98]

(d) The creation of the ill-starred Warrant Chief system in the former area of the Oil Rivers (or Niger Coast) Protectorate, which had been the province of Goldie's old friend Sir Ralph Moor, and (this above all) [99]

(e) Lugard's deliberate attempt, which even his most sympathetic supporters apparently now concede, to dismantle the structure of Indirect Rule which had been developed in the North under the guidance of Girouard and Bell (and Wallace, who had acted as High Commissioner longer than Lugard had actually served) and at the instance of Burdon, Hewby, Temple and others, of whom Palmer[100] was one of the more recent converts.

To detail this last item would be a work of supererogation in view of the excellent treatment aspects of it have been accorded by Dr. Mervin Hiskett in an admirable "Critical Introduction" to the second edition of Temple's book, which is an analysis of extreme sophistication and value by one of the leading authorities on Islam in Nigeria. [101]

The fact that remains, however, is that between 1912 and 1918, Goldie and Lugard parted ideological and social company for ever. The War no doubt assisted this process, though the opportunity for them to have met at intervals throughout it—had either of them so wished—was never absent. Flora's enmity, which, in the absence of any persuasive evidence to the effect that she was not Goldie's rejected lover is here taken for granted, was certainly a factor. How much Goldie was affected by Lugard's aberration into Ulster politics is unclear in the absence of data, but it can be regarded as likely that he agreed with Harcourt that it gravely called into question Lugard's judgement and discretion. [102] It should be remarked, however, that the impetus behind that incident appears to have been Flora's, a fact which, having in mind the pretty pass to which her misdirected enthusiasms over the Jameson Raid had brought the *Times,* quite certainly casts the most serious doubts on *her* good judgement! (103)

Temple's eclipse and his retirement in 1917 at the early age of forty-six —under a chain of circumstances that will be perpetually puzzling to an ex-Colonial Service Officer (for is not the *Governor* the person responsible for the provision of satisfactory answers to Parliamentary questions?) (104)—can not have been less unwelcome to Goldie than it was welcome to Lugard.

Lugard's retirement in 1919, when faced with a situation which made him feel, as Goldie too had felt in 1900, that he had been put out to grass while he still had useful work in him, probably presented the last opportunity at which a reconciliation could have been effected, but Goldie was then seventy-three to Lugard's sixty-one and had himself finally severed his ties with the L.C.C. that same year, and nothing came of it.

The publication of *The Dual Mandate* in 1922, and the applause that greeted that extraordinary admixture of seminal conceptualization and platitudinous over-simplification completes the picture. It is not surprising that Goldie's friends and admirers, confronted as they were with his present total withdrawal and, in 1925, his death (Lugard did not attend the funeral), whilst seeing during the same period the emergence of the beginning of the legend of Lugardian infallibility, reacted with a conviction that indeed Chersiphron and Metagenes were lost while Herostratus lived.

They did attempt a counterstroke. Lady Wellesley's book was part of it, and Darwin was both active and persistent. R. S. Rattray, himself no inconsiderable scholar, took issue with the myth, and in his turn had issue taken with him by Palmer—whose reply was really no answer to many of the points that Rattray raised. (105) Rattray also wrote an article which was published in *The Fortnightly,* (106) in April, 1935. It was not very well done and is somewhat scrappy and occasionally regrettably inaccurate, but it also gives the impression that the writer feels like a man who is trying to win a fist fight with a sack of feathers, so entrenched is the myth against which he is tilting. Two brief quotations will serve to demonstrate its direction.

"In *The Dual Mandate* . . . the only reference to be found to Goldie by name [occurs on page 14]. There seems nothing in Lord Lugard's work from which any person could assume that 'the present Government of Nigeria was based on Goldie's original scheme' to quote a claim which Lord Scarbrough has vouched for as being thoroughly justified.''(107)

It would be interesting, too, to confirm what it was that underlay Rattray's need, in the closing sentences of his article, to pen the following thoughts:—

[Goldie] . . . was an idealist with enough practical genius to carry his idealism through—indeed a rare combination. The cheapest of all attacks on his name and memory are those which hint at his lack of rectitude. He was too great—and I should like to say . . . too beautiful a character ever to be besmirched in such a manner.'' (108)

Unhappily, the probability is that his objection was to the phrase "Goldie was no more a plaster saint in his public than his private life revealed here in such human colours . . .'' which Miss Margery Perham (as she then was) used in the final paragraph of a review which she had written of Lady Wellesley's book. (109) She was immediately challenged by Stephen Gwynn to justify the innuendo. Goldie was, he admitted, "lax in sex-morality," but in public life, his honour was unsullied. Fairness requires that it be stated that Miss Perham's subsequent endeavour to defend her position was not overwhelmingly convincing.

How he would have regarded this last stand by his friends is not entirely clear. Gwynn maintains that during his lifetime, Goldie had had so little desire for counsel that he forbore to offer it to others! But there were one or two things, as Wellesley stresses, that he believed in with a burning conviction that he could never be stopped from pressing.

Chief amongst them was his passionate belief "in the civilizing influence of material prosperity" (110) — and for him, material prosperity was spelt T.R.A.D.E. This accounts for his meticulous insistence on the need always to ensure that the Company's shareholder's were fairly dealt with, an interesting example of which occurred in 1907.

On 29 November of that year, the Earl of Onslow, (111) delivered a somewhat overdue Presidential Address at a dinner of the African Society. This was after Goldie had actually succeeded him as President, and naturally, he was in the chair.

In the course of a rather florid and insubstantial speech, Onslow made a reference to the role of the Royal Niger Company, and said:—

"That Company [to which, together with Goldie, he had paid tribute as being the founders of the Protectorate] naturally considered the interest primarily of its shareholders, but, as we know in the history of England, a time generally arrives when the duties of a company to its shareholders must be incompatible with the interests of *the settlers in the country of its operations and for that reason the British Government took over Nigeria from the Niger Company, and made it a part of the British Empire.* "(112)

One can almost see Goldie explode! That he did so is patent from the remarks he made when replying to the formal toast, "The Chairman," which was proposed by Professor Wyndham Dunstan, F.R.S. They were devastating.

"I recognised [that a time always arrives when the duty of a company to its shareholders must be incompatible with the interests of the State] . . . before I founded the Niger Company and I put it in a memorandum before Lord Salisbury. I took care to let Lord Salisbury know, and also Lord Roseberry, that I should see that the shareholders, with whose money the Company was built up, were fairly treated. The phrase was that "the pioneer was always ruined" and I said that in this case the pioneer should not be ruined, and he was not. I had gone into the street, and induced people to give me a million to begin with. I was bound to see that they got a fair return on their money. If I had not done so, I should have been committing a breach of trust. My work was an international struggle to obtain British possession of that territory, and I may remind you that the work was brought to a successful conclusion before the Niger Charter came to an end. I think that you will agree with me that I was absolutely bound to protect the shareholders' interests in the first place, but "I may add that during the fifteen *(sic)* years the Charter lasted, we never once had a sustained remonstrance from the Foreign Office. I think that is a record for any Government. My whole interests were Imperial interests, and on the day of the transfer to the Crown, my work was done." (113)

This was the nearest Goldie ever came to a justification of his role, and it is sufficient! When he saw his great vision of the Niger Territory in 1879, (114) it was accompanied by the realisation that "the one thing needed there was civilized government, through which alone there could come about a great development of commerce, by giving to the people peace, justice and liberty." (115)

But, as he continually stressed, "Civilized Government" did not necessarily mean "Alien Government," and he was especially chary of such because, usually, it placed an almost uncontrollable power in the hands of a single official. "No man" he said, "is fit to be trusted with power."

The only other recourse, therefore, lay in reforming the indigenous systems themselves. Perhaps no better memorial can be given to him than Lord Scarbrough's unequivocal declaration:—"The policy of ruling through Native Chiefs was his, [the] prohibition of Liquor Trade in the Northern Province [and the] abolition of slave traffic, all his." (116)

For him, the work may have been all that mattered, but for us, the man is of no small account either!

(1) Herostratus was an Ephesian who set fire to, and partially destroyed, the Temple of Diana at Ephesus, one of the seven wonders of the World. This he did on the night that Alexander the Great was born, as he believed it, to ensure himself of immortality. Chersiphron of Crete and his son Metagenes began its construction in B.C. 541, and the total time abuilding was 220 years. I am indebted to Nicolson for pointing out the symbolism of this quotation on the fly-leaf of Lady Wellesley's book, though we disagree slightly on interpretation.
(2) See Goldie to Brettonet, 17 Feb., 1897. "[Please] reply in English or in French, as although I should understand the general meaning . . . in German I should not feel confident of seizing all the details . . ." (F.O. 402/248). On the languages, Markham made this statement on relinquishing the presidency of the R.G.S. to Goldie in 1905. We can only guess intelligently at what these languages were: English, French, German and Latin, certainly, together with Arabic for sure; Spanish and Greek probably—he travelled widely in Spain and Spanish-speaking lands—and, in view of his support of the Hausa Association, possibly Hausa, but more likely, Italian. Sir H.Rider Haggard also credited Goldie with speaking eight languages, see page 202.
(3) See pages 18, 19.
(4) Major Edward Lugard, 1865-1957, Lugard's younger brother "Ned," whom he described as his *alter ego,* and who exercised a certain censorship over the publication of the earlier diaries.

(5) Nicolson, I. F., *The Administration of Nigeria, 1900-1960,* Clarendon, Oxford, 1969; p. 156, fn. 4 and p. 191.

(6) Perham, Margery, *Lugard: The Years of Authority;* Collins, London, pp. 206-210.

(7) Markham, Sir Clements, 1830-1916; President from 1893-1905.

(8) See H. R. Mill, *The Record of the R.G.S., 1830-1930,* R.G.S., London, 1930.

(9) See page 108. Goldie admired Johnston and, clearly, was admired in return.

(10) See C.O. 446/1. Also Perham & Bull, *The Diaries of Lord Lugard,* Faber & Faber, London, 1963, pp. 397-419, and Perham *op cit,* p. 87ff.

(11) Willcocks, Colonel (later General Sir) James, 1857-1926. Served with Lugard in India; 1899, Colonel-Commandant of the W.A.F.F.; 1900, commanded Ashanti Campaign; 1906 returned to India and commanded the Indian Army in Europe. Governor, Bermuda, 1917-22. Author of *From Kabul to Kumassi,* Murray, London, 1904; *With the Indians in France,* Constable, London, 1920, and *The Romance of Soldiering & Sport,* Cassell, London, 1925.

(12) See page 160 *et seq.*

(13) See also Flint. *op cit,* p. 298 et seq. Somerset was the second son of the second Earl of Raglan, and thus the grandson of the Raglan who held overall command at Balaclava. He was a Captain in the Grenadier Guards, on secondment to the Frontier Force. He died in Liverpool in March, 1899, having been invalided home in February and barley surviving long enough to disembark. According to Willcocks, his nickname was *Oli Shango. Sango* is the Yoruba God of Thunder, but *Oli,* in either Yoruba or Hausa is meaningless. The nickname was probably *Halin Shango,* Hausa and Yoruba combining in *Barikanci* (Barrack Patios) to render "He of the thunderous disposition."

(14) Such a possibility can by no means be ruled out. There is considerable evidence that manufactured incidents were used to forward Lugard's plans for the occupation of Kano and Sokoto. See Muffett, D. J. M. *Concerning Brave Captains.* André Deutsch, London, 1964.

(15) C.O. 446/1.

(16) It is with a sense almost of shock that one sees the final paragraph of this letter "If a reign of the sword etc." quoted as evidence of Goldie's approbation of and support for a "tough" policy in dealings with "Nigerian rulers." See Perham *op cit.* page 88. Such an attribution ignores completely the heavy vein of sarcasm with which the whole passage is shot through and through. Goldie was not advocating such action. He was warning against it, and was also warning a year later that Lugard would not be able to withstand the pressures from the military officers (men like Somerset and Willcocks) to embark on military adventures. See Antrobus to Chamberlain, 18 October, 1899, C.O. 446/5. In the event, in regard to Abadie, Morland and others, Goldie was right, and it is interesting to note that it was Goldie's old officer, Burdon, who played the peacemaker and advocated a conciliatory approach to Sokoto and Kano. See Muffett, *op cit.,* especially p. 34ff.

(17) All the following extracts are taken from C.O. 446/1 655-673. Somerset's complaint that the Company neglected the Frontier Force is not born out by Lugard who, on 28 April, had written "The way some of these people expect the R.N.C. to dry-nurse them exasperates me . . ." and on 8 May recorded ". . . nothing could exceed the willingness and the efforts made by the local officials." Perham & Bull, *op cit.,* p. 408.

(18) Possibly "Mrs." was intended, but a son or other relative may be referred to.

(19) See footnote to page 24 (footnote 4 on p. 31.)

(20) On 27 February, 1881, a British force of 554 officers and men under Sir George Colley was cut to pieces by a Boer Commando at Majuba Hill, 92 being killed, including Colley, and 134 wounded. The British Government had begun peace negotiations before the battle, and in spite of public consternation persisted in its course. This is what Somerset has in mind!

(21) See the *Geographical Journal.* Vol XXIII, 1904.

(22) See Perham *op cit.,* page 207.

(23) Perham, *op cit.,* p. 64.

(24) E. Moberly Bell, *Flora Shaw, (Lady Lugard, D.B.E.),* Constable, London, 1947. Goldie is mentioned once, on p. 9.

(25) Wellesley, *op cit.,* p. 120.

(26) See footnote 19 to page 19 (p. 23).

(27) Perham *op cit.,* p. 65.

(28) *Ibid,* p. 55. Flora Louise Shaw was born in Dublin in 1851. In the words of the *Times* obituary (28 January, 1929), "she was a thoroughly womanly woman, young looking and with undoubted charm and even beauty . . ." It is not without significance that during her lifetime she became emotionally involved with the three men of her day who, above all others, epitomised the concept of "Empire," Cecil Rhodes, Goldie and Lugard. Her relationship with Rhodes seems to have been deep but platonic, that with Goldie was clearly sexual, and with Lugard again platonic and, initially, shallow.

(29) See pages 18 & 19.

(30) Perham *op cit.,* p. 65. For an account of the Celia episode see Vol I.

(31) *Ibid,* p. 68.

(32) *Ibid.*

(33) *Ibid,* p. 206.

(34) Mureji is opposite the confluence of the Niger and Kaduna Rivers, and the centre of the Kedde—hereditary canoe and ferrymen of the Middle River.

(35) Perham *op cit.,* p. 82. Italics added.

(36) *Ibid* p. 209. Lugard's echoing of Somerset's claim is not likely to have been lost on Goldie!

(37) *Journal of the Royal Society of Arts,* Vol. LII.

(38) *Journal of the Royal Colonial Institute,* Vol. XXV, June, 1904.

(39) In which class, unhesitatingly, must be included Nicolson, *op cit.,* which has gone far to redress the somewhat slanted picture otherwise presented.

(40) Joyce Cary to his wife. Letters dated 27 February, 1917, now in the Osborn Collection of the Cary Papers; Bodleian Library, Oxford.

(41) Among such must be included Perham. For example, Sir Percy Girouard (Lugard's French Canadian immediate successor) did NOT write to Palmer in 1909 *"I adhere absolutely to the policy laid down in Memorandum 18 . . ."* as Perham appears to believe, and as she quotes him as saying. Instead, he wrote "Until I can meet Residents in council and get views and cross opinions, *I adhere absolutely to the policy laid down in Memo. 18,* AND NOW BEING CARRIED A LITTLE FURTHER IN MY NEW MEMO." (upper case type added), which is a very different thing indeed. (See Palmer, Sir Richmond; *Journal of the African Society,* Vol. XXXIII, January, 1934, page 40, lines 15, 16 and 17.

For Hesketh Bell's real views, also quoted by Perham as an example of the "almost reverent acceptance" with which both the above regarded Lugard's work, see below. For Perham's use of these quotations, see *op cit.,* page 471.

(42) Mary Kingsley, *op cit.*

(43) This reference is from the *Periplus of the Erythrean Sea,* the first century sailors' guidebook. "Their own chiefs rule them under Charibael King of Mapharites."

(44) Mary Kingsley, *op cit.*

(45) *Ibid.* R. S. Rattray makes the same point about MacLean in his paper presented to the African Society (the one that evoked Palmer's response) and published in the Society's *Journal* Vol. XXXIII, 1934.

(46) Perham and Bull; *op cit.,* pp. 106-109.

(47) See Flint, *op cit.,* p. 298 *et seq.* It should be remembered, however, that until the publication of the *Dual Mandate,* Lugard's claim to absolute authority as the progenitor of Indirect Rule was by no means universally accepted. Nor, for a limited but informed section of the public, was it unquestioningly accepted afterwards either. It must be noted too that Willcocks learned his lesson. Writing on 11 January, 1899, a bare three months after the Somerset episode, he observed to Chamberlain:—"I am writing to the Agent General, Royal Niger Company, about [certain activities of the Emir of Kontagora which have been reported to me]; for although the attack was made on Imperial troops only, I do not again desire to deal with such Chiefs direct." (C.O. 879/58). Of the damage which the Somerset incident did to the Company, however, there can be very little doubt.

(48) Sir Henry Hesketh Joudon Bell, G.C.M.G. 1865-1952. 1882 Colonial Service West Indies. 1890-93 Gold Coast; 1894 Bahamas; 1899 Dominica (Administrator); 1906 Uganda; 1907 Governor, Uganda. 1909 Governor, Northern Nigeria; 1912 Governor, Leeward Islands; 1916-25 Governor, Mauritius. It is clear from what follows that in 1898 he was serving in the Colonial Office, possibly on a consultative basis. The author recalls with pleasure his occasional meetings with Sir Hesketh during the early years of his own colonial service.

(49) Kaduna, National Archives 4964/1909.

(50) *Colonial Reports—Annual, 1900-1911;* H.M.S.O., London, p.26.

(51) *Ibid.*

(52) Political Memoranda 1906. Waterlow & Sons, London, 1906. Memorandum No. 9, p. 190.

(53) *Ibid.*

(54) Letter from Secretary, Zungeru to Resident Sokoto, 28 October, 1909.

(55) Kaduna, National Archives 4964/1909. This throws a significantly different light on Bell's observation in his Annual Report for 1910-11, p. 32, that "the policy of ruling through and with native rulers . .». has been pursued with undeviating fidelity in the Northern Emirates" than that in which it is regarded by Perham, who sees it as an "almost reverent acceptance" of Lugard's policy.

(56) *Ibid,* p. 24.

(57) *Ibid.*

(58) For the source of this quotation see Muffett, D. J. M., "New Introduction," *loc. cit.*

(59) See Perham *op cit.,* p. 247 *et seq.*

(60) *Ibid,* p. 280. "When . . . Hong Kong was offered, Lugard accepted . . . and, as he thought, finally closed the book of his African record."

(61) See page 268 for example.

(62) See page 104 and fn.

(63) See Perham, *op cit.,* for accounts of the Lugards' seeking Goldie's assistance over the "Scheme." Especially pp. 240 & 245.

(64) See Muffett, D. J. M., *Concerning Brave Captains,* André Deutsch, London, 1964.

(65) According to local accounts, Hillary and Scott were taken alive and were then dismembered, their trunks being pounded to a pulp by women with pestles. The limbs were then "boned out" and the major bones were then sent to the district heads of the districts abutting on Satiru, together with invitations to join the revolt. The then Ardo Denge, who related this version to Mr. H. A. S. Johnston, from whom the author received it, was sent Hillary's shin bone with the suggestion that he should use it as a tethering post for a horse.

(66) See page 300.

(67) See Perham, *op cit.,* pp. 206-7.

(68) *Native Races and their Rulers,* by C. L. Temple, Argus, Cape Town, 1918. This is an incredible book, in which crass and sophomoric platitudes rub shoulders with sophisticated and illuminating analyses. There is no evidence that Temple, first Resident Bauchi, then of Kano, and then Lieutenant-Governor of Northern Nigeria, 1916-1918, ever met Goldie, but it is hardly to be credited that he did not. Many of their ideas were identical.

(69) Writing to King Edward VII, in respect of the Elgin Commission, Lord Esher (see below) observed:—"Your Majesty well knows that Royal Commissions are, as a rule, the expedient employed by politicians to relegate awkward and difficult questions to the official pigeon hole." Journals and Letters of Reginald Viscount Esher, London, 1934, p 419.

(70) See for example, M. Howard, *Soldiers and Governments;* Indiana U.P., 1957.

(71) Victor Alexander Bruce, 9th Earl, 1849-1917. Viceroy of India, 1893-98. Colonial Secretary, 1905-1908.

(72) Reginald Balliol Brett, 2nd Viscount, 1852-1930. P.S. to Lord Hartington (later Duke of Devonshire) 1878-1885. Deputy Governor, Windsor Castle, 1901, Chairman, War Office Reconstruction Committee, 1903. Co-Editor of *Queen Victoria's Letters,* refused editorship of *Daily News, New Review, Life of Disraeli,* as well as the War Office, Governorship of Cape Colony and the Viceroyalty of India.

(73) 1826-1904. A distinguished Indian Army Officer and Military Administrator.

(74) 1834-1916. Naval Lord of the Admiralty and Controller of the Navy, 1888-1892; C-in-C, North America and West Indies, 1892-96; C-in-C, Mediterranean, 1896-1899.

(75) 1841-1926.

(76) 1851-1919. Among the major works in which he had a hand were the Manchester Ship Canal, Tower Bridge, Simonstown Naval Dockyard, Dover Harbour, Singapore Harbour *et al.*

(77) The *Times,* loc. cit.

(78) See the *Times,* 11 Sept., 1902, p.7, cc. 5 & 6.

(79) Ponsonby, Sir F., *Recollections of Three Reigns;* Eyre & Spottiswoode, London, 1951, quoted by Leslie, *op cit.,* p. 324.

(80) *Ibid.*

(81) Esher *op cit.,* pp. 417, 418.

(82) See correspondence in the *Times* in August & September, 1903, and pages 204-208 below.

(83) R.G.S. meeting on 12 January, 1907 at the Queen's Hall. The address was by H.R.H. the Duke of Abruzzi on "Mount Ruwenzori" and the King and Prince of Wales were both present.

(84) See pp. 286-289 following.

(85) Lewis Harcourt, 1st Viscount, 1863-1922. Liberal M.P. for Rossendale, 1904-1916; Sec. of State for Colonies, 1910-15. A friend of Lord Esher's, with whom he founded the London Museum in 1911.

(86) See page 290.

(87) See page 184.

(88) See pages 290-294 below.

(89) See page 20.

(90) See page 113 ff.

(91) Published from March, 1883 to June, 1960. Darwin, had met Goldie when serving in the Intelligence Section of the War Office, and they became firm friends. When preparing his article he asked Goldie for help and " . . . he consented to discuss the whole subject with a shorthand writer to take down his exact words." *Journal* of the Royal African Society, Vol. XXXV, 1935, pp. 138-143. See also p. 19.

(92) *Journal* of the Royal African Society, *loc. cit.*

(93) Charles Strachey, Sir, 1862-1942. Foreign Office, 1885-99; Colonial Office, 1900-1927. Delegate to the Versailles Conference, 1919; Assistant Under Secretary, 1924-27.

(94) See Perham, *op cit.,* p. 473.

(95) *Ibid,* p. 405-6 and p. 433.

(96) *Ibid* pp. 433-436. By the time of the really serious disorder in 1918, Goldie had given up.

(97) *Ibid.*

(98) See page 300, fn. 13 (p. 302).

(99) Perham, *op cit.,* Cap. XXIII.

(100) *Ibid,* Cap. XXIV.

(101) Temple, *op cit.,* 2nd Edition, Frank Cass, London, 1968, pp. vii-xlii.

(102) Perham, *op cit.,* p. 621 *et seq.*

(103) *Ibid,* p. 61.

(104) *Ibid,* p. 477.

(105) See page 44.

(106) The *Fortnightly Review* began publication in 1865 and in 1935 changed its name to *The Fortnightly.* In 1954 it was taken over by the *Contemporary Review.* Two of its most famous Editors were John Morley and Frank Harris.

(107) "The Founder of Nigeria" by R. S. Rattray, *The Fortnightly,* April, 1935, pages 452-453. Hesketh Bell's minute to Burdon, given on page 47, startlingly confirms Scarbrough's hitherto unsupported conviction. See also page 57.

(108) *Ibid,* p. 454.

(109) See the *Spectator,* 21 December, 1934, p. 971, and 4 January, 1935, and 18 January, 1935. "Single men in barracks don't grow into plaster saints." (Kipling).

(110) See page 81.

(111) William Hillier, 4th Earl of Onslow, 1853-1911. Governor of New Zealand, 1889-92. Under Secretary, the Colonies, 1887 and 1900-1903. Alderman of the London County Council (as Goldie later was), 1896-99.

(112) Onslow, had been acting as Colonial Secretary in Chamberlain's absence during Lugard's Kano, Sokoto and Burmi campaigns in 1903. Who the "settlers" were that he had in mind is not clear, but he should have known better. Mr. Reginald Antrobus, who was present with his wife and who had been Onslow's Assistant Under Secretary of State (as he still was), must have blushed at his late Chief's ignorance—and bowed his head at Goldie's reply. (Italics not in original)

(113) This, and the previous quotation, can be found in the *Journal* of the African Society, Vol. VII, No. XXVI of January, 1908, at pages 206-7 and 118 respectively.

(114) Wellesley, *op cit.*, p. 142.

(115) Goldie used these words in accepting the gift of his portrait from the R.N.C. Directors and Shareholders in 1899. See *Ibid,* but also see the *Times,* 28 October, 1899, where the phrase used is "political acquisition or, in other words, the formation of a civilized government there . . ."

(116) Wellesley, *op cit.*, p. 156.

II

Articles in Books or Journals, Reviews,
Addresses Reproduced as Monographs
etc.:—

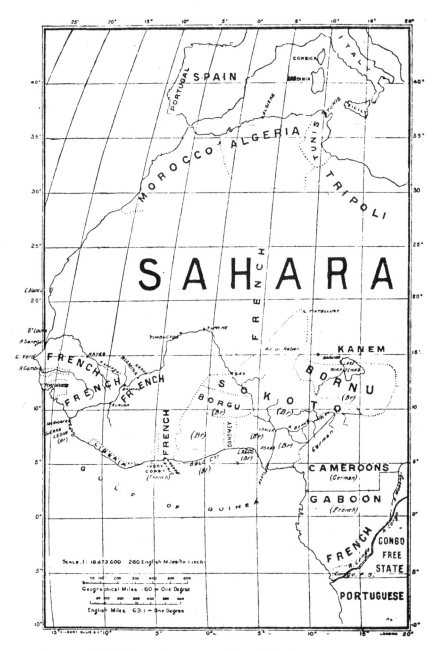

The map which Goldie used to accompany his article in the *Paternoster Review*.

I. FRANCE AND ENGLAND ON THE NIGER (1891)

This article first appeared in the January, 1891 edition of the *Paternoster Review*. It was then reprinted as *Africa Pamphlet* No. 4 of 1891. The present text, as reproduced, is taken from the earlier edition.

Goldie examines the question as to whether the policies then being pursued by the newly resurgent pro-colonial-expansion parties in France would inevitably bring France and Britain into confrontation within the foreseeable future in either the basin of the Niger, or in that of Lake Chad. His conclusion, erroneous as it turned out, is that it would not.

The article also gives a very clear picture of how Goldie regarded the merits of colonial government by Chartered Company over government by the Crown. He saw Company rule as possessing "internal and perennial sources of energy and being independent of Parliamentary crises and party necessities."

Examining the resources that he considers necessary to guarantee orderly development, Goldie rejects forest produce and ivory as providing an insufficiently reliable under-pinning. Instead, he bases the prospect of adequate future development squarely on the creation of a sufficient "agricultural wealth."

Assailing the critics of African development, Goldie especially singles out Sir John Pope Hennessy[1] and is not above a quiet dig at the Marquess of Salisbury either.

Most interesting of all, perhaps, is his endorsement of Dr. Blyden's campaign in the United States to "repatriate" American Blacks.

I must preface this article by two definitions. For want of a better concise name I shall use the vague term "Central Africa" to describe the more or less malarious portion of that continent lying between (say) the eighteenth parallels of north and south latitude, exclusive of the maritime regions within twenty or thirty miles of the seaboard, which can look to European fleets for protection of life and property. Central Africa, thus defined, is about thirty times the area of France, and fifty times that of the United Kingdom, and probably contains about one-twelfth of the population of the globe. In the second place, and for the same reason, I use the word "England" for "Great Britain and Ireland," and "Englishmen" for the inhabitants of this country. "Britain" and "Britons" are, unfortunately, considered pedantic in prose.

The Anglo-German and Anglo-Portuguese agreements of 1890 have induced a colonial movement in France which, in this age of electricity, may be described as a strong secondary current. Competent authorities tell us that this agitation is no longer confined to colonial enthusiasts, but has penetrated into the mass of the nation; and a number of expeditions have lately been dispatched from widely separated points of the African coast to extend French rights into the heart of the continent. The inadequate recognition in England of this movement may perhaps be attributed to a well-founded belief on the part of "Our own Correspondents" that the British public has lately had a surfeit of the Dark Continent.

It may seem illogical that the demarcation by other countries of spheres of influence in East and South Africa should affect the estimate which France had previously formed of the value of the regions bordering on her possessions in the north and west of the Continent; but it is not in France alone that the fever of annexation proves contagious. To this cause, principally, may be attributed the popularity of propositions for the immediate occupation of vast areas of Central Africa. Two minor causes have contributed to this movement. The first has been the downfall of the Boulangists, (2) who had opposed colonial adventures; partly no doubt from a belief in the necessity of concentrating the forces of France at home, and, perhaps, partly from a desire to oppose any policy which had been adopted by their *bête noire*. Now M. Ferry (3) having recognised the hegemony of Germany in Europe, had, during his tenure of power, sought to direct the energies of France to compensations abroad. The reaction against Boulangism has thus, indirectly, revived the popularity of colonial expansion. Less than thirty voices are now raised in the French Chamber against that occupation of Tonquin (4) which not only wrecked M. Ferry but endangered for a time the stability of the Republic. The second cause has been the interest aroused throughout the country by the attractive colonial section of the Exhibition of 1889. (5) Multitudes of all classes, who were drawn to Paris by M. Eiffel's master-piece, remained to enjoy the realistic representations of their African possessions, and carried back their enthusiasm into every commune of France. There was a grain of truth in the view of a rhapsodical journalist that the light of the great tower would penetrate from the Champs de Mars to (among other places) the plains of Timbuctoo.

The dangers of prophesying are proverbial; but it appears almost certain that this new-born movement will before long be stifled, as has always previously happened, by newer and more pressing interests; so that unless the French Government seizes this golden opportunity of inducing the nation to delegate the work to Chartered Companies, which would have internal and perennial sources of energy and would be independent of Parliamentary crises and party necessities, the present agitation will lead to no practical benefit whatever to France. Until the African races reach a level at which they can dispense with minute and incessant control of Europeans, civilization cannot cease to mount without falling back to its starting point. The special difficulty of the Central African question lies in this early stage, during which spasmodic efforts are a sheer waste of lives, money and energy. I do not, for a moment, wish to imply that France is peculiar in the want of steady continuity on the one hand, and judicious moderation on the other, in her African policy. M. Ribot, indeed, tells his Chamber that they do these things better in England. But here, too, the ebb and flow of opinion on this question during the last three centuries remind one of those fevers which form the chief obstacle to its speedy solution. In the delirium of the hot fits, Central Africa has figured as *"La Belle au bois dormant"* (6) ready to awake to full vitality at the first caress; while, in reality, it is a Pygmalion's statue, to which the gift of life will only be granted on the prayers of a fervent and constant wooer, after patient preliminary labours: "Interea niveum mira feliciter arte Sculpit ebur." (7) For, I would point out in passing, although ivory and other existing products cannot make Central Africa worth holding, they form the temporary basis on which the subsequent creation of agricultural wealth must rest. But the hot fits of enthusiasm have always been succeeded by periods of chill, lassitude and nausea, during which public opinion has blindly accepted assertions that Europe can never make any lasting impression on those regions.

The most trenchant assailant to-day of "The African Bubble" is Sir John Pope Hennessy, whose local knowledge as the Governor of the West African Coast Settlements in 1872, and whose general experience, since then, as a ruler of mankind from China (almost) to Peru, entitle him to a respectful hearing. It would be futile to attempt to disprove in a few paragraphs the justice of his conclusions. A separate article could hardly deal adequately with the methods of overcoming the two great difficulties of climate and labour. I will, therefore, only remark that the present "resources of civilization" differ widely from those of the seventeenth and eighteenth centuries, to the failures in which Sir John mainly appeals, and that the most widely known living authorities in this country are opposed to his views. Mr. Stanley's(8) opinions are familiar to the whole civilized world. Mr. H. H. Johnston's(9) delightful article, published in the "Fortnightly Review" for November, and others too numerous to quote here, have probably been read by all who are interested in this question. I have before me an unpublished statement drawn by Mr. Joseph Thomson,(10) just after his travels in the Sokoto empire in 1885, as to the potential wealth of these regions, which by the Niger Company's treaties from 1885 to 1890 have been placed within the British sphere of influence. Mr. Thomson intended this statement to form part of an address which he delivered in Birmingham; but he was good enough to omit it at a time when the scramble for Africa was at its height and the position of England in the Niger-Tchad basins was insecure. Commander Cameron(11)has written equally hopefully on those parts of Central Africa with which he is best acquainted. Finally, Sir Samuel Baker,(12) the value of whose opinion as an African explorer is greatly increased by his having so ably administered a vast equatorial province, now replunged in barbarism, is constantly urging the importance of it being occupied by England. Sir John Hennessy's premises, however, will be welcomed by persons whose lives are spent in disproving by practical results the soundness of his inferences. He has brought vividly before the attention of the uninformed public immense difficulties which are often ignored, and the rhythmical recurrence of the successive phases—enthusiasm, vacillation and abandonment—which have marked the ill-directed attempts of former generations.

Those who wish to form a just idea of the economic value of Central Africa should carefully study the work just published on "Applied Geography," by Mr. J. Scott Keltie,(13) whose authority on this subject is recognized abroad as well as at home. I may also quote the following extract from a speech delivered by Lord Aberdare in July, 1889:— (14)

"I have seen our position in Africa mentioned as resembling that of the foundation, from small beginnings, of our vast Indian Empire. Except that both undertakings sprang from a common spirit of commercial enterprise, the comparison is deceptive and misleading. The East India Company planted itself in countries already occupied by old civilizations, where the national intellect had been cultivated for untold ages, and commerce, with its attendant wealth, had long flourished; countries peopled by races inured to taxation, from whom large revenues could be raised without serious opposition. On the Niger there is no Pagoda-tree to be shaken with the accompanying showers of rupees. We do not, so far, raise from the natives one penny of direct revenue, the little we receive being indirectly through duties on the trade entering and leaving the country. Instead of vast populations with the inherited habit of labour, we have to deal for the most part with tribes ignorant, idle, and improvident, incapable of understanding, I need hardly say, not only the accumulation of wealth for future generations, but even the prudence of providing for their own sustenance during years of scarcity. They have not only to be taught how to work, but, what is more difficult, to be taught the habit of working.''

While insisting on the potential wealth of Central Africa, I have dwelt on the obstacles in the way of its rapid development and on the absolute futility of an intermittent or spasmodic policy, because these points are essential to the main object of this article, which is to examine whether the existing movement in France is likely, within any period worth considering, to bring her settlements—for passing expeditions leave no results—into close contact and therefore possibly into collision with England in the Niger-Tchad basins. At the time of the conclusion of the late Anglo-French agreement, it was said that Lord Salisbury, far from having removed, *pro tanto*, the danger of conflict between the two nations, had given them a common frontier and had therefore actually created opportunities for disputes. I shall endeavour to show the fallacy of such reasoning by a short examination of the conditions which Lord Aberdare, in another speech delivered last July, [15] summed up in the following words:—"Nature has placed between these spheres"—French and British—"formidable barriers, which could only be overcome by an initial expenditure out of all proportion to any probable return for many years."

There are six distinct directions from which French commercial or military settlements may advance into the neighbourhood of the British Niger Protectorate: namely, 1st, from Gaboon Colony northwards; 2nd, from the coast of Dahomey to the southern frontier of Borgu, one of the latest acquisitions of the Niger Company; 3rd, from Grand Bassam, on the Ivory Coast, to the western frontier of Borgu; 4th, from Bamaku on the Upper Niger due eastward to the limits of the Sokoto empire, about 60 miles west of Say on the Middle Niger; 5th, from the same position at Bamaku round the great bend of the Niger to Say; and 6th, from the Mediterranean by a Saharan railway to the northern shores of Lake Tchad.

The first of these routes—now being followed by the Crampel [16] expedition—is open, in an extreme degree, to some of the objections to the others. France has first to civilize her Gaboon colony, where, only the other day, the commandant of a station was killed and eaten by the natives. But this route may, I think, be summarily dismissed by the statement that it would involve hemming in the German Cameroons colony and thus cutting it off from its legitimate expansion eastwards. A similar policy was, indeed, successfully pursued by France towards British Gambia; but that was in the days of *laissez faire*, when it was the fashion in England to deplore the burden of empire and to contemplate with equanimity the prospective separation of even the richest colonies. In spite of the decided subsidence of the late colonial excitement in Germany, there is no probability of her permitting her Cameroons Colony to be burked in this manner, especially as she has taken much trouble to provide against similar action from the Niger Company by arranging a line of demarcation between their respective spheres of influence.

The second route, from the coast of Dahomey, would be practicable only after the complete subjugation of that country, a costly enterprise which is now postponed to the Greek Kalends.

The third and fourth routes, from the Upper Niger and the Ivory Coast

68

respectively, may be treated together, as they involve the same insuperable difficulty—that of exercising effective commercial or military influence in Central Africa at a considerable distance from either the sea, a navigable waterway, or an already settled, developed and therefore secure inland base of operations. France, whose Senegal Colony dates from the seventeenth century, was able gradually to establish her power on the banks of that river up to Kayes, the highest navigable point. Thence during many years of alternate energy and abandonment, which afford a striking example of the costly wastefulness of State vacillation, a few miles of railway have been constructed to Bafulaba, further up the river. It is said that this short railway involves a heavy annual cost to prevent its being submerged by sand-drifts. In 1881 there commenced a period of great military activity under the able and energetic colonels Desbordes, (17) Gallieni (18) and Archinard. (19) A succession of brilliant expeditions have enabled France to establish a line of military posts from Bafulaba to Bamaku on the navigable stream of the Upper Niger, on which have been placed three posts up to Kurusa and two down to Niamina. Treaties have been made with Samory (20) and Ahmadu, (21) two of the most powerful native rulers, which, under the principles of international comity, probably give France rights in those regions as against other European States; but they do not—at any rate as yet—give her a secure basis of operations from which to commence, without the aid of a navigable river, even a military occupation of the five hundred miles which separate Bamaku from the western frontier of the Sokoto Empire. On the contrary, the French position on the Upper Niger itself must long be one of watchful defence. Ahmadu is again at war with France, while the attitude of Samory is such as to demand serious sacrifices to defend the position even on the Senegal River. I am informed on good authority that not one French commercial establishment has been placed on the Upper Niger, so that the considerable expenditure of lives, heroism and money during the past ten years, has as yet been fruitless. The truth is that France has before her a herculean labour in pacifying, effectively occupying and developing the great triangle, 250,000 square miles in area, of which the sea-board from Cape Blanco to Mellicoree forms the western side; a line from Cape Blanco to Niamina, the north-eastern side; and the Upper Niger, from Niamina to Kurusa (with a prolongation to Mellicoree), the south-eastern side. When she has partially completed this preliminary task—be it twenty or fifty years hence—she may profitably commence a similar work to the east of the Upper Niger.

The occupation and development of the country between the Ivory Coast and the western frontier of Borgu, by the circuitous route necessary to keep clear of the British Gold Coast Colony, will be a still longer operation than that from Bamaku. The distance, indeed, is about the same, while the base of operations will be on the sea-board and therefore superior to the insecure footing on the Upper Niger; but the climate of the Gulf of Guinea, and the belts of forests that will have to be not only traversed but permanently occupied, will more than counter-balance this advantage. It is improbable that France will support, through a long period and under successive governments, the sacrifices necessary for pushing forward and maintaining lines of merely military posts, either from the Upper Niger or the Ivory Coast, leading to no lake or navigable stream and scattered over a hostile, unhealthy and barbarous country.

The fifth route is that from Bamaku, by the great bend of the Niger, past Timbuctoo and Tufilaten, where the first rapids occur, down to Say. An attempt to visit Timbuctoo was made in 1889 by the naval Lieutenant Caron, who descended the river from Bamaku in an armed steam launch. After a perilous voyage, he succeeded in reaching the port of Timbuctoo, but the attitude of the natives was so threatening that he was compelled to return up stream without even landing there. Nevertheless, it is probable that France will, before long, occupy Timbuctoo, not because of its intrinsic importance—for this, according to the best authorities, is small—but because its name is a household word, redolent of the poetry of the desert and of the mingled civilization and barbarism of Islam in Africa, which appeals to the imagination of the French electorate. To the more prosaic Englishman it is chiefly known by a doggerel rhyme. (22) From Tufilaten down to a little above Say, the Niger is so broken by rocks and rapids as to make its navigation impracticable to cargo vessels; while the country on either side for the greater part of the distance is rocky and sterile. There appears, indeed, to be much resemblance between this region and that bordering the Nile from Berber to Wadey Halfa. This is not surprising, as the Niger thrusts this great horse-shoe northwards into the same latitudes of the Sahara. French expeditions may reach Say by this route in canoes or perhaps even small launches; but it is highly improbable that, for many years to come, French settlements, commerce or even military posts will approach the British Niger from this direction.

The sixth route is that by the suggested railway from Algeria to the northern shores of Lake Tchad. It is difficult to consider this seriously as a question for our days. Certain stretches of Central African railway are indicated by nature as possibly worth laying at once as a means to future development. Such are the 300 miles in construction along the cataracts which have hitherto prevented adequate use being made of the magnificent waterways of the Congo. There is also much to be said in favour of laying rails over the 400 miles between Mombasa and the Victoria Nyanza, (23) and over the 300 miles between the coast and Lake Nyassa. These two lines would run through countries where it is not unreasonable to hope that extensive plantations may before long be formed, affording intermediate traffic; they would be in length only one-fifth to one-sixth of the suggested Saharan railway; finally, they would run to large navigable lakes, the shores of which will attract the trade of the surrounding regions; while a considerable portion of Lake Tchad is a marshy lagoon. Most practical men will agree that the desert railway should follow and not precede the development of the Central Sudan and that fertilization of the Sahara, which was a confidently discussed project of the immediate future at the time that I first visited Africa, nearly a quarter of a century ago. I do not mean that the immediate construction of this line would have no practical effect whatever. On the contrary, great benefits would result—to England. These would be both commercial and political in character. I propose to consider them in turn.

It must be borne in mind that the frontier line from Say to Barrua, drawn by the late Anglo-French Agreement,(24) does not follow a parallel of latitude, but is deflected northward, so as to include in the British sphere all that belongs to the Sokoto empire; that is to say, all the fertile lands which bound that portion of the Sahara on the south, including the oasis of Air or Asben. If this British sphere already produced a large value of articles demanded by the markets of Europe, the commercial prospects of the railway would be very different; but it can scarcely be too often repeated that the wealth of these regions, from a European point of view, is potential and not actual. Their dense populations are as yet able to draw little more than their scanty daily bread from a soil capable of ultimately producing immense quantities of raw material for exchange with the manufactured goods of Europe. Until security for liberty, property and life, is substituted for slavery, rapine and mutual destruction, and until the consequent production and accumulation of material wealth reaches considerable dimensions, the commercial value of the Central Sudan must be small. The forest products afford a six per cent. dividend to the Niger Company, and will, in time, with prudence and energy, pay twice this rate on a capital tenfold or twentyfold of that which can as yet be profitably employed. But from this point of view it will be a long step to the creation of a new India. No Englishman who grasps this situation could fail to welcome an undertaking, which, at the cost of others, would give an immense impetus to the agricultural development of regions secured to his country.

It is not easy to estimate to what extent the commerce of the British Protectorate, when developed, would pass by the railway to the Mediterranean instead of by the natural routes—the waterways of the Niger and Benue—to the Gulf of Guinea; because one cannot foretell with any certainty what classes of European goods the Sudan will then demand, or what kinds of tropical produce it will mainly export to the markets of Europe. At present, the principal goods are cottons, hardware and high dried salt, which Northern Europe can supply more cheaply than the Mediterranean regions. So again the bulk of the existing forest products, gum, gutta, percha, kernels, palm oil, peppers, rubber, etc., are chiefly absorbed by the Northern ports of Europe and by the United States. Most of these have, at present, no direct steam communication with either Algeria or the mouth of the Niger; but the rates of freight from Liverpool may serve for a comparison; those to Algeria being from twenty-five to thirty shillings a ton, and those to Akassa from fifteen to thirty-three shillings. Let it be conceded, however, for the sake of argument, that if French taxpayers or shareholders are content, for a long period, to forego any return for their original outlay of ten to twelve millions sterling on the railway, to contribute a large proportion of its annual expenses and costly maintenance, to pay for the military occupation of its line of route and to abstain from levying taxes on transit through Algeria, the trade of the northern belt of the British Protectorate would follow this direction. Why should England object to receive this magnificent bonus from France, which would thus bear the heat and burden of the day? Why should it grudge an ultimate, though long deferred, dividend to the French shareholders? Even the dog in the manger—on our resemblance to whom foreign journalists so amiably insist—might have favourably considered a proposition based on the doctrine of *'do ut des.'*(25) He would have shown himself wanting in common sense as well as in morals, if he had snarled at those who brought him his food. The only regret would be that the money should not have been more effectively and directly applied to the commercial development of our territories. But that France will be willing *'travailler pour le roi de Prusse'*(26) in this manner, is perhaps one of the most roseate of the dreams into which sanguine temperaments fall when they deal with Central African matters.

It may be asked whether French settlements might not be created in countries on the east of Lake Tchad, outside of the British sphere. This question leads at once to the *political* benefits to England of the railway. The regions between Bornu and the Nile form the very crater of the active Mohammedan volcano in Africa. Mahdists,(27) and Senoussists(28) would soon combine against the advance of the Nazarene. A great military nation such as France could undoubtedly "smash the Mahdi," and occupy those countries, if determined to make the necessary sacrifices; but it would have the constant disadvantage of its only line of communication being a desert railway 2,000 miles in length, menaced by the Tuaric tribes, by the possible hostility of Turkey on its Tripoli flank and by the probable disaffection of its Mussulman subjects in Algeria and Tunis. It needs no demonstration that the success of such a struggle against Islam militant would be of incalculable political advantage to England in its Niger Protectorate, in Egypt and in its East African possessions; but to anticipate having the chestnuts thus pulled out of the fire for us would be to reckon too much on French idealism.

These considerations, however, suggest a collateral and important question.

Assuming that my belief is wrong as to the necessary slowness of development in Central African regions, (29) and that the outposts of French settlements advance with rapid strides to our frontiers, ought this to be a subject for our regret? To me there seems but one rational answer. England, too, has a gigantic task before her in developing the half million square miles which fall within her sphere of action in the Niger-Tchad basins. Every new success of France in the work of civilization in her own sphere would not only encourage us in our labours, but would certainly afford us many new and useful ideas of procedure; while every passing failure—and there must be many—would teach us what to avoid. The two nations are so distinct in their genius and methods that each will have to learn from the other in the creation of agricultural wealth in these vast regions, where every feature is abnormal and where the experience of colonial expansion elsewhere is of little use. It cannot, indeed, be denied that there would be a tendency to friction on a long and not very clearly marked frontier line in the heart of Africa; but firm administration and friendly diplomacy should easily dispose of this difficulty. In any case it would surely be better to have on our borders a civilized nation, with interlacing interests in many parts of the globe and with much to lose from war, than barbarous, ferocious or anarchial tribes, to attack whom is like cutting water with a sword.

This doctrine applies not only to France and England, but also to the three other European nations—Germany, Italy and Portugal—principally interested in Central Africa. It is not the cant of those who cry peace where there in no peace, nor does it rely on the bruised reed of sentimentalism, which would fail at the first pressure put upon it. It is based on intelligent self-interest, which should recognize that, for many generations there will be ample work for the ambitions and energies of each nation in its own sphere. Central Africa is, indeed, almost the only remaining region on this planet, where the Abrahamic policy — "If thou wilt take the left hand, then I will go to the right"—is still practicable. It is for this reason that all who have studied the question rejoice in the extensive—but unfortunately not yet complete—application of the theory of spheres of influence. The marking out of certain wide limits for the operations of each nation removes, *pro tanto,* the danger of conflict through the action of ambitious and competing explorers, to whose rapid passage through Africa with treaties and flags there are no such obstacles as exist in the way of permanent and solid settlements.

If, as is often asserted, posterity will look upon the opening up of Africa as one of the salient features of the Victorian age, it will assuredly give a prominent place in this movement to the statesman whose commanding influence has made possible this policy of mutual non-intervention—a curious instance of the irony of fate, for Lord Salisbury's public utterances(30) show him to be somewhat sceptical as to the capabilities of Central Africa, and mainly actuated by the more pressing necessity of obviating disputes with our European neighbours.

It may be interesting, in conclusion, to consider the probabilities whether France or England will make more rapid material progress in its own spheres of action. I cannot see any ground for belief that the former is deficient in colonizing aptitudes. Want of space forbids an examination of the special circumstances in the history of the eighteenth and nineteenth centuries which have handicapped her in the race. Nevertheless, it seems certain that she will only waste her energies in attempting to rival us in Central Africa unless a great change takes place in the statistics of her population. It might be presumption in a foreigner to dogmatize as to the causes of a condition of things which has occasioned considerable difference of opinion among French thinkers. Still less would one venture to predict whether France will prefer continuing to support a moderate population at home in comfort, at the cost of colonial expansion, or to achieve the latter, as England has done, through an exodus of men pushed out of an overcrowded fatherland by the struggle for existence. It is admitted that the smallness of French families is more marked among the middle classes and superior artizans than among the peasants. Now it is the former that must furnish the victims (31) for developing Central Africa, which is, in the main, unfitted for European manual labour. Unless wholesale colonization by Chinamen or Indians were successfully adopted, the work must be done by Negroes under the constant supervision of vast numbers of educated Europeans, who must be content to spend the best years of their lives in unhealthy and barbarous regions, unenlivened by those social and cultivated pleasures to which Frenchmen attach so high a value. Even if it proves practicable to carry out the proposal—advocated for the last twenty years by Dr. Blyden, himself a remarkable type of the capabilities of the black race—to terminate the war of colour in the United States by the restoration of the Negroes to the homes of their forefathers,(32) the necessity for minute European supervision must remain for some generations. It is this which differentiates Central Africa from tropical Asiatic countries where a comparatively small European population can, as in India, reap the fruits of the labour of millions of industrious natives.

To England, where the cry "what shall we do with our sons" grows louder every year, the opening up of Central Africa is a pressing necessity; to France, it is the realization of a great idea. I do not give an opinion on the long-disputed question between the territorial aggrandizement of a nation and the material well-being of the individuals who compose it. France may elect to follow one or other of these principles, but not both; for there, as in other countries, *"il faut qu'une porte soit ouverte ou fermée."*(33) I have pointed out, above, the importance in Central Africa of one Abrahamic policy. There is another which seems an essential preliminary to France taking her full share in the opening up of that continent. She must be fruitful and multiply.(34)

GEORGE TAUBMAN GOLDIE.

(1) Sir John Pope Hennessy, 1834-1891. Colonial Governor and Member of Parliament; First Conservative Roman Catholic Member to be elected, 1859; Governor of Labuan 1867-71; Gold Coast 1872-73; Windward Islands 1875-76; Hong Kong 1877-82; Mauritius 1883-89. Whilst in Mauritius, he espoused the cause of the French-speaking Creoles on the Island, and was suspended from office. After a period of eclipse, and the issuance of a series of demurrers against any activity in Africa, Pope Hennessy was returned to Parliament in 1890 as an anti-Parnellite Home Ruler, but he died the next year.
(2) The followers of George Ernest Jean Marie Boulanger, 1873-91. French General; Minister of War; Boulanger led a brief but influential authoritarian movement and nearly toppled the Third Republic. Leader of the *revanche* movement against continued German occupation of Alsace-Lorraine he welded together a coalition of the Left, the Monarchists and the Bonapartists. In 1889, after B. had been dismissed from the Army, this group won every Paris seat but one. Urged to take over the Government, his nerve failed him and he dallied with his mistress the Vicomtess de Bonnemain instead, and then fled to Brussels, being tried in *absentia* for treason and banished. His mistress dying on July, 1891, B. committed suicide on her grave in September.
(3) Jules Francois Camille Ferry, 1832-93. Assassinated. Republican anti-clericist, pro-colonial expansion; Mayor of Paris during the Siege, 1870-71; largely responsible for the French acquisition of Tunisia, 1881; Tonkin, 1885; Madagascar, 1885; French Congo, 1884-85. Public anger at his Tonkin policy drove him from office in March, 1885. Re-elected to the Senate in 1891 from the Vosges; President of the Senate, 1893.
(4) Declared a French Protectorate in 1883, Tonkin was occupied in 1885.
(5) An unprecedentedly successful Exhibition. Centred on the Eiffel Tower, it contained 5,000 Art and 55,000 Industrial exhibits.
(6) "The Sleeping Beauty." Charles Perrault, *Contes de ma mère L'Oye* (1697).

(7) Ovid; *Metamorphoses* Book X. "Meanwhile with wondrous art he successfully carves a figure out of snowy ivory . . ." "Sculpit" should read "Sculpsit."

(8) Later Sir Henry Morton Stanley, 1841-1904.

(9) Later Sir Harry Johnston, 1858-1927.

(10) Mr. Joseph Thomson, famous as an explorer in Kenya (Thomson's Falls, Thomson's Gazelle), employed by the R.N.C. in 1885. See also p. 96.

(11) Cameron, Verney Lovett, R.N., 1844-94. Royal Navy, 1857; Abyssinia, 1868; Led R.G.S. expedition to aid Livingstone, 1873; Accompanied Burton to W.A., 1882; Retired from Navy, 1883. Wrote up his travels.

(12) Baker, Sir Samuel White, 1821-93. Explored Nile and its tributaries, 1862 onwards; Discovered L. Albert, March, 1884; Gold Medal R.G.S. 1865; Knighted, 1866; Accompanied Prince of Wales to Egypt and the Nile, 1869; Governor of Equatoria (as Pasha); 1869. He was often accompanied by his wife Frances.

(13) John Scott Keltie (Sir), 1840-1927; noted geographer and historian and Secretary and Librarian to the Royal Geographical Society.

(14) Chairman's speech to the ninth Ordinary General Meeting of the R.N.C. As Aberdare was suddenly indisposed, Goldie read it for him. He also, of course, almost certainly wrote it! The *Times*, 27 July, 1889.

(15) Quoted from the Chairman's (Lord Aberdare's) address to the tenth ordinary general meeting of the R.N.C., 29 July, 1890. See the *Times*, 30 July, 1900, page 12, Column 2.

(16) Crampel, Paul, 1864-1891. French explorer; opened up northern areas of French Congo and initiated policy of joining France's West African holdings by way of Chad and the Sudan to link Algiers with the Coast. Ambushed at El Kouti by Rabeh's men and killed, July, 1891. See also page 148.

(17) Borgnis-Desbordes, Gustave, 1839-1900; Surveyed Upper Senegal, 1880; Commanded three expeditions against Samory 1881-83; Built forts at Kita and Bamako; Transferred to Indo-China, 1884.

(18) Gallieni, Marshall of France Joseph Simon, 1849-1916. Governor of the French Sudan; fought throughout the area of the Upper Niger. His most historic moment came, however, in 1914 when he was Commander of the Paris Military District and moved the Paris Garrison, including units of his "beloved Senegalese" in the City's taxicabs to the Marne and thus materially assisted in halting Von Kluk's drive on the capital.

(19) Major Louis Archinard, Gallieni's firebrand successor and a fervent admirer of Borgnis-Desbordes. Archinard fought extensive campaigns throughout Senegambia and had a deserved reputation for ruthless impetuosity.

(20) Almami Samori, c. 1830-1900. Founded an empire c. 1875 based on Guinea; Fought against the French with the utmost skill and tenacity from 1881-1898; in 1887 a treaty was signed at Bisandugu under which France claimed protectorate rights. Samori skillfully played the British off against the French and in 1891 Archinard made a surprise attack towards the Upper Niger. Samori was finally captured in 1898 and exiled to Gabon. This ended the Dyula Empire and all resistance ceased. He died on 2 June, 1900.

(21) Eldest son of Haj Umar el Tijani (c. 1790-1864), founder of the Tukulor Empire, Ahmadu succeeded his father in 1864, but could not hold the alliegence of his followers. After temporising with the French under Gallieni, with whom he signed a treaty in May, 1887. Archinard, his successor, resumed hostilities and Ahmadu was finally defeated in 1892 and fled for protection to Sokoto.

(22) Goldie must have had in mind the "jingle" popular with English children even between the two World Wars, and attributed to Bishop Samuel Wilberforce:—

"Once there was a Cassowary
On the plains of Timbuctoo;
And 'e ate a Mission-ary,
With 'is Prayer an' 'Ymn-book too!

If *I* were a Cassowary
On the plains of Timbuctoo
I would eat a Mission-ary
Cassock, band an' 'Ymn-book too!"

Bishop Wilberforce was born in 1805 and died in 1873. An alternative second verse is:—

> "If *I* were a Cassowary,
> Pecking stones near Timbuctoo,
> *I* would eat that Mission-ary,
> *And* 'is Prayer an' 'Ymn-book too."

Wilberforce is also notorious for having engaged in the famous debate on Evolution with Thomas Huxley.

(23) For evidence of Goldie's continued interest in this line see pages 179-182.

(24) That is, the agreement of 1890. This was a historic document in a way, as it gave tacit international recognition to the Sokoto Caliphate.

(25) "I give in order that I may be given." i.e. "Cast forth thy bread" etc. Mediaeval Latin proverb. It is given in Walther, Hans, *Lateinische Sprich wörter und Sentenzen des Mittelalters*, (ed.), Götingen, 1963.

(26) Proverbial expression attributed to Voltaire, who spent the years 1750-1753 in the service of Frederick the Great in Potsdam. The last six months, however, were spent under house arrest and Voltaire and Prussia parted company under circumstances of some disenchantment. "To work for the King of Prussia" = work to no profit or purpose.

(27) Followers of Muhammed Ahmed Es Seyyid Abdullah El Mahdi, 1848-85. Defeated Gordon at Khartoum.

(28) More properly, *Sanusiyah*, members of a Moslem *sufi* (brotherhood) founded in 1837 by Muhammed Ibn Ali As Sanusi. Particularly strong amongst the Bedawi of Tripolitania, the movement has been marked as one of reforming zeal.

(29) It was, entirely wrong! By 1897, France had penetrated to the Middle Niger from Dahomey and had set in train those repurcussions that were to end the rule of the R.N.C.

(30) At the Mansion House Banquet on 6 August, 1890 (the day after the Anglo-French Boundary Agreement was signed) Salisbury has stated:—"Men have welcomed the agreements . . . because they recognise that [they remove] the most probable and the most dangerous cause of possible quarrel between nations who ought always to be at peace . . . We have been . . . drawing lines upon maps where no human foot has ever trod . . . We have been giving away mountains and rivers and lakes to each other, only hindered . . . [by the fact] that we never knew exactly where [they] were." The *Times*, 7 August, 1890. Neither Aberdare nor Goldie were listed amongst the guests, though the Governor of the Hudson's Bay Company was.

(31) In view of the enormous casualty rate amongst European officials and missionaries at this time the word is not ill-chosen.

(32) Goldie was intensely interested in Blyden's proposals. "[Goldie] urged the U.S. Government to deport without delay their entire Negro population to Africa. He actually worked out the cost of the scheme, discussed it with Sir Edward Grey, and presented it to the U.S. Government for consideration." Wellesley *op cit.*, p. 154. The R.N.C. employed several black District Agents and at least one Senior District Agent, and this as early as the 1880's. They moreover enjoyed the privileges of their rank such as tents, lamps, etc. and a special allocation of porters to transport their personal baggage when on tour. Lugard disapproved mightily. "The self-assurance and importance of these Anglicized Blacks is beyond calculation." Perham; *Diaries of Lord Lugard*, Vol. IV, Faber & Faber, London, 1963; p. 170.

(33) "Either a door is open, or else it is shut," i.e. "there is no middle way."

(34) The *Paternoster Review* was not the most successful of enterprises. It began publication in London in 1890, ran through six issues to constitute Volume I and folded in 1891.

II. FRENCH AMBITIONS IN AFRICA (1894)

This article was first published in the *Asiatic Quarterly Review* of April, 1894. The period is that immediately before the start of the "race for Nikki" between Lugard (as an employee of the Company) and Decoeur (as the agent of the French Government), and is one that was marked by mounting tensions on both sides.

It was, after all, only a few months earlier that the R.N.C. had finally rid itself of Mizon[1] even though the worst of his atrocities had been perpetrated well over a year before.

Goldie, moreover, having—as he thought—negotiated a cast-iron arrangement with Germany in the previous year[2] had seen it already begin to erode as a result of the 1894 Franco-German Agreement which had ceded to France access to the navigable Benue[3] and had thus opened up the prospect of a whole new series of confrontations with the Company on the eastern marches of its territory similar to the now familiar pattern of friction in the west.

Above all, however, Goldie could now see clearly the writing on the wall which presaged the evaporation of his fondest dream, the creation of a belt of British empire from the Atlantic to the Nile—and even, perhaps, to the Red Sea, a dream that was finally to recieve its quietus with the ratification of the 1898 Convention between Britain and France, which gave to her the eastern shore of Lake Chad and which thus fulfilled the French dream of a continuous band of French colonies from the Congo to the Mediterranean Sea. [4]

It was this vision which Goldie is now trying to articulate, to pre-empt, and even, hopefully, to exorcise!

Before dealing with the subject-matter of this article. I must make two prefatory remarks. The term "tropical Africa" is here employed, for want of a better, to describe those two-thirds of the continent—whether within or without the tropics—where Europeans cannot till the soil, nor rear their children to the third and fourth generations, and where, consequently, they, can only found what the French call colonies of plantation. This definition may avert objections from those who tell us that colonies of settlement may be successfully formed in Mashona and Matabele-land, the Shiré Highlands, Abyssinia and other regions lying within the tropics.

In the next place, this article is intended less for those familiar with African questions, than for the general reader, whose interest in the opening out of much needed new markets for our manufacturers is probably mingled with a desire to know how these enterprises affect our relations with France. The tension of those relations, during the last few months, has more than once burst the veil thrown over them by diplomatists, and I select three recent incidents which deserve special notice, as typical of the various aspects from which this matter is regarded from different standpoints.

One of these incidents was a temperate and lucid article in an English Review for March by M. André Lebon, a well-known deputy to the Chamber, who frankly admits the present "unfavourable current of opinion" among his countrymen towards England, which he attributes generally to our having shown a want of sympathy for their loss of Alsace-Lorraine and having joined in the "process of boycotting" France since the war of 1870: but amongst the immediate causes he gives the chief place to "the African question."

Another incident was a great banquet in Paris in connection with this African question, at which many leaders of public opinion were present, including a former Colonial Minister, when the following toast was given without any dissent being expressed, or at any rate reported:—"To all who struggle against our enemies, the English."

The third incident was the eloquent and statesmanlike speech of Lord Dufferin (5) at the late meeting of the British Chamber of Commerce in Paris, which has elicited all the latent good feeling of the French people towards England, and thus cleared, for a time, an atmosphere highly charged with electricity. The gist of his speech was that two such nations as France and England ought not to quarrel over the "distant cane-brakes of Africa, of the feverish jungles of Indo-China."

To the English mind, the idea of war on such grounds is absurd. But the old proverb that it takes two to make a quarrel is less true than its converse, that it takes two to keep the peace; and those who habitually study the French Press or have trustworthy information from French sources, appreciate the serious dangers through which diplomatists have had to steer; dangers with which Lord Dufferin must have been strongly impressed or he would not have thought it necessary to speak as he did. We English are often reproached with being an unimaginative race, and we certainly find it difficult to understand the intensity with which the French people pursue some abstract idea, more for the sake of its own grandeur than for defined and probable results. Of late years, few ideas have moved the French public more deeply than that of uniting their scattered colonies into a great African Empire.

It is a common mistake to suppose that the conception of France regaining in "Les Indes Noires" that colonial parity with England which she lost, last century, in the Eastern and Western worlds, has been confined to a small minority of Chauvinists, (6) who though active and earnest, have little influence over their compatriots. Even if this were true, it would not have sufficed to avert serious dangers, for reasons which I will presently mention. That it is not true might be shown by giving a list of the eminent statesmen and others, from the President of the Republic (7) downwards, who thought it necessary to countenance the African demonstrations in Paris in July and August 1892; but, to my mind, a more convincing proof of the hold that this conception has acquired on leaders of opinion is to be found in the fact that a philosopher such as M. Melchior de Vogué (8) has steadily supported the movement with the literary force and perspicuous calmness which mark his style.

It may, however, be asked why French ambitions in Africa need endanger the good relations between France and England? It may be said, with truth, that tropical Africa is large enough not only for both nations, but for all the civilized Powers who intend seriously to undertake the difficult task of developing it; that France has obtained the recognition of spheres of influence, which are, in the aggregate, nearly as large as Europe; that in tropical Africa there is no alluring pagoda-tree ready to be shaken, as in the wealthy Indies; and that whatever may ultimately come out of that region, a great deal of work and capital must be previously put into it. These facts are incontrovertible; but they are, unfortunately, on a totally different plane from those which must constitute a standing danger to peace, until the respective spheres of French and English influence are fully defined and until both nations insist that these shall be scrupulously respected.

One element of danger has arisen from the instability of the Parliamentary *régime* in France, owing to the number of indepedent and hostile groups. The result is that any important group can exercise much greater influence over the Government than it is entitled to do from its numerical strength. In the new Chamber of Deputies, the Colonial group is a powerful body, which by throwing its weight into close divisions on other questions, might be able to eject any Ministry from power. This increase of strength was due to several causes. The elections took place at a time when the national feeling against England was running strongly, so that the competitors of candidates known to be opposed to an aggressive Colonial policy found their opportunity in branding these as having English proclivities. Even the long services and great ability of M. Clemenceau could not save him from condemnation on this unpardonable charge. (9) Moreover a natural reaction had gradually set in against the bitter resentment so long displayed towards the late M. Jules Ferry and his supporters on the subject of Tonkin. To these causes may be added the justifiable enthusiasm and pride aroused by the exploits of recent French explorers, such as MM. Binger, (10) Crampel, Monteil, (11) Maistre (12) and others. There is no reason to suppose that the members of the colonial group, as a whole, are wanting in the good sense and equity of their compatriots; but their attention is, from the nature of their work, constantly drawn to the two unpalatable facts, that the colonial policy of England has been more successful than that of France, and that French merchants abroad cannot, generally speaking, hold their own against English merchants on equal terms. This seems at any rate the most reasonable explanation of the deplorable support recently given by the colonial group to openly avowed attempts to drive out the English—*"chasser les Anglais"*—from territories acquired by treaty and recognized by France as falling within the sphere of British influence.

A strong Colonial Minister, responsible to the country, would be able to enlighten public opinion and check excesses arising from these causes; but the recent French system seems the worst possible for this purpose. Formerly, the supreme direction of colonial affairs was entrusted to the Minister of Marine; but the colonial inferiority of France being constantly attributed to this subordination, the colonial office was made practically autonomous. Instead, however, of putting at its head a fully empowered Minister, sitting on equal terms in the Cabinet and sharing the responsibilities of his colleagues for peace or war, the appointment was given to an Under Secretary. Between his department and the military and naval officers in the Colonies, who count upon the support of their respective Ministers in the Cabinet, there has been constant friction, resulting in an almost complete want of control on the part of the Under-Secretary. The following incident exemplifies the normal condition of affairs. Towards the close of last year, M. Delcassé (13) found occasion to remove the military Governor of the French Soudan, Col. Archinard, perhaps the most

78

distinguished of the succession of brilliant soldiers, who have, since 1880, created that province for France. Col. Archinard having asked for certain explanations, the late Under-Secretary wrote him an exceedingly polite letter, conferring on him, for his services in Africa, the order of the *Green dragon of Annam;* whereupon Col. Archinard replied, in equally polite terms, that the order in question had no value for him, but that he had passed it on to one of his negro subordinates.

Under such a system it is not surprising if French explorers, who are generally officers, have obeyed their own patriotic impulses rather than the matured policy of a responsible Government. Every such officer has strong motives for endeavouring to extend the territories of his country, no matter how he may tread on the susceptibilities of other nations. Recent experience will have taught him, indeed, that the most solid services to France will not bring him so prominently and favourably before the public as those which enable him to assert that he has checkmated the English. A further proof of this occured lately, after the capture of Timbuctoo, contrary to explicit orders from Paris. The general tone of the newspapers was unfavourable to this movement as premature, but the strongest condemnation came from those papers which frankly pointed out that it was unnecessary, as its occupation would not be detrimental to English interests. (14)

Finally, it must be borne in mind that many Frenchmen, who earnestly desire the maintenance of amicable relations with England and who deplore aggressive action in Africa, feel bound to support such action after the event, on the sentimental ground of upholding the honour of the flag, at any cost. Herein lies the chief danger of collision; for England could not submit to be chased out of her territories by some irresponsible filibuster, sincerely anxious though she is to live on friendly terms with her nearest neighbour. It has been argued that tropical Africa is not worth the risk of war, and that it would have been sound policy to give France all that she so ardently desired in that continent, in exchange for concessions in other parts of the world. On this question I express no opinion here. But no strong and self-respecting nation can afford to yield to illegal force, even in the cane-brakes of Africa; as she would thereby encourage, in every direction, aggressions which she must ultimately resist or cease to be a Colonial or even a European Power.

French ambitions in Africa have, therefore, a deep interest for every Englishman apart from their intrinsic importance, and I propose to consider briefly—their nature; how far they are at present realized; whether valuable material results may be expected; and, finally, if in their completion, serious disputes are likely to arise between France and England.

France commenced her African career in the same manner as other European nations, planting her flag, by conquest or treaty, on widely distant parts of the coast, without any apparent thought of ultimate union. Before 1882, her activity in Algeria, and on the Senegal and Gaboon rivers aimed at local colonial development and not at a connected African Empire. It would, of course, be rash to assert that no such conception had ever been suggested previously. I remember that Mr. Joseph Thomson, in his work on Mungo Park, published some years after the issue of the Niger Charter, showed a great geographer, named McQueen, (15) had suggested such a Charter in the early years of this century, and had, with remarkable sagacity prophesied that this alone would prevent France from obtaining possession of the greater part of Northern Africa. I may admit that I had never before heard either of McQueen's name or his suggestion; and it is probable that corresponding theories from the French point of view may have been advanced, in former days, from time to time. But it was not until 1882—a year after the first application to the British Government for a Niger Charter—that any practical move was made for the union of the scattered French colonies in Africa, by the acquisition of the immense inland regions lying between them. In that year a Company, with a capital of £600,000, was formed at Marseilles, under the patronage of M. Gambetta,[16] for the double purpose of pushing up overland to the Upper Niger from the sea-board of Senegambia, and of entering the Lower Niger, at its mouth in the Gulf of Guinea, and working up the river to meet the advance from the west. In 1882, also, was first seriously mooted the idea of a Trans-Sahara railway. I cannot now remember whether the gentleman, who came to London to seek for English support in this matter, was the originator of the scheme or only an enthusiastic supporter; but out of the mass of details with which he favoured me, there was one which produced a lasting impression: namely, that the carriages were to be bullet-proof, without side windows, and with platform roofs for mitrailleuse guns for the benefit of the Tuaregs. Finally, it was in 1882, that M. de Brazza,[17] who had just succeeded in adding the great territory of the French Congo to the small coast colony of the Gaboon, commenced that northward movement towards the centre of Northern Africa, which has at last borne fruit in the Franco-German convention of 1894.

It must be remembered that in 1882, Germany had not commenced her colonial career or annexed the Cameroons; nor England acquired political rights in the basins of the Niger and Chad, or on the Oil Rivers; nor the International Association received recognition as the Congo Free State: so that the extension of French rights—as against other European nations—over more than half of the continent of Africa was no visionary scheme, but might have been realized without any very serious sacrifices. The effective occupation of those five or six million square miles would, however, have been a very different task.

M. Gambetta's fall from power, his death, and the disasters in Tonkin which practically put an end to the career of M. Jules Ferry, prevented this gigantic plan being pursued at the time when it was practicable. Its failure is still frequently deplored by the French Press, and was undoubtedly at the root of the recent attempts of the Colonial party to repudiate or evade the Anglo-French Convention of 1890,[18] which had secured to England the Niger and Chad basins to the south of a line from Say on the Middle Niger to Barruwa on Lake Chad. But the good sense of the French people ought to recognise that two powerful nations, desirous of keeping the peace, can only deal with facts as they are and not as they might have been under other circumstances. England cannot be justly blamed for having secured those Niger-Chad regions, which were far removed from any then existing French possession or sphere, and had been opened up to commerce by British enterprise alone—the French having only entered after the ground was broken; and having entirely disappeared after a few years of fruitless struggle.

Meanwhile, France had advanced from her position on the Senegal over extensive inland regions and had also taken possession of the hinter-lands of British Gambia and Sierra Leone, which she hemmed in closely to the sea; thus impairing the present value of these British colonies, besides effectually preventing their future extension. England might have reasonably refused her recognition to this procedure, inasmuch as France, in the negotiations for the Say-Barruwa line of 1890, had rested her case on the right of Algeria to a hinter-land 1,500 miles in depth, although at that date no Frenchman—explorer, merchant or official—had ever even visited the Central Sudan. But England, in her desire for peace, has always wisely shown a respect for French territorial claims, which has not been uniformly reciprocated. It would greatly serve the interests of peace and good feeling if these facts could by any means be placed temperately and without any shade of reproach before the general French public, which at present hears only unfounded accusations of grasping action on the part of Great Britain, in tropical Africa.

The public interest aroused by the conclusion and discussion of the Anglo-French agreement of 1890, gave a fresh impulse to the idea of uniting in some manner the African colonies of France, to which the valuable addition of Tunis had meanwhile been made. Large sums of money were found by the State and public subscription, and a stream of explorers extended French rights in every direction. The French Sudan was carried down to her possessions on the Ivory Coast and eastward to the rear of our Gold Coast colony. Admirably conducted military operations placed Dahomey under French rule, while the French Congo was pushed northwards toward Lake Chad behind the German colony of the Cameroons. An agreement has at last been concluded between France and Germany which enables the former country to complete the union of her colonies, by a circuitous route to the east of Lake Chad, and thus form her African possessions into a connected Empire. The advantage of the completion of this scheme to the cause of peace cannot be over estimated, as the advocates of an aggressive African policy will now have to convince their compatriots of the adequate benefits to be secured by each new aggression and will no longer be able to rest their case, as heretofore, on the sentimental idea that the French possessions in Africa should be united across the continent, even at the risk of collision with England.

The attractions of this territorial continuity, for which so much has been sacrificed and risked, seem to be purely ideal. It can hardly be doubted that the commerce of Senegambia will always pass to and from the Atlantic coast and not over thousands of miles of land transit to the French Congo or Algeria; (19) and so on *mutalis mutandis.* However this may be, England has never opposed or displayed jealousy of the scheme, which is at any rate innocuous, and with which we have no concern whatever. I urge this, because the French Press constantly asserts the contrary. Scarcely any statement about a nation is true of all its individual members; but it is certain that most Englishmen are completely indifferent to the fact that France has now acquired, or rather excluded from foreign interference, nearly one-third of Africa; while many of us rejoice at this extension, as tending, when the frontiers are finally agreed, to preserve the peace of Europe by giving France ample employment abroad for her energies and revenues.

It is a notable fact, that although the French, as individuals, have a reputation for greater prudence and economy than the English, they have, as a nation, shown far more liberality in expenditure on building up colonies for the benefit of future generations. During the sixty-three years' occupation of Algeria, the mother country has already contributed over £160,000,000 to the expenses of that colony, and still pays for the entire maintenance of the army and for much of the expenditure on public works. In the other African colonies the amounts have not been so formidable up to now; but in all, with the exception of Tunis, the mother country supplies the annual funds without which they would cease to exist.

I cannot resist comparing these facts with the attitude of England towards her West African possessions. I refer especially to the Niger Territories, because I can place complete reliance on my information in that instance. The British taxpayer has contributed nothing whatever either to the acquisition of these half million square miles or to their subsequent administration. No doubt this system tends to encourage self-reliance and energy, just at the hardiest children are those who have been allowed to run loose in all weathers: but some do not survive this bracing process, and it is difficult for limited private enterprise to contend successfully with prolonged hostile operations supported by public subscriptions and State funds.

In considering the question whether France will reap such a harvest from her possessions in tropical Africa as will repay her for her present sacrifices, I am leaving the realm of fact for that of inference. But I have never yet heard any valid reason for doubting that tropical Africa—excepting in the sterile soil of the desert and the swamps of river mouths—will gradually become as productive as other tropical regions of the world. It is said that the negro races will never take kindly to industry, and this view is generally supported by the two assertions, that the natives do not work at present, and that the freed negroes of our West Indian colonies and elsewhere are incurably idle. The former propostion is certainly inaccurate in respect to large populations of Western and Central Africa. I venture to think that the average European, if placed under similar political and social conditions, exposed at all times to slavery or violent death and to the seizure of the fruits of his labour by a stronger than himself, would not display more industry than the native of Africa. As to the argument drawn from our West Indian colonies, it must be remembered that the slaves exported from Africa belonged mainly to less energetic tribes which had been gradually driven down to the coast from the interior by higher races.

It cannot however be denied that to develop general and active habits of industry amongst the natives of tropical Africa and to introduce the growth of indigo, coffee, tobacco and the many other products which will pay for export, the tuition and supervision of great numbers of Europeans will long be needed. The insignificant proportion of Europeans who suffice for this purpose in Asiatic countries, where the birth of civilization and industry dates from prehistoric times, would be ineffective in moving the *inertia* of the Dark Continent. This may prove a serious stumbling-block to the full satisfaction of French ambitions in Africa. I shall not dwell on this point, because I dealt with it fully some years ago in an article which earned the approval of so high an authority as M. Barthélemy Saint-Hilaire; (20) but I may point out that Frenchmen can hardly be induced to settle in sufficient number even in the delightful climate of Algeria, within easy distance from France, and that only the pressure of over population can produce the necessary supply of men willing to pass the best years of their lives in unhealthy and depressing climates, far from the comforts and interests of civilization and with little society but that of lower races with whom they have hardly an idea in common.

A glance at any map of the present partition of Africa, since the Franco-German convention of the 15th March, 1894, will show that while about one-half of the area of the French empire in Africa, is fairly accessible to commerce and military force, she is not so well placed as other European Powers in respect of the far inland half, of which it may be safely prophesied that it will be the latest part of the Continent to bear fruit, the most costly to develop and the least profitable to work.

Another obstacle to the early success of the French Empire in Africa lies in the nature of some of the races within her sphere. One is apt to forget that in speaking of a State possessing a sphere of influence, the primary meaning is that other European States have agreed not to encroach or exercise political influence within it. Such international conventions are, it is true, generally based on previous treaties with the native rulers, but the effective concilliation or subjugation of these potentates is generally a later consideration. So far as the tribes of the Sahara, or potentates such as Samory, are concerned, the difficulties of France are probably not much greater than those with which Englishmen have to deal, both in East and West Africa, or have lately successfully dealt in South Africa. But in her newly-acquired sphere, running from the French Congo to the east of Lake Chad, she has a task before her which will severely strain her resources. She has entered here into a hornets' nest of Moslem fanaticism and of fighting races, in the very centre of the continent. The new sphere will be altogether valueless unless France deals vigorously with the fanatical states of Baghirmi(21) and Wadai,(22) which are not likely to make any voluntary concessions to the hated and despised Nazarenes.(23) The conditions in this eastern region are entirely different from those in portions of the Western Sudan, where masses of the populations are Pagan at heart, and so little attached to their Moslem rulers that a small European force would suffice to break a native kingdom to pieces; and where the rulers themselves, either from the knowledge of this fact or from the absence of fanaticism are generally willing to concede to Europeans, for a consideration, at any rate the political rights necessary for the security of commerce. If, however, France subjugates this nucleus of militant Islam to the east of Lake Chad, she will have rendered a great service to all the civilized Powers having possessions in Northern Africa, and England especially will have cause to rejoice at her having at last realized her dream of uniting her colonies.

It is to the east of Baghirmi and Wadai that the principal danger of future dispute may arise. But the intrusion of France into the basin of the Upper Nile(24) would be a gratuitously unfriendly act, as she has no possessions on the East Coast from which she could reach that basin, and could not possibly hold and develop territory so remote from her bases of operations on the Atlantic and Mediterranean coasts; while that region lies clearly within the natural hinterland of the British East African Protectorate. There are, happily, distinct signs of a better understanding than has lately existed between the two countries; and, so long as that lasts, it may be hoped that no French Government will encourage or recognise such a useless and agressive wild-goose chase to the east. Passing westward from Wadai, there can be no element of dispute till Morocco is reached. As this country falls within general European politics rather than African politics, I shall venture no opinion on its future. France and England are, fortunately, not face to face with this problem, in the solution of which Germany, Spain and other nations will claim a voice. Moving southward from Morocco to the region which the French designate *le boucle du Niger,* (25) where the frontiers have yet to be settled between France and Sierra Leone, our Gold Coast Colony and the Niger Territories, there is still plenty of work for diplomatists, but no great cause for anxiety. Each nation has its treaties with native rulers and its rights to a reasonable hinterland for its existing possessions; but there is no important principle at stake as in recent disputes elsewhere.

The Anglo-German agreement of November 1893, and the Franco-German agreement just concluded, may appear to some as made at the expense of England alone; but, if so, she may console herself by the assured possession of as much of the richest portion of tropical Africa as she can digest within two or three generations. It may perhaps be reasonably hoped that the race for Africa is now practically at an end; and that the time has come when European nations, no longer able to enjoy the dramatic spectacle of a struggle for the possession of a continent, must be content with more prosaic rivalry in the settlement and development of their respective spheres. This task will be more arduous than that of exploration or treaty-making. Regions as large as Europe have to be effectively occupied and governed; the paralyzing effects of native misgovernment from time immemorial have to be modified; and a new order of ideas gradually introduced amongst a hundred million inhabitants of tropical Africa; but six European nations, with all the resources of modern civilization, have pledged their credit to carry out this work, and though progress must be slow at first, its ultimate success may be confidently predicted. (26)

(1) Mizon, Louis Alexandre Antoine, 1853-1899. French sailor, explorer and administrator, and an avowed Anglophobe. From 1880-1883 he co-operated with de Brazza in the Congo and then embarked on a career of African exploration alone. Appointed an agent of the French "African Committee," Mizon entered the Niger and Benue twice, once in 1890-92, and again in 1893. His exploits in Muri, when he used his own forces (notwithstanding his claim to be on a purely scientific and exploratory expedition) to assist the Emir of Muri in attacking Kona, led eventually to his exposure. In spite of this, however, he remained a hero to the French "Colonial Faction," even though largely discredited elsewhere. Mizon was lost at sea in the Indian Ocean in 1899. When at Yola he presented the Lamido with two brass cannon which for long graced the lawn of the Residency, Kano. The whole *affaire Mizon* is discussed at some length in Part III.

(2) "I induced the British Government to grant a great strip of Nigeria to Germany . . .; it was worthless." Wellesley, *op cit.,* p. 97.

(3) Flint, *op cit.,* p. 184 *et seq.*

(4) "Never now shall Nigeria and Uganda join hands." Mary Kingsley to Stephen Gwynn, quoted in Wellesley, *op cit.,* p. 22.

(5) Delivered 5 March, 1894. The speech was conciliatory to French ambitions and was hailed in glowing terms by the French Press and all shades of French politcial opinion. Lord Dufferin was British Ambassador to the Third Republic at the time he made the remarks. Goldie quotes from the speech. See the *Times* 6 March, 1894, p. 5.

(6) Literally a group of super-patriots who took their name from Nicolas Chauvin a Republic and Empire soldier celebrated for his degree of patriotic dedication. See also succeeding footnote and page 203 for details of the concept of "Les Indes Noires."

(7) President Marie-Francois-Sadi Carnot, 1837-1894. Fourth President of the Third Republic; Assassinated on 24 June, 1894 by an Italian anarchist.

(8) Vogüé, Marie-Eugène-Melchior, Vicomte de, 1848-1910. French historian and member of the Academie. De Vogüé wrote the preface to Colonel Monteil's book *De Saint-Louis à Tripoli etc.* He was also French Ambassador to Turkey and to the Austro-Hungarian Empire. See also page 203. De Vogüé coined the phrase "Les Indes Noires" as the title to a brochure which he wrote in 1890. It fascinated Goldie!

(9) Clemenceau, George, 1841-1921. Jules Ferry's most dedicated and redoubtable opponent; defeated in the elections of 1893 and withdrew temporarily from politics, resuming his career in journalism. In 1902 he was re-elected to the Senate and remained active thereafter until defeated in the Presidential Elections of 1920, after which he finally retired. Revered during World War I as "Tiger" Clemenceau.

(10) Binger, Louis Gustave, 1856-1936. French Explorer and Administrator who operated in the *"boucle du Niger"* in 1887-89. Governor of the Côte d'Ivoire, 1893; Director, African Affairs, Colonial Ministry, Paris 1897.

(11) Monteil, Parfait Louis, 1855-1925: In 1890-92, he made a journey from St. Louis, Senegal to Tripoli via Say, Sokoto, Kano and Chad. French Congo, 1893; Ivory Coast, 1895. Author of *De St Louis à Tripoli par le lac Tchad,* Paris, 1895.

(12) Maistre, Paul André Marie, 1858-1922. French General most famous as the Commander of the French Divisions sent to Italy after Caporetto in World War I. Between 1892-93, he explored the Upper Benue.

(13) Delcassé, Théophile, 1852-1923. Journalist and politician; Under-Secretary of State (1893) and then Minister of Colonies, 1894-95; Foreign Minister 1898-1905; Anglophile and a proponent of the *Entente.*

(14) Timbuktu was occupied by a French force under Major (later Marshal of France) Joseph Jacques Césaire (Pappa) Joffre in 1894, after Colonel Bonnier had been murdered by Tuaregs. Joffre, an Engineer, then built Fort Bonnier and Timbuktu became the Headquarters of an administrative *cercle.* Joffre was born in 1852 and died in 1931.

(15) Goldie's self-professed ignorance boggles the mind! James MacQueen 1778-1870, was probably the most famous of all "theoretical geographers." His attention was first drawn to West Africa by reading Mungo Park's *Travels* (1799). At that time he was in charge of a sugar plantation in the West Indies. There he began to question Mandingo

slaves on the plantations and to interrogate the captains of slavers and their crews. An enthusiasm for African Geography developed. In 1821 MacQueen became Editor of the *Glasgow Courier,* and in that same year published his book . . . *a particular account of the course and termination of the Niger,* in which he theorised that the many rivers in the Bights of Benin and Biafra would prove to be the mouth of the Niger. He was absolutely right!

(16) Gambetta, Léon, 1838-82. Lawyer and Liberal politician; Escaped from Paris during the Siege in a balloon, 7 Oct., 1870 and rejoined the Government at Tours as Minister of War and of the Interior. He refused to sign the treaty ceding Alsace-Lorraine. Later, he floor-managed the acceptance by the National Assembly of the Constitution of the Third Republic in the face of the opposition of the Monarchist majority. Prime Minister, 1881. Advocated a liberal platform, but voted out of office in January, 1882, before he could implement it.

(17) Brazza, Pierre Savorgnan de, 1852-1905. Italian born French explorer, naturalised 1874; explored Gabon and Congo between 1875-78 and 1879-82; subsequently, administered French Congo.

(18) In fact, the Say-Barruwa line was not upset until the Anglo-French Agreement of 1898, although France did gain some slight advantage in the Lake Chad area as a result of the Franco-German Agreement of 1894.

(19) Stephen Gwynn, in Wellesley *op cit.,* p. 23, notes an axiom of Goldie's. "Trade," he said, "seeks the sea by the shortest route." Gwynn adds " . . . there remained clear in my mind . . . a perception that . . . the natural lines of intercourse ran across, not lengthwise" throughout the African continent.

(20) Barthélmy-Saint-Hilaire, Jules, 1805-1895. Philosopher and statesman; Foreign Minister under Jules Ferry, 1880-1881. The reference is clearly to the article "France and England on the Niger," which is reproduced above.

(21) Bagirmi—an area of some 20,000 sq. m. south-east of Lake Chad. The Bagirmi waged internecine war on Bornu, but about 1890 were over-run by Rabeh Zobier, after whose death at the battle of Kusseri in 1900 and that of his son Fadr-Allah at Gujba in 1901, Bagirmi finally was subjected by the French.

(22) Wadai—a buffer between Kanem and Bagirmi, Wadai was finally annexed by France in 1909. An area of 150,000 sq. m. in the Chad basin, the country had a mixed population of Arabs, Fula, and Tubu under a Maba ruling elite. Warlike and intractable they fiercely resisted penetration. In 1910, Boyd Alexander, the first Briton to explore Wadai was murdered there, and in the same year, a French column 300 strong under Colonel Moll was attacked by a force of 5,000. Moll and a hundred of his men were killed before the attack was finally repelled.

(23) i.e. The followers of the "Man from Nazareth," Christians.

(24) This, of course, is exactly what happened in 1897. Jean Baptiste Marchand, 1863-1934, a French officer who had served in Senegal in 1889 and who in 1890 had led an expedition to explore the source of the Niger, later exploring extensively throughout the Western Sudan and the Ivory Coast hinterland, was sent by the French Government in January of that year, to interpose a French presence between British moves to join up Uganda and the Sudan. Marching from Brazzaville he arrived at Fashoda on the White Nile in July of 1898. A crisis in Anglo-French relations ensued. Eventually Marchland withdrew. Mary Kingsley always claimed that there was a secret deal—Marchand for Goldie. Ironically, Vandeleur was present at Marchand's withdrawal.

(25) i.e. "the Niger bend."

(26) The *Asiatic Quarterly Review,* in which this article appeared, was issued under that name from 1886-1913, with a brief period as the *Imperial and Oriental Review and Colonial Record.* From 1914 to 1952, it ran as the Asiatic Review.

III. THE WEST AFRICAN LIQUOR TRADE (1895)

The following statement was made by Sir George Goldie before the Native Races and Liquor Traffic United Committee on 27 February, 1895. It was published in the same year by Shaw & Sons, London.

GENTLEMEN,

As you know, Lord Aberdare died only the night before last, (1) and I should have asked you to excuse me from keeping this appointment but for the urgency of the question to be discussed, and for my knowledge that he would have strongly desired that there should be no delay, on personal grounds, in a matter in which he was so deeply interested. But you will understand that I am not so fully prepared to meet you as I should have been but for this unexpected and most painful shock.

I had the pleasure of addressing you some four or five years ago, but probably some of you were either not present on that occasion or have not a distinct memory of the points I then raised. I think, therefore, I had better briefly explain my own *locus standi* in the matter, so I will read a short extract on the repression of the liquor traffic from a speech delivered to the Shareholders of the Royal Niger Company in July, 1890, by Lord Aberdare. (2) He said—

"I believe that the Company was the first public body to enunciate and urge upon the Government this principle in regard to Central Africa. At the time of the meeting of the Berlin Conference in October, 1881, the Native Races and Liquor Traffic United Committee, which has since done much admirable service, had not come into existence. A reference to the Blue Book, Africa, No. 4 (1885), will show, what is, moreover, well known at the Foreign Office, that this question had been warmly urged on the British delegates by your Deputy-Governor, Sir George Goldie, who was acting as the Company's representative at the Berlin Conference, and who, in so doing, was only giving effect to the deep conviction he had long entertained, and which he had succeeded in impressing on his colleagues in the Council. These opinions were adopted by the British Delegates, and were pressed by them on the Conference, before the earliest representation had been made by any public body in England to our Foreign Secretary. Her Majesty's Government were unable to carry their proposal at the Berlin Conference, owing to the opposition of certain other Powers; but, largely in consequence of the strenuous efforts of the United Committee, the policy advocated by Sir George Goldie at Berlin has, within the last few weeks, been adopted by Europe at the Brussels Conference. We have lost no time in taking advantage of this International Agreement, and we have this morning made a regulation absolutely prohibiting the importation of spirituous liquors, for sale or barter, into any place within the jurisdiction of the Company north of the seventh parallel of north latitude (3) —that is to say, into about nineteen-twentieths of the regions over which the Company has treaty rights of jurisdiction. We trust the day is not far distant when the same policy may be enforced in the remaining twentieth of our Territories; but until the Company's military force is greatly strengthened, the attempt would inevitably be attended by disastrous failure.''

I may remind you, in passing, that a disaster, such as was here foreshadowed, has now actually occurred, owing to the Niger Company being unaware that some 1,500 rifles and machine guns had been smuggled into Brass in the neighbouring Oil Rivers (Niger Coast) Protectorate, in defiance of the Brussels Act. The Niger Company could not, of course, maintain its legislative restrictions on liquors, if it were liable to many such unexpected and disastrous blows. (4)

You must not imagine from the above extract that the Company had awaited the Brussels Act to *commence* its work. The heavy duty on spirits was imposed within three weeks of the issue of the Charter in July, 1866, four years before the Brussels Act, and the total prohibition of the sale of spirits in one (inland) third of its sphere was dated on the 29th April, 1887, three years before the Brussels Act. The Niger Company, therefore, distinctly led the way, which was afterwards followed by other Governments. But the Brussels Act, 1890, made possible wider measures, which would previously have raised protests from foreign Powers. Malicious or ignorant assertions have been made that the Company has only prohibited the traffic in Mohammedan countries which do not want spirits. I must point out the absurdity of this statement. It might, perhaps, apply in some degree to a very small portion of Sokoto; but by far the greater part of that empire is only Moslem in name, the ruling caste of Fellatahs being scattered in small numbers over extensive regions, inhabited by races essentially Pagan in nature. This remark applies also to nearly the whole of the empire of Gandu. The regions south of the Benue, below Ibi, are entirely Pagan and under tribal rule. So are the regions near the Niger, below Lokoja down to Asaba, while the great Kingdom of Borgu is also entirely Pagan. Out of all these vast regions into which the importation of spirits is now prohibited, the only place where the rulers ever showed even a nominal opposition to the liquor trade was Nupe; and it is unnecessary to point out to your Committee the large extent of the spirit traffic in Nupe in the days prior to the Charter of the Niger Company, because this has been often referred to in your earlier publications. I venture, indeed, to suggest that in future reprints of the letter of Maliki, Emir of Nupe, (5) to the late Bishop Crowther, you should append a note to the effect that the action of the Niger Company during the first three years after receiving its Charter, entirely destroyed the liquor traffic in Nupe. This instance of Nupe shows that Moslem rule is no bar in Central Africa to an almost unlimited extension of the liquor traffic. The Company may fairly claim that, but for its timely work of prohibition, the liquor trade would soon have spread over its inland Territories, by far the most populous region of tropical Africa. The consumption over this region, if taken only at the same rate as in Great Britain, would be about thirty million gallons a year; while now, entirely through the exertions of the Company, the former spirit traffic in this region is abolished by law, and future traffic there rendered impossible, except in smuggled liquors.

I may tell you a fact related to me by Sir Claude MacDonald, the present Administrator of the Oil Rivers, or (as it is now called) the Niger Coast Protectorate, and who is a frank and avowed opponent of government by Chartered Companies. He was sent by the British Government some five years ago to make a confidential and independent report on the Niger Company's Territories. In one part, I think in the Anambra district, (6) after examining the Chiefs about their treaties to see if they understood them, he asked if they had any grievance. There was a unanimous reply in the affirmative. On asking what the grievance was, the Commissioner was informed that now the Chiefs could get no drink.

Happily in that region the Company is sufficiently strong to resist any attempt at serious insurrection on that account, though the consequent expense, work, and anxiety of maintaining order are very considerable; but the smuggling of spirits into those inland regions is difficult compared with the ease with which smuggling into the delta can be carried out. It must not be forgotten that an enormous amount of spirits—said to be two million gallons—is imported annually into the small neighbouring colony of Lagos, and a similar amount annually into the strip of the Oil Rivers, now known as the Niger Coast Protectorate. The pressure, therefore, on the delta of the Niger in the Company's Territories is very serious, and every outbreak amongst the natives there is utilized by the persons interested in the liquor traffic to denounce the Company as unfit to rule, and to urge that the delta should be handed over to the Coast Protectorate.

Yet you must not think that this difficulty is in the delta alone. In a report just received from Captain Lugard, that experienced and intelligent officer writes as follows about the Mahomedan province of Illorin and the neighbouring country of Yoruba. He says:—

"Unfortunately, however, the main article imported into the country, in exchange for its products, is one which tends to deteriorate the people, instead of raising them in the plane of civilization. Lagos gin, from which almost alone the wealth of Lagos accrues, is found in every town and village from the coast to the far Northwestern boundary of Yoruba, and penetrates even to Borgu. Since its sale has been prohibited by the Royal Niger Company (above Lat. 7 deg.) Illorin has become the depot whence the river stations of the Niger are supplied from Lagos with spirits. From Illorin gin is brought to Jebba and to Egga, and even, I am told, to Lokoja, and throughout Nupe. Thus, this illicit traffic not only supplies the basis of trade to Lagos in its own Hinterland, but defrauds the Niger Company of a portion of its legitimate trade in its own territories. I trust that on these representations the Directors may see their way to take action with a view to protecting their own commercial interests." (7)

It is evident then that the Brussels Act is, as regards spirits, a dismal failure. What is the use of prohibiting the import of liquors into the vast inland regions with frontiers too large and too unsettled for effective customs surveillance, when only light duties are levied on the coast line from which spirits are allowed to penetrate freely inland?

The average import of spirits into the Company's Territories since the issue of the Charter has been only 163,000 gallons, as against the immense quantities imported into the neighbouring Oil Rivers (Niger Coast) Protectorate and Lagos. Last year, indeed, was a record year in the Niger Company's Territories, not a single pint of trade liquors having been imported during the year. This was the first time since the opening of the Niger to European trade. But this state of things cannot last, cannot probably even be repeated, unless restrictive measures are taken in respect to the trade in neighbouring regions.

What then is to be done? On the 3rd May, 1887, I addressed a full letter on the subject to the Marquis of Salisbury, in which I advocated the bringing about of an international agreement—practically with France and Germany—by which a uniform duty should be imposed on spirits (from Senegal to the Cameroons inclusive) not less than the duty on spirits imported into Great Britain, which is, I believe, 10s. 6d. a gallon. The duty in Lagos is, I understand, 6½d a gallon. But much experience has been gained since I wrote that letter in 1887, and I would now advocate the total prohibition of trade spirits into West Africa, from the Southern frontier of Morocco down to the Northern frontier of the Cape Colony. If England, France, and Germany were agreed, Portugal and the Congo Free State would not be likely to refuse to join. The difficulties in the way of such an agreement are now far less than at the time of the meeting of the Berlin Conference in 1884. On the 14th May, 1889, the German Reichstag adopted almost unanimously a resolution "to request the Federal Governments to again take into consideration whether, and how, the trade in spirits in the German Colonies can be effectually opposed either by prohibition or limitation." It would seem, therefore, as if public opinion in Germany were ripe for effective action in this direction. If England and Germany were united on this question, it is extremely improbable that the French nation would accept the odium of taking up an adverse attitude. The object is, at any rate, worth a strenuous effort on your part.

It may be asked whether smuggling could be effectually prevented over such a long line of coast. But spirits can only be shipped to West Africa in steamers or sailing vessels of considerable tonnage. The African rivers are now sufficiently occupied to make it impossible for such vessels to enter them without the knowledge of the Customs officers,and all along the line of coast the surf breaks with such force as to make discharging cargo a slow process. Moreover, vessels found suspiciously close to the shore in places not near a port of entry would naturally be examined. As all the colonizing Powers maintain gunboats in West Africa, the cost of patrolling the coast would be insignificant. But it might also be asked whether in many parts of West Africa commerce, as a whole, would not greatly suffer from a prohibition of the sale of spirits. No doubt the aggregate of trade would diminish temporarily, but the question which merchants have to put to themselves, and which the Powers have to ask, is that which the Council of the Royal Niger Company put before the shareholders. Is it not better to suffer a temporary diminution of trade with the prospect of reaping the permanent benefit which must accrue from putting commerce on a sounder foundation? Unless this question is answered in the affirmative, as it was at once answered by the shareholders of the Company, all hopes of developing Africa and raising it to the standard of Europe must be abandoned.

It is on this practical ground alone that I have for so many years urged this question. At the risk of alienating your sympathies, I must tell you frankly that I am not an ardent supporter of total abstinence, even for myself—nor even of temperance, except for myself—and that I am not altogether in accord with the views which you put forward in your publications. (8) But, although our ultimate motives are distinct, we have, apparently, one common immediate object, namely, the suppression of the West African Liquor Traffic, and I have no hesitation, therefore, in saying that if your Committee wishes to do effective work in this direction, the time has arrived for making a special effort both abroad and at home.

(1) For the obituary, published in the *Geographical Journal,* and written by Goldie, see pages 213-215.

(2) 10th Ordinary General Meeting, held at Surrey House, 29 July, 1890.

(3) That is, approximately anywhere north of Idah, some 45 miles down river from Lokoja.

(4) Here, and before an especially receptive (and not un-influential) audience, Goldie moves on to the offensive against the "Liverpool Merchants" and others, (including Sir Claude Macdonald) who were supporting, either overtly or covertly, the campaign to shift at least the major share of the blame for the Brassmen's raid on Akassa almost exactly two months earlier.

(5) Maliki 4th Emir of Nupe, 1884-1895, had urged Bishop Crowther to press the Church Missionary Society to agitate for a ban on the importation of spirits, and especially gin. Naturally, the Missionaries made as much of this letter as they could.

(6) The area on either side of the Anambra River, in the modern Igala Division and then on down towards Onitsha. McDonald was appointed Sole Commissioner to "investigate" the R.N.C. in 1889. An account of the mission is contained in A. F. Mockler-Ferryman's book, *Up the Niger etc.,* (London, 1892).

(7) At this time, Lugard, having succeeded in the race for Nikki, was fixing the Lagos-Ilorin boundary, in company with Captain R. L. Bower, who, between 1893 and 1897 was British Resident, Ibadan.

(8) This was bearding the lion in its own den with a vengance! Only a person as supremely assured as Goldie was would have dared to take such a position. But, as has been shown, his stand on liquor was impeccable. It was the prohibitionists who needed Goldie and not the other way round. That is not to say, however, that in his battles with Liverpool and with the Government, Goldie did not take full advantage of his alliance with the anti-liquor lobbies.

IV. BRITAIN'S PRIORITY ON THE MIDDLE NIGER (1897)

This article appeared in the *New Review* of June 1897. [1] The highly successful Bida and Ilorin campaign had been concluded in February and the Company's prestige had never stood higher. This was the year of the Diamond Jubilee. The Constabulary had marched in the processions and had been part of the Review by Her Majesty of the Colonial Contingents in Regent's Park.

But it was also the year in which the Company found itself challenged on the Middle Niger in force by the French. Goldie himself had clashed with Bretonnet, and Chamberlain was on the point of putting into effect his "chequer-board policy" that would need Imperial troops properly to effect it.

In using the word 'priority' in the title, Goldie is doing so in the sense of "right to precedence." There is no suggestion at all of the modern connotation. Thus, in this presentation, which he stresses is directed at reasonable men on both sides of the Channel, an attempt is being made to establish the historical precedence of British activities on the middle section of the Niger below the agreed 1890 boundary mark which was the town of Say.

The article is, in a sense, a provocative one in that it challenges France on specifics, and specifics which, moreover, are irrefutable. Some aspects, indeed, such as the role of Dr. Baikie, he seems to play down; the Model Farm Project of 1841, gets no mention at all. But as a brief though authoritative synopsis of British enterprise in the hundred years up to 1890, the material is well presented.

One word however is beginning to emerge as almost a "Goldie-ism," and that is "calumny." It will appear with added frequency later and it may be that its appearance presages a certain morbidity on Goldie's part, all one with the intolerance of misrepresentation which he expressed to Leonard Darwin in 1911. [2]

Two things of especial interest emerge from the article. First, the veil is drawn just a little bit on the National African Company's treaty making activities and some new names appear; Hamilton, an ex-naval officer, Greenshields "a Scotch commercial agent" and, later, Lister, a senior executive officer of the R.N.C.

Secondly, there is a fascinating discussion of the minutiae of the drafting and execution of the Protocols of the Berlin Conference, and of their subsequent breaching by France. In all this there should be borne in mind, less than four months before, Goldie's confrontation with the French Lieutenant Bretonnet[3] who had led a military patrol into Borgu and had occupied Bussa while the Company's troops were actually engaged in fighting in Nupe and Ilorin.

Goldie, in fact, first heard of the appearance of a foreign force in Borgu early in February, 1897, from Lieutenant Barton, the commander of the Company's troops at Fort Goldie. Barton was a man for whom Sir George had not very much time, having described him in a letter to Scarbrough a bare month earlier[4] as "not much better" than a fool.

So scrappy was his information that he wrote on 17 February from "The Emir's Palace Ilorin" in order to enquire of the interloper whether he was German (as was suspected) or French. The reply that he received from Bretonnet was clearly a shock to him.[5]

During the subsequent correspondence, which involved the exchange of three letters in all, Goldie took up a position very close to that which he repeats in his monograph, with regard to effective occupation being required for "coasts" only as opposed to "hinterlands," and was at pains to point out that this had been agreed at the initiative of the French Plenipotentiary, M. le Baron de Courcel.

Amongst the political questions which call for solution, there are few more important to the progress of the world than the prevention, if practicable, the occasional irritation displayed in France towards Great Britain. While the material advantage to civilization of cordial relations between the two greatest colonizing Powers is obvious, most thinking Englishmen desire also, as a matter of sentiment, to be on good terms with a people to which they are indebted for so much that makes life worth living from both the mental and the physical point of view. I propose to touch on one only of the minor causes of irritation with which I happen to be familiar: the controversy, namely, as to French and British rights in the regions of the Middle Niger.

It would be vain to hope to modify the attitude of the extreme section of the French Colonial party, which, in order to attain legitimate aims in Africa and Asia, has exerted itself to foster Anglophobia in France. In the eagerness of pursuit, that section has thrown off all sense of fairness towards opponents. In its ably-written organs, calumnies from obviously prejudiced sources are published as proved facts; while personal attacks are so persistent and so numerous that even a summary of those relating to the Niger Company alone would fill a good-sized volume. Two amusing instances will suffice as types of the whole series.

When the French gunboat, the *Ardent,* [6] was stranded for several months in the Lower Niger without provisions and with a fever-stricken crew, a well-known Parisian newspaper protested against the barbarity shown by the Niger Company's officials—one of whom was specially named—in refusing assistance to these Europeans in distress, and declared that, being "scarcely human," they were fitted only for residence "in a zoological garden." The substance of the article, which was couched throughout in similar language, was reproduced in many French newspapers. The humour of the incident lies in the fact that the

French Government had just before transmitted to the Niger Company, through the British Government, its thanks for the prompt and effective assistance of every kind afforded to the *Ardent*. The second instance occurred at a later date, when another highly respectable organ of the colonial group adopted, for the first time, the system of cross headings in capitals, simply in order to give prominence to the epithets "négrier," "voleur," "menteur," "assassin," which it applied to myself, and developed with more vehemence than logic in the text under each heading.

It is desirable to allude to this attitude of the extreme colonial group in view of Sir Charles Dilke's [7] recent contention in the House of Commons: that the Niger Company should meet its traducers with contradiction instead of silence. Now, the policy of exposure was in one case fully tried. [8] It resulted ultimately in giving to the author of the calumnies of that day the very notoriety at which he had aimed; as, on each occasion, he and his supporters ignored the refutations by the Niger Company, and utilised the public attention attracted by those refutations to restate all the original calumnies as if they were undisputed. To repeat this error would be to aggravate an evil as yet insufficiently known: namely, that French officers who leave Africa grateful for the kindness of Englishmen there, find their work ignored by the colonial party if they acknowledge British services, and their careers assured by advertisement if they consent to insinuate that they have had to struggle against the English. It is to the honour of most French officers in West Africa that they have resisted this constant and powerful pressure to sacrifice their consciences to their careers.

But while it is useless to appeal to the extreme colonial section, the case is entirely different as regards the general French Press and public. The perusal, as part of my daily work, of everything written on Western Africa by both Parisian and provincial newspapers, has convinced me that the occasional irritation on Nigerian questions of the general public has arisen from a mistaken impression that France possesses, by priority of exploration and interests, sentimental rights to the regions of the Middle Niger, where the British are supposed to have made their appearance at a later period, and to have shown a spirit of aggression or at any rate, of desire to interfere with the legitimate expansion of a friendly nation. It is not surprising that, under this impression, even moderate minds in France should feel inclined to condone efforts to violently dispossess Great Britain of political rights acquired under the recognised rules of international comity.

Let me not be misunderstood as supposing that priority of exploration or commercial interests in uncivilised countries is admitted by the Governments of colonising Powers as a sufficient basis of political rights. My point is that public sentiment is a force which neither Parliaments nor Foreign Offices can long resist, and that public sentiment in France has been misdirected owing to forgetfulness or want of knowledge of the modern history of the Niger. Since Great Britain cannot afford, as a matter of general policy, to allow her long acquired and publicly notified rights to be "jumped" by armed aggression, it is a matter of no little importance to remind the public on both sides of the Channel of the often told story of the great West African river. I propose then to give a brief historical summary which, if admitted as correct, clearly shows the priority of Great Britain in that region, and which, if contested, will be open to correction.

Some definition of the term "Middle Niger" is desirable at the outset. Neglecting the highest, the practically unnavigable, waters near the sources of the Niger in the Sierra Leone hinterland, now handed over to France, the river falls naturally into three fairly equal divisions. The term "Upper Niger" is generally applied to the long stretch of navigable river downwards from Bamako past Timbuctoo to the earliest rapids. Great Britain has always admitted the political claims of France to the regions on both banks of this section, owing to their proximity to the French colony of Senegambia, from which that part of the river can be best approached for the practical purposes of commerce. The name "Lower Niger" is given to the section navigable for purposes of commerce from the sea to the lowest rapids. The political rights of Great Britain over the regions on both banks of this section are, I believe, not disputed by any person of authority in France. The Middle Niger is the section, from 600 to 1,000 miles in length, which, though navigable in parts, is not practicable for the transit of commerce by water from the Lower Niger to the Upper Niger or *vice versa.* It is true that this unnavigability of the Middle Niger for commercial purposes, which Great Britain put forward uncontested at the Berlin Conference '84-5, has since been denied by one French traveller, and consequently by a number of French writers in the Press; but the question has been finally set at rest by the recent journey from Bamako to the mouth of the river by Lieutenant Hourst [9] and his companions. The difficulties encountered by Lieut. Hourst, owing to the natural obstacles of the Middle Niger, render his journey one of the most remarkable among recent travels in Africa. I have designedly stated the length of this unnavigable section as from 600 to 1,000 miles, in order to avoid controversy on an immaterial point. The lowest estimate, 600 miles of unnavigable river, is sufficient to dispose of the absurd assertion, recently disseminated through the Press, that the jealous action of the British Niger Company is blocking the natural road from the ocean to the French possessions on the Upper Niger. The recent striking speech of M. Chaudié, Governor-General of French West Africa, pointing out that France's proper road to the Niger is from the Senegal coast on the west, should be weighed by every Frenchman who desires to promote the interests of his own country and not merely to annoy the English. It will be found in the last January number of the *Bulletin du Comité de l'Afrique,Française,* the official organ of the colonial group.

In dealing, however briefly, with the modern history of the Middle Niger, it is impossible to exclude all reference to that of the great river as a whole. Its modern story commences with Mungo Park, [10] who, starting from the Atlantic coast a little more than a century ago and travelling through regions now part of French Senegal, was the first European to reach the river. He struck it at Sego, below Bamako on the Upper Niger, a large section of which he then explored. But his more celebrated journey was that commenced in January, '05, in which, again reaching the Niger basin from the Atlantic coast, he followed the Upper Niger and Middle Niger down to a little below the town of Boussa, the capital of a country of the same name, which now extends from between Say and Illo down to the frontier of Ilorin. Here Park lost his life. If priority of exploration could sustain a claim to political preponderance, the life and death of Mungo Park, the first explorer of the basin of the Niger, would undoubtedly confirm that preponderance to Great Britain. The next European to reach the Niger was another Scotchman, Major Laing, of the Yorkshire Light Infantry, [11] who after preliminary travels in the Sierra Leone hinterland, decided to change his base of operations to the Mediterranean coast. He left Tripoli in '25 and on the 18th August, '26, reached Timbuctoo, near which city he was soon afterwards murdered. Laing was interesting as being the first European who actually visited Timbuctoo; but as he did not explore the Middle Niger region, his travels give no special claim to priority in that direction. The same remark applies to Réné Caillé, [12] the first, and for many years the only, Frenchman to visit the Niger basin, as his travels were also confined to the regions of the Upper Niger. Réné Caillé, who had been aroused by reading the *Travels* of Mungo Park, adopted like him the route from the West or Senegal Coast, and leaving the Rio Nunez on the 19th

April, '27, reached Timbuctoo just a year later. Thence he travelled to Fez and Tangiers. The hardships undergone by Caillé were almost incredible, and his name is rightly cherished by Frenchmen as one of the most courageous and successful of African explorers. So far, however, Mungo Park remained the only explorer of the Middle Niger regions. In '23 to '25, Major Denham(13) and Captain Clapperton(14) made their celebrated journey on behalf of the British Government from Tripoli to Kano and Sokoto and arrived within five days' march of the river itself. The countries explored by that expediton are, indeed, Middle Niger regions; but, being on the east of the great river, where no serious French claim is made, British priority in that direction needs no confirmation. The journey led, however, to one of the greatest geographical discoveries of the age, involving more than one exploration of the Middle Niger regions. Captain Clapperton, disappointed at not having reached the river, induced the British Government to allow him to change his base of operations to the Gulf of Guinea, and within two months of returning home from his long wanderings in the Central Sudan, he sailed for Badagry near Lagos. Thence he led an expedition northward through Yoruba land, Boussa city, and the Middle Niger regions to Sokoto, where he died, about twenty months after leaving the coast. Captain Pearce, of the Royal Navy, Dr. Morrison, naval surgeon, and Dr. Dickson, a Scotch medical man, had previously succumbed to the climate or the treachery of the natives.(15) Clapperton's servant, Richard Lander,(16) whose statue dominates the highest eminence near Truro in his native county of Cornwall, found himself the only European survivor at Sokoto of the expedition. It was then that Lander proved that his humble origin, his imperfect education and his want of adequate support could not discourage his heroic determination to solve the problem of the course of the Niger to the ocean. After an adventurous journey to Kano and a journey southwards in the vain hopes of finding in that direction the unknown course of the river, he returned to Sokoto and thence retraced his steps through the Middle Niger regions by Boussa city to Badagry on the Guinea Coast. On reaching England, he, after great efforts, induced the British Government to contribute a parsimonious sum which only enabled him to take with him his brother John. They followed on this occasion a somewhat different route from Badagry to Boussa city, and thence traced the Niger down to its mouths on the Gulf of Guinea in '30 and '31. The explorations of MacGregor Laird(17) resulting from Lander's great discovery, and the commercial voyages up the Niger under his auspices, fully established the priority of British exploration and commerce on the Lower Niger.

The next exploration of the Niger regions was that organised by the British Government in '49 under Mr. Richardson, (18) to which was appointed a German, Dr. Barth, (19) who after Richardson's death took command. If Mungo Park was the first and Richard Lander the most successful of Nigerian explorers, Dr. Barth merits the name of the "complete traveller," from the extent of his explorations and the wealth of information that he gave the world in his remarkable book, which remains the best handbook of Sudan travel. But while Germany is rightly proud of Barth's nationality, it must always be remembered that the expedition was a British expedition, equipped by the British Government and reporting to British authorities. Barth explored more throughly than had before been done the Middle Niger regions, crossed the river at Say, and travelled direct across the great bend of the Niger to Timbuctoo, whence he returned to Say, following the banks of the river. The remainder of his travels from Sokoto to Tripoli and his previous journeys to Bornu, Baghirmi and Adamawa, does not affect the subject of this article.

The first journey to Boussa by way of the Lower Niger, from its mouth on the Gulf of Guinea, was made in '57-58 by Lieut. Glover, (20) R.N.—afterwards celebrated as Sir John Glover—who accompanied Dr. Baikie (21) in his expedition up the Niger in the *Dayspring,* on behalf of the British Government. Glover's charts up to Boussa are still the official Admiralty charts. A most interesting diary of this expedition has just been lent to me by one of the survivors, Inspector-General Francis Davis, R.N. It is well worthy of publication.

I shall but refer in passing to Germany's great travellers, Rohlfs, (22) Oscar Lenz, (23) an Austrian in German employ, and Flegel, (24) and to those of Italy, Matteucci (25) and Massari; (26) partly because, with the exception of Flegel, they only approached, and did not enter, the Middle Niger regions with which this article deals, partly because their labours do not affect the question of priority as between France and England, and partly because in their time the age of exploration had given way to the age of commerce and political influence.

In '79 the British trading companies, which had for some years previously been opening up the Lower Niger to commerce, amalgamated into the United African Company. Being the only Europeans in the Niger, they carried their operations up to the commencement of the Middle Niger, and in imitation of the East India Company in its earlier stages, they began to exercise political influence over the tribes and states bordering the whole Lower Niger, their object ('79 to '82) being to acquire a position which would justify a demand for recognition by Royal Charter. (27)

Two years later France made her first advance from Senegambia into the basin of the Upper Niger under Gallieni—at that time a captain—and gradually established herself in that region; but she never approached the Middle Niger, by exploration, by occupation, or commerce, until after Great Britain had in '90 concluded (1) the Anglo-French agreement known as the Say-Barua line, and (2) through the Niger Company, a political agreement with Boussa.

It is unnecessary to say much on the ephemeral appearance in the Lower Niger of two powerful French Companies, inasmuch as their operations commenced long after those of the British Companies. (28) They never penetrated to the Middle Niger, and all their interests were, after a few years' intense struggle, bought out by the National African Company, just before the meeting of the Berlin Conference.

In '85 the National African Company, as the United African Company had now become, recognised that the time had arrived to extend its influence into the Middle Niger regions. It accordingly dispatched Hamilton, an ex-naval officer, and Greenshields, a Scotch commercial agent, to Boussa city to conclude a treaty with the King. On their arrival they found that he had left his capital for Kunji, one hundred and twenty miles further up stream. They accordingly followed him. there, and at last obtained a treaty which, though partly commercial in character, also placed the foreign relations of the kingdom of Boussa in the hands of the British Company. Similar treaties were obtained at Sokoto and Gandu by Joseph Thomson in the same year, and subsidies have been regularly paid to all three potentates since that date. The following year the National African Company at last obtained the long sought-for Charter, and thus secured validity for political rights which previously had no international value.

In '89, the Niger Company received an intimation that it might be well to have a more clearly political treaty with Boussa, and early in '90 Mr. Lister, a senior executive officer of the Niger Company, concluded such a treaty, which has more than once been published in the British Press and copied in its essential points into the French Press. The treaty among other things placed under British protection the entire Boussa territory which, as far as the west bank of the Middle Niger is concerned, extends from the frontier of Ilorin on the south to a little beyond Illo, a town not far below Say, on the north. Later in the same year France and Great Britain agreed on a line of demarcation from Say to Barua separating the French and British spheres.

This completes the summary of historical facts establishing Britain's priority on the Middle Niger in exploration, commerce, and political treaties with native rulers, at a time when no French explorer, merchant, missionary or political agent had ever approached that region; but it may be useful to add a few words on the recent contention of the unofficial French Press that, under the General Act of Berlin '85, the establishment of a military post by one European Power in any spot where another Power has no military post, overrides previous treaty rights of that other Power. No one can contest the authority of "The Protocols and General Act of the West African Conference" ('85) as agreed by the Plenipotentiaries of the fourteen nations represented at Berlin. There are two points worth noting. Art. 34 of the General Act restricts to possessions on the *coasts* of the African Continent the obligation of a Power assuming a Protectorate to notify the fact to the other Signatory Powers. As a matter of fact, England has notified her Protectorate of Boussa territory to France; but there was no necessity for her doing so. Art. 35 of the General Act also restricts to possessions on the *coasts* of the African Continent "the obligation to ensure the establishment of authority sufficient to protect existing rights." A curious point is that these restrictions to the *coasts* were solely due to the representations of the French Plenipotentiary, M. le Baron de Courcel, (29) since then the Ambassador of France in London. On page 209 of the British Blue Book, Africa No. 4 ('85) will be found (Protocol No. 8—sitting of January 31st, '85) the following paragraph:—

"In the same connection, the French Plenipotentiary placed it on record that new occupations on the coasts of the African continent were alone alluded to in the Declaration."

Again on page 214 of the same edition—under the heading "Annex 1 to Protocol, No. 8, Report of the Commission charged with the examination of the Project of Declaration respecting the new Occupations on the Coasts of Africa"—will be found in the following remarks:—

"The Project of Declaration only had the African coasts in view. The fitness of this restriction has been questioned. The Enlgish Ambassador would have preferred that the rules which are about to be settled for the acquisition of new possessions in Africa should be made applicable to the whole African continent. In support of his proposal he quoted this fact: that the African coasts are very near being occupied for the whole of their extent, and that, if reduced to this zone, the formalities we have in view will have but little practical value. The French Ambassador did not share this feeling. Granted that there existed but little available territory on the coast, these territories make amends by possessing an importance which justifies new arrangements of which they would be the object. Along the sea-shore, moreover, the ground is clearly defined, whilst, in regard to territorial delimitations, there is much that is uncertain and unknown in the interior of Africa. M. Busch, Under-Secretary of State, had not, for his part, declared himself hostile in principle to Sir Edward Malet's (30) proposal; but he remarked that it necessarily implied the precise and early settlement of the state of possession of each Power in Africa."

The principle for which Baron de Courcel thus successfully contended was, in my humble opinion, imperative in the interests of Europe in general and of France in particular. The early effective occupation of the vast African continent, with three times the area of Europe being impracticable, the necessity of effective occupation to validate treaty rights would have destroyed the foundations of the principle of spheres of influence, but for which a general European war could hardly have been averted. As regards France, that Power had in '85, and still has to-day, within her spheres of influence, a larger unoccupied area in the interior of Africa than any other colonizing nation. To-day, as in '85 France is the power which can least afford to throw over the principle propounded by her in Berlin and agreed to by the fourteen Signatory States. Her existing rights behind the British Colonies of the Gambia, Sierra Leone, and the Gold Coast have been entirely based on treaties with native potentates. On this ground she has successfully relied in all the West African arrangements made during the last ten years with the British Government. Nor is that sound principle ignored by those responsible for the conduct of public affairs in France, as appears from the following evidently inspired article in the *Temps* of the 8th April last, which I commend earnestly to the attention of both French and English readers:—

Under the heading of "Political Confusions in the bend of the Niger" the Cologne Gazette *publishes an article of which we reproduce the essential passage. After recalling the rights acquired by Germany and declaring that, since '95, France has inaugurated a new theory in colonial matters, that of "effective occupation," the* Cologne Gazette *adds:*

As the final delimitation of contested territories in the Sudan must sooner or later be made in Europe by a Diplomatic Act, it is doubtless indifferent whether ambitious French lieutenants install in the bend of the Niger a few more or less posts; and the existing facts only merit being regarded in the most serious fashion because they again throw light on the system approved in high places of "effective occupation."

After the event, as before, we maintain that the creation of French military posts at Kiriki and Bassila, in the Tchantcho, is equivalent to a violation of incontestable rights of Germany, and we think that the appointment by M. Ballot, Governor of Dahomey, of Lieutenant Baud as resident at Gourma, constitutes a blameable and absolutely one-sided anticipation on the diplomatic solution of the question of frontiers on the Niger. The altogether extraordinary proceeding of the French authorities is so much the more strange as we have hitherto, by reciprocal chivalric condescension, arranged in the most cordial fashion with the French Government in colonial questions.

There are two things to consider in this article: the appeal to the viligance of the German Government, and the disputing the French rights which the French exercise in Gourma. The first observation being a question of internal policy does not concern us. But, in regard to the second, we shall not cease to repeat that the political rights exercised by our officers over certain territories in the bend of the Niger result from treaties concluded by our explorers with the native chiefs. German explorers have concluded with other native chiefs other protectorate treaties. Which are the genuine treaties? That is what will have to be determined by the French and German negotiators, who will have to arrange the questions in dispute, or the arbitrators, who will have to control these negotiations, if it happens that they are not able to come to terms among themselves.

It can hardly be doubted that the sound doctrine here laid down by the *Cologne Gazette,* and accepted by the *Temps,* is that held by the responsible Government of the Republic. No one will believe that France while admitting this doctrine in her dealings with Germany, will attempt to override it by violence in her dealings with her no less friendly neighbour, Great Britain: which has no reason to fear the most searching examination into the validity either of the Lister treaty with the Kingdom of Boussa or of the subsequent Lugard treaties with Kiama, Kishi, Niki and other places to the west of the Middle Niger.

GEORGE TAUBMAN GOLDIE.

(1) Published in London between 1889 and 1897, after which it was superseded by the *Outlook.*

(2) See page 20 above.

(3) Bretonnet, Henri-Etienne, 1864-99. In 1882, Bretonnet was a junior officer in a French Naval expedition up the Benue to Adamawa; promoted lieutenant, 1894; 1896-7, Dahomey and the Middle Niger; 1898, Secretary to the French Geographical Society; 1898, French Colonial Service, Chari; 1899, killed at Tobago, when the force he commanded was ambushed by Rabeh's men and massacred.

(4) Wellesley, *op cit.,* p. 59.

(5) F.O. 403/248, p. 180-183.

(6) *Ardent* was the French gunboat that "ran" into the Forcados mouth of the Niger in November 1894, to synchronise with Cmdt. Toutée's push into Borgu. She then promptly ran aground twice, being refloated on the first occasion with the aid of the Company. On the second occasion, she stuck fast and was aground until the River rose during the next rains, July 1895.

(7) Dilke, Charles Wentworth (Bart.), 1843-1911. Radical, Republicanist, M.P. from 1868-86 when disgraced in a celebrated divorce suit. Again from 1892-1911. Vehement opponent of Chartered Companies. Gwynn and Tuckwell, however, in their *Life,* claim that Dilke's opposition to Goldie stemmed from R.N.C.'s policy of "contractual censorship of its agents" against which he railed in Parliament. Goldie is referring to this here.

(8) i.e. *"L'affaire Mizon."* For further details see Part IV.

(9) Hourst, M., Lieutenant. Started from Timbuktu in January, 1896, and navigated the Niger from thence to the sea, carefully surveying and charting as he went. His book *Sur le Niger et au Pays des Tuaregs,* Paris, 1898, is marked by an extreme Anglophobia.

(10) Park, Mungo, 1771-1806. First European explorer of the Niger to return safely, 1795-7. Second expedition financed by the British Government resulted in the loss of the whole expedition and Park's own death at Bussa. Hausa nickname *Ban ci ba,* (I have not eaten).

(11) Laing, Alexander Gordon, 1793-1826. Credited with being the first European to reach Timbuktu, though it is now known that Benedetto Dei, a representative of the Florentine banking house of Fortinari established himself there as a trader in Lombardy cloth c. 1470. Laing came overland from Tripoli and was murdered after reaching Timbuktu on 26 Sept., 1826.

(12) Caillé, René, 1799-1838. Mastering Arabic and native customs, Caillé passed himself off as an Eygptian prisoner of the French and made his way to Timbuktu in April, 1828, proceeding thence to Rabat in Morocco where he arrived on 14 August. Died of tuberculosis in 1838.

(13) Denham, Dixon, 1786-1828. A member of the Oudney expedition to Lake Chad in 1823-25, he established friendly relations with Sheik Muhammad El Amin El Kanemi of Bornu. Appointed Inspector of Freed Slaves in Sierra Leone in 1827 and Governor in 1828, he died of fever that same year. Nickname *Rais Khalil.* An abbreviated and annotated edition of the Bornu section of Denham's *Journal* can be found as Johnston and Muffett, *Denham in Bornu;* Duquesne University Press, 1973.

(14) Clapperton, Hugh, R.N., 1788-1827. The first European to visit Sokoto and return. A member of the Oudney expedition, he continued on from Chad with Oudney towards Sokoto. Oudney died at Madachi in 1824, and Clapperton went on alone, returning to England with Denham in 1825. Almost immediately he left again for Badagry with three companions and a servant amd made his way to Bussa and thence once more to Sokoto. He died at Jungevi near that city in 1827 and was buried by his servant Richard Lander.

(15) Clapperton's travelling companions at the start of the second journey.

(16) The Lander brothers, Richard (1804-34) and John (1807-39). After Clapperton's

death, Richard Lander made his way first to Kano, thence to Badagry and home. In 1830, having agreed with the Government in a sum of £100, with a similar sum to be paid to his wife for her maintenance, Richard and his brother John retraced their steps and made their way to Bussa. After exploring upstream about 100 miles, they then headed down river and after many vicissitudes, including capture and ransom, emerged at the mouth of the Brass River. Richard Lander again returned to the Coast with MacGregor Laird's first expedition, but died at Fernando Po on 6 Feb. 1834 from wounds received in a clash with tribesmen on 20 Jan. John Lander entered the Customs Service on return from Africa, but died in 1839 from a disease which he had contracted there.

(17) MacGregor Laird, 1808-1861. Scottish merchant, pioneer of British trade on the Niger. Operating from Liverpool, and with the backing of the family ship-building firm, Laird accompanied a privately financed expedition under the command of R. A. K. Oldfield up the Niger, travelling in the *Alburkah,* the first iron vessel to make an ocean voyage, and in company with two other ships, 1832-34. Thirty-nine of the forty-eight Europeans on board died of fever. Though never returning to the Coast, Laird persisted in his efforts to open up the Niger. He financed the 1854 expedition under Baikie, but passionately opposed the Model Farm Project of 1841. It proved to be a disastrous failure.

(18) Richardson, James, 1806-51. Leader of the expedition of 1850 from Tripoli to Lake Chad. Died in 1851, leaving Barth and Overweg to go on together. Overweg, Adolf, 1822-1852, an Austrian, was the expedition's geologist/astronomer. He died at Maduwari in Bornu also in 1851.

(19) Barth, Dr. Heinrich, 1821-1865. Geographer, scholar, and probably Africa's greatest explorer. In 1851-54 he journeyed from Tripoli to Timbuktu and back. His book, *Travels and Discoveries in North and Central Africa,* in five volumes, remains all but faultless. His nickname was *Abdul Karim.*

(20) Glover, (Sir) John Hawley, 1829-85. A naval officer, Glover accompanied Baikie's expedition of 1857 as cartographer. In 1863 he was appointed Administrator of Lagos, and remained there until 1872. In 1873, Glover volunteered to try and enlist the support of other tribes against the Ashanti, with little success, but in 1874, in command of "Glover's Hausas," he assisted in the capture of Kumasi. Governor of Newfoundland in 1875, of the Leward Islands, 1881, Newfoundland again, 1883, died in London, 1885. When *Dayspring* was wrecked at Jebba, Glover went on to Bussa by horse.

(21) Baikie, Dr. William Balfour, R.N., 1825-1864. In 1854 took over command of *Pleiad* on Consul Beecroft's death, and explored the Benue for 250 m. from the confluence. Quinine was given under supervision and no casualties resulted from fever. Founded Lokoja as a trading settlement. 1857, British Consul on the Niger. Same year, *Dayspring* Expedition wrecked on Juju Rock near Jebba. Visited Kano in 1862. Hausa nickname *Da Gudu* ("In a hurry").

(22) Rohlfs, Friedrich Gerhard, 1831-96. Joined the Fr. Foreign Legion: raised to Chevalier de la Legion d'Honour for bravery. 1865, journeyed to Bornu, Bauchi and (via the Benue) to Lokoja, thence to Raba, from where he went overland to Lagos. Recipient of the R.G.S. "Patron's" Medal.

(23) Lenz, Oscar, 1848-1925. Austrian explorer; 1874-77, expedition to Equitorial Africa. 1879-80 went to Timbuktu and on to Senegal disguised as a Turkish Medical Doctor; 1885-87 unsuccessful attempt to rescue Emin Pasha. Professor of Geography at Prague University, 1887-1907.

(24) Flegel, E. R., 1855-86; German explorer; 1879, went up the Benue 250 m. in C.M.S. launch *Henry Venn;* 1880 visited Sokoto and obtained permission to explore Adamawa. 1882-84, did so and located source of Benue. Died at Brass on third expedition 1866.

(25) Matteucci, Pelegrine, 1850-1881; in 1880 he led an expediton from Suakin (27 March) to Wadai, Bornu, Kano, and thence by way of the Niger to Akassa, where he arrived on 3 July, 1881. Died of fever in London on voyage home.

(26) Massari, Alfonso Maria, 1844-1939. Accompanied Matteucci and took command of the expedition on his death. In 1933 was awarded a gold medal by Mussolini as a "Pioneer of Italian Colonization."

(27) "I attribute the success of the Company . . . chiefly to our following a definite plan from the commencement instead of growing up by accident . . . in the main the policy conceded on the Niger in 1877 . . . has been played out like a game of chess." Wellesley, *op cit.,* p. 28.

(28) Goldie is being less than truthful here! Commandant Mattei *did* establish successful trading stations on the Middle Niger and Benue—in spite of the opposition of the R.N.C.

(29) Later French Ambassador to the Court of St. James.

(30) Malet, Sir Edward (Bart.), 1837-1908. British chargé d'affaires Paris, 1871; Ambassador to Brussells, 1883; to Berlin, 1884-95. He was instrumental in settling rival German-British claims in both Africa and in Samoa.

V. THE FUTURE OF THE NIGER TERRITORIES (1897)

This address was delivered on 6 July, 1897, before a special meeting of the London Chamber of Commerce and its invited guests. The place was the Hall of the Salters Company, one of the City of London Livery Companies, and one moreover from which the Royal Niger Company, because of the extreme importance of the salt trade on the Coast, could have expected every consideration.

Goldie was taking the occasion to fly two trial balloons. The first was an adaptation, if not an even closer reflection, of a plan which Mary Kingsley is known to have been actively supporting, namely that Nigeria should be governed by a "Committee" of merchants, overseeing the actions of executive officers. [1]

The second was a proposal that The Royal Niger Company as such should continue the administration of the Niger Territories, but that as a condition of it so doing, should cease its activities as a *trading* company. The precedent for this, as Goldie pointed out in his address, was the Honourable East India Company.

It is interesting, moreover, to note that Goldie had first referred to the possibility of this occurring as early as 1896, when he wrote to Lord Scarbrough on 11 December of that year:—

"If we succeed in this campaign (and *of course* we shall succeed) we must not take the terms which I offered Lord Salisbury through Kirk and subsequently through Moor. We are now risking the whole existence of the Company, against immense odds, *and if we give up commerce*[2] we must have an equivalent for this risk. Besides, we shall have the public on our side . . . when we succeed." [3]

The significant phrase is "if we give up commerce;" not "are bought out" or "taken over" etc.

The idea that Goldie was now putting forward in public therefore, was one that had been uppermost in his mind for some years. Its inception can be traced back to the revolt of the "Brassmen" in 1894. On 29 December of that year, the Brassmen (more properly, Nembe) had raided the Royal Niger Company main depot at Akassa and had sacked it.

The British Government, the Nembe being in fact within its jurisdiction and not in that of the Company, had quickly mounted a punitive expedition, but the reaction in Britain, both to the raid itself and to the expedition which followed it was ambivalent to the point of paradox, much sympathy being evinced for the Nembe and a great deal of condemnation being expressed for the Company and the Government.

The agitation was greatly exacerbated by the fact that Sir Claude Macdonald, Governor of the Niger Coast Protectorate in which the Nembe resided, almost openly sided with them in their grievances against the Company, as did the opinion of the politically powerful "Liverpool" trading community, so long opposed both to Goldie and to the Charter.

The upshot of all the pressure was that the Government felt bound to appoint a Commission of Enquiry. The Commissioner selected was Sir John Kirk, formerly Dr. John Kirk, a friend of David Livingstone. In 1866, he had been appointed British Consul at Zanzibar and his unquestioned probity coupled with his zeal to suppress the slave-trade, allied to a considerable administrative talent, quickly marked him out as a major force in contemporary African affairs.

Subsequently, he and six others founded the Imperial British East Africa Company, [4] bought out early in 1895 under circumstances of the utmost parsimony on the part of the Government. The dissolution of the Company had, however, made Kirk available and the Liberal Government promptly made him the Sole Commissioner.

Kirk's Report, whilst not exonerating the Company by any means, and whilst recognising a certain validity in the Bill of Particulars drawn up against it, nevertheless refused to condemn its administration and, above all, refused to recommend a revocation of its Charter, a course for which both Macdonald and "Liverpool" were by now avid.

Instead, he proposed a plan (omitted in the final printed version) [5] similar to the one that Goldie was now advancing in his address. Flint in fact argues [6] that Goldie may have "fed" Kirk the plan for inclusion in his report in the first place, and quotes the letter reproduced above as confirmatory evidence in support of this theory.

If this is sustained, however, it would be necessary to accept the reference to Salisbury as being in error, since Salisbury was not in office in August 1895 when Kirk delivered his report.

The probability would therefore seem to be that when Salisbury did resume office once again as Prime Minister later in 1895, Goldie used first Kirk and later Sir Ralph Moor to "refresh" the issue with the new Administration, a possibility that Flint also recognises.

Sir John Kirk joined the Council of the Royal Niger Company immediately after his Report was submitted. He was still there in 1897 when Goldie was speaking, and it is obvious that, revocation of the Charter being clearly foreshadowed, his counsel—in view of his experience with the winding up of the IBEAC—would have been heeded in any discussions about this touchy issue.

It is also beyond all possible question that the two proposals now being advocated entailed a radical departure from the accepted norms of colonial administration, in that the territory would be governed *from London*. That is to say that the chief executives would not reside on the

Coast, and would make only intermittent visits there. This was, in fact, the way Goldie had operated with Flint and Wallace, and it had worked.

This suggestion so closely parallels the famous "Scheme" which Lugard put forward in 1904 that it is not conceivable that he was doing anything more than up-dating it and re-writing it.

"The Lugard Scheme for Continuous Adminstration," as Perham describes it, [7] was the product, she believed, of both Sir Frederick and of Flora. It entailed the appointment of:

" . . . a Lieutenant-Governor with a Second or Deputy Lieutenant-Governor to act in [my] absence [shades of Flint and Wallace!] who would carry out the routine government . . . [and] leave me free to deal with all legislation . . . and matters of general policy. I would . . . have an office in London and remain there for half the year, visiting Nigeria only in the winter for 5 months at most." [8]

Perham is convinced that the plan was Lugards'. Why, is not clear as the evidence would appear to be overwhelming that Goldie was its originator. Nothing came of the Lugards' efforts, however, in spite of the most intense lobbying that they could mount. In fact, Flora seems to have overplayed her hand quite disastrously, alienating many who could have helped in bringing it to fruition.

All this, however, was in the future. That night in the Salters Hall, Goldie was to some extent embarking on his last campaign, opening public discussion on the future of his own special creation. The very existence of his Company was at stake, and it, as he remarks during the course of his speech, had been founded for one purpose and one purpose only—and that was *not* for commerce; it was to aid the fulfillment of his childhood dream of colouring the map red—for "Empire." In the course of this address, in addition to developing the points already discussed, Goldie gives several insights into his thoughts on other issues.

The meeting was under the chairmanship of Sir Albert Rollit, the President of the Chamber and a Member of Parliament. The guest-list included Mary Kingsley, Sir G. Baden-Powell, the elder brother of the victor of Mafeking the founder of the Boy Scout movement, and the Earl of Scarbrough. The French Ambassador was represented by the Vicomte de Manneville. Leonard Darwin was present, as were Vandeleur, Wallace, Burdon, Craster, Castelotte, Dangerfield, Hewby and others who had served the Company in the recent campaign, as well as James Pinnock, and Alfred Miller from the Board of Directors. Robinson and Jones (late Home Secretary of the London Missionary Society) represented the Church and there were representatives also of several of the more prominent of the philanthropic societies such as the Anti-Slavery Society and the Liquor Traffic United Committee, with both of which Goldie was in very good standing.

After the Chairman had introduced nim in the most glowing terms, Goldie said:—

If I make a very brief acknowledgement of the kind words of Sir Albert Rollit, do not imagine that it is because I do not appreciate the cordial manner in which you have received his remarks, but the best way, I think, in which I can show gratitude is to commence at once with the address, after thanking you for the reception you have accorded me. The Niger territories is the official name of the sphere acquired for Great Britain by the Royal Niger Company and governed by it under Royal Charter. Within the last few months a shorter and more picturesque name has been given by the Press to these territories, and has been generally adopted by the public—Nigeria. (9) The British sphere of Nigeria is divided, roughly speaking, into two sections, as widely separated in laws, government, customs and general ideas about life, both in this world and the next, as England is from China. Endless misconceptions have arisen from neglect of this fact, some writers having discussed the Lower Niger, or in other West Coast possessions of Great Britain, while some writers have treated it as if entirely composed of organised and semi-civilised Mohammedan States. The southern third of Nigeria, lying on either side of the Lower Niger and to the south of the river Binue *(sic)*, is for the most part inhabited only by Pagans, occupying as yet only a low rank of civilisation. They are divided into hundreds of tribes, most of which, before the advent of British power, were not only addicted to practices of outrageous cruelty, but were also constantly warring against each other, chiefly for the purpose of capturing slaves. This southern third of Nigeria—and especially the maritime and most barbarous portion—has naturally been more frequently visited by Europeans than the regions of the far interior, so that to many persons the word Niger conjures up only a picture of mangrove swamps and tropical forests, inhabited by semi-nude savages living under the terrors and horrors resulting from witchcraft and fetishism. During the last six months, this impression of Western Africa, generally has been widely disseminated among the public by the large circulation of the valuable work written by one of the most remarkable travellers of the Victorian era, Miss Mary Kingsley, (10) who is present here to-day. Her principal travels have indeed been amongst races of a different family from the negroes of Nigeria. But the picture of West African life drawn by her is, in general outline, applicable to the southern third of Nigeria, though it should be pointed out that even in this purely Pagan region, the inland tribes are, on the whole, of a higher order (11) than those nearer the seaboard—milder in manners, less influenced by the witch doctor or fetish men, and, if this is a sign of civilisation, more fully clothed. Yet within the last few days it has been found necessary to give instructions to send a small punitive expedition against a tribe, about 150 miles from the seaboard, which has indulged in human sacrifices of a very revloting kind, notwithstanding the order and pacification which the Company has gradually introduced into this region. I do not propose to say much to-day about this southern third of Nigeria; because, although the forests teem with valuable products, such as rubber, and there seems little doubt that the trade of this region, in forest products alone, will at no distant time attain such dimensions as to count materially in the volume of trade of the British Empire, a considerable period must elapse before these inferior tribes, who have, doubtless, been gradually driven south towards the sea by the pressure of higher races advancing from the north, acquire the industrious habits on which alone a wealthy civilised State can be permanently built up. To most of this region applies the popular idea of the negro as a somewhat indolent person, with moderate wants and little ambition. Very different, however, are the conditions of the inland two-thirds of Nigeria lying between the Great Sahara on the north, and the two great branches of the rivers Niger and Benue on the south. This region covers the larger portion of the Central Sudan. It is specially important to bear in mind its Sudanese character, at a time when the attention given by the Press to Egyptian questions tends to confine to the Eastern or Egyptian Sudan a name which, as every geographer knows, applies to all the black man's lands under

105

Moslem influence. The Sudan extends some 3,000 miles across Africa from the frontiers of Abyssinia on the east to those of Senegal on the west. No adequate policy can be framed for dealing with the northern two-thirds of Nigeria without due recognition of its close connection with other Sudanese regions, a connection due partly to unity of religion and partly to the constant intercommunications maintained by the streams of Hausa caravans, bent on trade or pilgrimage or both combined, which flow from Kano and other great cities of Hausaland into almost every part of Africa north of the equator. To this larger, more important and more interesting part of Nigeria, I wish to draw your especial attention to-day. For the sake of brevity it is desirable to find an appropriate name for the whole of this Sudanese region, and I know of none more suitable than that often given to it,—Hausaland. It is true that in considerable districts, for instance in Northern Nupe, the inhabitants are not Hausas, but have a language of their own; yet even in these portions, the civilised habits and modes of thought of the Hausas are predominant, the caravans which pass almost continuously along the bush tracks in every direction are Hausa, the merchants in the towns are Hausa, and the *lingua franca* is the Hausa tongue. But the Hausas are not rulers even in their own provinces. Supreme political power in Hausaland is held by the Fulah race, an alien people of uncertain but probably Eastern origin, who in the early part of this century conquered the seven old Hausa kingdoms, whence they gradually extended their power southward and eastward, thus forming the vast empire known as Sokoto Gandu, or, more briefly, as the Fulah empire. The Fulahs, when of pure breed, have light complexions, regular and fine features, and oval faces, and some of the women are possessed of striking beauty both of face and figure. But as Fulah men frequently intermarry with women of Hausa and other African races, many of the ruling caste are now of negro colour and feature. The conquest of the immense and fairly civilised populations of Hausaland at the beginning of this century by a comparatively small number of Fulahs has often excited surprise. The Fulahs are undoubtedly inferior to the Hausas in the arts of peace, and so far as is known, they have not introduced any single element of civilisation into Hausaland, (12) while their passion for slave-raiding has impoverished and depopulated those regions. Their military success has doubtless been partly due to religious fanaticism and to personal courage. Their reputation in this respect was fully justified by the manner in which, during the two days' battle outside Bida on January 26th and 27th last, they sustained the heavy artillery fire brought to bear on them, to say nothing of the Maxim guns and the well-directed volleys of the Hausa troops. To these qualities of the Fulahs of fanatical and first-class fighting men must be added their astuteness as diplomatists and their knowledge how to "divide and govern." The proud character of the race is well described by the proverbial saying that a Fulah man slave will escape or kill his master, and a Fulah girl slave will rule the harem or die. But the main secret of the Fulah conquests and of their present power is the fact of their being an equestrian race. Their cavalry, armed like our own with lances and swords, is formidable to disciplined troops, and is irresistible against an untrained enemy on foot. History tells us that this rule has been universal. The part played by the horse in the conquest of Mexico by Cortes is too well known to need more than passing reference. So, too, in Europe, a mere handful of knights used to put to flight masses of sturdy "villeins," until Morgarten and Crécy (13) showed how disciplined infantry could resist cavalry. The thorough training and leading of Hausa soldiers by British officers, and the introduction of modern artillery into the Sudan regions have commenced, and will, before long, complete the enfranchisement of Hausaland from the unceasing slave-raiding which has been so terribly destructive to human life, and an absolute barrier to prosperity. This summary of the political and social situation in Hausaland has been necessary, because misgovernment has been the main obstacle to progress there. At the International Geographical Congress two years ago, Sir John Kirk very aptly described tropical Africa as "a lost continent owing to the misrule which has pervaded it." His description is true of all tropical Africa, but it is specially applicable to Hausaland, where , but for native misgovernment, all the elements of a great civilisation are present. The Hausas are possessed of remarkable energy, judgment, and intelligence. They are skillful, and almost artistic workers in metals, leather, and other materials. They possess histories, songs, and tales written in their own tongue. Some of you may remember Stanley (14) telling this Chamber, two or three years ago, that of all the African races, the Hausa alone valued a book. They have the advantage of a fertile soil, and they display that eager desire to get on in the world, which is so unpleasing in the individual but so valuable for the State. (15) Above all, they are unlike most African races in that they are extremely industrious, notwithstanding the little inducement to display this virtue in a land where the acquisition of wealth has too frequently led to the loss of liberty or life. Many competent authorities have accordingly declared Hausaland to be by far the most valuable section of tropical Africa. For excellent reasons, its mineral resources have not yet been explored, although some deposits are already known to exist. (16) In this connection, it is well to remember that only thirty to forty years ago, the immense mineral wealth of South Africa was so little suspected that a considerable section of the English Press used to advocate retirement from South Africa, excepting Cape Town, which was to be held as a coaling station on the road to India. But although minerals are most valuable to give a start to a new country, the only foundations of permanent prosperity are the industry, intelligence, and prolificness of its inhabitants combined with fertility of soil. All these conditions are united in Hausaland. The manner in which population there rights itself after the wholesale destruction resulting from slave raids, is hardly credible in colder climates where infancy is prolonged, while at least six times the existing population could support themselves in comfort. If properly administered, Hausaland would, at no distant date, become as valuable as any equal area of British India, but patience is needed. The vital question to consider is how to maintain and increase British power there pending the final pacification of the country and the consequent development of a revenue sufficient to support normal colonial administration. The initial labours of opening up Nigeria and of laying the foundation of British justice there have so far been successful. The bugbear of Fulah power, which the official documents of ten years ago declared would crush the Niger Company at the first impact, has been, at any rate partially, laid by the recent campaign. (17) The international struggles of the last fifteen years with France and then Germany and then again France, have been gradually reduced to modest proportions. The most cogent motives for absolute silence have ceased. It seems to me the time has come to discuss publicly the methods calculated to lead to success as well as those certain to lead to failure. In discussing this subject I am confronted with a personal difficulty. Being connected with the company which governs Nigeria, it may be thought that my views are necessarily prejudiced. Let me, then, briefly state, once for all, that I have no mandate from the Niger Company, that the views advanced are purely personal, that these views are consistent either with the continuance of the company or its disappearance, and that I shall place myself at an entirely outside standpoint. I should, indeed, be grateful to be relieved of the almost overwhelming labours, to say nothing of the responsibilities, weighing upon me, if I could be assured that the fabric so painfully raised by an abnormal and specially-devised system (18) would not collapse under the premature application of costly and unsuitable methods. It is not a simple matter to found civilised Government in vast inland regions of Equatorial Africa—(hear, hear)—where commerce, and therefore revenue, is undeveloped. There are only six other regions where the experiment has been tried. There is the French Sudan, which during the sixteen years since the first advance of Gallieni has drained enormous sums from the mother country without any material return. There are the French Congo and German East Africa, to which, in a lesser degree, the same observation applies. There is the Congo Free State, built up on the private fortune of King Leopold and on the liberality of the Belgian Parliament. There is the territory founded and formerly administered by the British East Africa Company. This Imperial possession has been started under favourable financial conditions, not only by the simple process of not paying to the Chartered Company the value of the work it had done, but also by very large sums voted by Parliament, and by considerable direct and indirect Imperial expenditure every year. But it is doubtful whether such expenditure will suffice to develop the country. The sixth instance is the region known as British Central Africa, and after reading the admirable book published two or three days ago by Sir Harry Johnston, (19) I felt tempted to say, "Here is the exception that proves the rule." Thanks to the extraordinary energy, ability, and experience of Sir Harry Johnston, marvellous progress has been made, but I hear rumours on every side that it is doubtful if he will return to his post. If not, the continuity essential for opening up Inner Africa is broken, as it is also whenever the climate compels an administrator to come home for his health. I shall advert later to the abnormal means of meeting this difficulty adopted in Nigeria—that of administration from home. My present point is the financial one and on this you will note in Sir Harry Johnston's book that the revenue of British Central Africa is 22,000l., and that all beyond that has to be found by the Imperial Treasury. Possibly the present Parliament might be willing to do for Nigeria what has been done for Uganda and British Central Africa, and what the French, Germans, and Belgians have done for their Equatorial possessions, on the large scale necessary for dealing, under normal Imperial methods, with the powerful organised forces existing in Hausaland; but there is no security that future Parliaments would continue that policy until the general pacification of Nigeria and the development of a commerce and revenue commensurate with its vast area are accomplished facts. Great Britain is at present in a hot fit of empire-making which, like African fever, has its alternation of cold fits. So lately as 1865 the House of Commons Select Committee appointed to examine into West African matters reported as follows:—"That all further extension of territory, or assumption of government, or new treaties offering any protection to native tribes would be inexpedient." It was, perhaps, partly due to this resolution that, until the Royal Niger Company stepped in and acquired half a million square miles of the most valuable part of tropical Africa, not a single step into the interior was taken by any of the West African colonies, which allowed another colonizing Power to hem them in to the sea and deprive them of their *Hinterland*. If a few failures or disasters, such as must occassionally occur in building up empire, were to happen, we should probably see the same policy revived. If the quondam author of "Greater Britain" (20) urges our retirement to coast spheres in Africa, at a time when colonial expansion is at fever heat, what will others of his opinion say (and do, in power) when, as must inevitably happen, temporary misfortunes and disappointments occur, when reaction succeeds the outburst of energy displayed since Germany commenced as a colonising power just thirteen years ago, and when the watchword *"Imperium et libertas"* gives way to the "Rest and be thankful," against which we used to chafe twenty to thirty years ago? There would be little chance, in such circumstances, of Parliament continuing the financial support which would certainly be required by Nigeria during its infancy to support the costly methods of normal Imperial government. (Hear, hear.) The inevitable results would be failure, disappointment, and abandonment. Assuming that enough has been said to show the necessity of continuing in some shape or other the existing abnormal system which has enabled Nigeria to pay its way without the assistance of a single shilling from the Imperial Government, the next point to consider is how much of this is essential. The only vital condition to my mind is that Nigeria should continue to be administered as heretofore by a permanent council, [21] untrammelled by bureaucractic formulae, experienced in African questions, corresponding somewhat with the Council of the Governor-General of India, controlled, as are both Chartered Companies and Governors of Crown Colonies, by a Secretary of State, but no more subject than British India is to constant Parliamentary interference, and above all administering, not locally, like Crown Colonies, but from home, as the Council of the Niger Company has always done. The permanence of the members of such a council, subject, of course, to changes made by the Secretary of State, seems to me to be of vital importance. Let me say, with all respect, that I look on the appointment of the present Secretary of State [22] for the Colonies as likely to mislead the public mind in regard to the true principles for dealing with inner African dependencies. Mr. Chamberlain's extraordinary vigour, rapidity, voracity for work, and willingness to accept responsibility before Parliament are likely to give the Colonial Office a reputation of suitability for creative administration which cannot be expected to survive his tenure of that particular office. The second vital point is that the administrative council should govern from home and not locally in Nigeria. This is the only possible way of securing continuity of administration of a region where no local continuity can be obtained at present, owing to the nature of the climate, in which Nigeria has perhaps greater difficulties to meet than the other European possessions in Equatorial Africa to which I had referred. There are, indeed, high ranges of plateaux in the far interior where white administrators could retain their activity and powers of work for long periods, but these Simlas of the Central Sudan [23] are not yet effectively occupied, so that for some years to come they must be left out of account. Yet I desire to draw your close attention to them, as they will afford, the ultimate solution of the difficult question of the administration of Nigeria. Meanwhile it must be taken for granted that no local continuity of government is at present practicable, and this in regions where continuity is of vital importance, owing to the enormous difficulties to be overcome. In the Coast possessions of West Africa, where European administrators and traders live on or near the seaboard, and are practically under the protection of the Imperial Navy, and where powerful native governments [24] do not exist or can be dealt with by Imperial troops, as in the Ashantee war of 1874, local administration is not open to the same objections, although it is well known that the Colonial Office is compelled to exercise a larger share in the actual government of West African colonies than it does in Crown Colonies in healthier climates, where continuity of local government can be maintained. In Nigeria, ever since the issue of the Charter, the two Agent-Generals, [25] or local heads of the Niger Government, have been only executive officers, with considerable lattitude in carrying out their instructions, and they relieve each other at short intervals to allow of their renewing their vigour at home. The real work of administration, the work performed by Governors (or by Governors and Councils) in Crown Colonies, or by the Council of the Governor-General in India, has been dealt with day by day by a Council living in the temperate and healthy climate of London, where not only can men work continuously for twice as many hours a day as they can in West Africa—a vital matter in an emergency—but where the character and effectiveness of the work done is entirely different. To this system, and not to any individual merit, has been due the successful administration to which both Lord Salisbury and Lord Kimberley bore such striking and gratifying testimony the other day in the House of Lords. (26) Whether this system continues as heretofore under the Chartered Niger Company, or whether, that Company retiring from Nigeria, a Governing Council is created *ad hoc.*, is only an accidental, I do not say unimportant, feature. If anyone has attended here in the expectation of some suggestion as to which of these alternatives is likely to be adopted, he will, I fear, be disappointed; for I do not know, and if I did know, I could not say. But this much may, I think, be safely prophesied, that if the company is permitted to continue its work, it will, sooner or later, have to face a dissolution of its dual positon of adminstrator and trader. As it was founded, and as it bought up all trading interests, whether British or foreign, for the purpose of obtaining a charter, (27) and thus creating a British West African Empire, I feel confident that if its work of administration and development were transferred to other hands it would not elect to continue as a trader, although, doubtless, to protect its capital, it would continue to hold its extensive and valuable private rights as a limited company. (28) A simple and natural alternative seems to be that it should abandon the purely trading side of its operations and confine itself, like all other chartered companies, to the sufficiently onerous labours of developing and administrating its vast estate on behalf of Great Britain. As you know, the British East African Company was practically not a trading company, but one of development and administration, its purchases of ivory in the far interior being too small to be taken into account, and moreover not competitive with independent traders. The British South African Company again is not a trader, for the owning of lands and minerals in every civilised country is a permissible monopoly, and therefore on a different footing from trade. The legitimate work of the South African Company has been that of development and administration. The same remark applies to the only other existing Chartered Company, that of North Borneo, which does not trade itself, but administers and develops its territory for the benefit of independent traders. The greatest and most striking example, however, is that of the Hon. East India Company, which in 1833 was at last forbidden to trade, and the succeeding twenty-five years formed a useful period of transition to direct Imperial administration in 1858. The advantages of some such intermediate system appear to me considerable. It would avoid the dislocation resulting from the withdrawal of the Company from trade before it had transferred its commercial assets to independent traders, it would provide a ready-made fleet of extremely light draft steamers and launches for the use of independent traders during the difficulties and costly navigation of the eight months of the dry season, a need which independent steamship companies would not be disposed to meet until a large growth of commerce had taken place, it would maintain an existing local organisation which is known to and liked by the native populations, it would secure an experienced administration at home which has never allowed itself to be trammelled by red tape or blind respect for precedent, and amongst other minor advantages it would, without cost to the Imperial Exchequer, enable the subscribed capital of the Company, fixed interest on which could be paid out of the revenues of Nigeria, to be employed in the work of development. But this question of Company or no Company is, in the future history of Nigeria, but an accidental feature. The one essential element is that continuity shall be maintained by permanent, unwearying, and bold administration from home, as heretofore controlled, but not conducted, by the office of a Secretary of State, until the Simlas of Hausaland, to which I have already alluded, are occupied and utilised, and a sufficient volume of commerce and therefore revenue is created to permit local government of the normal type. When that day arrives the foundations of Nigeria will have been fully laid, and it may be left to natural causes to raise that great structure of Nigerian prosperity which I shall not see, but in which, under reasonable conditions, I have the most absolute faith. (29)

(1) See Flint, *op cit.,* pp. 304-306.

(2) Italics added.

(3) Wellesley, *op cit.,* p. 65. Sir Ralph Moor was Governor of the Niger Coast Protectorate and successor in that office of Sir Claude Macdonald. Later on, he was also a colleague of Goldie's on the Selborne Committee.

(4) The Imperial British East Africa Company was granted a Charter in September, 1888 to develop British East Africa, rather on the lines that the R.N.C. was perceived to be developing the West Coast. The aims, objectives and methods were however, dissimilar, and the venture was not commercially viable. The Charter was revoked as from 1 July, 1895.

(5) See F.O. 83/1382 of 25 August, 1895. The printed version is Parliamentary paper 1896 LIX Ms p. 361.

(6) See Flint, *op cit.,* p. 212, fn. 2.

(7) See Perham M. *Years of Authority;* Collins, London, 1960; p. 225 *et seq.*

(8) *Ibid.,* p.226. Letter from Lugard to Sir John Kirk, broaching the "Scheme." Kirk must have been amused, if not astonished, to read Lugard's opening gambit—"I would propose . . ."!

(9) The name "Nigeria" was first coined by Flora Shaw (later Lady Lugard), in an article which she wrote in the *Times.* She was that paper's Colonial Editor.

(10) *Travels in West Africa* by Mary Kingsley; Macmillan & Co., London, 1897.

(11) Goldie's references to "higher" and "lower" orders of development grate on the modern ear. They are, however typical of the times in which he lived, a time when the full implications of Darwin's theory were but little comprehended and when the theory itself was somewhat grossly interpreted. (e.g. "Social Darwinism")

(12) Goldie is here grossly unfair to the tradition of piety and learning that marked the Fulani elite, especially at the time of the Jihad. That Sultan Bello asked Clapperton for a copy of Euclid in Arabic (his own having been lost in a fire in his home) was on record, as was Barth's very high opinion of the administrative machinery which they oversaw.

(13) The Battle of Morgarten was fought on November 15, 1315 between the forces of the new Swiss Confederation and the Austrian Hapsburghs. Crécy was fought on August 26, 1314 when the Black Prince's archers routed the French cavalry. Both engagements are models of their kind.

(14) Sir Henry Morton Stanley, 1841-1904.

(15) Goldie's acknowledgement of the value of ambition is not without its irony, in view of his expressed abhorrence of it.

(16) It is now almost certain that the R.N.C., thanks to Wallace's sojourn at Ibi on the hulk *Emily Waters,* had been aware of the existence of the Plateau tin-fields to a fairly accurate degree, though not precisely, since about 1885. See also page 293.

(17) That is the 1897 campaign against Bida and Ilorin, which Goldie accompanied and for the details of which he was entirely responsible. It too was a model of its kind!

(18) Goldie's concern is understandable. The Earl of Scarbrough always claimed that the R.N.C. "was a one man show." (See Wellesley, *op cit.,* p. 25.) Here, not only is the danger inherent in such a system looming, but also the prospects of an endeavour to establish "Direct Rule" *à la* the Lagos model, and an abandonment of Goldie's "gradualist" approach.

(19) *British Central Africa: An attempt to give some account of a portion of the Territories under British influence north of the Zambesi* etc., etc., by Sir Harry Johnston, G.C.M.G., K.C.B., (1858-1927); Methuen, London, 1897.

(20) Sir Charles Wentworth Dilke, 1843-1911. Author of *Greater Britain: A Record of Travel in English-speaking Countries during 1866 and 1867,* Methuen, London, 1868. Dilke, though a "Radical Imperialist," was Goldie's *bête noir.*

(21) This is a reference to the "Kingsley Plan."

(22) The Rt. Hon. Joseph Chamberlain, P.C., M.P., Lord Mayor of Birmingham 1873, Secretary of the Colonies, 1895-1903. Originally a Liberal, he broke with Mr. Gladstone over Irish Home Rule. He suffered a stroke in 1906 and was paralized until his death.

(23) The Second World War saw the erection of "The Jos Hill-Station" precisely on the model that Goldie was advocating and for the precise purpose he had in mind.

(24) This observation foreshadows the arguments later to be made in favour of "Indirect" versus "Direct" Rule.

(25) Joseph Flint and William Wallace. As has been noted above, Lugard copied this procedure slavishly in advocating his own "Scheme."

(26) John Wodehouse, Baron Wodehouse and 1st Earl of Kimberly (1866). 1826-1902, Colonial Secretary, 1880-82, India Office, 1882-1885, and 1886, Foreign Secretary, 1894-5; Leader of the Liberal Party in the House of Lords, 1891-1902.

(27) Goldie here states categorically the driving force behind all his amalgamations and all his commercial activities—Empire!

(28) Nevertheless, the Niger Company *did* remain as a trading company on the River. The remark may go some way to explaining Goldie's severance from it however.

(29) The speech as given in its original form was first published by the London Chamber of Commerce Incorporated as Number 25 in its Pamphlet Series, and was priced at 3d.

VI. INTRODUCTION TO C. F. S. VANDELEUR'S
CAMPAIGNING ON THE UPPER NILE AND NIGER
(1898)

As has been noted, Goldie considered this to be far and away the most important exposition of his philosophy of Government. It was written to fulfil a promise made to Lieutenant (Brevet Major) Cecil Seymour Vandeleur [1] of the Scots Guards, one of the volunteers serving with the Royal Niger Constabulary in the Bida and Ilorin campaign.

"I have more than one man's work to do" he told Stephen Gwynn, "but I gave eight hours to dictating that paper. That will tell you if I attached importance to it." [2] That remark was made to Gwynn, moreover, not at some remote and detached later date, but in the same year that the book was published, in 1898. Gwynn, a man whose reputation as a scholar, journalist, author, poet and Irish Nationalist stood high enough on its own account, had sought a meeting with Goldie "not as an interviewer, but as a seeker after knowledge," and it was during the course of this conversation that Goldie made his observation after having first referred Gwynn to the book in question as containing the essence of his views on government in relation to the African continent. [3] It is as such therefore that this monograph stands alone, a magnificent compostion, lucid, easy to read, concise but comprehensive, setting out a philosophy in both ideological and practical terms.

The monograph reveals Goldie as the gradualist that he was. But what it does still more is to establish him beyond any possibility of contradiction not only as the man who first expounded the practicality of "Indirect Rule" as being the policy most likely to be successful if adopted, but also as the practitioner prepared to put it into effect. No doubt too, at this time, he still saw the role of the Chartered Company as that of being the most likely instrument of its application even though, before he set off to the Coast to put the Bida campaign in motion, he knew that a revocation of the Charter was in the wind. What he hoped for, however, was clearly an abandonment by the Company of its *trading* role, and a concentration instead on its *administrative* function.

What he did NOT know, if Mary Kingsley is to be believed, was that when it came to the pinch, the British Government was going to be both ready and willing to "sell him down the river," and would make a deal with France.

"They [France] got for Fashoda (i) Sir George Goldie's head on a charger; (ii) Article ix (whose terms indirectly but greatly favoured their commerce); (iii) the East shore of Lake Tchad (along which they could link up North Africa to their possession of the Congo)." (4)

Had he known this, then it is at least doubtful whether Goldie would have embarked upon either the Nupe or the Ilorin campaign when he did.

But it is unprofitable to speculate too long on imponderables of this nature. Goldie must have known of the likelihood of French moves towards Borgu, or he would not have promised Chamberlain not to take the Company troops north of Jebba.

By the time the book was ready for publication Vandeleur was away on the Nile, preparatory, as has already been noted, to assisting Marchand on his way from Fashoda, and Goldie was deeply involved in a "quasi-official" capacity in the negotiations in Paris which were destined not only to deal with Borgu, but also with the Nile and the Gold Coast hinterland as well. They were also, as it happened, going to produce the 1898 Anglo-French Boundary agreement which would finally determine what the boundaries of Nigeria were to be, from an international standpoint, until the Treaty of Versailles. When Bretonnet had appeared in Bussa, therefore, he had been the chorus, as it were, almost of a Greek Tragedy that was finally going to destroy his work.

But, because at this time he had no inkling of what was in store, and because he was leaning over backwards to be punctilliously correct and conciliatory to France to boot, Goldie felt it necessary to preface his remarks with the following disclaimer:—

"Some months ago I promised Lieutenant Vandeleur, who has since gone to the Upper Nile, to write an Introduction to his book dealing with the Nupe War. I could do no less for one of the thirty-four officers whose high qualities carried us successfully through perhaps as hazardous an enterprise as any in which so small a force has ever been engaged. It did not at that time seem possible that the negotiations in Paris would not have come to a close before the book appeared. I have no reason to suppose that the author has inserted anything that could give offence in France or prejudice the negotiations; but in view of my quasi-official position, I feel bound to take the precaution of saying that I have not yet read the book, and must not be considered as endorsing anything contained in it. G.T.G."

There was really very little danger of Vandeleur taking any umbrage at Goldie's action in this respect, for the two had grown to be remarkably close. This is hardly to be wondered at. Their backgrounds and antecedents were precisely similar, their inquisitive scholarship was complementary and they were both out of the same mould—landed gentry with a heavily military family tradition behind them. (5)

If Goldie was somewhat the deeper thinker and more mature philosopher, then it should not be surprising.

The text of Goldie's monograph follows:—

If, in the year of grace when Her Majesty was born, (6) a traveller had combined in a single volume his experiences on the Nile and Niger, the incongruity of the subjects would have then appeared almost as great as though the rivers had been the Ganges and St. Lawrence. We now know that the vast regions between the Nile and the Niger are so closely connected by unity of religious faith and by internal commerce, that political events on the one stream react upon the other; we recognise that the Nile and Niger questions are not disconnected, but are two sides of a single question—that of the Sudan.

In treating this subject it is well to remind the general reader of the geographical position of the Sudan; as, since the British occupation of Egypt (7) and the military operations in the Egyptian Sudan, (8) a slipshod habit has crept into some English newspapers of applying to the latter alone a name which belongs properly to the whole of Negroland under Mohammedan influence or visited by Mohammedan trading caravans. *Chamber's Encyclopaedia*, in 1860, defined the Sudan as "bounded on the north by the Sahara, on the west by Senegambia, on the south by Upper Guinea, and on the east by Kordofan"; but it would be inconvenient to treat the Sudan to-day as ending on the western frontier of Kordofan, for the regions between it and the Red Sea, north of Abyssinia, are now habitually included in the term. With this amendment the definition above given will serve all practical purposes. The French, who during the last seven years have become far more fully informed than our compatriots about Africa north of the Equator, are strictly correct in naming their vast sphere to the east of Senegambia the French Sudan. The question is not one of geographical accuracy alone. It involves a recognition of the essential homogeneity of this great belt of Africa, on which important point I propose to touch presently.

In 1819, only those interested in geographical research were familiar even with the name of the Niger, or knew that its upper waters, down to Bussa, had been traced fourteen years before by a Scotchman, Mungo Park, the father of African exploration in modern times. It was only in 1831 that the lower waters of the Niger and their path from Bussa to the ocean were discovered by an equally great Englishman, Richard Lander. A like mystery veiled the sources and upper waters of the Nile until Speke, (9) Baker and other explorers, during the sixties, connected them geographically with the Nile of Nubia and Egypt.

Between these great rivers of East and West Africa lie regions of the breadth of the entire continent of Europe, regions which were, in 1819, altogether unknown and believed to be but sparsely inhabited. It was not until Major Denham and Captain Clapperton, in 1823-25, and Dr. Barth, in 1849-55, explored this vast area on behalf of the British Government, that the civilised world recognised that this heart of Africa was no barren desert. They found that it was filled with populous and organised States, that is possessed a fertile soil and intelligent and industrious inhabitants; but they did not sufficiently recognise—and this discovery was reserved for our days—that the considerable civilisation of the Sudan could make no further progress, that this lost thirtieth of the human race could have no adequate connection through commerce with the outer world, until a sound basis was substituted for that on which the social system in those regions has hitherto rested.

No student of history can, indeed, assert that the institution of slavery in its customary forms is an absolute barrier to intellectual progress and the creation of wealth. Greece, Rome, and the United States of America have afforded a sufficient answer to that extreme view. Nor can the slave *trade* be such a barrier, if the word be confined to its usual and proper meaning of buying and selling of slaves; for this has been the natural course in all ages in all slave-holding countries; while the capture of slaves in war has proved, at anyrate, preferable to the more ancient practice of killing all prisoners.

The radical vice of the Sudan, the disease which, until cured, must arrest all intellectual and material progress, is the general, constant, and intense prevalence of *slave-raiding.* It is not possible, in a brief preface, to present any adequate picture of a system under which considerable towns disappear in a night and whole tracts of country are depopulated in a single dry season—not as a result of war, but as the normal method of the rulers for collecting their human cattle for payment of tribute to their suzerains or for sale to distant parts of the continent. Much has been written on this extraordinary subject. It may suffice to refer the reader to Canon Robinson's(10) *Hausa Land,* and to Sir Harry Johnson's *(sic) Autobiography of a Slave,* (11) which, though presented in the form of fiction, is an understatement of the facts. But perhaps a more vivid picture is given in *The Life and Travels of Dorugu,* (12) dictated by himself, a translation of which appears in Dr. Schoen's(13) *Magana Hausa,* published by the Society for Promoting Christian Knowledge. Dorugu was a native of the Niger Sudan, who was ultimately brought to London by Dr. Barth. The merit of his story lies in its artlessness and brevity. His childhood is largely filled with sudden flights into the forest or hills to escape the slave-raiders. His family rebuild their burnt farmhouses, or change their homes with philosophic equanimity like that of vine cultivators on the slopes of a volcano. The simplicity with which Dorugu relates the fears and dangers of his boyhood shows that to him they seemed as inevitable as measles and school to an English boy. At last he is caught in his turn; his parents, brothers, and sisters, for whom he evidently had a strong affection, vanish suddenly and entirely out of his life, and he himself becomes one of the millions of pieces of human currency which pass from one Sudanese State to another.

At first sight it seems impossible to reconcile this universal and continual slave-raiding in times of peace with the considerable civilisation and complex political organisation of the Sudanese States. The system probably originated from the great demand for negro slaves that has existed from time immemorial amongst the lighter coloured races of mankind. The docility of the negro, combined with his intelligence and capacity for work, must have given him a special value in the slave markets of antiquity, as in those of modern days. The growth of Mohammedanism, with its polygamous institutions, during the eight centuries after the Hegira, gave an immense impulse to the export slave trade of the Sudan to Asia, Europe and North Africa. At the commencement of the sixteenth century the philanthropic efforts of Bishop Las Casas(14) laid the foundations of the negro slave trade to the New World. Three centuries of this export trade on a large scale must have contributed to confirm and develop the old slave-raiding habits of the Sudan, though it seems unjust of certain writers to lay the entire blame on Christendom for a social canker which had existed in Africa for many hundreds of years, before Charles V.,(15) out of pure benevolence, permitted the import into St. Domingo of slaves from the Portuguese Guinea Coast. But although the qualities of the negro and the demand for his services by lighter coloured races in all ages account for the inception of the remarkable system of slave-raiding, the number of slaves exported has probably been insignificant compared with the number dealt with in the internal traffic of Negroland.

To understand this question properly, it must be remembered that the value of a slave is extremely small near his place of capture. His initial price is often lower than that of a sheep, which has less tendency to escape. As the slave is taken farther away from his home, his value rises rapidly; so that it is commercially a sound transaction to send a hundred slaves, say, from Bornu to Darfur, while bringing a hundred others from Darfur to Bornu. No doubt they have also a value as transport animals, but I venture to assert that this feature of the traffic has been over-estimated, especially as camels are plentiful in the northern regions, while horses and donkeys are largely used and might be cheaply bred to any extent throughout the Sudan. While, therefore, a well-planned system of Sudanese railways would have a considerable indirect effect on the internal slave trade, and consequently on slave-raiding, it would not, as generally believed, directly touch the root of the evil. This can only be eradicated by the same vigorous means which we employ in Europe for the prevention of crime and violence. It is, I fear, useless to hope that commerce with Europe will, by itself, suffice to alter a social system so deeply ingrained in the Sudanese mind; for the creation of commerce on a large scale is impossible until slave-raiding is abated.

Let me not be misunderstood as preaching a crusade of liberty against the Sudanese States. To this policy I am strenuously opposed. Force must indeed underlie all social action, whether in Africa or Europe, whether in public life or in the more intimate relations of parent and child, schoolmaster and pupil. But there is a wide difference between its necessary and constant display and its unncessary use. The policemen of our towns have not their batons habitually drawn, though they do not hesitate to use them on occasions. There is probably no part of the world where diplomacy is more effective than Negroland, provided it is known that behind diplomacy is military power. There is certainly no part of the world where the maxim *Festina lente* (16) is more applicable.

It was the just perception of this principle which led France, at the Berlin Conference, to induce the civilised States to agree that, except on the *coasts* of the continent, (17) effective occupation—or, in other words, forcible occupation—should not be a necessary condition of political influence. The French Ambassador at Berlin pointed out very clearly the distinction in this respect between the coasts and the interior of Africa, and the disadvantages of requiring early effective occupation inland. The adoption of his view by the fourteen States represented at Berlin has consecrated this important principle as a recognised rule of international law until otherwise decided by the signatory nations. International rivalry is thus reduced to reasonable limits, and time is given for the gradual and natural growth of European influence in those regions.

When, however, the application of force becomes absolutely necessary, it ought surely to be thorough and rapid. Yet last spring, after the completion of the operations described by Lieutenant Vandeleur in the latter half of this book, one of the most able and respected organs of public opinion in this country questioned the morality of "mowing down natives with artillery and Maxim guns." (18) Now, these "natives" were the fighting organisation of great regions which they—though in a comparatively small minority—held down with a hand of iron, treating the less warlike inhabitants as cattle to be raided when wanted. The death of each Fulah killed at Bida secured the lives and liberty of scores of peaceful and defenceless natives. If Europe had no material interests to protect and develop in Africa, it would still have the same right, the same duty to extirpate slave-raiding that a man has to knock down a ruffian whom he sees mal-treating a woman or child in the street.

While, however, this consideration should satisfy the consciences of persons interested in the welfare of the oppressed millions of Africa, the material importance of opening up the Sudan cannot be overlooked by any European State which subsists largely on its manufacturing and shipping interests. On this point it will be well for me to confine my remarks to the region lying between Lake

Chad and the Niger, to which my studies of the last twenty years have been mainly directed. This region has been known of late under the name of the Niger Sudan. It comprises Bornu and the Fulah or Sokoto-Gando Empire, the greater and more valuable portion of which is mainly peopled by the civilised, commerce-loving, and industrious Hausas, who form about one-hundredth of mankind, and whose intellectual capacity H. M. Stanely has aptly emphasised by describing them as the "only Central African people who value a book."

In dealing with the value of the markets to be developed in the Niger Sudan, it is difficult to decide on how much must be said and what may be assumed as known. On the one hand, all geographers and many publicists are familiar with the fact that the region in question possesses populous towns and a fertile soil, and, most important of all, races whose industry is untiring, notwithstanding the discouraging and paralysing effects of insecurity of life, liberty, and property. They know that these races are possessed of high intelligence and considerable artistic skill, as displayed in their fine brass and leather work. They know that the early marriages in those latitudes, and the fecundity and vitality of the negro races, have, through countless generations, largely counteracted the appalling destruction of life resulting from slave-raiding, and that under reasonable conditions of security the existing population might soon be trebled and yet live in far greater material comfort than at present. They know, in short, that all that is needed to convert the Niger Sudan into an African India is the strong hand of a European protector. But, on the other hand, the general public and a considerable section of the press seem still inclined to confuse the Niger Sudan with the very different regions which border the Guinea Coast. The well-clad, intelligent, and fairly civilised races of the interior are constantly referred to as half-naked and indolent savages; the fine country which forms three-fourths of the Niger Sudan is confounded with the swamps of the Niger Delta. It is not difficult to recognise how this delusion originated and is maintained. The Niger Sudan is separated from the civilisation of the Mediterranean regions by a thousand miles of the Sahara, which the Tuareg and other wandering tribes render well-nigh impassable. It is separated from the Guinea coast-line by a maritime belt, malarious in climate, and inhabited by lower races who have, perhaps, been gradually pushed seawards by the successive waves of higher races coming from the North. The vast majority of Englishmen—whether soldiers, officials, missionaries, or traders—who have visited West Africa have seen only the coast-line or, at most, the maritime belt, and their impressions of this small section of the continent have very naturally been accepted by uninformed readers as applicable to the vast *Hinterlands.* The difficulty of access to the Niger Sudan regions accounts amply for this important and valuable portion of the earth's surface having been cut off from outside intercourse for all practical purposes until the last quarter of the nineteenth century. The barriers which from time immemorial have separated the Sudanese races from the remainder of the human family have at last been effectually broken down, and it may be safely prophesied that within twenty years the union will be complete, provided vital errors of policy are avoided. The two principal dangers can hardly be too often urged, and I propose to deal with them briefly in turn. (19)

Central African races and tribes have, broadly speaking, no sentiment of patriotism, as understood in Europe. There is therefore little difficulty in inducing them to accept what German jurisconsults term *Ober-Hoheit,* which corresponds with one interpretation of our vague term "Protectorate." (20) But when complete sovereignty, or *Landes-Hohiet,* is conceded, they invariably stipu-late that their local customs and system of government shall be respected. On this point they are, perhaps, more tenacious than most subject races with whom the

British Empire has had to deal; while their views and ideals of life are extremely difficult for an Englishman to understand. It is therefore certain that even an imperfect and tyrannical native African administration, if its extreme excesses were controlled by European supervision, would be, in the early stages, productive of far less discomfort to its subjects than well-intentioned but ill-directed efforts of European magistrates, often young and headstrong, and not invariably gifted with sympathy and introspective powers. If the welfare of the native races is to be considered, if dangerous revolts are to be obviated, the general policy of ruling on African principles through native rulers must be followed for the present. Yet it is desirable that considerable districts in suitable localities should be administered on European principles by European officials, partly to serve as types to which the native governments may gradually approximate, but principally as cities of refuge in which individuals of more advanced views may find a living, if native government presses unduly upon them; just as, in Europe of the Middle Ages, men whose love of freedom found the iron-bound system of feudalism intolerable, sought eagerly the comparative liberty of cities.

The second danger to be apprehended—a war of religions—will probably present itself to every thoughtful European. Fortunately for the Niger Sudan, Moslem fanaticism in this region has not the intensity of that now existing farther East— in Wadai, Darfur, and the Nile provinces. Yet ill-advised legislation, a careless administrative system, or a bad selection of officials, might well create an entirely different state of things. Twenty-five to thrity years ago one was able to travel in the Egyptian Sudan without escort, and without even keeping watch at night. With what incredulity would one have then received a prophecy that only ten or fifteen years later that district would become a hotbed of Mohammedan fanaticism, and would be absolutely closed to Christendom for a long period of years! The danger in the Sudanese States is accentuated by the close connection between them, due not only to a common faith and similar modes of life, but also to the constant communications kept up by the Hausa trading caravans which radiate from Hausa-land into distant parts of the continent. Prior to the Mahdist conquests, the pilgrim caravans from Central and Western Africa used to pass through Darfur to the Red Sea. I have travelled with no less than eight hundred Hausa pilgrims in a single caravan between Khartum and Suakin. The rise of Mahdism has temporarily diverted these pilgrim travellers northward from Lake Chad to the Mediterranean; but every part of the Sudan is still permeated by trading caravans constantly passing to and fro, and carrying news, almost always distorted and exaggerated, from one part of this vast region to another. About twelve years ago a placard issued by the late Mahdi was found posted in a street of Bida, no less than two thousand miles distant across country from Khartum; while one of the incidents that precipitated our war last year was the receipt of letters from the Khalifa at Omdurman by the Sultan of Sokoto and the Emirs of Nupe and other provinces of the Sokoto Empire, urging them to drive the Christians out of their country.

The similarity of the Sudan regions from east to west may be further illustrated by a striking fact of no little importance to the British Empire, and in which personally I take more interest than in the commercial development of the Sudan. Its entire northern belt, from Senegambia to the Red Sea, is inhabited by races at once capable of fighting and amenable to discipline. The value of the Sudanese regiments of the Egyptian army is widely known. Less has been heard, as yet, of the splendid qualities of the Hausa as a soldier when well officered. In the campaign described by Lieutenant Vandeleur, these qualities were fully proved. On the rapid and arduous march of seventeen days from Lokoja to

119

Kabba, and thence to Egbon *(sic.)*, and again on the march to Ilorin, with serious scarcity of water, and at times shortness of rations, our troops were always good-tempered and cheerful; and, although in heavy marching order, would pick up and carry the seventy-pound loads of the porters who fell by the way. In camp their conduct was exemplary, while pillaging and ill-treatment of the natives were unknown. As to their fighting qualities, it is enough to say that, little over 500 strong, they withstood for two days 25,000 to 30,000 of the enemy; that, former slaves of the Fulahs, they defeated their dreaded masters; that, Mohammedans, they fought for their salt against their brethren of the faith; and finally, that though they had never before faced cavalry, they stood firm under charges *home* on to the faces of their squares, maintained perfect fire-discipline, and delivered their volleys as steadily as if on parade. Great Britain has had to rely too much of recent years on Indian troops for tropical climates. This is not a healthy condition of things, for many reasons. She may well find an independent source of military strength in the regions bordering the southern limits of the Great Sahara. (21)

I have necessarily touched very briefly on the main features of the Nile and Niger question,—one which must inevitably become better known in the early future. When the history of the Victorian age is written from a standpoint sufficiently removed to allow a just perception of proportion, the opening up of Tropical Africa will probably stand out as a prominent feature of the latter half of that era. The fifty years that followed 1492 formed by no means the least interesting period in the domestic and international history of England, France, Germany, or Spain, or in the history of freedom of human thought and action; yet no events of that half century appear to us now more important than the discoveries of Columbus and the conquests of Cortes and Pizarro. The results of opening up Tropical Africa cannot, of course, be on a similar scale; yet it seems to me that they must be so great as to dwarf many contemporaneous questions which now occupy the public mind in a far higher degree.

The share that Great Britain may take in this movement depends on the condition of the national fibre. A statesman of the early Stuart period would have deemed it impossible that these little islands could control an empire such as that of the days of Chatham; while the Great Commoner himself might have felt misgivings could he have foreseen the Greater Britain of the Diamond Jubilee year. Yet the growing burden of empire has brought with it a more than equivalent accession of wealth, vigour, and strength to maintain it; and although it may be that the British Empire has now reached its zenith, (22) and must gradually decline to the position of a second rate power, we are not bound to accept such assertions without the production of more valid evidence than has yet been adduced in their support.

GEORGE TAUBMAN GOLDIE.

NAVAL AND MILITARY CLUB,
16th February 1898.

(1) *Campaigning on the Upper Nile and Niger:* Methuen, London, 1898. The author, Lieutenant C. F. S. Vandeleur, D.S.O., F.R.G.S., was an officer of the Scots Guards who later transferred to the Irish Guards on the formation of that Regiment. He was born in 1869 and was killed at Waterval North in the Transvaal on 30 August 1901, when the train in which he was travelling to join a new command was blown up by an Irish train-wrecker named Hindon and the passengers ambushed by men of Commandant Byer's Commando.
(2) Wellesley, *op cit.*, p.24.
(3) *Ibid*, pp. 23 & 24.
(4) Wellesley, *op cit.*, p. 69.
(5) For details of Vandeleur's career, see Muffett D. J. M., "New Introduction" in Frank Cass' re-print of the 1898 edition of the Vandeleur book, 1974.

(6) 24 May, 1819.

(7) 1882.

(8) 1885-6 & 1897-8.

(9) Speke, John Hanning, 1827-64. The first European to reach Lake Victoria, 30 July, 1858. Speke accompanied Burton on the 1855 expedition to Somaliland where he was seriously wounded. He rejoined Burton during 1856-58. In 1860 he and Grant embarked upon a second expedition to the Lake which lasted until 1863. In that year, Speke and Grant met Baker and his wife Florence at Gandokoro on their way up the Nile. He returned to England in 1864 and was to have debated Burton on 15 Sept. on the source of the Nile. He met with a fatal shooting accident the afternoon before.

(10) Robinson, Canon Charles Henry, 1861-1925. Missionary, lexicographer of Hausa, linguist and authority on Hausaland.

(11) Published in the U.S. as *The History of a Slave,* New York, 1889, the author being Sir Harry Johnston.

(12) Dorugu, c. 1837-1912, a Hausa slave whom Barth acquired in the Kano slave market. He, and a similarly obtained Marghi lad named Abiga, returned to Britain with Barth and were educated there. In 1862 Dorugu returned to Africa and disappeared. Lugard used to tell a story about his reappearance. Apparently Captain Abadie, Lugard's A.D.C. in 1900-01 was reconnoitring Abuci in Nupe:—
A ragged whitehaired old gentleman [Lugard called him a "savage"] came to Abadie's door and Abadie said to him "Well, Father Christmas! Who are you?" He was shocked at receiving the answer, "Young man! And who are *you?*" Sir Percy Girouard met him at Zungeru in 1907 and sent him to teach in Sokoto. In 1908 he again met him there, somewhat unkempt and dishevelled. He rebuked him saying that his clothes were unworthy of his occupation. To do this Dorugu, completely unabashed, replied "Sir, I am only teaching savages." (Journal of the African Society, Vol. XI, 1911-12, pp 468-9 & 471). In 1971 Yale U. Press republished Dorugu's story as part of *West African Travel and Adventures,* edited by A. H. M. Kirk-Greene and Paul Newman.

(13) Schoen, James Frederick, 1803-89. Missionary, linguist and the first lexicographer of Hausa.

(14) Bishop Bartolomé de Las Casas, 1474-1566. Opposed slavery for the Caribs and persuaded Charles I of Spain in 1517 to permit instead the importation of Africans for that purpose.

(15) Charles I of Spain and V of the Holy Roman Empire, 1500-1558. He assumed the rule of Spain in 1516.

(16) "Hasten Slowly." According to Suetonius this was the favourite proverb of Caesar Augustus.

(17) Goldie is somewhat repetitive in his determination to hammer this point home! Obviously it is a crucial one to win if the Company's position was to be secured.

(18) This would appear to be a reference to an Editorial in the *Liverpool Journal of Commerce* on 10 March, 1897, which, whilst deploring the relative lack of public attention directed to the success of the Benin Campaign which was conducted by a Royal Naval force operating on land, against—according to the *Journal*—"the most wicked and deeply dyed dusky despot on earth . . . and his sable satellites" (Mr. Agnew did not, apparently, invent alliterative invective!) was equally scathing in its criticism of the Company's campaign and to its policy of "baptism of fire and Maxim shot" as a replacement for Christian endeavour and conversion, and "the unwarranted mowing down of hundreds of the poor fellows" in the Nupe Army. The same *Journal* had, on 12 February, also protested "the horrible slaughter of thousands by means of the Maxim and other such machines of civilization." These criticisms infuriated Major Burdon, who noted them down in the "scrap-book" he prepared for his mother, and which was kindly placed at my disposal by Mr. A. H. M. Kirk-Greene, fellow of St. Antony's College, Oxford.

(19) Goldie was always haunted by the prospect of experimentation and a too hasty innovation in the government of African peoples. He was, as has been pointed out, a gradualist in approach. Avoidance of the two pitfalls that he now describes, would, of course, be absolutely fundamental to the execution of a policy of Indirect Rule.

(20) A more usual modern rendering would be "Suzerainty."

(21) Goldie maintained an acute interest in matters of the "logistics" of National Defence. Further reference will be made to this interest in Part III.

(22) It is possible, however, that Goldie did move towards that view in the months

121

immediately preceding the outbreak of the 1914-1918 War, or in the early months of it, not so much because of fear for its immediate outcome but of its longterm results. It was at this time that his public activity ceases and it was at this time also that he destroyed his papers, saying that his story was "deprived of value" and that "since the War I feel that I am out of date." See page 30.

VII. REVIEW OF *THE AUTOBIOGRAPHY OF SIR HENRY M. STANLEY* (1909)

This review was first published in *The World.* It was then reproduced, by permission, in the Journal of the African Society, Vol. IX, 1909-1910, from where this text is taken. It is an important document in that in addition to revealing much about Stanley's character, it also gives a number of new insights into Goldie's as well.

Fugaces labuntur anni!(1)It is difficult for those of the older generation to realise that, to perhaps one-half of the English-speaking people, Henry Morton Stanley, who seemed to us the incarnation of unquenchable vitality, is to-day only an historical personage. (2) Thirty-nine years have passed since he left Asia for Zanzibar to search for Livingstone, and nineteen since he brought to a close the extraordinary series of African journeys which made him the most effective of explorers since the discovery and opening up of the New World. Those who wish to study the rough-hewn Stanley of history have the materials to their hand in his three principal books, *How I found Livingstone,* (3) *Through the Dark Continent,* (4) and *In darkest Africa,* (5) or in extraneous literature of that period. If they wish to understand the preparation which wide travel gave to him for his great achievements, they can read *My Early Travels and Adventures in America and Asia.* (6) They can derive from these sources a clear perception of his energy and versatility, and of his greatness as an explorer and administrator; but they can form no true estimate of the *man* as known to his friends. Stanley's abnormal reticence towards the outer world, (7) the inevitable result of his abnormal environment from birth until his marriage at fifty years of age, gave rise to serious misconceptions by the general public of his real sentiments and character.

Lady Stanley (8) has, therefore, fulfilled a manifest duty in publishing, as Stanley had desired, the complete autobiography of his earlier years, of which even intimate friends had only vague and general knowledge, and in appending to this a concise and connected narrative of his later life "by interweaving strands gathered from his unpublished writings," such as diaries, note-books, lectures, and letters. But her book is much more than a sacred duty to Stanley's memory. The autobiography, which has strong dramatic interest, gives also a valuable insight into the psychology of a modern hero, and shows by what strange chances this *Bula Matari* (Breaker of Rocks), (9) as the natives named him, was welded into a hammer which could open up a lost continent to modern civilisation. The story in its earlier stages would be poignant reading if Stanley's keen sense of humour had not provided an antidote to melancholy. The tragedies of the early lives of David Copperfield and Oliver Twist sink into insignificance beside it. Dicken's kindly nature made him use his rights as a creator to mitigate the loneliness of David's childhood by the warm affection of a Peggotty. Oliver's troubles were short-lived compared with the prolonged sufferings of Stanley, who was clearly a highly strung, sensitive boy, thirsting for human love and finding only brutality and neglect. (10) Yet when one notes the futility and callousness of so many nurtured in comfort and affection, and remembers not only the effective work which Stanley's tempered mind and body enabled him to perform, but also the kind and just heart which beat under a somewhat fierce and dominating exterior, one is tempted to ask whether the educational methods of ancient Sparta were not preferable, both from an individual and from a national standpoint, to the pleasanter but more enervating methods of modern civilisation.

It is not within the scope of a brief review to deal fully with Stanley's voyage to America and the story of his varied life there; but most readers of the autobiography will share the regret that the latter is not described in greater detail. The narrative is as vivid as if it had been written from day to day, and not a word is wasted. His fifty-two days of torment on the *Windermere* will recall to readers of Clark Russell (11) the purgatory of sea life only half a century ago, and the remarkable changes which steam, a free press, and the growth of the public conscience have brought about in the commercial navies of England and America. Stanley's reason for joining the Confederate Army on the outbreak of the Civil War is at once amusing and characteristic. It was the receipt of a parcel containing a chemise and a petticoat. On such trivial events do our lives turn.

This may be a convenient place to note a fact with which all Stanley's friends were familiar, the chivalrous delicacy of his relations with women. A delightful story, very concisely told, is that of his brief friendship for a certain "Dick." This youth ultimately proved to be a girl who had run away from Liverpool and had crossed to America as a cabin boy. On the discovery of her sex, she displayed a delicacy no less marked than that of her young friend; for, without a word of farewell, she disappeared for ever from his life. Both humorous and idyllic is Stanley's account of his semi-engagement, nine years later, to a demure and charming Greek girl, named Virginia, in the island of Syra. Chivalry, in all the relations of life, was a feature of Stanley's character which impressed itself on those who had the opportunity of penetrating his real nature. That opportunity did not come to me until the autumn and winter of 1884, during the General Conference of Berlin. (12) The heavy labours of the day could not exhaust Stanley's energy, and he would often come to my rooms and sit up until the small hours, discoursing delightfully of all things in heaven and earth. Until then, our acquaintance had produced on me only the superficial impression, correct as far as it went, of colossal force, ability, and tenacity. Special circumstances were needed to break down his excessive reserve, due partly to the hardships of his earlier years, but maintained and intensified by the loneliness of his life in Africa.

It is hardly possible for those who have always lived in civilisation, or have travelled only with congenial companions on terms of equality, to understand the reserve, the secretiveness engendered by life in barbarous lands, either alone with natives on a lower plane of thought, or with white men whom the severe discipline essential in positions of grave responsibility forbids one to admit into intimacy. The shyness—the word is Stanley's—produced by such a life is forcibly depicted by him in Chaper XIX. of the autobiography, written on his return to Cairo in 1890, after the Emin relief expedition. Moreover, Stanley was, by nature, a dreamer of dreams, as have been most men who have achieved greatness on original lines. (13) Even alone with friends, he would often sit musing and apparently abstracted until roused by some remark. Then, rather slowly, he would begin to speak, and, from that moment, one "could not chose but hear"; (14) for although his public speeches were somewhat too ornate for the English taste, he was the best talker in more intimate circles than it has ever been my fortune to meet. Like the Merry Monarch, "he never said a foolish thing," even when discussing trivialities. His grip of every subject he treated, and his intensity of thought, were always relieved by a running accompaniment of irresistible humour.

The reputation of hardness, which some of his less competent subordinates—both Belgian and English—successfully attached to his name, was the result of his sense of duty and of justice. In barbarous regions, where the white men are a handful in the midst of savage populations, both duty and justice compel an administrator or explorer to put aside the luxury of sentimentalism. He is bound to enforce the strictest discipline and to eliminate incompetence or insubordination at the cost of making many enemies. (15) The persistent calumniation of Stanley perhaps reached its climax in the story circulated of his having thrown a baby into the Congo. This ludicrous tale was so widely believed that it was repeated to Lady Stanley, soon after her marriage, by a lady friend with "tears in her eyes." The autobiography gives the true and touching story of the baby. Stanley, like most men of intense character, was drawn to all weak and helpless things, as those knew who visited him during his simple and happy life at Furze Hill. His devotion to his adopted son was a lesson to fathers. Doubtless, he was affected also by the memory of his own too brief good fortune, in the cruel days of his youth, when Mr. Stanley, a New Orleans merchant, adopted him and gave him the name which he made famous. Mr. Stanley's death was a grave personal loss to his adopted son, yet, had he lived, a vivid and valuable chapter of history would never have been written across the equatorial regions of Africa.

The autobiography deals somewhat briefly with Stanley's parliamentary career from 1895 to 1900 (16) —a career for which nature had not equipped him. In 1899, when the Niger Act had received the Royal Assent, and my active life was drawing to a close, he asked me whether I would not stand for Parliament. I confidently promised to do so, if he would assure me of his satisfaction with his life there. His forcible reply recalled to my mind remarks, similar in effect, but differing *toto caelo*, (17) in phraseology and methods of delivery, which John Stuart Mill(18) had made to me, at Avignon, nearly thirty years earlier, and which had greatly affected my life. The philosopher and the man of action, each in his own way among the greatest that the century had produced, and perhaps as diverse in nature as was possible to two civilised men, agreed in the verdict that Parliamentary life was unsuited to those who were not born partisans. (19) Yet Stanley had strong political convictions, especially as regarded *(sic.)* the necessity of extending and consolidating the Empire, in view of the expansion or consolidation of other nations during the latter half of the century. The autobiography shows how earnestly Stanley had desired that the Congo should become British. His efforts in this direction were frustrated by that apathy and that want of foresight of British statesmen from which other makers of Empire suffered up to July, 1886. (20) If his efforts had been successful, the opening up of Africa, one of the greatest episodes of history since the discovery of America, would have been free from those stains which have shocked the conscience of impartial observers and tended to obscure the incalculable blessings that the partition of the Continent has elsewhere brought to the cruelly oppressed natives. (21)

Lady Stanley publishes (pp. 534-7) an extract from a notebook written in Africa in 1876, which clearly explains the sentiment of freedom which again and again drew Stanley to the wild. The following sentences give the keynote, "No luxury in civilisation can be equal to the relief from the tyranny of custom. The wilds of a great city are better than the excruciating tyranny of a small village. The heart of Africa is infinitely preferable to the heart of the world's greatest city."

Lady Stanley shows also how Stanley (22) rejected his many opportunities, which most people would have considered legitimate, of becoming wealthy, and was contented to live on a moderate income, derived mainly from his books and lectures. It is well for the nation and the world to read the life of a modern hero and a noble soul, who disdained to worship the golden calf. (23)

GEORGE T. GOLDIE:

(1) Goldie, as he had a penchant for doing, is adapting a Latin quotation—hardly a tag—for his own purposes. This time, it is from Horace (Quintus Horatius Flaccus, 65-8 B.C.). The full text is

"Eheu fugaces, Postume, Postume,
labuntur anni, nec pietas moram
rugis et instanti senectae
adferet indomitaeque morti."

"Oh! Postumus! Postumus! The fleeting years are slipping by, nor will piety stay for a moment the onset of wrinkles and hurrying old age or of death the indomitable." The passage can be found in *Lambi, xiv,* 1.

(2) Stanley died on 10th May, 1904.

(3) Published in 1872.

(4) Published in 1878.

(5) Published in 1890.

(6) Published in 1885. The correct title is " . . . *and Asia Minor.*"

(7) It is odd to see Goldie referring to "Stanley's 'abnormal' reticence towards the outer world."

(8) Lady Stanley was the former Miss Dorothy Tennant.

(9) Ki-Kongo for "He who smashes rocks."

(10) Stanley was born in Denbigh in Wales under he name of John Rowlands, and because he was abandoned, he was reared in St. Asaphs Workhouse as a "Workus brat."

(11) Clark Russell, 1844-1911. The author of some sixty popular nautical tales, some of which were instrumental in mobilizing public opinion to compel the amelioration of conditions of service "before the mast" in merchant ships.

(12) Goldie and Stanley were both "Advisors" to the British delegation at the Berlin Conference of 1884, which gave rise to the General Act of 1885. At that time, Stanley was without doubt the more "weighty."

(13) "All achievement begins with a dream. My dream was to colour the map red." See page 15.

(14) S. T. Coleridge; *The Rime of the Ancient Mariner,* Part I, v. 5.

"The Wedding Guest sat on a stone,
He can not chose but hear,
And thus spake on that ancient man
The bright eyed Mariner."

(15) Goldie was widely criticised himself for his order to shoot absconding carriers if their departure threatened the well-being of the column marching on Bida in 1897. There are echoes here of the Zweifel case and the straits to which that put Wallace, Goldie's admired and admiring subordinate on the Niger in 1888-89. See p. 136 and footnote.

(16) Stanley was Member of Parliament for North Lambert.

(17) Goldie is using the phrase both inaccurately and out of context. The proverb is first found in Macrobius (early 5th Cent. A.D.), *Saturnalia* 3. 12. 10. Here it means "In the whole Heaven" to be interpreted as "Way off beam." Goldie uses it in the sense "Heaven alone knows," which strains the meaning.

(18) John Stuart Mill, 1806-73, was a Member of Parliament from 1865-68. He stood only on the condition that he would neither campaign nor work for the Party in any way, nor would he ever give an account of his stewardship. From 1868-73, Mill had a summer

residence in Avignon and divided his time there. Mill started his career as an economist employed by the East India Company.

(19) In 1900, Goldie was urged to stand for Parliament and the seat at Oldham was offered to him—before it was offered to Winston Churchill.

(20) i.e. the year of the granting of the Charter.

(21) As can be seen when the above is compared with earlier views, Goldie's assessment of the Administration of the Congo underwent an agonising re-appraisal.

(22) Stanley suffered a paralysis in April 1903, and was unable to speak or move until his death thirteen months later.

(23) *The World: a Journal for Men and Women,* was published in London from July, 1874 to May, 1920, when it closed down. It was a weekly.

The S.S. *Yakoba* at Onitsha, Lower Niger. *Courtesy U.A.C. International.*

The Niger Company's S.S. *Nigeria* on the slipway for repairs. *Courtesy U.A.C. International.*

III

Letters to *The Times,*
Interviews with Correspondents and
Reported Comments on
Matters of Public Interest

A "field correspondent" in camp. See pp. 73 and fn. and 160 ff. *Courtesy U.A.C. International.*

The comfortable verandah of an office. *Courtesy U.A.C. International.*

LETTERS TO THE TIMES

During his active career Goldie wrote twenty-eight letters to the *Times*. None appear to have been published before 1888 and no more appeared after 16 September, 1913.

As could be expected of someone whose nature was so intensely private, his relations with the Press were ambivalent. According to Lady Wellesley, he loathed it and all that it stood for.

"I never knew a man who so loathed the press, who so despised its values—those ready-made opinions served up in slabs on the breakfast table every morning. He never grew accustomed to it, being one of these people who are born perpetually young, perpetually indignant . . . He died before the mania for self-advertisement had engulfed the world. Certain aspects of this would, I think, have driven him to desperation." [1]

Yet for all that, he knew full well how to use the power of the press, and how to harness it to his own requirements. Some of his letters can hardly be described as such, being rather "position papers" running to many hundreds of words. Although, according to Lady Wellesley again, he had no literary ambitions [2] his writing, as was to be expected of a man of his time and of his background, was clear, explicit and easy to read with some enjoyment. His hand can readily be detected in the speeches which Lord Aberdare, as Chairman, delivered to the Annual Meetings of both the National African Company and of the R.N.C.

In addition to the actual letters to the Editor, signed by himself, the *Times* also carried a number of articles during the same period, all of which were entitled "Sir George Goldie on . . ." These have also been reproduced, as have two letters also from Lord Aberdare and the response to one.

Goldie also gave at least two interviews [3] to a Reuters' Special Correspondent. Those of 1897 have been reproduced from the *Times,* since they purport to be verbatim. That of 1899 presented rather more difficulty. Despite the best efforts of Messers. Reuters, it has proved quite impossible to recover the original text.

The letters fall quite naturally into distinct categories which, moreover, appear to be governed as much by time as by subject. There is also a clear indication of Goldie's willingness to "go public" more readily as a President of the R.G.S., or in some similar capacity, than there was as "Administrator" or Deputy Governor, or as Governor of the Royal Niger Company. Two of the letters, those in which he mourns the passing of a near relative and of a friend—in this case none other than Cecil Rhodes—are entirely private. They are also extremely moving, and the last especially seems to give some indication of what Goldie himself regarded as a fitting accolade for a life well spent in honourable and worthwhile endeavour—a memorial in Westminster Abbey.

The first letter in the series is one dated 19 December, which appeared in the *Times* of 21 December, 1888, page 14, column 5. It and its immediate successor, written only a few days later, as well as the other correspondence on the issues raised, justify their allocation to a subcategory of their own.

(1) Wellesley, *op cit.*, p. 158.
(2) *Ibid.* p. viii.
(3) The phraseology used above is deliberate. Two Reuters' interviews, those of 6 April 1897 and 23 October, 1897 have been located and are reproduced. However, Stephen Gwynn, in Lady Wellesley's book, insists that there was yet a third one which occurred on 5 July, 1899, and he quotes extensively from it. It has therefore been possible to reconstruct a text.

I. LIVERPOOL AND PARLIAMENT

1. 21 December, 1888.

THE NIGER TERRITORIES.

TO THE EDITOR OF THE TIMES.

Sir,—Every active institution possesses the wholesome, though unpleasant, advantage of having critics whose number is in direct ratio and whose scrupulousness is often in inverse ratio to the energy and success which arouse their animosity. The governor and council of the Royal Niger Company have therefore not shown any undue sensitiveness to any anonymous or incorrect statements that have been made from time to time as to the administration of their territories. Now, however, that certain members of Parliament [1] have had their good-natured credulity imposed upon and have actually taken a division on the subject in the House of Commons, I would ask permission to give, through your columns, a concise refutation of the absurd assertions credited by them. These are that "the company is ruining the country. Their charter was granted in 1886. In that year the produce shipped homewards from the Niger amounted to 10,900 tons; in 1887 this had fallen to 8,630 tons; and in the first half of 1888 only 2,055 tons were shipped." The original authority for this ingenious statement should have known that the exports from the territories are always comparatively small during the first half of the year, owing to the main Niger and its numerous tributaries being to a great extent unnavigable from December to July, when launches and special steamers of three or four feet draught can alone bring produce down from Central Africa to the Ocean. As a matter of fact the tonnage already exported from the territories this year is about 12,500 tons, and is thus greater than in any previous year.

Moreover, according to advices dated the 25th of October, there were 3,000 tons more of this year's trade ready for export, which had been exceptionally delayed in the interior by an unusually early fall of the water, but which are expected to be shipped, as usual, before the close of the year. The export trade for 1888 is thus about 15,500 tons, or very largely in excess of that for 1886, when Mr. Gladstone's Government took the wise, and, indeed, only practicable decision to grant the charter, rather than allow the territories to fall into the hands of foreign Powers who had striven hard to obtain them. It is therefore indisputable that the above statement is misleading and that the company has, on the contrary, been successful in developing the resources of the territories under the exceptional difficulties arising from the universal depression of trade during the last three years. It is true that 1887 showed a slight decrease in the tonnage of exports—incorrectly stated as 8,630 tons—as against 1886, but this was entirely due to the important restrictions enforced by the company on the import of spirits. Although these had never formed so predominating a feature in the trade of the Niger territories as is the case in the adjacent coast regions, yet the 75 per cent. reduction within a very short period in the annual import of spirits could not but inflict a passing blow to commerce. It is satisfactory to note from the large increase of trade in 1888 that this effect was only temporary, and that useful manufactured goods—cottons, silks, woollens, earthenware, hardware, copper ware, tin ware, cutlery, fancy goods, etc., on which, as Lord Aberdare lately pointed out, (2) only a 2 per cent. *ad valorem* import duty is imposed throughout the seaboard zone of the territories—are more than filling the gap created by the diminution of the spirit traffic.

The critics of the company find it convenient to ignore the difficulties inherent to breaking into Central Africa. France has expended large sums and many lives in military expeditions in order to add an Upper Niger province to Senegambia, where she has been established for hundreds of years; but as yet she has not created any commerce nor has she derived any advantage whatever from these sacrifices. The Imperial British East Africa Company has only quite lately commenced its important mission, and has its experience to gain.

The German East African Company has learnt in a severe form the lesson which Central Africa sooner or later teaches to all who attempt to open it to commerce and civilization. The only remaining Central African Government—the Congo Free State—can assuredly confirm and sympathize with the difficulties to be overcome, although it has had, and still has, the advantage of very large endowments by the King of the Belgians. The British taxpayer has done nothing to help the cause. (3) At its sole cost, at its sole risk, and by its sole exertions during a bitter international struggle which lasted for three and a half years the Niger Company has secured to British influence the largest and most valuable part of the Niger basin, which, though necessarily slow of development, will assuredly prove of immense future importance to the working classes of Great Britain.

The chief existing difficulty of the company lies in the smallness of the administrative expenditure. This is as yet between £40,000 and £50,000 a year—fourteen-fifteenths (4) being paid by the company, which, having had at the time of the granting of the charter the whole of the European trade in the territories, has now—as lately stated by Lord Aberdare—about fourteen-fifteenths of that trade. Not a penny of the administrative revenue goes to swell the commercial revenue or dividends of the shareholders, who are at present, owing to the depression of prices in Europe, only earning about 5 per cent. per annum on their investment, notwithstanding the enormous commercial advantage the company possesses in being an amalgamation of all those whose business talents created the Niger trade, and in having a staff built up during a long period of continuous organization. The company itself has more than half a million sterling of subscribed capital which it is still unable to employ with any hope of profit. These facts destroy the absurd accusations of the company being monopolist in character.

As the critics of the company, relying on the ignorance of the public, have based their complaints on a comparison of the administrative expenditures of the Niger and Lagos, I would point out that the latter diminutive colony—with its 50,000 to 100,000 inhabitants and its small strips of seaboard territory, relying entirely for protection on the British fleet, towards which it subscribes nothing—actually expends more than the Niger Government, and is barely able to meet this expenditure, in spite of its long-established trade, of its fortunate geographical position, and of stamps and other duties at present impracticable in the Niger territories. The Niger Company has to maintain the best order it can among 300 barbarous and mutually hostile tribes, inhabiting extensive populous, and newly-settled regions, everywhere inaccessible to gunboats during nine months of the year, and in most parts at all seasons. To administer these countries according to colonial ideas(5) tenfold the present annual expenditure would not be sufficient. The existing lack of revenue is, however, implemented by the admirable energy and tact of the company's local officials, whose long experience and commercial training enable them to maintain excellent relations with the natives.

A well-known authority on West Africa (6) has repeatedly and ably exposed the incapacity of the British colonial system for opening up Africa. This does not arise from any fault of the Colonial Office, nor of those who are sent out to administer, but from a radical vice in the system of government. Inner Africa, out of reach of gunboats and unfitted for European military operations, cannot be ruled mainly by force, which should be used only to repel the invasions of surrounding predatory tribes and to protect to commerce-loving majority of the natives from the outrages and attacks of turbulent minorities. But the general maintenance of order must rest on the recognition by the mass of the inhabitants of their direct interest in the Government. (7) They yield a ready obedience to those who, like a commercial and industrial company, bring them material prosperity as an equivalent for the surrender of their previous tribal independence; but many years must elapse before they become sufficiently civilized to understand the advantages, or even the justification, of an Administration which does nothing but govern. In the Congo Free State, which is a purely philanthropic undertaking of the King of the Belgians', without any idea of commercial gain, trading with the natives is carried on at each of the stations; and, to a remark of surprise at this fact one of its highest officials lately said, "If we did not trade with them the natives would ask, 'What are you doing here?' "

I am, Sir, your obedient servant,
GEORGE TAUBMAN GOLDIE,
Political Administrator.
Surrey-house, Victoria Embankment, Dec. 19.

It took nearly two weeks for a reaction to come to Goldie's letter, The *Times,* which had published his letter within two days of his writing it, now delayed for four before publishing its riposte. Part of the reason may have been that the signature was "African Merchants" and though not unknown, it was not usual for the *Times* to publish letters which the correspondents were unwilling to sign with their proper names. On 3 January, 1889, however, the letter appeared. It was a long one.

In it, the writer reviewed the events leading up to the grant of the Charter, and accused the Company of now actively applying pressure to have it extended over the Oil Rivers. Such, the letter held, would increase the already illegal but nonetheless pervasive tendencies towards monopoly which had always been evinced. Accordingly, the writer called for no action by the Foreign Office unless and until the question of any extension of the R.N.C. Charter had been fully investigated by a House of Commons Committee.

After referring to both Goldie's letter and to the Debate, the letter then demanded that if, in spite of the objections, an extension of the

Charter was permitted, then the Royal Niger Company should be required to administer the territory only, and to disassociate itself from trading. Failing that, then let the administration of the Oil Rivers remain as it was, and let the Company, if it wished, come in to trade in a purely trading capacity, their objections not being to the Company *per se,* but to the Company in collusion with "certain departments of the Foreign Office."

Goldie's response was prompt.

2.   4 January, 1889. Page 4, Column 6.

THE ROYAL NIGER COMPANY

TO THE EDITOR OF THE TIMES

Sir,—I have read with much interest the letter from "African Merchants" in your issue of to-day. I admit that if their premisses were sound I could not myself avoid arriving at some, at least, of their conclusions. I trust you will allow me space for a short letter showing that they are building on an entirely imaginary foundation.

I would like, however, to begin by saying that I have not in any way questioned the scrupulousness of "African Merchants." I unfortunately do not know who they are, and their letter in your issue of to-day is—except in two minor particulars, to which I need not refer—fair and temperate in tone. The persons "whose scrupulousness is often in inverse ratio to the energy and success which arouse their animosity" are those who—locally informed of the real facts of the case—originate statements that the trade of the company's territories is diminished instead of increasing, and that troubles with some of the 300 tribes are more frequent (instead of far less frequent) than they used to be prior to the issue of the charter: who rake up as a new event the old story which appeared in the newspapers last July of the deplorable mutiny of the Zweifel(8) exploring expedition in March last, when the white men in charge were compelled, in defence of their lives and to save a native town from being wrecked, to shoot down seven out of 150 mutineers; who magnify these seven deaths to 15 or 20, and characterize this deplorable but necessary loss of life as a revolting massacre; and who, finally, make utterly unfounded and unjustifiable assertions that the proved conscientious and tactful officials of the company in the territories are discourteous and arrogant to natives and Europeans.

With regard, however, to the "African Merchants' " letter, I would point out that their arguments and fears entirely rest on two erroneous assumptions—first, that the Niger Company has applied to Her Majesty's Government for an extension of its charter over the Oil Rivers; and, secondly , that if such extension were to take place the shareholders of the Niger Company would reap commercial advantage therefrom.

The plain facts are these. The majority of the Oil River merchants—representing, as I am informed, seven-eighths of the Oil River trade—expressed some months ago their hope that Her Majesty's Government would extend the charter of the Niger Company over the Oil Rivers, on the ground that, in their opinion, the regions in which they carry on their operations could not (at any rate for many years) be satisfactorily administered and developed as a Crown Colony. The Niger Company thereupon expressed its concurrence, provided that the following fundamental principles were secured:—1) That the existing commercial interests of the present shareholders of the company should not be in the slightest degree prejudiced thereby; and 2) That these interests should not be commercially benefitted thereby, inasmuch as the company could not admit that it should hereafter be alleged that it had desired, for unfair commercial advantage, the extension of a charter granted for the general benefit of commerce.

These conditions were fortunately reduced to writing and largely circulated long before the commencement of the present agitation, so that the most sceptical critic will find it difficult honestly to throw doubt or ridicule on the *bona fides* of the Niger Company. On the other hand, "African Merchants" will, I trust, now recognise that it was never contemplated that their interests and those of everybody concerned should not be duly considered, or, I may add, that the very principles which they advocate in last paragraph of their letter should not be carried out.

I do not deny that the Niger Company would be glad, for administrative reasons, to see an extension of the charter over the Oil Rivers, subject to the above conditions. The peaceful settlement of the interior of Africa at the back of these rivers, corresponding to that which has, so far, been successfully carried on in the company's territories, (9) would have a most beneficial political effect on the latter. These now have contiguous to their long and straggling frontier barbarous countries given over to incessant inter-tribal wars, slave raids, and cannibalism, as were formerly, and still are to some extent, the tribes in the company's territories. With the introduction of commerce, and, later on, of agriculture, (10) these neighbouring regions would gradually become peaceful and cease to be a source of danger to the territories. Moreover, the council of the company have—incredible as it may seem to *les esprits forts*—a strong and disinterested ambition, as they had when they founded the company, to see these regions, with which they are so closely connected, grow under their auspices from barbarism to civilization, from anarchy to order, from slavery to freedom, and from universal poverty to a source of wealth both to the natives of the country and to the overcrowded working classes of Great Britain. (11)

I am, Sir, your obedient servant.
GEORGE TAUBMAN GOLDIE,
Political Administrator.
Surrey-house, Victoria Embankment, Jan. 3.

(1) They were:—Mr. James Picton, Radical, Leicester; Mr. Legh, Lancashire, S.W.; Mr. Henry Labouchere, Northampton; Mr. W. F. Lawrence, Liverpool; Sir George Campbell, Newton; Mr. Molloy, King's Co., Birr; Mr. Conybeare, Cornwall, Camborne. The House divided on Picton's motion to reduce the salary of the Consul at Old Calabar by £100. The motion was defeated by a majority of 93 with 50 votes for it and 143 against. The debate was notable for Picton's extreme hostility to the R.N.C., and to the proposal then being mooted to extend its Charter to take in the whole of the Oil Rivers Protectorate (later to be the Niger Coast Protectorate). The Consul at Old Calabar was Consul Hewitt. Picton was at pains to point out that he had no complaint with his performance, only with the R.N.C.'s. Hansard, 17 December, 1888. 562-572.

(2) See Lord Aberdare's speech at the eighth ordinary general meeting of the R.N.C., held on 31 July, 1888. Report in the *Times,* 2 August, 1888. Aberdare also stated, however, that in the much larger inner zone, consisting of all the territory over 300 miles from the coast, the duty was at 12% *ad valorem*—a fact which Goldie does not disclose in his letter.

(3) Not unnaturally, Goldie was fond of pressing this point, which had a considerable appeal to an economy-conscious Treasury and Parliament. His appreciation of the Congo situation at this period, however, was somewhat ingenuous, not to say "starry-eyed."

(4) Also in Aberdare's speech at the 1888 R.N.C. Annual General Meeting.

(5) The beginning of a recurrent theme. Goldie always claimed that it was this rule by methods other than "colonial ideas" that differentiated the R.N.C. from any similar

organisations. He is here putting heavy weight on "the civilizing influences of trade," see pages 225-226 and (especially) page 109.

(6) A suitably vague reference that could apply to either Stanley or Johnston, both of whom Goldie was very fond of quoting.

(7) Here is the first trace of a fundamental principle of the Doctrine of Indirect Rule. At the moment, Goldie seems to be groping towards an understanding of the logical conclusion of his argument. His reference to the Congo looks almost like special pleading.

(8) "The Zweifel Case," as it came to be known, very nearly provided a *cause celèbre* of the utmost embarrassment to the Company. In March, 1888, a Swiss national, Herr Joshué Zweifel, who had formerly been in the employ of the French "Verminck" Company, and who had joined the Niger Company after 1884 when Goldie had bought the French Companies out, had just returned to Lokoja from a botanical exploratory expedition on behalf of the R.N.C. On 21st of that month, his carriers, mostly from Sierra Leone and the Gold Coast, "mutinied." Wallace, the Senior Executive Officer on the spot, and a small force of five other Europeans and twelve Gold Coast constables, together with a contingent of "Lokoja Warriors," tried to overawe the carriers and make them hand in their axes, knives, and matchetes. In the process, a ringleader was perceived to be assaulting the police, and Wallace shot him dead. The police then opened fire and a number of the carriers were wounded, some later dying. The affair did not become known until the July, when several papers "ran" stories on it emanating from Lagos, Freetown and Accra. Salisbury and the Foreign Office inclined to side with the Company, but the Colonial Office under Lord Knutsford, was avid for Wallace and Zweifel being tried for murder, though, in the end, nothing came of it.

(9) This claim, of course, constitutes an effective counter to Flora Shaw's assertion that the R.N.C. exercised very little influence or control in the hinterland.

(10) Goldie's references to the solid base of future development which agriculture alone provides have been noted before.

(11) Mary Kingsley echoes these sentiments faithfully in her book *West African Studies,* published in 1899 by Macmillan & Co. It should be noted, however, that when the issue finally came to be resolved, the Company's Charter was not extended to cover the Oil Rivers. Instead, the area became "The Niger Coast Protectorate" and then, in 1906, a part of Southern Nigeria.

II. THE HOENIGSBERG CASE AND CONFLICT WITH GERMANY

Mary Kingsley, whose style was often refreshingly racy, stated unequivocally that "Liverpool . . . hates the Royal Niger Company like the devil."[1] This situation the previous correspondence reflects. She also, however,ascribes this animosity to the Company's policy in regard to the Liquor Trade (a policy which this selection of Goldie's thinking makes abundantly clear) and to its tendency to "keep its ain guts for its ain sea mews." It can readily be appreciated therefore, that if "Liverpool" chafed under the system, others, like France and Germany, were likely to do so even more.

The first challenge to the Company, outside that of "Liverpool" of course, came from Germany, a newcomer to the Colonial field, but one which already had acquired a considerable influence in the territory contiguous to the Niger Delta as a result of it having snapped up the colony of Kamerun under the nose of a dilatory Foreign Office in 1884.

In the pre-Charter period, the Company had won out over several private or semi-official attempts to advance Germany's claims in the Niger basin. After the granting of the Charter, however, the struggle was renewed on an official basis, with Bismarck himself taking a hand.

The result was that in 1887, under the stimulation of the Hambourg liquor interests according to Goldie, a series of complaints began to filter back to the German Foreign Minister alleging discrimination by the Company against a Herr Jacob Hoenigsberg, whose activities, it was alleged, the Company was seriously curtailing. There is a great deal of evidence now available to indicate that the whole complaint was a put up job, a situation, incidentally, which Goldie always stoutly maintained to be the case. At all events, Hoenigsberg now started actively to intrigue with the Emir of Nupe Maliki (1884-1895) against the Company and with every indication of some success, [2] so much so that the Company's position began to be seriously affected. This was in December of 1887.

The Company, therefore, began proceedings against Herr Hoenigsberg before its Chief Justice, Sir James Marshall who sentenced him to be deported. In accordance with this sentence, he was escorted out of the Company's territory and took up residence in Lagos, where he again started a business.

The diplomatic repercussions, however, were considerable. Both the British and German Governments appointed Commissions to investigate. The British Commissioner, Major, later Sir Claude MacDonald, after a long and scrupulous enquiry, found unhesitatingly in favour of the Company. The report of the German Commissioner is the subject of Goldie's communication to the *Times*.

It is difficult to classify this communication as a "letter." It is, in fact, much closer to being a "Position Paper." As such it constitutes a very valuable exposition of Goldie's reaction to the whole affair.

In the event, the whole matter fizzled out, greatly assisted by Bismarck's fall, and by the signing of the Anglo-German "Heligoland" Treaty in 1890.

3. 23 December, 1889. Page 12, Column 2.

GERMANY AND THE NIGER COMPANY

As the German government have published in a White-book their Consul's [3] report of his late visit to the Niger territories, without awaiting the return of the British Commissioner, [4] the Governor and Council of the Royal Niger Company have drawn up for the shareholders the following memorandum:—

1. The complete inaccuracy of all the statements on which the German Consul bases his attack on the general methods of the company's government, and on British rights of jurisdiction (through the company) in certain districts, can only be explained by a reference to the struggle, prior to July, 1886, between the company on the one hand and the late Herr Flegel, [5] supported by the German Colonial Society, on the other hand for the present central African zone of the Niger territories. This struggle, which had previously been carried on with extraordinary energy by Mr. David M'Intosh, then agent-general of the company, ended in July,1886, in favour of Great Britain—first, through the treaties made by Mr. Joseph Thomson, [6] on behalf of the company, with the Sultans of the empires of Sokoto and Gandu, after an exciting race with Herr Flegel; secondly, through the death of Herr Flegel; thirdly, through the issue of a Royal charter to the company by Mr. Gladstone's Government; and, lastly, through the agreement of 1886 between that Government and Prince Bismarck.

2. By that agreement a demarcation line was drawn between the spheres of influence of the two countries in their respective regions of the Cameroons and the Niger. Great Britain engaged not to make acquisitions, accept protectorates, or interfere with the extension of German influence to the east of that line, thus leaving Germany a free hand in extending her Cameroons possessions over a vast section of Africa. Germany entered into similar engagements as to the Niger regions west of that line.

3. In consequence of that agreement the company at once abandoned its previously-acquired treaty rights over a district to the east of that line and to the south of the Upper Benue, where, however, no German treaties have even yet been made, where no German merchant has even yet ventured, and where no German official has even yet penetrated. [7] Moreover, having learnt by long experience that no European merchant can permanently and safely carry on trade in inner Africa without the protection of European law, the company simultaneously abandoned its commerce in that district. No more convincing

140

proof could have been given of its desire to carry out faithfully the terms of the agreement between Great Britain and Germany.

4. The agreement of 1886 was thus more to the advantage of Germany than of Great Britain, and was no doubt meant to be loyally adhered to by the Governments of both countries. But the powerful liquor and shipping interests in Hamburg, irritated by the high duties imposed by the company on spirits, by the licences for their sale, and, later on, by their total prohibition in one-third of the company's territories, have persistently ignored the international compact thus entered into by the German Chancellor, and have strenuously supported the late efforts of Herr Hoenigsberg, now agent at Lagos of the principal Hamburg distillers, to undermine the company's jurisdiction within the British sphere. No one can doubt this attitude who has read the virulent articles published in 1888 in the German colonial organs and the petition of the Hamburg Chamber of Commerce to Prince Bismarck, dated the 3rd of September, 1888. In these documents the long political struggle with Herr Flegel, prior to the agreement of 1886, is raked up, distorted, and exaggerated, and is made to serve as the basis of the attack on the rights of jurisdiction of Great Britain (through the company) in Central Africa. No one could deny the great ability, energy, and patriotism which were displayed by Herr Flegel, who refused the offers of the company to establish and support him liberally as a trader if he would abandon his efforts to shake its political influence, which at that time (November, 1884) was very insecure. (8) But the Sokoto and Gandu treaties, the issue of the charter, and the Anglo-German agreement have consecrated the British rights as a *fait accompli*, just as similar treaties, charters and Anglo-German agreements have consecrated less effective German rights in the interior of the territories of the German East African Company, and in Germany's possessions in South-West Africa—the only difference being that these rights of Germany are respected by Englishmen.

5. Every effort has also been made by the liquor and shipping interests in Hamburg to lead the public in Germany and Great Britain to believe that numerous German traders have had occasion to complain of the action of the Niger Government. It is therefore well to point out again—although it will certainly be ignored, as heretofore, in the next attack from Hamburg—that, since the first discovery of the Lower Niger by an Englishman in 1829, there has never been a single German trader established in any part of the company's territories excepting Herr Hoenigsberg. The latter had not, prior to the issue of the charter ventured into those inland regions of Africa, where, but for the company, the lives and property of traders would be at the mercy of capricious and grasping native chiefs. About 18 months after he established at Egga, the late Sir James Marshall sentenced him to imprisonment (with the option of leaving the territories) for intrigues bringing danger on the whole European community. (9) Sir James Marshall was at that time the company's Chief Justice, but he had previously been well known for years as Chief Justice of the neighbouring Gold Coast Colony. If the agreement between Germany and Great Britain had not existed, the action of Herr Hoenigsberg, who spared himself no pains in setting at defiance the laws of the territories, and who, it is said, openly boasted that he would "burst up the charter," might have been considered politically justifiable as a patriotic endeavour to wrest these regions from British influence, however deplorable it was in the general interests of European commerce and civilization. But in view of that agreement, the company trusts that the Imperial Government of Germany will, on consideration, see the justice of Sir James Marshall's decision, and will not endorse the German Consul's assertion that it was "quite unjustifiable," and seemed "to be a kind of revenge on Hoenigsberg."

6. The above preliminary remarks appear essential to explain the extraordinary inaccuracies in the report of the German Consul of his late visit to the Niger territories. His two companions were Herr Hoenigsberg's son, who acted as his "protocolist," and Davis—a negro—who acted as his "interpreter." This selection of Abdurraham Davis(10) was peculiarly unfortunate, as he had been Herr Flegel's interpreter during the "scramble for Africa," and was known to be one of the most bitter enemies of the company. The result of relying on such an interpreter is shown in the German Consul's report of the extraordinary statement supposed to have been made to him by the Emir of Nupe, a tributary of the Sultan of Gandu. The important question as to jurisdiction in Nupe—on which alone is based the assertion that the company has infringed the Free Transit Act of Berlin, and should therefore compensate Herr Hoenigsberg—cannot be dealt with fully in this short memorandum; but the absolute untrustworthiness of the negro Davis as an interpreter so vitally affects the value of the German Consul's report in other matters, when he was equally dependent on Davis's translation, that it is necessary to refer briefly to the Nupe interview. The German Consul states that the Emir Moleki (whom he styles "the king") of Nupe, having informed him that he had made a treaty with the Royal Niger Company, said, "All Englishmen living in the territory of Nupe are exempted from the jurisdiction of the king, and subject to that of the company's agent at Egga." "On my (the Consul) asking whether this meant really only Englishmen, or also representatives of other European States, Moleki declared that he could not enter into such nice distinctions; that when he concluded the treaty he thought that all the white men belonged to the same race, and naturally stood under the direction of the chief of the company, and that there really only were Englishmen with some subordinate varieties." Now, while it is satisfactory that the Emir of Nupe is thus admitted to have asserted that he had by treaty conferred rights of jurisdiction on the company, it is incredible that he should, even as a jest, have attempted to impose so grossly upon the German Consul as to pretend that he—of all African potentates—had believed at the time of the treaty that "all white men belonged to the same race," and that "there really only were Englishmen with some subordinate varieties." The only legitimate conclusion is that the negro dragoman(11) Davis played his part in the matter that might have been expected; and if so in this instance, what value can be attached to other parts of the report based on his translations? The astonishing thing is that the German Consul should have accepted and reported such a statement as the above. There is probably not an Emir of any single province in the empires of Gandu and Sokoto who is not aware of the mutual independence of the leading European nations. The constant movement of pilgrims to and from Mecca keeps every Emir informed, though of course tardily and imperfectly, of the rumours of the bazaars of Cairo and Constantinople. But the Emirs of Nupe have had exceptional sources of information. Their capital has been visited during the last 60 years by white persons of various nationalities. No one will believe that Herr Flegel, during his long and bitter struggle, allowed the Emir of Nupe to think that Germans were only a variety of Englishmen, or in any way under the company. Moreover, two powerful French houses had, previously to the treaty, been contesting with the company for influence in the Niger, and especially in Nupe, and had only retired after strenuous efforts, continued for over two years, and after the loss of large sums of money. It is certain that the French agents during this rivalry did not represent their country as a dependency of England, nor themselves as only a variety of Englishmen. For the German Consul to have accepted such an incredible statement from his interpreter he must have entered the Niger with his mind too ready to endorse all the unfounded assertions in the above-mentioned

142

Hamburg documents, and to accept unquestioned everything told him by Abdurrahman Davis.

7. It is specially worthy of note that at the close of this interview with the German Consul the Emir of Nupe sent a letter in Arabic to the company at Egga, expressing his loyalty to his treaty with the company, and saying, among other things, "He, the stranger (i.e., the German Consul), said he is the Queen of England's messenger, but I could say nothing at all to him until I see you;" and again, "The stranger said he is a messenger from the Queen. I do not dispute that, whether true or false." (12) The company is unwilling to imagine that the German Consul really tried to pass himself off as a messenger from Her Majesty; but if the above is a specimen of the way in which Abdurrahman Davis translated the German Consul's speeches, it is not surprising that the latter should be so completely mistaken as to the general facts on which he bases his criticism of the system followed by the Niger Government. His misstatements (presumably based on Davis's information) and the real facts in reply to them will now be indicated.

8. He says, "The large towns have simply been closed and all traffic with them forbidden, as in the case of the populous towns of Onitsha, Idah, etc., as in them there would have been competition of other merchants." This is a mistake. It is impossible to say what towns he includes under "etc.," but not only has the Niger Government never closed Idah to trade, but that place has actually been a port of entry for vessels ever since the issue of the charter. As a matter of fact, Onitsha, the most turbulent place in the territories, and the scene of constant trouble prior to the charter, is the only town that has ever been closed to trade. The prohibition, of course, extended as fully to the trade of the company as to that of other foreigners. As the company at that time (1886) was the only European trade in the territories, and had large commercial establishments at Onitsha, it cannot be seriously contended that the closing was in order to prevent competition. Moreover, in another part of his report, the German Consul says that "competition with the powerful and admirably organized company is as good as impossible in the same locality," which, whether true or not, is plainly inconsistent with his previous and absolutely unfounded imputation of motives for closing "Onitsha, Idah, etc."

9. He says, "This principle is brought into startling relief by the legal regulation, that foreign merchants may only found factories and carry on trade where a factory of the company already exists. As competition with the powerful and admirably organized company is as good as impossible in the same locality, the monopoly is clearly expressed thereby." This is a mistake. No such regulation exists. The company, as a trader, is as much a "foreigner" in the Niger, and is subject to exactly the same restrictions, as any other merchant. (13) Disturbed districts may occasionally have to be absolutely closed for administrative reasons; though only one such instance—that of Onitsha—has actually occurred on the Niger since the issue of the charter, more than three years ago. But, subject to such possible dispositions in the interests of order, merchants and others, including the company, may live, build, and travel where they will. Trading vessels, including those of the company, may of course only call where there are custom-houses. This principle is more or less stringently followed in every river where free transit is in force, as otherwise it would be impossible to prevent smuggling; but it is especially necessary in the Niger owing to the great number of creeks through which the main river may be reached from the sea, and to the necessity for preventing the smuggling of rifles, cartridges, and spirits. (14) A free transit river, and especially where the revenue will not permit of coastguard supervision along thousands of miles of river bank in a wild and malarious country, must be treated in this respect like a sea coast, where vessels may only

communicate with the shore at certain points, although merchants and others may build, trade, or reside where they please on the land. As there are no less than 20 ports of entry on the 300 miles of the lower Niger, between Akassa and Lokoja, and a large number also on its tributaries or creeks and on the river Benue and the middle Niger above Lokoja, this necessary system imposes no hardship on the commerce either of the company or of other traders in the territories, who are in every respect on the same footing as the company.

10. After a hurried visit to the Niger, and without the least pretence of going into figures as to the amount of revenue raised, he declares that the taxation in the territories must be reduced, and says further "the assertion of the company that they pay these dues as well as other firms can be easily proved on paper and even almost demonstrated by accounts, but the sums in question merely pass from one pocket to another belonging to the same person." And again, "all European commercial establishments subject to the company are systematically ruined and rendered impossible and an artificial commercial monopoly of unexampled exclusiveness is created and strictly exercised." He adduces no evidence in support of these assertions, which are simply quotations, very slightly altered in words, from the above-mentioned Hamburg documents of 1888. They might have been as satisfactorily copied without the trouble of a visit to the territories. Here are the facts in reply to them:—

(a) At the time of the issue of the charter, the company was the only European trader in the territories. It is, therefore, impossible to argue that the charter created a monopoly.

(b) After the charter, two important British firms—who have lately amalgamated—established themselves in the territories, and as they have lately extended their operations, it may be presumed that their profits are not at a lower rate than those of the company, which after several years without dividends, only earns 6 per cent. per annum, a scarcely adequate rate for the risks of trade in inner Africa. It is therefore also impossible to argue that the charter has led to a monopoly.

(c) Since the charter, and in spite of the serious disturbance to trade caused by the restrictions on the liquor traffic, the total commerce of the territories has developed under the government of the company, so that the latter is carrying on an increased trade. At first it paid all the taxation of the territories. It now pays towards administrative expenses 14-15ths of the taxation, and other traders about 1-15th. If the comparatively heavy administrative expenditure of a yet undeveloped but extensive region of inner Africa, incapable of protection by European fleets, demands a higher rate of taxation than suffices for long-settled and developed sea-board colonies, it is the shareholders of the company who have most cause to complain of the nature of things, as merchants of all nationalities will be at all times free to share in the benefits of development due to the expenditure of the company's money during this early stage, when the commerce of the Niger is in its infancy.

(d) If the German Consul's views were correct, and the company really paid no taxes, the administrative revenue would be only £3,000 to £4,000 per annum, which is a *reductio ad absurdum.* (15)

11. He also states that every foreign firm has to pay a £50 general trading licence, and adds:—"Here, therefore, the law makes a clear distinction between foreigners and the company, who may carry on the trade in question without paying for a licence, having consequently an enormous advantage over all competitors." This is a mistake. The company as a trader is as much a "foreigner" in the Niger as any other merchant, and its commercial accounts are duly debited and its administrative accounts duly credited with its licences. In no

144

respect is the company, as a trader, placed on any other footing than that of other foreigners. As to the amount of the licence (£50), it may be pointed out that the German Consul was lately the temporary administrator of the neighbouring German colony of the Cameroons, where the licence is £100. (16)

12.   He considers it a decisive proof of unequal taxation or unfair treatment by the company that three petty traders besides Herr Hoenigsberg (not Germans) commenced operations on a very small scale, soon after the issue of the charter, at Egga, about 400 miles from the sea, and withdrew after 12 or 15 months; yet elsewhere, arguing against ports of entry, and not with reference to taxation, he urges that "competition with the powerful and admirably organized company is as good as impossible in the same locality." Now, the company, during the period in question, was unable to earn a profit at Egga. This was partly owing to local bad trade, and partly to the low price of shea *(Bassia Parkii)* in Europe. No petty merchant without a fixed establishment, and therefore free to move his capital to some more secure or more remunerative spot, would employ it without a profit in Central African commerce in hopes of future development or better times; so that the retiring of these small traders only proves that the company, which is obliged for political reasons to maintain permanent establishments at Egga and scores of other places, during bad times as well as good times and at all seasons of the year, is *pro tanto* at a disadvantage with others who may come and go when and as they please. It is true that the disadvantage may be more than compensated by the admirable organization to which the German Consul alludes; but this is the result of the accumulation of the experiences of many years, and has nothing to do with the charter or inequality of taxation or unfair administrative treatment. When the prices of African produce in Europe revive, or the volume of the Niger trade increases so as to permit the earning of profits adequate to the risk, numbers of small traders will, no doubt, at once enter the Niger, and, whether English, German, or of any other nationality, will certainly be welcomed by the company as fellow contributors to the burdensome taxation necessary for the development of the territories and the maintenance of security, justice, and order.

13.   There is one argument which entirely disposes of the German Consul's repetition of Herr Hoenigsberg's charge that "the company crushed his trade so as to prevent competition," as if the petty trade done by him could have perceptibly affected the volume of the company's trade. During the dry season which followed Herr Hoenigsberg's establishing at Egga he lost the small steam launch which constituted his only means of taking his goods from the sea to Egga, 400 miles up the river, and of bringing his native produce down to the coast. As he could not have obtained another suitable launch from Europe for a long time, his trade, but for the company, would have been stopped, while his expenses at Egga, which in inner Africa are always extremely heavy in proportion to the turnover, would have continued. The company was not then aware of the intrigues which Herr Hoenigsberg was carrying on to undermine the treaty rights of the company, and therefore allowed him to ship his merchandise in its light draught steamers. Freight was, of course, charged on these cargoes, but such a policy would certainly not have been followed by a company which wished, as the German Consul says, to ruin its competitors. During that period also Herr Hoenigsberg frequently enjoyed the hospitality of the company, and, needless to say, without charge. Yet the German Consul, to strengthen his case, asserts that it is the policy of the company to "grudge even a glass of water." This particular reproach should not have come from the German Consul, who received unstinted hospitality from the company during his visit, and travelled without charge on its steamers. The following more generous recognition of the methods of the

company has been received from Baron von Soden, the Imperial Governor of the Cameroons, in a letter to the company, dated September 3, 1889:—

(Translation.)

"The mail which has just arrived brings me news from Ibi, on the Benue, of the German traveller, Dr. Zentgraff, who left Cameroon at the end of last year and had not been heard of since.

"I hasten to render you my best and cordial thanks for the hospitable reception and effectual assistance which the German traveller has received at your hands and those of the officials of your company, and which he acknowledges with high praise."

14. If the company were to reverse its policy in regard to the liquor traffic, if it were to abolish its spirit licences and its high duties on spirits, if it were to repeal its total prohibition of the liquor trade in the Benue regions of its territories, and to abandon its declared intention of similar prohibition in the Middle Niger regions above Lokoja, the liquor and shipping interests in Hamburg and their energetic representative in the Reichstag—Herr Woermann—would no doubt declare it to be a model government and would cease to dispute the rights of Great Britain within the British sphere of influence, while the persistent calumnies against the company by the petty coloured and white traders in Lagos and on the neighbouring coast would no longer be invented. But such a reversal of its policy would mean not only an immediate return of the liquor traffic in the Lower Niger regions from the present insignificant amount to the far larger dimensions of a few years ago, but the flooding with spirits of the extensive and populous regions lately opened up to European commerce by the efforts of the .company. The Governor and Council have never put forward any philanthropic motives for their policy in this respect, but have always stated their belief that the permanent interests of the company, both pecuniarily and as a government, are bound up with those of the peoples of the territories. They are convinced that, with an unrestrained liquor trade, no progressive and permanent commerce, no general development of agriculture, and no widespread introduction of the industrial arts can be expected in those regions of tropical Africa where, fortunately for the natives, they cannot be improved off the face of the earth by European colonists, as in other and healthier parts of the world. (17)

GEORGE TAUBMAN GOLDIE, Deputy-Governor.

London, Dec. 16.

(1) See Kingsley to Edward Clodd. Letter dated 16 February, 1898, in Edward Clodd, *Memories,* Chapman & Hall, London, 1916, page 80.

(2) See F.O. 84, 2109 X/J 5351. The Author has also in his possession a copy of a letter from the Emir to Willian Wallace, the Company's Agent at Lokoja, in which his view of the proper relationship between the Company and himself is radically different from those that the Company entertained! This aspect is not suitable for consideration here as discussion of it would need to be extensive.

(3) The German Commissioner was Jesco von Puttkammer (b. 1855). Prussian Civil Service, 1883, German Consulate, Chicago. 1885, sent to Kamerun as "interim Chancellor," being later appointed German Consul, Lagos. In 1889, he undertook the German enquiry into the Hoenigsberg case. 1891, appointed Administrator of Togo; 1895, Governor of Kamerun. 1906, recalled on account of his severity in dealing with native rulers, in particular the Duala Chief Dika Akwa. Von Puttkammer was Bismarck's wife's nephew.

(4) Major (Sir) Claude Macdonald, later of the Oil Rivers Protectorate.

(5) See page 96.

(6) See pages 74 footnote; 234-5 and 239-40.

(7) Goldie's real reason for the abandonment of this "narrow" strip of country are dealt with elsewhere.

(8) An interesting confession of weakness, the validity of which is not often appreciated.

(9) Macdonald considered this fear to have been justified. Even the most recent data, however, hardly bears out so extreme a view, though judging from hindsight is often distorting.

(10) Abdurrahman Davis was a Moslem Sierra Leoneian.

(11) Goldie's use of the Turkish "Dragoman" *is*, of course, deliberate and is intended to contrast this "tourist guide" with the Company's own "Native Diplomatic Agents." See page 161.

(12) This letter is not available. A much stronger letter is, however, the existence of which would seem to deny the authenticity of the one referred to.

(13) A quotation from Lord Aberdare's address to the R.N.C. Annual Meeting. See page 134.

(14) This prophecy proved only too true in 1894 when the "Brassmen" revolted against the Company's Customs restrictions.

(15) According to the arguments here advanced by Goldie, the Company's Administrative Expenditure works out to about £55,000 per annum.

(16) Von Puttkammer must have found this point well taken, though it all depends on whether a Licence Fee is levied in concert with or in lieu of other exactions.

(17) No-one, reading this passage can fail to be convinced of Goldie's unfailing respect for native culture and native institutions. In the context of his day, the view as he expressed it was almost revolutionary! Goldie's sentiments are reflected in the motto of the Company, Ars, Jus, Pax.

III. L'AFFAIRE MIZON

4. 11 August, 1891. Page 18 Column 4.

THE CRAMPEL MASSACRE

TO THE EDITOR OF THE TIMES

Sir,—The French Press, from the *Gazette de France* down to, or up to, the *Intransigeant,* hints or asserts boldly that this disaster—deplorable in the common interests of European prestige in Africa—is due to the intrigues of the Royal Niger Company. May I point out, once for all, that the Niger Company had no interest in the failure of M. Crampel's expedition? The kingdom of Bornu is clearly reserved to the sphere of influence of the company by the Anglo-French agreement of August, 1890, and the company, with half a million square miles of tropical Africa to develop, has no desire to enter into conflict with Mahdism and Senoussism between Lake Tchad and the Nile. I should be sorry to see England engage in this costly and unprofitable enterprise, which is better suited for the more ideal ambitions of France.

As I have mentioned Lake Tchad, I would point out the extraordinary ignorance of the French Press in treating this region as unknown, except from the travels of Barth and Nachtigal. The Niger Company has been for some years in constant communication with this region, from which it draws a considerable amount of commerce. Only last year one of the company's expeditions visited Kuka (on Lake Tchad), the capital of Bornu, and the European leaders of the expedition apparently thought no more of their journey than does the British householder at this holiday season of his trip to Eastbourne or Trouville.

I am, Sir, your obedient servant,
GEORGE TAUBMAN GOLDIE.
August 10.

Goldie had a clear justification for complaint on this and allied issues. The vituperation to which the activities of the R.N.C. were subjected in the French Press was, in the main, inexcusable, frenetic and hysterical. Goldie does, however, have cause to be grateful for its sensationalism at a later stage of *L'Affaire Mizon,* when the accusations of Dr. Henri Ward received the fullest publicity. For a note on Crampel, see page 68.

This letter also has significance in view of Goldie's disapproval of part of Lugard's paper to the R.G.S., which involved this very issue of the ability of the Company's servants to move about freely.

L'Affaire Mizon, of which the preceding letter was merely a prelude, was the most bitter and far-reaching confrontation between France and the Company. Goldie, in fact, attributes to it and to it alone the cause of the, as he saw it, premature revocation of the Charter. In historical perspective, it appears that, far more so than in the Hoenigsberg case, the Company was utterly and completely justified in the stand that it took and Goldie is not to be blamed when later he underlines this fact. In view of the importance of this case, letters both by Mizon and by Lord Aberdare have been introduced to permit sides to be presented. The correspondence opens as follows:—

5.   21 December, 1892. Page 3 Column 6.

ENGLAND *and* FRANCE *on* LAKE TCHAD

TO THE EDITOR OF THE TIMES

Sir,—In view of the personal aspersions with which almost every French newspaper liberally bespatters such of its compatriots as happen to differ from its opinions, it is not possible to feel much indignation at the assertions in Paris, reported in your telegraphic news to-day, that the Niger Company's expedition to Bornou delivered to the Sultan a forged letter from Her Majesty. But as the accusation has been made, it may be well to point out the stupidity of this particular calumny. The Royal Niger Company is the authorized representative of Her Majesty in the Central Sudan, and if it had considered that the delivery of a Royal letter would have been useful, it would no doubt have obtained one. The Earl of Scarbrough and myself had the honour this year of delivering such a letter to another Mohammedan potentate in those regions. (1) The invention is, therefore, unintelligent in character, and fit only to rank with those monstrous charges of assassination which M. Mizon and his friends preferred against the company last summer, and which Lord Aberdare so completely rebutted and discredited. (2)

I am, Sir, your obedient servant,
GEORGE TAUBMAN GOLDIE.

Royal Niger Company (Chartered and Limited), Surrey House,
Victoria Embankment, W.C., Dec. 19.

26 July, 1892. Page 8 Column 3. (Note date.)

LORD ABERDARE'S LETTER

LIEUTENANT MIZON'S STATEMENTS

TO THE EDITOR OF THE TIMES

Sir,—In the course of my address last week (3) —full copies of which either in English or French can be obtained at the Company's offices—I read a letter from Lieutenant Mizon to our Agent-General, Mr. Flint, which, as I pointed out, must convince every impartial mind that Lieutenant Mizon, seven or eight months after the Patani (4) attack, did not believe in the complicity of the company in that incident. I further showed that, as he was then nearly 300 miles distant from the scene of that attack and was moving up to Adamawa and thence to the Congo, he could not have acquired any subsequent information to modify his views. Lieutenant Mizon has not failed to grasp this complete destruction of his credibility as a witness, and he has therefore endeavoured to lessen the force of this evidence in his own handwriting by two assertions.

The first assertion is that the letter in question was addressed personally to Agent-General Flint. Now as all the orders from home on political matters pass through Mr. Flint, who is the ruler in Africa of the Company's territories, and as Mr. Flint was in the delta region at the time of the attack and personally received Lieutenant Mizon and his party at Akassa immiediately after their rescue by the Company, it is difficult to see how the fact of the letter in question being addressed personally to Mr. Flint weakens its value as evidence against its author, for no one but Mr. Flint could have instructed the Patani savages to murder the French party.

Lieutenant Mizon's second assertion is, however, more extraordinary. It is that he only wrote the letter under compulsion, because Mr. Flint refused otherwise to order the Company's engineers to repair the French launch, and that the cordial expressions in the letter meant no more than "Lord Aberdare when he concludes with 'your humble servant' means that he is humble to or the servant of the person to whom he is writing." The best answer to this is to give Lieutenant Mizon's letter in full and in his own English, as I read it in my address.

Lokoja, June 1, 1891.

Dear Sir,—I have the honour to inform you that within a few days my party will go up Benoue River with my barges, and that I will follow as soon as I will be able to steam my launch, when the broken pieces of machinery will have been repaired according to orders you have sent to the superintendent engineer at Akassa. I know that you seldom go up Benoue River in the dry season, and that you will go home the next month. So I will not be so lucky to meet you again in Niger Territories, but I hope I will do so in Europe after my travel. Will you permit me to offer you my best thanks for all the kindness you have had for my party and for myself when living in Lower Niger. I accept with full heart the expressions of goodwill made by you last Saturday for the success of the mission under my commanding.

I am, dear Sir, yours truly,

L. MIZON.

To J. Flint, Agent-General, Niger Territories.

The terms of this letter deserve careful attention, especially Lieutenant Mizon's desire, very natural according to my view, to meet Mr. Flint again on his return to Europe, his gratitude for all the kindnesses received during the whole of his seven months' residence on the Niger, and his "full heart" for Mr. Flint's good wishes. When Lieutenant Mizon asserts that, simply in order to get his launch repaired, he wrote such a letter to a man who had incited savages to murder him, his French colleagues and his numerous escort, he reduces his credibility as a witness to a lower point, if possible, than it stood at before his explanation.

His position is indeed most unfortunate. When, at a later period, he invented this and other atrocious charges against our officials, in order to magnify the dangers and risks of his journey, he had no doubt forgotten having thus put into writing a final and effective reply to his charges. Nor is he able to contravert my statements that he and his followers had on five separate occasions been given passages on the Company's steamers over a distance, in the aggregate, of over 500 miles, that he received every care and kindness from the Company's medical and

150

other officers in our territories, and that he obtained from our local authorities assistance, including an unsecured loan of over £400, without which he could not have continued his journey.

Having thus shown that no reliance can be placed on any statement of Lieutenant Mizon, it is unnecessary for me to ask you to find space for the very long and detailed address which I delivered on this matter to our shareholders last week, translations of which into French have been despatched to the leading organs not only of France but of Europe; but I would wish, through your columns, to expostulate with papers held in such high repute in this country, no less than abroad, as the *Journal des Débats* and the *Temps,* for adding the weight of their authority to the extravagent inventions of Lieutenant Mizon. The conductors of these papers are far too well acquainted with the English character to suppose that the seven gentlemen in this country, without whose authority nothing of importance is done by their Niger officials, had dabbled in murder and in such villainous or contemptible plots as those imputed to them. These consist of myself as Governor, of Sir George Goldie as Deputy-Governor, of the Earl of Scarbrough, of the Hon. Charles Mills, and of Messrs. Miller, Edgar, and Croft, three gentlemen long acquainted with African trade, and of unblemished personal character. (5)

The mischief of this readiness to believe in British perfidy is very serious. It tends to embitter international relations, and to foster and seemingly to justify national prejudices and antipathies. Observe the immediate consequences of Lieutenant Mizon's accusations. Frenchmen exclaim, "Are we not right in our estimate of English egotism and unscrupulousness, when even a company managed by men apparently respectable, employing agents also respectable, can deliberately plot and endeavour to execute wholesale assassinations and be guilty of every form of meanness, and of the basest intrigues?" And the Press, even in its best representatives in France, instead of calming the excitement, hastens to increase it by adopting these wild statements without one title of trustworthy evidence. Nor is the mischief confined to France. Englishmen, not believing a word of these accusations, who feel convinced of their absurdity and baselessness, draw the natural conclusion that, in spite of near neighbourhood and long friendly relations, the French people and French Press are ready to believe, on the slightest evidence or on no evidence at all, that the English, not only on the Niger but everywhere else, are capable of acts of ferocity and treachery which the most barbarous savages could not exceed. French speakers seem to be surprised at the warmth with which, on the part of ourselves and our officials, we repel these charges of assassination and treachery. What would be their tone if the case was reversed, if the events had taken place on the Senegal or Upper Niger, the accuser being an Englishman, the accused French?

I am, Sir, your obedient servant,

July 25, 1892.   ABERDARE.

27 July, 1892. Page 5 Column 1.

LIEUTENANT MIZON AND LORD ABERDARE
PARIS, JULY 26.

Lieutenant Mizon has forwarded the following letter to Dalziel's Agency for publication, in reply to Lord Aberdare's communciation, which appeared in the English Press this morning:—

"Sir,—Lord Aberdare was not satisfied with bringing a regular list of accusations against me at the annual meeting of his company, but must needs reiterate his charges in a letter, which you have been good enough to communicate to me, and which appears to contain no fresh allegations against me.

"Lord Aberdare in his hostility still confounds me with the whole of the French Press, whom he accuses of partiality. I am not going to pretend to defend the newspapers; but all the same I may remark that they have all reproduced Lord Aberdare's charges against me much more fully than have the English Press, although it is true that this does not show that they are convinced of the truth of the accusations.

"I accuse the Royal Niger Company of forcibly ensuring respect for its flag, and allowing it to be understood, in contravention of the duties imposed upon it by the Treaty of Berlin, that it was indifferent to the respect meted out to other flags, which, as all those who know Africa are aware, is nothing but an instigation to pillage and assassination. That is the original cause of the attack of which I was the victim on the river Forcados.

"Lord Aberdare, to prove that this opinion of mine is a recent one, only publishes the letter which I addressed to Mr. Flint on June 1, 1891, in which I thanked him for his personal attention to me. Lord Aberdare ignores the fact that I wrote this letter at Mr. Flint's own request. However, to refute this puerile argument, I respond:—

"(1) That in the letters which I wrote at Assaba in January, 1891, and which were published in May by the *Bulletin du Comité de l'Afrique Française,* I expressed the same opinion on the attacks of the Patanes as I do to-day, and I even added that Mr. Bedford, one of the company's agents, said that if I had been attacked by the Patanes it was because I had not respected the rules of the company. Lord Aberdare cannot ignore this communication of mine, as it has been the basis of diplomatic *pourparlers.* How, then, can he now pretend that my opinions have changed on this point?

"(2) I repeat once more that I have no reason whatever to complain of Mr. Flint's personal attitude towards me. Even had there been reason to do so, I should certainly have avoided such a proceeding at a time when I was entirely dependent on the good-will of Mr. Flint. I was at that time exhausted by fatigue and illness, and was inspired with the sole aim of reaching Yola at any cost, although every means was used to prevent me.

"(3) In addition to the attacks by the Patanes and numerous petty vexations that I was forced to undergo, I have to complain of another agent of the company, Mr. Mackintosh, who, according to the statements obtained by me at Yola, took measures for having my party massacred while going up stream, although he had given me a cordial welcome. With this object, he did not hesitate to spread lying reports concerning me. These statements were not obtained by me, as Lord Aberdare affirms, on the testimony of a single person, but from Sultan Zoubir himself, (6) from his Ministers, and numerous others. Not believing it possible for a civilized man to be guilty of such abominable conduct, I asked my friends to maintain silence with regard to the disclosures which had been made to me, and for four months I thoroughly investigated the question at Yola and at Garoua. I now accuse Mr. Mackintosh, supported by the confirmatory evidence adduced in the course of this inquiry.

"(4) Above all, I have to censure the general spirit in which the conduct of the Royal Niger Company is conceived, as it is manifestly opposed to the provisions of the Berlin Treaty, to the principles of humanity and good sense, and the commonest loyalty. My opinions on this point were explained last year in a document published by the *Bulletin du Comité de l'Afrique Française,* and I have further strengthened my conclusions by facts which none have disproved. It is quite surprising to find that Lord Aberdare has not transferred the discussion to this most important ground. Have I any need to repeat once more that I openly complain of the general spirit in which affairs are conducted by the Royal Niger Company? If I am forced to consider certain of their agents to be malefactors in view of their conduct, I have, on the other hand, no reason, as Lord Aberdare seems to think I have, for bringing a sweeping accusation against the English, among whom I have many friends, or against the agents of the company as a body, some of whom have shown the greatest courtesy towards me.

"I do not follow the example of Lord Aberdare, who in his letter did not hesitate to indulge in calumnies and insinuations, and to accuse a French officer of bad faith who has had 23 years of honourable service. I shall not cast suspicion on his good faith; but, in view of the facts brought forward by me and the vague contradictions they have called forth, I consider myself justified in saying that Lord Aberdare is either most prejudiced or gifted with little clearness of perception if he imagines that he will succeed in obtaining justification before the eyes of impartial men in all countries for the proceedings to which the company over which he presides has had recourse against Flagel and myself, and which the company contemplate enforcing against merchants of all countries.

"I am, etc.,

"L. MIZON, Lieutenant de Vaisseau."

—*Dalziel.*

28 July, 1892. Page 7 Column 4.

LIEUTENANT MIZON AND LORD ABERDARE

A representative of Dalziel's Agency called upon Lord Aberdare at his residence, No. 39, Prince's gardens, yesterday afternoon to obtain his views concerning Lieutenant Mizon's rejoinder, which was published in *The Times* of yesterday. Lord Aberdare stated that he had had no intention of making any public reply to the grave insinuations contained in Lieutenant Mizon's letter, because he did not deem them worthy of discussion. In the course of conversation he reviewed the matter as follows:—

"Lieutenant Mizon is endeavouring to divert public attention from my charges by discussing questions of the policy and the administration of the Royal Niger Company, which he asserts to have been in violation of the Treaty of Berlin. I never had any intention of discussing these important subjects with him. The company may or may not be right in their view of these matters, but they are wholly outside the subject of my letter. He began by charging the company with having laid plans for his assassination. He then, apparently, on ascertaining that neither I nor my colleagues were capable of such atrocities, charged them on our agents. The publication of his letter to Mr. Flint, however, compelled him to release Mr. Flint from any complicity, and he now throws on Mr. Bedford the charge of having incited the Patanes to attack him on his first entrance into the Niger district and on Mr. Mackintosh that of having, eight months later, suggested his murder to the Sultan of Yola.

"The attack by the Patanes, with the contrivance of which M. Mizon charges Mr. Bedford, presupposes, if his account be true 1) Mr. Bedford's knowledge of the expedition, of which he and the company knew absolutely nothing; 2) Mr. Bedford's knowledge that M. Mizon, against all probability, would enter the Niger by the unused branch called the Forcados instead of by the usual route up the Nun from Akassa; 3) that Mr. Bedford knew that M. Mizon would fall short of fuel exactly where he did fall short—namely, on the banks of the river occupied by the Patanes, and that Mr. Bedford, foreseeing all this, had

153

arranged this murderous attack with a tribe not only under the jurisdiction of the Royal Niger Company, but bitterly hostile to us. I need not say that all these suppositions involve improbability amounting, in fact, to an impossibility. Lieutenant Mizon has so far modified his charge against Mr. Mackintosh as to assert that, although he did not directly incite the Sultan of Yola to assassination, he made such suggestions about the objects of M. Mizon's mission as would have infallibly led to his murder. Of course Mr. Mackintosh indignantly denies all this story, and he has in favour of his credibility not only his well-known loyal character, but the fact that the Sultan treated Lieutenant Mizon and his mission, so far as we can ascertain, with the utmost kindness.

"When, on the reception of the news of the attack on M. Mizon by the Patanes, the French Press generally represented it as the work of the Royal Niger Company, we of course indignantly denied it. I had occasion last year to see some eminent members of the French Government, and then I expressed my astonishment that M. Mizon, a member of a most honourable profession, had not, whatever cause he might have of complaint against the Royal Niger Company, hastened to relieve them from all complicity in the attack upon him. He must have known that his entrance by way of the Forcados was unknown to the company's officers, and that therefore these grave charges were untrue; but he never said a word on the subject until he arrived in Adamawa, when he adopted all the worst accusations of the French Press, and sanctioned them by the authority of his name and his profession. I, therefore, accuse Lieutenant Mizon of a conscious falsification of the facts and of doing his best to arouse and aggravate international jealousies between France and England."

4 August, 1892. Page 3 Column 2.

FRANCE

PARIS, AUG. 3.

Lieutenant Mizon will take leave of M. Carnot at Fontainebleau to-morrow, and will embark at Bordeaux next Wednesday. He intends to ascend the Niger and the Benue up to Yola, whence he will make explorations and endeavour to create commercial relations with the natives.

Lord Aberdare's letter on Lieutenant Mizon, 14 September, 1893, Page 9 Column 4.

THE ROYAL NIGER COMPANY

TO THE EDITOR OF THE TIMES

Sir,—The publicity given to the articles of the *Temps* and *Figaro* denouncing the action of the Royal Niger Company in refusing to assist M. Hoelle in his mission to the expedition lately under the command of Lieutenant Mizon makes it expedient that its reasons for the course pursued should be made known.

I need only revert to the atrocious charges of Lieutenant Mizon against the company in 1891-2 of attempts to murder, of treachery, fraud, etc., for the purpose of explaining the reasons why they strongly objected to his being permitted to take the command last year of a so-called "scientific expedition" through the Niger territories to the upper waters of the Binue. That expedition, which included 12 of Lieutenant Mizon's compatriots, some 40 soldiers from Senegal and Gaboon, with two pieces of artillery and some 30,000 cartridges, was represented by the French Government as a "quite pacific enterprise," and the fullest assurances were given that not only should British interests be respected, but that Lieutenant Mizon would conform scrupulously to their instructions to observe "the very special obligations imposed upon him by the strict observance of the dispositions of the Brussels Conference." The company deferred reluctantly to the pressure of the Foreign Office, with the result that our worst forebodings were realized. They were far exceeded.

Lieutenant Mizon ascended the Binue with two vessels during the brief season when that river is navigable. When he reached that part where both banks are under the rule of the Emir of Muri, a vassal of the Empire of Sokoto, who had entered into a treaty with the company, the validity of which had been recognised by the French Government in 1890, and never questioned since, he contrived to run his larger vessel aground on an island or shoal and to remain there until the waters fell, with the prospect of retaining that position for nine or ten months. It may be said that this might have been an accident; but the two French officers who formed part of the expedition, and who returned to France about May last, declared it to have been purposely done, and all Lieutenant Mizon's subsequent proceedings confirm their statement.

I stated at the general meeting of the company on July 13, the use which Lieutenant Mizon made of his voluntary detention. He declared our treaty with Muri void. He made one himself with the Emir. He established several factories for commerce in the Muri territory. He proclaimed what he called a "French Protectorate of the Central Soudan." He joined his forces to those of the Emir, captured a pagan town in the territories of the company, where 50 natives were killed and 2,000 reduced to slavery. These facts rest not only on the authority of our officials, but of the French officers above mentioned, who had been entreated by their French companions to enlighten the French public on the facts of the case. These facts became, of course, known to the French Government, who, however—so far as I know and believe—took no steps to repress Lieutenant Mizon's lawless proceedings, nor expressed any regret for them either to the British Government or to the company. It was only when the Royal Niger Company acquainted the Foreign Office with their intention, as soon as the rising of the waters in the Binue permitted, to attack, take, or destroy this lawless expedition, which, under the guise of scientific discovery, had committed acts worthy of pirates, that their communciations with the French Government roused M. Develle to the necessity of clearing the French Government from the appearance of conniving with the perpetrators of deeds so injurious to French honour and to the rights of a friendly nation. Lieutenant Mizon was recalled, and the Foreign Office was assured that his vessels would be removed beyond the territories of the company. In the meantime the French flag was flying not only on the French vessels but on their factories. They were carrying on an unlawful trade, they were openly flouting and defying the officials of the company, and were shaking and undermining its authority far beyond the limits of Muri. Strong measures became necessary, and a blockade of the Muri waters was proclaimed by the company. Such being tne state of the case, the company were invited to give a passage on their steamers to M. Hoelle, who was sent to take charge of the vessels of the expedition. But at that time the company had received no information as to the resolution taken by Lieutenant Mizon nor of the movements of the vessels, and the blockade was in full force. They therefore declined to assist M. Hoelle, without otherwise interfering with his full liberty of movement and action. Up to this moment we know not whether M. Mizon intends to obey or disregard the summons of his Government, nor where he is nor what he is doing. We have been informed that since our refusal of a passage to M. Hoelle the French vessels have been moved up to Yola, which I may say in passing, having reference to the town, not to the province, is within the territories of the company. Our officers found the French flag still flying on the Muri factories after the departure of the vessels. These circumstances appear to me to justify the refusal of the company to afford M. Hoelle the assistance we recently and gladly gave to M. Maistre. Until every vestige had disappeared of an expedition which, whatever its original object, had assumed so hostile an attitude towards the company, and whose continued presence in the waters of Muri was to the native Princes the symbol of French triumph over British rights, we persisted in refusing to give any facilities to the movements of French emissaries. Enough mischief had already been done without running the risk of more.

In conclusion, I venture to say that, while I have a great admiration for the ability of the *Temps* and *Figaro,* and equal respect for their character as journals, I cannot but be disappointed at their allowing conduct such as Lieutenant Mizon's has been shown to be to pass without one word, one hint, of moral disapprobation.

I am, Sir, your obedient servant,

ABERDARE, Governor of the Royal Niger
Company.

Duffryn, Mountain Ash, South Wales, Sept. 12.

6. & 7. 30 December, 1893 and 1 January, 1894. Pages 8 Column 2, and 10 Column 3 respectively.

LIEUTENANT MIZON

TO THE EDITOR OF THE TIMES

Sir,—The Niger Company has no intention of discussing at present the rights of Great Britain and France in the Niger basin. But I see that the Paris telegram of your issue to-day quotes from the *Temps* the following question, which demands an immediate answer:—"Will the Niger Company, moreover, deny the authenticity of a certain map published by it in 1886, and just sent to the *Temps* by its Liverpool correspondent," etc.? I reply that the Niger Company has never published any map defining its territories. But I recognize without difficulty, the source from which this error has sprung, and I shall be prepared to expose it fully when the proper time arrives.

I am, Sir, your obedient servant,

GEORGE TAUBMAN GOLDIE.

The Royal Niger Company, London, Dec.29.

LIEUTENANT MIZON

TO THE EDITOR OF THE TIMES

Sir,—I see, by the Paris telegram in your issue of to-day, that the *Temps,* abandoning its assertion that Mr. Morley, the secretary of the Niger Company, had repudiated the letter on June 26, written by him at the direction of the council, now attributes this repudiation to Lord Aberdare, the governor of the company.

Such an allegation, made by a newspaper of the position of the *Temps,* demands an immediate contradiction; and, as Lord Aberdare is not in London at present, I hasten to state that there is no foundation whatever for this new assertion. On the contrary, Lord Aberdare, in his speech at the annual meeting of the company on July 13 last, was most careful to point out that a collision on the Benue could only be avoided by Lieutenant Mizon ceasing to carry on war and to interfere politically in a region which was reserved to British influence by the Anglo-German agreement of 1886 and the Anglo-French agreement of 1890. I may add that Lieutenant Mizon himself had, with the assent of the French Government, recognised this region as British in his letter to Agent-General Flint of December 9, 1890.

I am, Sir, your obedient servant,
GEORGE TAUBMAN GOLDIE.

The Royal Niger Company, London, Dec. 30.

(1) The Emir (then "Chief") of Bussa. See page 196.

(2) This correspondence is reproduced on the pages immediately following. For Goldie's attribution of the revocation of the Charter to the Mizon case, see page 172, and also page 93 with regard to Goldie's views on the publicity which surrounded it.

(3) The Annual Meeting of Shareholders. The 12th Ordinary General Meeting, 20th July, 1892. For a note on Mizon, see page 76.

(4) Shortly after entering the River in 1889, Mizon's boats were attacked by a war-party from the Patani tribe, inhabiting the area around Forcados. One boat was seriously damaged, and the party was only saved by the timely intervention of the Company, which came to the rescue, salvaged the boat, repaired it, and then re-equipped the expedition.

(5) This group, known on the Coast as "The Seven," formed the "Council" of the R.N.C. and were its governing body.

(6) This reference is to Zubeiru, the 4th Lamido (Emir) of Adamawa, with whom Mizon established close relations, and to whom he gave two brass cannon. Zubeiru ruled from 1890 to 1902.

IV. THE RACE FOR NIKKI AND OTHER PROBLEMS ASSOCIATED WITH IT

8. 31 December, 1894. Page 7 Column 5.

THE SCRAMBLE FOR AFRICA

TO THE EDITOR OF THE TIMES

Sir,—The *Débats,* according to your Paris telegram to-day, asserts that the regions in which Captain Lugard is travelling "are simply those over which formal Acts signed by the Bingers, the Crozats, and the Monteils (1) have established" a French protectorate. If it were so, it would be a serious indictment against a friendly nation; but I venture to assert that the *Débats* is mistaken.

The regions in question cover an immense area in what is known in France as *le boucle du Niger.* (2) They are bounded on the south by the ninth parallel of north latitude, which is the limit of the several international agreements between Great Britain, Germany, and France on the Slave, Gold, and Ivory Coasts. They are bounded on the west by Tiebu's country (3) and the French possessions on the Upper Niger, and on the north by the great bend of the Niger to the east of Timbuctoo. They are bounded on the east by Gurma, a province of the Sokoto-Gandu empire within the Niger Company's territories, and by Borgu, with which the company concluded a treaty on January 20, 1890, placing that country under British protection, as fully and clearly announced by Lord Aberdare in July of the same year.

The mass of information collected by the officials of the Niger Company during many years establishes the fact that these regions are not divided into a few large States, but contain great numbers of independent jurisdictions. French readers may arrive at the same conclusion from a careful study of Captain Binger's great work. (4) Now, Messrs. Binger, Crozat, and Monteil have concluded a very limited number of treaties within these vast regions, the greater part of which is still open to the enterprise of England and Germany as well as France. The *Débats* is apparently unaware that England has already acquired the rights there through the exertions of Mr. Ferguson, and that a German expedition from Togoland is now securing portions of those very regions for Germany.

Having had occasion for some years to peruse all cuttings from the Parisian and provincial Press relating to Western Africa, sometimes hundreds in a week, I am struck with the unanimity with which it is held that every portion of Africa north of the Equator not actually secured by another Power, and some portions that are so secured, must be within the French sphere of influence. Undoubtedly,

158

"to him that hath shall be given," and France has achieved much since 1880. On the theory of *Hinterland* alone, and without the support of a single treaty with the natives, she induced England in 1890 to admit the extension of her possessions in Algeria and Tunis to the far-distant Say Barua line, while at the same time France, in complete disregard of the *Hinterland* theory, was hemming in our promising colony on the Gambia, reducing it to a few square miles, and pushing between the Upper Niger and Sierra Leone, thus injuring the existing trade of that colony and destroying its future. France is now similarly threatening the *Hinterland* of our Gold Coast colony. It is with this operation that Captain Lugard, if successful, will interfere; but he has strict instructions to avoid any conflict with French expeditions or trenching in any way on French rights.

I, have the honour to be, Sir, your obedient servant,

GEORGE TAUBMAN GOLDIE, Deputy-
Governor, Royal Niger Company.
London, Dec.29.

9.   2 March, 1895. Page 5 Column 6.

THE SCRAMBLE FOR AFRICA

TO THE EDITOR OF THE TIMES

Sir,—The criticisms on the Niger Company made by M. Deloncle in the Chamber of Deputies, as telegraphed by your Paris Correspondent, call urgently for reply. M. Deloncle, in his usual reckless manner, which, I may point out, is too often shared by most of the Deputies of the colonial party and by newspapers of such high repute as the *Débats* and the *Temps,* asserts that the Niger Company has sunk or otherwise injured the French gunboat Ardent, which lately ascended the river. (5) The best reply to this reckless and unfounded assertion is that the French Government has, through Her Majesty's Secretary of State, quite lately expressed its thanks to the company for the assistance which has been given to the Ardent in its serious difficulties.

As M. Deloncle referred also to Captain Lugard's expedition, I may add that the treaty made by that officer with Nikki has just been received here and proves to be in due form. Your readers will remember that some weeks ago the French semi-official newspapers announced that Captain Decoeur and M. Albi had made a treaty with Nikki, giving France rights over the whole of Borgu, but they made no mention of the fact that Captain Lugard, with a very large expedition, had been there just before. Thereupon the whole French colonial Press denied the British claims to a treaty with Nikki, and, very naturally, ridiculed the idea that so large an expedition could have been at Nikki only a few days before the French travellers without their knowledge. When, a little later, it became certain that Captain Lugard had distanced his French competitors a change of tactics was adopted, and it was asserted that, though it was always well known that Captain Lugard had been at Nikki, the King had declared that no treaty had been made. This assertion also is now disposed of by the arrival of the treaty itself.

I am, Sir, your obedient servant,

GEORGE TAUBMAN GOLDIE.
London, March 1.

10. 5 September, 1896. Page 7 Column 6.

M. THAREL AND THE FRENCH
NIGER COMPANY

TO THE EDITOR OF THE TIMES

Sir,—I have read with the greatest surprise the Paris telegram in your issue of to-day, from which I learn that a M. Tharel controverts with extraordinary vehemence statements which he assumes me to have recently made as to French and British interests to the west of the Niger.

I cannot remember having publicly alluded to this question during the last 12 months. In my speech last month, at the annual meeting of our shareholders, I carefully abstained from any allusion to France or to any conflict of interests to the west of the Niger. May I also add that I am not aware that there is any French company operating in those regions? I cannot, therefore, account for M. Tharel's diatribes otherwise than as an attempt of the extreme section of the colonial party in France to put pressure on the French Government to reopen the Mizon question, on which public opinion in this country long ago pronounced itself.

I am, Sir, your obedient servant,
GEORGE TAUBMAN GOLDIE.
The Royal Niger Company, London, W.C., Sept. 4.

11. 21 November, 1896. Page 10 Column 2.

THE NIGER COMPANY AND THE ILORINS

TO THE EDITOR OF THE TIMES

Sir;—I could not deal adequately with the political questions raised by the letter in your issue of to-day from the Governor of Lagos (6) without repeated references to confidential despatches exchanged during the last ten years between the Foreign Office, the Colonial Office, the Government of the Royal Niger Company, and the Government of Lagos itself.

This seems to me to form a serious objection to the new departure established by Sir Gilbert Carter of the Governor of a Crown colony commencing a public controversy with the Government of a neighbouring British possession, especially at a time when this washing of linen in public is calculated to injure British interests threatened by foreign aggression.

There is, however, one point raised by Sir Gilbert Carter on which I am at liberty to speak, and which calls for immediate reply. He says:—

"Ilorin, unfortunately for the interests of the colony of Lagos, is within the sphere of influence of the Niger Company, though, so far as I am aware, the company has never taken any steps to make this influence felt in any practical manner. No white official has ever been permitted to pay a visit to Ilorin from the Niger Company, except this merit can be claimed by a gentleman who entered the town with his face blacked and in Mohammedan costume, and in this fashion had an interview with the Emir, who would not have been permitted by his people to publicly receive a white man."

If, on the one hand, Sir Gilbert Carter is referring only to the town of Ilorin, his mistake probably arises from the fact that the Niger Company's first treaty with Ilorin, on the 18th of April, 1885, was negotiated by Mr. M. Benson Nicol, one of the numerous coloured diplomatic agents who have rendered such remarkable services to British interests in the Niger territories since the commencement of the "scramble for Africa,"[7] just as the well-known coloured traveller, Mr. Ferguson,[8] has rendered distinguished political service to the British colony of the Gold Coast. Sir Gilbert Carter appears, however, to be unaware that the second treaty with Ilorin, of the 9th of August, 1890, was publicly negotiated in the town of Ilorin by Mr. Watts,[9] a white gentleman who holds the post of executive officer for those regions, and who was received by the reigning Emir and his chiefs with the greatest cordiality.

If, on the other hand, Sir Gilbert Carter is referring to the country of Ilorin, and not only to the town, I must point out that it has been repeatedly travelled over by the officials of the company, including, amongst others, Captain Lugard, that officials of the company are now moving about Ilorin, and that a fort occupied by a considerable force and commanded by an officer in Her Majesty's service was established in Ilorin territory in the early part of this year.

Sir Gilbert Carter's attitude to the Niger Company has been so consistent and is so well known that his really humorous attack would only excite a smile if it were not for the international aspect of the question. Your readers will appreciate the extreme joy with which Sir Gilbert Carter's assertions will be welcomed by the French Press, which is already carrying on a vigorous campaign in the hopes of compelling the French Government to disregard British rights in the valuable territory of Ilorin. It is, therefore, desirable to point out that by the third clause of the Niger Company's treaty of the 9th of August, 1890, the Emir and chiefs of Ilorin agreed as follows:—

"We will not at any time whatever cede any of our territories to any person or State, nor enter into any agreement, treaty, or arrangement with any foreign Government except through and with the consent of the company, or if the company should at any time so desire with the consent of the Government of Her Majesty the Queen of Great Britain and Ireland and Empress of India;" while, by the fourth clause, they agreed to place their country under British protection.

I am, Sir, your obedient,
GEORGE TAUBMAN GOLDIE, Governor of
the Royal Niger Company.

London, Nov.20.

By any standards applicable to it, Governor Carter's letter to the *Times* was an extraordinary document. In the first place, it must be regarded as unusual, if not irregular, for the Governor of a Crown Colony, subordinate to the Secretary of State for the Colonies, to engage in the public airing of a dispute with an organisation (such as Goldie's was) for which the Foreign Office was ultimately responsible. In the second place, his letter is shot through with inaccuracies, special pleading and mis-statement of fact. In the cold light of hindsight, Goldie's reply to this intemperate outburst must be regarded as a model of restraint! Governor Carter wrote:—

November 20, 1896. Page 8 Column 4.

THE NIGER COMPANY AND THE ILORINS

TO THE EDITOR OF THE TIMES

Sir,—I shall be obliged if you will correct an important error which has occurred

161

in your report of an interview between a representaive of Reuter's Agency and myself in regard to the Ilorins in your issue of to-day.

In this report I am represented to have said:—

"With regard to the criticisms passed upon the Lagos Government I am quite aware of extenuating circumstances which should deter the Niger Company from taking measures to reduce their people to submission and to prevent future inroads upon the Lagos sphere."

My statement was directly contrary to this, and should have been that I was not aware of the "extenuating circumstances" claimed for the Ilorins by the writer of the article headed "The Royal Niger Company" in *The Times* of the 16th inst.

Ilorin, unfortunately for the interests of the colony of Lagos, is within the sphere of influence of the Niger Company, though, so far as I am aware the company has never taken any steps to make this influence felt in any practical manner. No white official has ever been permitted to pay a visit to Ilorin from the Niger Company, except this merit can be claimed by a gentleman who entered the town with his face blacked and in Mohammedan costume, and in this fashion had an interview with the Emir, who would not have been permitted by his people to publicly receive a white man.

Ilorin has been for years a menace to the Yoruba country, which is the *Hinterland*(10) of Lagos, formerly a Yoruba town and the headquarters of the Generalissimo of the Yoruba army. An ambitious functionary, named Alfonja,(11) rebelled and invited some warlike Foulahs and Gambaris from across the Niger to assist, the result being the conquest of the whole Yoruba country by the strangers, who professed the Mohammedan religion. Alfonja was killed when he could be made no further use of, and thus the strangers remained masters of the country. Yoruba remained under their yoke for many years, but at length the inhabitants of a large town called Ibadan rose, reconquered all the old Yoruba towns, and drove the invaders back to Ilorin. This was the state of affairs when I arrived in Lagos in 1891, but a desultory war was still in progress, its sole object on either side being the maintenance of the slave trade. The Ibadan army, consisting of about 20,000 men, was encamped at a place called Ikirun, and the Ilorin army, which was much smaller, but had the advantage of troops of cavalry, was settled at Offa a few hours march from Ilorin.

The object of this so-called war was, of course, not to kill, but to capture slaves and to plunder, and it will be readily understood that neither side was anxious to come to a permanent settlement. It was, however, felt at Lagos that while such a state of things lasted it was impossible that any industry could flourish or that the trade upon which Lagos depended could materially develop. Successive administrations had, therefore, endeavoured to put an end to the existing state of things, but without success.

It is true that two very material obstacles stood in their way—viz., the attitude assumed by two independent States which stood between Yoruba proper and the Lagoon—Jebu(12) and Egba.(13) The authorities of these two States insisted upon acting as middlemen between the Yoruba country and Lagos, and their geographical position enabled them effectively to do so. All native produce had to be sold in their markets, and at their price, and upon the smallest provocation the roads were stopped and no produce was permitted to reach Lagos. The Jebus especially were a savage, intractable people, practising human sacrifices and other barbarous rites. Owing to the wilful violation of a treaty and the threat to kill a white officer who was sent to demand explanations, an expedition was sent against the Jebus in 1892, resulting in the subjugation of that country. A further result of this expedition was that the Egbas were brought to

162

reason, and sent a deputation to Lagos inviting the Governor to visit Abeokuta, the capital of the country, a courtesy which had been denied all previous Governors.

It was now considered that the state of the country was ripe for the peaceful expedition to the Yoruba country which followed in 1893 to endeavour to induce the Ibadan and Ilorin armies to return home; this, as is well known, was successfully accomplished, and steps have since been taken, by a military occupation of important points in the Yoruba country, to prevent the recurrence of the inter-tribal wars which so seriously interfere with trade and the general prosperity of the country.

It is perhaps hardly to be expected that the Ilorins will acquiesce quietly in a policy which has deprived them of what doubtless they conceive to be a legitimate means of subsistence—viz., slave-raiding and robbery, and possibly this is what is meant by the "extenuating circumstances" claimed by the Ilorins. It is, however, hardly the *rôle* of a civilized Government to look at the question from this point of view. There is no question as to the beneficial results of the policy which has been followed during my five years' administration of the affairs of Lagos. Thanks to the splendid services of that distinguished officer Captain Bower (14) slave raiding in the Yoruba country has practically ceased to exist, and the natives are now enabled to settle down peaceably to agricultural pursuits, which is the natural industry of the people.

I am, Sir, your obedient servant,
GILBERT T. CARTER, Governor of Lagos.
November 19.

We regret the mistake to which Sir Gilbert Carter refers. Reuter's message reached us correctly. (15)

(1) See page 78.

(2) i.e. "The Niger Bend."

(3) By "Tiebu's country," Goldie has in mind the area in modern Mali between the Bagoé and Black Volta Rivers. It was then ruled by "King" Tiéba of Sikasso who warred with Samori from c. 1870 onwards along his eastern frontier, often in a sort of alliance with the French. In 1888, Tiéba signed a treaty accepting French protection, but in 1898, Sikasso was occupied, and his successor, Ba Bemba, seeing the town being sacked, committed suicide.

(4) *Du Niger au Golfe de Guinée par le Pays de Kong et le Mossi; Par le Capitaine Binger (1887-1889)*, Hachette, Paris, 1892.

(5) See page 92. The Deputy François Deloncle, an ardent colonialist!

(6) Carter, Sir Gilbert, c. 1844-1927. 1864, Royal Naval detachment, Ashanti Campaign; 1875; P.S. to Governor, Leeward Islands; 1879, Collector of Customs and Treasurer, Gold Coast; 1882, Treasurer and Postmaster, Gambia; 1888, Administrator, Gambia; 1890-98, Governor, Lagos; 1898-1904, of Bahamas; 1904-1910, of Barbados.

(7) See pages 141-142. The Company's record in respect of the promotion of African Staff was excellent.

(8) George Ekem Ferguson, the main agent for the spread of British rule in the Northern Territories of the Gold Coast. See also pages 158 and 201.

(9) Watts, Walter, FRGS. A long-time Agent-in-Charge at Eggan, and a key man on the Middle Niger. One of the few Europeans who spoke fluent Nupe, his Hausa nickname was *Biri* (Monkey). In 1900, Watts became one of the re-organised Company's Agents-General.

(10) It is not without a certain piquancy to see Sir Gilbert invoking the *Hinterland* doctrine in the same way that would have been appropriate in dealing with a Foreign Power.

(11) Actually it was Afonja, c. 1785-1831. Afonja (L'aya l'oko; "Brave Warrior in the Bush") rebelled against the Alafin of Oyo, Aole, in 1817. He then invoked the aid of

Mallam Alimi, a Fulani Preacher living in Ogbomosho. Afonja was killed in a civil war fomented by Mallam Alimi's sons shortly after he died in 1831.

(12) For an excellent account of the Ijebu War see R. Smith "Nigeria—Ijebu" in Crowder *West African Resistance,* Hutchinson & Co., London, 1971.

(13) None the less, Egbaland had a cast-iron "Treaty of Independence" with Britain which was re-affirmed in 1893. Its existence caused Lugard much chagrin.

(14) Bower, Capt. (later Sir) Robert Lister, 1860—1929. Political Officer, Ijebu, 1892-1893, having taken part in the expedition against that state in 1892. From 1893-1897, he was British Resident, Ibadan. With Lugard, he delimited the boundary between Ilorin and the Lagos Protectorate in 1894-95, when Lugard was employed by the Royal Niger Company.

(15) Flora Shaw was the *Times* Colonial Editor. It is not known who edited the Reuters' despatch, but the omission of the negative did, as Carter complained, radically alter the impact of the message.

V. HAUSA, HAUSAS AND THE HAUSA ASSOCIATION

In 1892, *The Hausa Association* was founded in memory of Rev. J. A. Robinson, a Missionary of the Church Missionary Society, who had died at Lokoja on 25 June, 1891. Its avowed objective was "For promoting the Study of the Hausa Language and People."

The Association was "governed" by a General Council which included the Archbishops of Canterbury and Dublin, four Bishops, the Duke of Westminster and Field Marshal Lord Wolesley, two other peers and a host of lesser luminaries, numbering twenty-nine in all.

Day to day administration was in the hands of an Executive Committee, of nine, the Chairman of which was Goldie, who became, in fact, not only the Association's driving force, but also its chief propagandist. In his activities on the Association's behalf, he was greatly assisted by his friend Leonard Darwin, also a member of the Executive Committee.

12. 14 May, 1894. Page 11 Column 5.

THE HAUSA ASSOCIATION

TO THE EDITOR OF THE TIMES

Sir,—Some eighteen months ago you published an account of the Hausa Association, then being founded for the purpose of opening up the Hausa language to Europeans. As the first student returns to England next month after his preliminary residence in Tripoli and Tunis and will start almost immediately for the Central Soudan by way of the Niger, it may be interesting to note what progress has already been made, and what programme has been settled for carrying out the important object of the association.

That this object is of national interest scarcely calls for proof. Great Britain has now a sphere of influence covering half a million square miles in the basins of the Niger and Tchad. The only widely spread language of that populous region is Hausa, which is spoken by not less than one-hundredth of the human race. The Niger Company, as the official representative of the Empire, successfully carries on its political and commercial operations in this early stage of development chiefly by means of interpreters; and, although it has subscribed liberally to the Hausa Association and will doubtless give every facility to the students, its limited funds are scarcely sufficient for the more immediately necessary work of maintaining order in the occupied portion of its territories. The work of the Hausa Association may, perhaps, not bear full fruit until after the company's task is complete and it has ceased to exist, at any rate as a Government. (1) But those whose minds are fixed on the permanent civilization and development of the populous and fertile regions of the Central Sudan must recognize the hopelessness of success without the medium of a common language.

Mr. Charles Robinson, the first Hausa student, has not allowed the grass to grow under his feet in North Africa. He has mixed intimately with the Hausa visitors and residents there; he has acquired a knowledge of their habits of thought as well as of their language, both of which are essential conditions to useful residence in the Central Sudan, and he has, among other linguistic work, translated part of the Gospels into Hausa.

It should be pointed out here that, while the association has the sympathy of certain missionary societies, it is really an eclectic body of men who recognize that the interests of the Empire, of science, or of mission work in these regions can only be advanced by making the language of the country accessible to Europeans by full and accurate vocabularies, grammars, and translations. It was on this ground that the noblest work in the English tongue was unanimously accepted as the most suitable translation with which to commence.

Mr. Robinson has been assisted in his work at Tunis by a qualified surgeon, Mr. Tonkin, who accompanies him to the Central Soudan, where a doctor can often obtain access to circles to which the ordinary traveller would not be admitted. Mr. Tonkin has made a special study of ophthalmia, which is so prevalent in Hausaland that at Kano there is a "blind town" ruled over by a blind king or chief. Mr. Tonkin will also look after other scientific branches of the expedition. While their principal stay will be at Kano, "the Manchester of Central Africa," they will also visit other important towns, where somewhat different dialects of Hausa are spoken, so that the proposed vocabularies may be of service to future residents in various parts of the Hausa States.

The expedition will remain in the Central Sudan sufficiently long to enable Mr. Robinson and his assistants to complete amongst the Hausa people the work commenced in North Africa. They then propose to return with a Hausa caravan across the Great Sahara to the Mediterranean. It is one of the most interesting features of this intelligent and industrious Hausa people that they radiate out in every direction over the continent of Africa. In 1870 I travelled with some 800 of them from Berber to Suakin, 2,000 miles from their homes. (2) They are to be found on the Gold Coast and in Senegal, and their caravans are penetrating further every year into the basin of the Congo.

Great Britain has thus an unrivalled opportunity for spreading her civilization over the northern half of the African continent, and I venture to appeal to all who sympathize with this object to send their subscriptions to Mr. J. H. Tritton, at 54 Lombard-street, E.C., who kindly acts as hon. treasurer of the Hausa Association.

I am, Sir, your obedient servant,

GEORGE TAUBMAN GOLDIE, Chairman of the Executive Committee.

London, May 10.

166

13. 20 August, 1895. Page 15 Column 2.

THE HAUSA ASSOCIATION

TO THE EDITOR OF THE TIMES

Sir,—Nearly three years ago you published an article describing the foundation and objects of the Hausa Association, and I should be grateful if you could find space for a brief account of the progress made.

Public attention has lately been much directed to the northern half of tropical Africa, and it is not necessary to dilate on the importance of establishing linguistic communication with no less than one-hundredth of the human race, that being a reasonable estimate of the Hausa-speaking people. Lest, however, some of your readers should imagine that the objects aimed at are, on the one hand, of merely philological interest, or, on the other hand, impracticable in their nature, I would ask leave to quote a few words from addresses delivered last year to the London Chamber of Commerce.

Mr. H. H. Johnston, whose experience as a successful explorer and administrator of so many distinct regions of Africa gives great weight to his opinion, said that—

"In the course of his African travels he had been struck by the almost greater spread of the Hausa people as travellers and of their language than of any other tribes in the northern part of Africa. The importance of the Hausa people and their language was shown in the fact that they were beginning to cover the whole part of Northern Africa. That nation which was to acquire the greatest control over the Central Sudan, the greatest influence in politics and trade, must first of all acquire a supreme influence over the Hausa people. Fortunately for Great Britain, the Hausa home and all the bulk of the people were within the Niger territories, which were under British influence. The Hausas were a very valuable people to get hold of. They were an extremely industrious people; they did not seem to have inherited the curse of Mahomedanism—a sort of sanctified idleness. He sincerely hoped some day to see a chair founded in our great Universities for the study of Hausa."

Mr. H. M. Stanley said that—

"In his journeys across Africa he never came across any other nation that esteemed a book. All but the Hausas regarded books at rubbish. The Hausa people covered an enormous territory, and the Hausa language might be said to cover roughly a territory measuring a thousand miles north and south and a thousand miles east and west. To him, so long familiar with Africa, the project was a very taking one. To distribute books among illiterate pagan tribes would be the height of absurdity; but to disseminate them among a people who had been called by all travellers the literary race of Africa seemed as wise as it was statesmanliike. It was the hope of the association to render proficiency in Hausa as indispensable for success in Western Africa as proficiency in Hindustani, Persian, and Arabic was indispensable for promotion in the Civil Service in the East."

Mr. Clements Markham (3) said, "That the council of the Royal Geographical Society took a very great interest in the aims of the association. He had not the slightest doubt that in the first investigation and exploration of a country it was essential to study its language."

Major Leonard Darwin, who spoke from the experience gained during four years' charge of the African section of the Intelligence division of the War Office, said that—

"Of the British possessions in Africa, Hausa was the one to which we ought certainly to direct our earliest attention. He wished to dissipate the idea that the Hausa Association were a set of faddists, who merely wished to spend a vast amount of time or money to introduce some civilization into a small African tribe, and that their object was hardly large enough to be worthy of their efforts. That was a total mistake, for the Hausas were in every sense a nation, who could spread our influence over the whole of the northern portion of Africa.''

The first step of the association was to appoint a student, the Rev. Charles Robinson; not because he was a clergyman, for the association is not a missionary society, and it comprises "all sorts and conditions of men," but because he was the most competent applicant, a man of academic distinction, varied experience, and tried capacity in Oriental travel. The next step was to despatch him to Tripoli and Tunis, where extensive Hausa colonies exist, so that he might carry on his preliminary studies in a healthy region before proceeding to the heart of Africa. To Mr. Robinson were joined a qualified medical man, Mr. Tonkin, and an assistant, Mr. Bonnor. The third step was for Mr. Robinson and his companions to proceed by way of the rivers Niger and Benué to Loko, and thence by a difficult and toilsome overland journey of about 350 miles to Kano, the commercial centre of Hausaland, and while probably the most populous, certainly the most important, town of all tropical Africa. It may be interesting to state that on his return journey Mr. Robinson followed a different route, some 425 miles overland, part of which had never before been traversed by any European, and leading from Kano to Egga, on the Niger. He and his companions arrived safely in England on the 24th ult.

The main result of his work may be briefly summed up as follows. He has not only carefully revised and corrected Dr. Schon's dictionary, the imperfections of which that eminent philologist was the first to recognize, but he has added to it no fewer than 3,000 new words. He has the materials for an adequate grammar of the Hausa language. He has collected a number of native manuscripts consisting of history and of historical and religious songs, and he has translated these with a view to publication. (4) He has prepared accurate translations of two of the Gospels into Hausa, in the form of Arabic character used in that country. Dr. Tonkin's scientific observations will be communicated to the proper societies.

Unfortunately, the funds of the association are now exhausted, and, unless assistance is forthcoming, it cannot continue its work. May I then conclude by saying that Mr. J. H. Tritton, of 54, Lombard-street, E.C., is our hon. treasurer?

I am, Sir, your obedient servant,

GEORGE TAUBMAN GOLDIE.

11, Queen's-gate-gardens, Aug. 17.

14. December, 1895. Page 10 Column 6.

OUR HAUSA TROOPS

TO THE EDITOR OF THE TIMES

Sir,—Now that the Ashanti expedition is bringing the Hausa troops of the Gold Coast before the notice of the public, while the Hausa Association is preparing to issue books and documents on the Hausa language, it might be well if some uniform orthographic system were adopted in respect of the Hausa name. I doubt whether the ordinary newspaper reader of Reuter's telegrams recognizes that the "Houssa" troops belong to that interesting Hausa people whose language is spoken by one hundredth of mankind, and whose caravans carry the Hausa influence from the Central Sudan to the Red Sea, the Mediterranean, the Atlantic, and the Gulf of Guinea.

Whether the consonant in the name is single or double is not very important, though the Rev. Charles Robinson, the student of the Hausa Association who has recently returned from Kano, the "Manchester of Central Africa" and the capital of Hausaland, confirms the opinion of all experts that the duplication of the consonant gives the name an incorrect sibilant sound; but the quite incorrect form "Houssa" leads to a mispronunciation which effectually disguises the true name.

Perhaps I may mention that since you last noticed the work of the Hausa Association its general committee has been joined by the Duke of Westminster, Viscount Wolseley, Lord Loch, Lord Lamington, Sir John Kirk, Sir Albert Rollit, Sir Brandford Griffith (late Governor of the Gold Coast), the President of the Royal Geographical Society, Captain Lugard, and Sir Francis Scott, who is now using these valuable soldiers of the Hausa race in his advance into Ashanti.

The University Press of Cambridge, Mr. Robinson's *alma mater,* has kindly undertaken the publication of some of the valuable Hausa documents which the student has brought back from Kano.

I am, Sir, your obedient servant,

GEORGE TAUBMAN GOLDIE.

11, Queen's-gate-gardens, S.W., Dec. 14.

(1) This observation confirms the view that even at this comparatively early stage Goldie envisaged the revocation of the Charter.

(2) See also page 17.

(3) Markham was now in his second year as president of the R.G.S.

(4) In addition to the letters to the *Times* reproduced above, Goldie was the author of a nine page pamphlet entitled *The Hausa Association* published in 1895 in 8° form, British Museum Catalogue number 12901 K33(10). This is also reproduced as an appendix to Robinson's book.

VI. ECHOES OF L'AFFAIRE MIZON

When Lieutenant Louis Mizon made his second push up the Benue in 1892/93, he did so in the face of the most determined oppostion from Goldie who, however, was over-ruled by a timorous Foreign Office anxious to avoid an international confrontation. In the event, Goldie was right, and by no stretch of imagination was the new Mizon expedition the purely scientific and commercial enterprise that the French Government certified it to be.

The party consisted of over a hundred men, all of whom were armed, and it was transported in two vessels, one of twenty tons and the other of eighty. One of them was the *Sergent Malamine.*

A full account of the expedition, and of the complications which it entailed, are related by Flint [1] and need not be enlarged upon here, it being sufficient merely to note that by the time he was recalled to France in September, 1893, Mizon had signed a treaty with the Emir of Muri, Muhammadu Nya, 1874-1896, under the terms of which he had declared the "French Protectorate of Muri," in the process entirely disregarding the fact that beyond question Muri was a dependency of Sokoto from a treaty with the Sultan of which the Company drew its own claim to territorial legitimacy; assisted in the sack and pillage of the Jukun town of Kona; distributed a considerable quantity of modern weapons, and made the Emir Zubeiru of Yola a gift of two brass cannon. [2]

On his evacuation of that city, he had left behind a dozen Senegalese and an Algerian Zouave, together with his bigger vessel, the *Malamine.* This Wallace, who had been standing by on the Company's stern-wheeler *Nupe,* promptly seized by the simple though direct means of threatening to hang the French agent in charge if he demurred. Goldie responded to the Mizon episode by lodging a formal claim for £100,000 damages. Against this, the French Government made a counter claim alleging that the vessel had been illegally seized. It was this issue that had now been made the subject of an arbitration award.

THE SERGENT MALAMINE ARBITRATION. (3)

TO THE EDITOR OF THE TIMES

Sir,—Last week was laid before Parliament the award of M. le Baron Lambermont (4) on the question of seizure, eight years ago, by the late Royal Niger Company of the French vessel Sergent Malamine. (3) This was one of the incidents of the complicated *affaire Mizon* which, as Lord Rosebery well knows, would have brought France and England into collision, but for the substantial additions then recently made to that fleet now gathered in these waters. (5) Even those little concerned with African questions will remember the enthusiastic reception given throughout France to the late Commandant Mizon, the heated debates in the Chamber, the banquet of the Municipality of Paris, the diamond necklace presented by them to M. Mizon's Nigerian slave girl, Snabou, (6) and her being publicly embraced by the then President of the Republic. (7) Now that the happy consummation of the Coronation may have relieved the pressure of your columns, I venture to ask for space for a few remarks on the decision of Baron Lambermont, which is so completely satisfactory from the British point of view.

It is true that he awards to France the sum of £6,500; but he is careful to point out that he was constrained to do this by the terms of "the Arbitration Convention signed by the two Governments on the 3rd April, 1901"; and he emphatically and repeatedly justifies the action of the British authorities—the late Royal Niger Company—and condemns the illegalities of the French expedition. Whether the British Government was wise, as a matter of State policy, to sign that convention, and thus to give away a case which the arbitrator has now incidentally decided in their favour, may be a matter of dispute. Some will doubtless hold that an amicable settlement of a long-standing controversy *vaut bien une messe* (8) and is cheap at £6,500. Others will undoubtedly maintain that the payment of Danegelt is an expensive process in the long run. But on this I offer no opinion, because the object of this letter is to press three more important points upon the attention of the public.

The first is that of historical justice. One of the chief features of the last quarter of a century has been the partition of Africa. When its full and, as yet, partly secret history is published a leading place must be given to the Royal Niger Company, not only because it was the earliest of the three African chartered Governments, but chiefly because its efforts alone, from 1881 to 1886, brought about the revival of that policy which the abolition of the Honourable East India Company and of the Hudson Bay Company was supposed to have destroyed for ever—I mean the policy of governing through chartered companies territories within the British Empire. (9) It was the granting by Mr. Gladstone and Lord Rosebery of the Niger Charter in 1886 that enabled Lord Salisbury, without fear of serious opposition, to grant to Sir W. Mackinnon his charter for the Imperial British East African Company in 1887, to bring British North Borneo within the Empire in 1888 by making it a Protectorate, and, finally, to grant to Mr. Cecil Rhodes, in 1889, his charter for the British South Africa Company. Perhaps I dwell unduly on this point because my really useful work in life (10) has been the conception in 1877, and the final carrying through in 1886, of the principle of temporary chartered government for new and barbarous regions, in face of the refusals of three successive Governments and in face of the declaration, still in my possession, of the then Law Officers of the Crown that it was no longer within the competence of the Sovereign to grant a charter authorizing the exercise of sovereign rights within the limits of the Empire. (11) But, seeing that the late

Royal Niger Company has such a far-reaching record, and seeing that the Mizon affair, with the consequent campaign of the French Press, brought about the premature revocation of the charter, it is clearly a matter of historical justice to the company to place on record, once for all, that an impartial arbitrator, recognized as one of the highest living authorities on international comity, has amply and emphatically justified the action of the company.

My second point is that this arbitration on the Sergent Malamine incident will not be the last word in the Mizon affair. The British Government, as the residuary legatee of the late Royal Niger Company, as an administrative body, have a far larger claim—which I put forward prior to the French counter-claim—against the Republic, for the almost incredible illegalities of the Mizon expedition, which, curiously enough, were first denounced by M. Henri Rochefort in the *Intransigeant*. (12)

My third point is of wider importance. Is it too much to hope that when Anglo-French disputes arise, as cannot fail to be the case, in other parts of the world, the eminently peaceful, practical, and sober-minded people of France, as distinguished from the noisy and intemperate minority, may be influenced by the memory that the Sergent Malamine incident, on which rested for years such a volume of hatred and suspicion of England, has now been proved to have been a mare's nest?

I am, Sir, your obedient servant,

GEORGE TAUBMAN GOLDIE.

Aphrodite, R.Y.S., Ryde, Aug. 11.

16. 22 August, 1902. Page 6 Column 5.

THE BRITISH NORTH BORNEO COMPANY

TO THE EDITOR OF THE TIMES (13)

Sir,—I have just read Mr. Martin's letter in your issue of yesterday. I note that he wrote it from Homburg; and it is reasonable to assume that he had only seen a summary of my letter to you. For, if he had read the letter itself, he would not have failed to see that I had carefully (and twice) used the expression "within the Empire" in speaking of the late Royal Niger Company as the first of the modern chartered companies. He would also have seen that I drew special attention to the fact that the British North Borneo Company—which, as every one knows, received its charter in 1881—was brought within the Empire in 1888 by extending British protection to it. But Mr. Martin himself makes the earlier position of the Borneo Company quite clear by his reference to Mr. Gladstone's speech about "not hindering the enterprise of Englishmen beyond the borders of the Empire."

This position would have been of no use to the three African companies—the Royal Niger Company, the Imperial British East African Company, and the British South Africa Company—as these were founded by Sir William Mackinnon, Mr. Rhodes, and the writer expressly for the extension of the Empire. (14)

May I, in conclusion, express my agreement with Mr. Martin as to the importance of British North Borneo to Great Britain as a strategical position, and add my belief, based on long examination of the subject, in the great commercial future that lies before the company of which he has so long been chairman.

I am, Sir, your obedient servant,

GEORGE TAUBMAN GOLDIE.

Aphrodite, R.Y.S., Cowes, Aug. 20.

172

(1) See Flint, *op cit.*

(2) Additional detail has also been taken from *The Gazeteer of Muri Province,* Waterlow & Sons Ltd., 1922, based on the account of W. P. Hewby, the R.N.C.'s agent at Ibi from 1894-1899 and afterwards Resident, Bornu.

(3) Sergent Malamine was a Senegalese *Tiraillear* promoted to that rank by De Brazza in 1880. He was then left at Stanley Pool as De Brazza's representative to "hold the fort" while De Brazza was away. This he did with skill and honour even against Stanley himself, who arrived shortly afterwards to claim the station on behalf of King Leopold. De Brazza's successor—none other than Mizon—dismissed Malamine in Feb., 1882, and returned him to Senegal where he died in penury in 1885, denied both pay and pension by bureaucratic incompetence. See *Brazza of the Congo* by R. West, Jonathan Cape, London, 1972. The naming of the vessel, and its being left behind is not, therefore, without its irony—or its symbolism.

(4) Lambermont, Baron, 1818-1905. Belgian elder statesman who represented Belgium and the Congo at the Berlin Conference and who was the mutually agreed arbitrator in this case.

(5) This refers to the Coronation Naval Review in Cowes Roads, in which Goldie as a member of the Royal Yacht Squadron, from whence his letter is addressed, participated.

(6) The proper name was *Zainabu.*

(7) President Sadi Carnot, 1887-1894.

(8) "Paris is at least worth saying a Mass for!" A *bon mot* attributed to Henry of Navarre, who converted to Catholicism in order to gain the Crown.

(9) This phrase is important as it gave rise to the subsequent correspondence.

(10) It is interesting to see Goldie's unequivocal assertion of what he perceives to be the really important issue.

(11) Note the flat attribution of the revocation of the Charter to this single cause.

(12) It must further be borne in mind that at the time when Goldie was writing this letter, the Public had been made aware of the fact that at least one other French West African expedition had been proved to have acted in a manner not dissimilar from the way he had always claimed that Mizon had behaved. In 1899, the Voulet (Paul, 1866-1899) and Chanoine (Charles Paul Jules, 1870-1899) expedition had set off for Chad from Say on the Niger. After the most horrendous stories of its rapine and pillage filtered back, Colonel Klobb (Jean Francois Arsène, 1857-1899) had been sent to take command. Voulet murdered him at Dankari. Subsequently, both Voulet and Chanoine were shot by their own *tirailleurs,* and Capitaine (later General) Jules Joalland (1870-1940) was sent after the mutineers to bring them back to their allegiance and resume the march to Chad. Chanoine was the son of the Minister of War in the Dreyfus case.

(13) This letter, which at first sight appears to be almost completely out of context, reveals a great deal about Goldie. On 19 August, 1902, the *Times* had published a letter from Mr. R. B. Martin, the Chairman of the British North Borneo Company, in which he stated that Goldie was "in error in stating . . . that the charter issued . . . to the Niger Company was the first one granted since . . . the East India and the Hudson Bay Company . . . [because] the grant of [the British North Borneo Company's] charter was made in 1881, five years before that to the Niger Company." Goldie could well have ignored the fact that Martin had clearly mis-read his letter, since he went on to make the very point that Goldie had, *viz.* that the Borneo Charter was for an area *outside* an internationally recognised British sphere of influence, which the Niger was not. Martin had taken issue, and the issue must be countered.

(14) This positive statement of intent is interesting.

VII. MOURNING AND REGRETS

17. 11 July, 1898. Page 12 Column 3.

THE LATE CAPTAIN CHARLES GOLDIE TAUBMAN

TO THE EDITOR OF THE TIMES

Sir,—I should be obliged by your correcting a not unnatural error in your obituary notices of to-day. Captain Charles Goldie Taubman, of the King's Own, whose death during the recent military operations in Nigeria is announced, was the son not of myself, but of my brother, Sir John Goldie Taubman, of the Nunnery, Isle of Man.

I would add that the only possible alleviation to the grief of his sorrowing parents and others is that he died in the active service of his country, as he would have chosen.

I am, Sir, your obedient servant,

GEORGE TAUBMAN GOLDIE.

Naval and Military Club, July 9.

Captain Charles Goldie Taubman, Sir George's nephew, was serving with the West African Frontier Force on secondment from his Regiment the King's Own (Royal Lancaster). He died of "fever" on 23 February and the *Times* published an Obituary Notice on July 9th. His grave at Gulu near Lapai in Niger Province is marked with a stone obelisk that Goldie had shipped out and erected.

18. 25 December, 1899. Page 4 Column 6.

This is the last letter that Goldie wrote while still Governor of the Royal Niger Company, Chartered and Limited. Six days later, the Charter was revoked.

THE LIVINGSTONE EXHIBITION

TO THE EDITOR OF THE TIMES

Sir,—Will you allow me to place before the notice of the public the objects of the Livingstone exhibition, which will be held at St. Martin's Town-hall, Charing-cross, during the first five days of the New Year, from 11 a.m. to 10 p.m., except that it will close at 7 p.m. on the 2nd and 4th, to permit of evening meetings of the Royal Geographical Society and of the London and Liverpool Schools of Tropical Medicine? The formal opening ceremony will take place at 3 p.m. on Monday, January 1.

As it may be thought that the present crisis makes this an unsuitable period for a new exhibition I may state that the project was largely organised before the outbreak of war in South Africa. But, were it otherwise, I would deprecate allowing the current of our daily lives to be chilled by a passing cloud. It is right that those who have the good fortune of being able to render active assistance to the South African question should devote their time to it; but it would be a matter of regret if our general national enterprise, whether public or private, were to diminish in vigour simply because we have not yet completed our military preparations to overcome a resistance which proves greater than we had anticipated, but which must ultimately yield to the weight and energy of the British Empire. Those who advocate a "day of humiliation" must have allowed the emergency of the moment to obscure the teachings of history; our habit of under-estimating our enemies, our customary reverses during the early stages of a great war, and our dogged persistence, which has carried us successfully through difficulties greater than those which we are now encountering. The one apparent exception, the American War of Independence, need not discourage us. We had then on our hands a struggle with three European States; we were fighting our own countrymen in an indefensible cause, and our difficulties of ocean transport were very different to those of the age of steam. That before long—it may be next Christmas, it may be two or three years hence—the South African troubles will be a matter of history seems to me as certain as that the sun is shining behind the grey pall under which I am writing, but which must, in due time, disappear.

The Livingstone exhibition will be of considerable value to those who intend to serve or travel in tropical, unhealthy, or rough countries. It should therefore interest all who have friends in such regions. Its principal object is to display in a practical form the equipment, kit, clothing, food, medicines, and other articles which, directly or indirectly, may help in the preservation of health or the treatment of accident or disease. Young officers and civil officials are generally completley at sea on these points when ordered out for the first time; and doubtless this applies also to missionaries and scientific travellers. It must be admitted that a passing exhibition does not meet the full requirements of the case, but it is a first and important step towards a permanent exhibition.

Her Royal Highness the Princess Christian, in accepting the position of patron, has shown the sympathy always felt by the Royal Family in such movements.

Lord Salisbury, Lord Landsdowne, Lord George Hamilton, and Mr. Chamberlain have expressed their sympathy on behalf of the Foreign, War, India, and Colonial Offices, while the Royal Geographical Society is lending its valuable collection of objects of interest connected with the lives of Livingstone and other travellers, to which will be added loans from various other quarters.

I may say, in conclusion, that the credit for the conception and organization of this valuable exhibition belongs to the Livingstone College and its indefatigable secretary, Dr. Harford-Battersby.

I am, Sir, your obedient servant,
GEORGE TAUBMAN GOLDIE.
Naval and Military Club, Christmas, 1899.

When this letter appeared, the War in South Africa was going very badly for Britain. Defeats, set-backs and military ineptitude were being reported daily. As a result, a growing sentiment began to be canvassed for an official Day of Prayer and National Humiliation to be announced, at which time the Nation would seek a spiritual renewal the better to steel itself for its task. The proposal did NOT meet with Goldie's approval!

Nor did it meet with Queen Victoria's! According to Ponsonby[1] the Queen told him that she was much opposed to the whole idea. She objected on principle to people being ordered to pray; she added that "if we were justified in going to war and if we thought we were doing right by South Africa, there was no reason why we should 'humiliate' ourselves, but if, on the other hand, we thought we were wrong, the sooner we stopped the war the better."

Goldie's view of the American Revolution is forthright and enlightened. The anti-Colonial myth which grew up in the years of massive immigration has only just begun to give way to a perception of the intense opposition to Government policy that was manifest in some circles in Britain, though serious scholarship has always been aware of it. Unfortunately, serious scholarship does not always mould or condition national attitudes!

The Princess Christian referred to in the letter was the Princess Helena Victoria, third daughter of the Queen, who had married Prince Christian of Schleswig-Holstein. Dr. Harford-Battersby had served as a medical missionary in Lokoja in the "Hausa Mission," organised by that muscular Christian G. Wilmot-Brooke. Though it did contribute indirectly to the stimulation of the study of the Hausa language, the mission itself was a dismal failure, Wilmot-Brooke and Robinson dying, and Battersby being invalided home. The basic philosophy underlying it, namely that missionaries ought to sink themselves into the culture and social customs of those they try to serve, rather than exist as agents of an alien and often hostile culture was very sound, though Wilmot-Brooke himself often appears in a rather unattractive light, especially in regard to his attitude to Bishop Crowther.

19.   28 March, 1902. Page 8 Column 6.

TO THE EDITOR OF THE TIMES

Sir,—It is difficult to realize that Cecil Rhodes is dead. [2] Just a month ago he and I were flying in his motor-car round the roads of the Wynberg district—he, outspoken as usual, full of his plans for the future, passing judgments on men and things with his customary frankness. His appetite was good, and he transacted business and responded to telegrams with the decision and promptness that must always have distinguished him from weak and vacillating minds.

His first greeting to me had been, "Well! they've squeezed you out; but they won't squeeze me out," and when I advised him to arrange for the transfer of Rhodesia—as I had for the transfer of Nigeria—while he had health and vigour to see some justice done to his shareholders[3] he touched his heart significantly, and, of course, I said no more. But, later on, he spoke of his great railway scheme and the projected bridge across the Zambesi in a tone that convinced me that he had no premonition of any immediate evil.

My object in writing this letter, however, is to put on record the surprising fact that all the Boers to whom I spoke of him expressed their respect and liking for him.

One expected that fervent loyalists in South Africa should look to him as the one necessary man; but that their admiration should be shared by the other side is, to me, convincing proof of the greatness of his character.

Like most strong men, he had many enemies, but Britons do not carry animosity beyond the grave; and if, as I hope, the authorities of Westminster Abbey admit his monument to the precinct where the memories of other great Englishmen are preserved, few, if any, voices would be raised against their decision. (4)

Your obedient servant,

GEORGE TAUBMAN GOLDIE.

Naval and Military Club, Piccadily, W., March 26.

(1) See Ponsonby, Sir F.; *Recollections of Three Reigns,* Eyre & Spottiswoode, London, 1951, p. 77.

(2) Cecil Rhodes died on 26 March, 1902, after a long history of heart trouble. He never married.

(3) For Goldie's extreme touchiness on this issue, see pages 199; 280; 281.

(4) There is a certain poignancy in Goldie, the declared agnostic, suggesting enshrinement in Westminster Abbey as a suitable memorial!

VIII: THE YEARS OF ENFORCED LEISURE AND OF DIVORCE FROM AFRICA

20.   18 January, 1901. Page 6 Column 1

SIR G. TAUBMAN GOLDIE AND IMPERIAL FEDERATION.—Sir George Taubman Goldie writes:—"As I have already received several letters on the subject and do not wish for more, may I ask you kindly to correct a slight stenographic error in the report of my remarks at the Royal Colonial Institute meeting on January 15? The measure which I hoped might be consummated even in my lifetime was Imperial Federation, and not Australian Federation."

This is the first intimation that the *Times* received that Goldie was "back in circulation." Since the letter on the Livingstone Exhibition he had been silent. Much of 1900, of course, he had spent on a trip to China, which he appeared to have thoroughly enjoyed. He had, however, been back in time to attend the "20th ordinary general meeting of the Niger Company (Limited and Reduced)" held at Surrey House on 10 August, 1900. He took no part in the proceedings and made no contribution, his presence, presumably, being occasioned by the fact that the Report and Balance Sheet under consideration related to a period when he had jurisdiction.

Now, on 16 January, 1901, the *Times* had carried a report of a meeting held the day before by the Royal Colonial Institute, with Goldie in the chair. The Speaker had been Major A. St. Hill Gibbons, who had read a paper entitled "The Nile and the Zambesi as Waterways."

The meeting had, however, been opened by Goldie reading out the draft of a telegram which had been sent to Lord Hopetoun, [1] Governor-General of Australia, conveying greetings on the inauguration of the Australian Commonwealth two weeks earlier.

After Major Gibbons had spoken, Goldie added a few laudatory remarks, during which he said:

" . . . that the subject of waterways, though of the greatest intrinsic interest, was very little understood yet by the general public. Major Gibbons has not exaggerated the enormous importance of utilizing these great waterways, especially in new and tropical countries. Great Britain had far greater advantages than any other country for acquiring, holding, and developing great river systems, and yet those advantages had been too often forgotten. In our long struggles with Spain this country never thought of acquiring the Plate river system, and during the 60 years in which we had been harassing China with demands we might better have concentrated our attention on establishing our position on the Yang-tsze and the West rivers. That could have been done at one time without exciting jealousy or undertaking huge burdens. Of the four great river systems of Africa we did, indeed, control three; but the acquisition of two of them had been due solely to the action of chartered companies. The lessons of the last 15 months had taught us that for the immediate future all true Imperialism must concern itself with the consolidation of Empire, rather than with acquisition, under the penalty of the Empire's dropping to pieces from the want of adequate organisation. (Cheers.) Occupying the chair at this the first meeting of the new century, he could not conclude without expressing the passionate hope that the great measure of Australian federation would find its full consummation even within the lives of many who had already passed the zenith of their days. (Cheers.)

It was to this last sentence, as mis-reported in the *Times*, that Goldie is now objecting. Flora Shaw was listed as being present. Although the crisis in their emotional affairs had occurred in 1898, and another nine months were to elapse before her engagement to Lugard was announced, Bell makes quite clear that she was then still working full-time and was thus the reporter in question. She left England for South Africa in December as a Special Correspondent after having resigned her full-time work in September. Although Perham only refers to her having meetings with "Milner downwards,"[2] it is inconceivable that she did not again meet Cecil Rhodes. It would be interesting to know what passed between them.

21.   20 January, 1902. Page 7 Column 5

THE UGANDA RAILWAY[3]

TO THE EDITOR OF THE TIMES

Sir,—The telegraphic news that the first locomotive has reached the inland terminus on the shore of the Victoria Nyanza will have revived the interest of the public at home in the Uganda railway; and, as this subject must engage the attention of Parliament in the coming Session, your readers may perhaps be glad to hear the impressions of one who, never having been a Government official, cannot be open to the suspicion of bias through gratitude for past favours or hopes of favours to come. I assume that it is generally known that considerable portions of the track now followed are diversions of a temporary nature, that the steel work has still to be erected on 28 viaducts on the permanent line, and that the railway is not expected to be completed until September next or, more probably, the end of 1902.

   The first question of interest to the taxpayers at home is that of the capital account of the railway—that is, whether the work has been done judiciously and economically, so that there will be intrinsic value to show for the total capital sum expended when the line is completed. After seeing the line, throughout (practically) its whole length, and visiting its fully-equipped workshops, stores, and other accessories, I have no hesitation in answering this question in the affirmative. In arriving at this conclusion, three attendant circumstances had to be borne in mind—the general difficulties inseparable from all enterprises in equatorial Africa, the extraordinary local difficulties of railway construction in the East Africa Protectorate, and the political reasons for speed of construction. Of the first I shall say nothing; for those who have not personally experienced them during long years of disillusion and disappointment cannot fully appreciate them. As regards the special local difficulties, these were graphically and accurately described by Colonel Gracey, R.E., in his critical but, on the whole, favourable report of last March (Africa, No. 6, 1901); and, in view of the current fashion of treating British inventiveness and organizing power as things of the past, I venture to say that you would be doing a public service in reprinting the extract from that report which I enclose herewith. It is a just and certainly not over-coloured tribute to a work of which our countrymen may be proud:—

Extract from Africa, No. 6, 1901.

"After considering MacDonald's and other reports, the Government finally decided, in 1895, to construct a metre-gauge railway from the sea to Lake Victoria, and early in 1896 Mr. Whitehouse, (4) the Chief Engineer, and a small staff had arrived at Mombasa, and had commenced the surveys for the line.

The task before them was immense. A railway 583 miles long had to be accurately located and staked out, in many places through dense thorn jungle, where the survey parties could not see more than a few yards in front of them. The country was for great lengths waterless, without resources, and very sparsely populated, the only inhabitants being naked savages, without industries or arts, and for the most part quite unused to any form of labour. The route to be traversed was mountainous, rising to 7,000ft. near mile 350, falling to 6,000ft. near mile 425 in the great central rift, again rising to 8,300ft. at mile 490, and finally falling to 3,700ft, at the terminus at mile 583 on the lake. Very little unskilled, and no skilled labour was procurable in the country, and this necessitated the importation from India of an army of 20,000 navvies and artisans, who had to be fed, housed, clothed, and provided with tools, and all stores required for these purposes had to be brought from England or India, necessitating foresight of the same kind as would be required to place an army in the field. The difficulties of procuring labour and stores from England and India were furthermore greatly enhanced by the engineering strike in the former and the plague restrictions in the latter. Even when the men had been placed on the ground, and importation of all stores required for them had been arranged, the difficulties were not at an end, as the construction had to be carried through dry tracts 20, 30, or even 60 miles in length, where water had to be carried out to the labourers, where no transport animals could live owing to the tsetse fly, and where, consequently, work could only proceed a few miles in advance of the railhead. In some parts the country was very unhealthy and infested with jiggers, which were the cause of many severe ulcers amongst the workmen. In other parts the labourers were constantly being frightened off the work by man-eating lions. Landing jetties, hospitals, police, and post and telegraph services had to be organized, and a recruiting and supply agency established in India."

It is probable that money might have been saved if time had been no object. Some of the temporary diversions, which have enabled material, labour, food, and water to be extended rapidly along the projected line, would have been unnecessary. But the railway was not primarily a commercial speculation, and the public will not have forgotten the international situation up to 1899. Whether Uganda should ever have been occupied, whether the upper waters of the Nile were worth the imminent risk of war with a great Power, and even whether Egypt itself will be held permanently, are all points on which intelligent men have differed. These may, therefore, debate, till the crack of doom, whether the Uganda Railway should ever have been commenced; but all will probably agree that if it was to be done "then 'twere well it were done quickly." I have been strongly impressed by the vast superiority of this railway both in construction and in equipment over similar railways in several other parts of the world, though I will not incur Mrs. Malaprop's censure by mentioning names. (5) Indeed, I must confess that my first feeling was that the line had been built too solidly; that its *maximum* grades of one in 50 and its sharpest curves of 800ft. radius showed excess of caution, and that the really notable workshops and other accessories at the headquarter at Nairobi were better suited for Crewe than for a place within a few miles of the Equator. But the peculiar conditions of the East Africa Protectorate soon asserted their voice. As the line has, in regard to labour, been constructed from India, so for many years it must be maintained from India, involving heavy expense and serious delays in case of those special repairs of which rougher mountian lines have frequent need. Under these unusual conditions, the policy adopted will probably prove the cheapest in the end. The credit for the satisfactory construction of this truly national work rests in the first place with the Uganda Railway Committee selected by Lord Salisbury for this purpose. They have done yeoman's service for five or six years; but, undoubtedly, their most important single act was the appointment of Mr. George Whitehouse as chief engineer. The language of eulogy is apt to be wearisome; so I will only express the hope that the Government may find is possible to utilize in the task of making the railway a paying concern the energy, organizing genius, and fertile inventiveness which have enabled Mr. Whitehouse to construct the road so rapidly and economically in the face of exceptional difficulties.

The second question of interest to the taxpayers at home is that of the revenue account of the railway; in other words, how many years of loss or mere covering of annual expenditure must be expected before the Treasury receives its first dividends. I mistrust all prophecies on this question of time, though I feel not a shadow of doubt as to the line ultimately proving a sound commercial speculation for a nation which can afford to lock up securities for years in its strong box. But I wish to urge that the happy day may be hastened by very moderate expenditure in assisting to develop the East African Protectorate. Its two needs are irrigation and population. For these we must look to paid Indian experience and assisted Indian immigration, excepting in that white man's country which the railway traverses between Kiu, 267 miles, or perhaps Nairobi, 327 miles from Mombasa, and, roughly speaking, Fort Ternan, 542 miles. (6) The breadth of this healthy zone in a bee line is of course considerably less—perhaps 160 miles in all; but it affords an ample field for settlers who are content not to make fortunes, but to provide prosperous livelihoods on the land for themselves and their descendants. It may be that Great Britain is no longer able to supply agricultural colonists of this stamp. The constantly acclerating migration from the country to the towns at home arouses reasonable doubt on this point. But if it is so, I suggest that we may learn à useful lesson from Argentina. Concessions of land in the white man's country may be granted on moderate terms to British resident capitalists, both great and small; and the manual labour can be supplied by Italian immigrants who will remain, as in the regions of the Plate, for ten or twelve years, until they have amassed sufficient savings to enable them to live in comfort at home. Sir Charles Eliot, who has wisely devoted his first year of administration to constant travel throughout his extensive province, making himself acquainted with the wants and possibilities of the country, will certainly do all in his power to initiate and advance the development of his protectorate; but, if Great Britain wishes for a harvest, she must undoubtedly lend the seed more liberally than heretofore, especially in view of the large province that the protectorate will take over from Uganda on March 31 next.

Before concluding, may I venture on a word of warning addressed both to the public at home and to residents in the East Africa Protectorate? The railway is the alimentary canal of East Africa; but Mombasa is its mouth, and will consequently make its voice chiefly heard in the Press. Now for six years Mombasa has been living and growing (indirectly) on its toll on the millions advanced by the British Treasury for railway construction. Residents here point with pardonable pride to the creation in six years of a civilized and prosperous town out of an Arab village; but they hardly seem to have realized that by the end of 1902 nine-tenths of the 20,000 coolies employed on the construction of the railway will have returned to India; that a large proportion of the white and coloured railway officials will also have left East Africa; and that some years must elapse before the development of the interior can compensate for the cessation of the influx of British money. After seven years of the fat kine there must be seven years of the lean kine; and, although the country, as a whole, may be steadily and even rapidly advancing, the appearance will be that of retrogression. We may be sure that this state of things will not be overlooked by politicians at home averse to expenditure on our over-sea possessions.

I am, your obedient servant,
GEORGE TAUBMAN GOLDIE.
Mombasa, Dec. 22.

22.   18 September, 1902. Page 6 Column 2.

THE WAR INQUIRY

TO THE EDITOR OF THE TIMES

Sir,—While gratefully appreciating the very flattering reference to myself in your leading article of the 11th inst., which I have just received on my return from cruising, it is only fair to the Government to amend somewhat the statement that "though he has held office under the Crown, it has not been under the ordinary conditions." For, in a large number of the "Press cuttings" sent to me, I note that this view of my position as the founder of the Royal Niger Company has been misinterpreted and used as a basis for criticisms on the composition of the Royal Commission. (7)

Now, not only have I never held office under the Crown, but my work from 1881 to 1900, in regard to the issue, working, and abrogation of the Nigerian Charter, was in constant, though amicable, antagonism to six successive Ministries and quite a number of Public Departments. It is true that Great Britain, as the protecting Power, was entitled to object to the legislative and executive actions of the Royal Niger Company; but the Secretary of State had no voice in the appointment, promotion, or emoluments of any of its officials, nor, a fortiori, of myself.

I regret having, on public grounds, to trouble you with this personal matter; but, as the mis-apprehension has evidently been due to my having sedulously kept myself, as far as practicable, outside of public view, the present exception will not be misunderstood by those whose opinion I value. Une fois n'est pas coutume. (8)

I am, Sir, your obedient servant,
GEROGE TAUBMAN GOLDIE.
Aphrodite, R.Y.S., Plymouth. Sept. 15.

23. 6 July, 1905. Page 8 Column 1

TO THE EDITOR OF THE TIMES (9)

Sir,—A strenuous effort is being made to negative the second reading of the Administrative County of London and District Electric Power Bill, with a view to preventing its merits being proved before a committee of the House of Commons, as they were conclusively proved before a committee of the House of Lords, during an investigation extending over six weeks, when every conceivable objection was heard and dismissed. The following are some of the facts then established.

Hitherto, the supply of electric power to the manufacturers of London has been practically untouched; for, although the metropolis has numerous electric light undertakings by companies and municipal bodies, only 6¼ per cent. of their revenue is derived from the sale of power, and 93¾ from lighting, etc.—a proportion which should almost be reversed. This state of affairs has lasted for years, and would apparently have continued indefinitely but for the action of the electric power company which has taken up this new development. Nor can the electric lighting companies or municipal authorities be blamed for their long inaction, seeing that, with their varying systems, they cannot deal effectively with a problem involving concentration of production. Their average price of power to-day is, naturally, over 2d. per unit, whereas the standard price for the electric power company under the Bill will be ¾d. per unit. There is also over half a million horse-power of plant in London at present driven by steam which could be driven by electricity at ¾d. per unit, with a saving to manufacturers of some millions of pounds per annum. It is not, therefore, surprising that manufacturers employing 100,000 hands have petitioned Parliament to pass the Bill, nor that the leading railway, dock, and steamship companies are in favour of it. London, on account of its size, can, by adopting this proposed concentration in production, be supplied with electric power more cheaply than any other city in the world, or even than is Buffalo from Niagara. The Bill confers no monopoly whatever; it gives the right—but no exclusive right—to supply cheap electric power in cases where the Board of Trade considers it necessary and fixes the conditions.

Such is the outline of the position and, the question now arises why the Bill should be opposed, seeing that the House of Lords, which is not usually a contemner of reasonable vested rights, has introduced most effective clauses to protect the interests of the existing companies and municipal bodies, clauses which deserve the careful consideration of a committee of the House of Commons and cannot be fully dealt with in a second reading debate. The main opposition comes from two quarters—the existing electric lighting companies and the London County Council—for the smaller municipal bodies are divided in opinion, no fewer than seven of those within the area of the Bill having already withdrawn their opposition, and some having expressed an intention strongly to support it. The electric lighting companies appear to fear that, when their consumers of light see electric power being distributed in the industrial area at ¾d. per unit, they will put pressure on the companies to reduce their present average rate to householders of 5d. per unit; but, in the first place, the consumers cannot compel the lighting companies to do this, and, in the second place, these companies, while continuing with their existing plant to supply all the light they now distribute, would be able to increase their business to an extent now impossible by taking further current in bulk from the electric power company at less than half their present cost of production. The result might be a very large reduction in the cost of electric light to the householders in the metropolis with the maintenance (or even increase) of the dividends of the electric lighting companies. Why, then, do they not recognize this fact? A similar question arose, some 70 years ago, when the earlier railway schemes were keenly opposed by landowners whose successors competed equally keenly to have their estates developed by railway extensions.

But, in the present case, the vague and ungrounded fears of the electric lighting companies have undoubtedly been intensified—I suspect that they were originated—by the active spirit who has at last drawn the London County Council into a similar opposition. I have known him for a quarter of a century (from his early days in Nigeria) as a most upright and public-spirited man. (10) I have always admired his power of convincing and carrying with him, by sheer force of character, men of opposing opinions; and I do not know that he has ever shown this capacity more clearly than in organizing the present opposition and in misleading some members on both sides of the House. But too much municipalism has made him blind to the serious dangers that the ratepayers incur through the County Council entering into vast commercial speculations which it cannot conduct on sound commercial lines. Moreover, when he throws his energy into the debate on the second reading he will be in the strange position of a Socialist arguing against a measure which will benefit some two millions of the working classes, on the ground that it may injure vested interests which the House of Lords considers sufficiently protected.

He may reply that I am more likely to be biassed than himself by the fact that I am a subscriber to the expenditure for carrying this beneficent measure through Parliament. As I have never used my name for personal profit, (11) I wish to meet any such view by the promise that, if the Bill goes through this Session and I receive back the £900 I have subscribed for this purpose, I shall hand it over to the National Military Education League, which I am about to organize on the lines laid down in my separate report on the South African War Commission, (12) and endorsed by Lord Esher and other members of the Commission. But while I do not wish to make a personal profit on a public question to which I give public support, I must not be precluded, when the time comes, from investing largely, with (and on the same terms as) the general public, in an undertaking which I believe to be sound from the engineering and commercial standpoints, as well as of great importance to both the operatives and the ratepayers of London, and which will be no inconsiderable factor in placing Great Britain ahead of the enterprise of Germany and the United States instead of lagging behind, as it has done for the last generation.

I am, Sir, your obedient servant,

GEORGE TAUBMAN GOLDIE.

The Athenaeum, July 3.

24.   29 November, 1906. Page 7 Column 3.

DIPLOMACY AND GEOGRAPHY

TO THE EDITOR OF THE TIMES

Sir,—My attention has been drawn to Sir Edward Grey's reply, last Friday, to Sir Clement Hill's (13) question as to geography ceasing to be a subject in Diplomatic and Foreign Office entrance examinations. The Secretary of State said that "although a knowledge of geography is no doubt very useful, it is a subject with which men of general education are generally acquainted, and which is easily acquired after entry into the service." I wish that I could agree with him. Perhaps in the circumstances, you will be able to find space for the following extract from my Edinburgh address to the Royal Scottish Geographical Society on opening their session last Thursday night, a summary of which appeared in *The Times* of Friday. (14)

I am, Sir, your obedient servant,
GEORGE TAUBMAN GOLDIE, President R.G.S.
1, Savile-row, Burlington-gardens, London, W.,
Nov. 27.

Extract.

In an address which I delivered at York last August before the British Association I pointed out the advance in the appreciation of the importance of geography displayed by the governing classes. A case of atavism, recently brought to my notice, makes me fear that I was too sanguine as to the permanence of that advance.

In November, 1899, regulations were laid down for the examinations for the Foreign Office and Diplomatic Service which naturally (and I believe merely in repetition of earlier regulations) made geography an obligatory subject. A notice has lately been issued, to come into effect after July 1 next, under which geography will not only not be obligatory, but will altogether cease to be one of the subjects of examination. I have not time to give you a list of the many other subjects for which marks will be given to candidates, and which do not seem to be as important as geography to a Foreign Office clerk or to a secretary of an Embassy. I will only select six rather striking examples—animal physiology, physics, chemistry, moral and metaphysical philosophy, Sanscrit, and zoology. The last, of course, may be useful if he spends his leave in a country where big game is plentiful. In these six subjects the candidate might make 3,600 marks out of the *maximum* of 6,000 which he is not allowed to exceed. One is reminded of Mr. Gilbert's pattern of a modern major-general, in *The Pirates of Penzance*. who was an adept in every branch of knowledge excepting tactics and strategy.

The urgency of the case impels me to narrate an incident not yet published, especially as the principal actors in the scene are dead, so that no one's feelings will be hurt. A good many years ago a territorial arrangement with France was in discussion, and I was invited to consider it. The French proposals appeared to the Foreign Office satisfactory. On examination I found that they were expressed, as might have been expected, in longitudes reckonend from the meridian of Paris, while the map with which our Foreign Office were considering the proposals was made in Germany and reckonend its longitudes from the meridian of Greenwich. The arrangement in question was never completed.

This was an instance which came under my personal observation, but it is a matter of notoriety that some of our most serious international disputes of recent years have arisen from the faulty geography of the negotiators of treaties in the darker ages. Our Foreign Office and Diplomatic Service for years past have included men with geographical knowledge; but this improved condition will not last if geography is to be eliminated from the examinations, and Great Britain will see its future diplomatists contending with bows and arrows against foreign diplomatists armed with the best weapons of the 20th century. The most serious feature of the case, however, is that such an official denial of the national importance of geographical education is to-day possible. It shows the immense obstacles that still confront our geographical societies before they can make great and lasting advance in what seems to me one of their most urgent duties—that of educating the classes of Britain.

HIMALAYAN BARRIER

TO THE EDITOR OF THE TIMES

Sir,—On returning to England, I have found so much dissatisfaction in various scientific circles at the ultimate refusal of the Home Government to permit the ascent of Mount Everest that I shall be grateful if you can find space for the only three official letters, within my cognisance, on the subject. Mr. Morley telegraphs that he has no objection whatever to their publication.

The conception of this important scientific expedition was due to Lord Curzon; and as I am neither an original promoter of the scheme nor an Indian expert, I leave it to others to comment on the regrettable interposition by a Liberal Government of a Himalayan barrier to the advance of knowledge in this direction.

I am, Sir, your obedient servant,
GEORGE TAUBMAN GOLDIE, President R.G.S.
1, Savile-row, March 16.

Memorandum
1, Savile-row, Burlington-gardens, London, W.,
Jan. 23, 1907.
Scientific Expedition to Mount Everest

1.   Finance and Authority.—The funds are found by members of the Alpine Club; but the expedition is also under the auspices of the Royal Geographical Society.

2.   Leaders.—The expedition will be commanded, if the Government of India permit, by Major the Hon. Charles Bruce, M.V.O., of the 5th Gurkha Rifles, and son of the late Lord Aberdare. (15) Every one in India or in geographical circles at home will know that Major Bruce is exceptionally qualified for this work. Next to him is Dr. Tom G. Longstaff, M.A. (16) of Oxford (Christ Church), and who has also taken there a medical degree—M.D. In 1905, with the sanction of the Government of India, Dr. Longstaff accompanied Mr. Sherring, (17) I.C.S., in his extensive journey through Western Tibet and attained a height of about 23,000ft. Next to him is Mr. Arnold Mumm, late hon. secretary of the Alpine Club, who travelled last year in Uganda with Mr. Douglas Freshfield. Mr. Mumm is the partner of Mr. Edward Arnold, publisher to the India Office.

3.   Composition of Party.—The above three gentlemen, with three Alpine guides, two of whom were in Tibet in 1905 with Mr. Sherring, I.C.S., and showed great tact and consideration in all dealings with the inhabitants, while the third guide displayed conspicuously the same qualities in 1905 with Mr. Douglas Freshfield in Uganda. There will also be half a dozen Gurkhas from the 5th Rifles or other regiments; but these will go without their arms, so as to avoid the possibility of trouble. For the same reason no down-country native servants will be taken. Porters and baggage animals will be obtained, as usual, in concert with the local authorities.

4.   Nepaul.—Nepaul territory would be avoided. The party would travel from Darjeeling north to Kampadzong, just on the Tibetan side of the Indian frontier. There it would turn sharply and nearly due west to Kharta, from near which point it would commence the ascent and scientific observations. Whether successful or not, it would return by the same route, so that the Nepaul territory would nowhere be violated; moreover, there would be no appreciable inducement

to pass through Nepaul if the ascent is to be tried from the north, although it might be a convenience if the monthly supplies of provisions, sent to restock the party and in charge of natives, were allowed to cut the corner of Nepaul territory; but this is in no way essential.

5. Tibet.—As the expedition would turn its back on Lhasa directly it left Indian territory, and as the regions through which it would pass are very sparsely populated, there can be no question of Tibetan timidity or anxiety being aroused or of any friction or trouble occurring during the journey. It would not resemble Mr. Sherring's mission in 1905, which penetrated into the heart of Western Tibet, and which, nevertheless, encountered no opposition whatever.

6. General.—The party undertake that all monetary transactions with the natives shall be directly dealt with by the English leaders, and that no precaution shall be omitted to avoid any cause of friction.

GEORGE TAUBMAN GOLDIE, President R.G.S.

To the Right Hon. John Morley, M.P., etc., Foreign
Office, S.W.

India Office, Feb. 8, 1907.

Dear Sir George Goldie,—I have given full consideration to the proposal in your memorandum of January 23 that a British party should be given facilities by the Government of India to attempt the ascent of Mount Everest from the Tibetan side, avoiding Nepalese territory. And I am sorry to be obliged to refuse the present request for the same reasons which, as stated in the official letter from the Under-Secretary of State to the Royal Geographical Society of March 28 last, made it necessary for me to my great regret to decide that it was not possible, consistently with the interests of the policy of his Majesty's Government, for the Government of India to give encouragement or help to exploration in Tibet. There has been no change in the political situation since the letter of March 28 from this office to modify the considerations of high Imperial policy which led his Majesty's Government to decide that it was inexpedient to raise the question of facilities for travellers in Tibet with the authorities of Lhasa. And there can be no doubt that a British expedition proceeding by the route proposed through Tibetan territory, furtively as is suggested, and without previous notice to the Lhasa Government, would raise the question which his Majesty's Government, wish to avoid, in a more embarrassing form than if an application were made to the Tibetan Government for their consent.

I would add that this decision is based solely on considerations of public policy, and personally I am very sorry for the disappointment which it will cause to Major Bruce and Mr. Longstaff.

Yours sincerely,

JOHN MORLEY.

1, Savile-row, Burlington-gardens, London, W.,

Feb. 9, 1907.

Dear Mr. Morley—I am grieved at the decision announced in your official letter of the 8th inst., less on account of the public-spirited men who were prepared to risk their lives or spend their money on a scientific object than of the cause of knowledge itself which would have been promoted by the observations of various kinds made during the ascent of Mount Everest. I desire to disclaim very clearly and positively two assumptions on which your official letter appears largely to rest.

First, it never occurred to me that the expedition would be in any way "furtive." (18) I assumed that the Government of India would notify the Lhasa

Government that a purely scientific party desired to move from the British frontier along the sparsely populated inside edge of Tibetan territory to the summit of Everest, keeping its back turned on Lhasa for the whole of that journey. I do not believe in "furtive" policy except in war, when deceiving the enemy is recognized as fair.

Secondly, I submit that such a journey has nothing substantial in common with an exploration, such as was refused in your letter of March 28, 1906, which would have penetrated a considerable distance into a populous part of Tibet and largely in the direction of Lhasa.

I am yours faithfully,
GEORGE TAUBMAN GOLDIE, President R.G.S.
To the Right Hon. John Morley, M.P., etc.

26.   26 December, 1907. Page 6 Column 3

NATIONAL DEFENCE

TO THE EDITOR OF THE TIMES

Sir,—This day eight years ago, when the nation was in a state of discouragement now difficult to realize, I wrote to you to protest (19) against the undignified proposal, then widely advocated, to set aside a day of national humiliation, and I pointed out that before long not only the Boer war but also its salutary lessons would be practically forgotten. Your having published that letter emboldens me to ask for space to give full publicity for the first time to the policy of our association, which was formed in May, 1906. Its objects are as follows:—

1.   To assist, by the action of its members, in the maintenance and co-ordination of land forces adequate to the needs of the United Kingdom and the Empire.

2.   To support such expenditure upon the land forces as the security of the Empire necessitates.

3.   To promote continuity in our military policy, and to assist in removing military questions from the arena of party politics.

Our efforts in excluding party politics from our discussions during the last year have been entirely successful, thus proving that a large body of men of various shades of political opinion may find common ground in regarding Army questions from a national instead of a party point of view.

I need not enter here into our attitude towards the Territorial scheme, as that important point was amply dealt with at our recent annual general meeting, a full report of which can be obtained by writing to our hon. secretary, Mr. R. A. Johnson, 15, Tedworth-square, S.W., to whom also application should be made by those desiring to join our ranks. (20)

There is, however, another widely discussed question on which our association feel that their position should be made absolutely clear. Whatever views we may hold individually as to adopting compulsory adult service for the home Army or, on the other hand, maintaining a voluntary system, we are agreed on the urgent need for a powerful association, uncommitted to either of those policies, and engaged in keeping public attention alive not only to the general principle of possessing an adequate Army both for home and oversea service, but also to the subsidiary and often vital questions which will constantly arise in connexion with this principle. To make the utmost, at all times, of the system that we happen to live under has therefore been adopted as the basis of our association. It is outside of our sphere to criticize other societies or individuals in

188

their endeavours either to bring about compulsory service of adults or to maintain a voluntary system. We believe that by carefully refraining from any corporate pronouncement on this highly controversial subject we may be able to exercise an influence on all Army questions such as we could not possess if we were able to take sides in a polemic involving political and social considerations which lie at the root of our national life and necessarily arouse strong personal feeling. We have thus been able to enlist in our ranks supporters of both these principles, as well as others who are as yet unpledged to either. Moreover, in any appeal that we may make to Parliament or to the public, our arguments are likely to receive more unprejudiced consideration than would be the case if we approached them as partisans of a cause to which at any rate a large section would be vehemently opposed.

On these grounds we confidently appeal to men of all parties in the State who are convinced of the necessity of maintaining a degree of military strength commensurate with our responsibilities to give effect to their convictions by joining our association.

I have the honour to be, Sir, your obedient servant,
GEORGE TAUBMAN GOLDIE.

National Defence Association, London, Dec. 25. (21)

27. February, 1909. Page 8 Column 6

THE SITUATION IN VENEZUELA

TO THE EDITOR OF THE TIMES

Sir,—Having often derided the political tourists who hasten to instruct their countrymen about some distant land where they have been spending a few weeks, I am anxious not to join that army of bores. But there are two reasons which may justify my sending you, in brief form, my impressions on the present interesting situation in the capital of Venezuela.

The first is that there seems to be no other compatriot here whose position would permit of his doing so. The British colony consists of a Minister, a chaplain to the Legation, a Vice-Consul, and some half-dozen railway officials. There are no British merchants, no visitors, no independent residents, such as one might expect to find in perhaps the most perfect climate in the Tropics, and in a land where every prospect pleases. The Castro régime (22) was not calculated to encourage the influx of foreigners. Indeed, it was almost as difficult then to leave the country as to enter it.

The other reason is that the immediate future of Venezuela rests entirely on the character of General Juan Vicente Gomez, (23) and that no story of the dramatic events of last month could give a true picture of that character unless supplemented by personal impressions derived from conversation with him since he attained unlimited power. For there is no question that his power is absolute so long as it endures at all. I do not doubt that he could change his whole Cabinet every month without prejudicing his personal hold on the country. The host of newly-born newspapers—most of the old ones have disappeared like last year's snow—speak constantly of the President and never of his Ministers. It has always been so in Venezuela. The Liberator (24) was as absolute in his time as Castro in his; it was a matter of fortune alone that Bolivar was a hero and a patriot. Guzman Blanco (25) might have remained a dictator until his death, if he had not rashly, like Castro, placed the Atlantic between himself and his country, and, at that distance, quarrelled with those he had left in power. The tendency of the Spanish Americans, especially in the equatorial regions, towards absolute submission (tempered by insurrections) to any exceptionally energetic or reckless individual may be reasonably traced to their inveterate idleness or carelessness, partly induced by climate and partly inherited from Old Spain. (26) This national characteristic explains the anxiety with which so many here have asked me whether Castro's operation was not likely to incapacitate him permanently; while others have assured me that unless Europe prevents his returning here he may, in a single day, once more become master of the country. In that case he would again find at his feet those who are now outstepping the bounds of decency in vilifying and ridiculing him.

It is at this point that the full character of General Gomez becomes of vital importance to Venezuela. Although he had the reputation of being the real organizer of Castro's military victories, he was apparently unambitious and he had, at any rate, no opportunity of making his mark as a statesman during the recent dictatorship. Gifted with an open, cheerful, and highly sympathetic manner, which covers, I feel confident, unsounded depths of diplomacy, he leaves one not quite certain whether he was goaded unwillingly into action by his colleagues, by the popular demonstration of Sunday, December 13, and by the (alleged) telegram from Castro urging his assassination, or whether he had fully determined on his coup d'Etat from the moment that the tyrant left the country. But we do know that during that long period of delay, when his own life was not worth a week's purchase, he neither hurried nor lost his head, but gradually and secretly brought trustworthy troops into Caracas until, on Friday, December 19, he was ready for action, when he arrested the hostile colonels and politicians in the midst of their followers and with his own hands.

This remarkable union of the patient and intrepid soldier with the urbane and cordial diplomatist gives me strong confidence in the stability of his rule. I cannot conceive his ever suffering from nerves, such as undoubtedly lay at the root of that ferocity which brought upon Castro the hatred of all. The calm strength of General Gomez will deal promptly and effectively with any attempt of the late President to seize the reins.

As regards his future relations with Europe, we are bound to believe his friendly assurances. A sceptical attitude towards the new *régime,* however justified by Venezuelan history, would be no less impolitic than impolite. "Tell them in England that my policy is liberty at home and peace abroad." I believe him implicitly, were it only that he can best sustain himself by acting on lines exactly opposed to those of his predecessor. General Gomez has already redressed some serious injuries which Castro had inflicted on British subjects. It seems probable that he will pursue this policy to the end. I do not mean that he is the man to concede one iota to certain claims which some of our countrymen have put forward; and I earnestly trust, for the credit of England, that the Foreign Office will not press these unduly. But there are other claims, national and individual, which must be satisfied if British Commerce, or indeed any commerce, is to enter this country with confidence. Fortunately, we have in Venezuela a British Minister of exceptional judgment, power of work, and quiet insistence, who can be trusted both to advise the Home Government soundly and to negotiate ably and smoothly on the spot. It is surprising to me how we get a man of that calibre to serve in Venezuela. We may feel assured that Sir Vincent Corbett (27) will press no claim which cannot be fairly sustained, but that he will not rest until all sound claims have either been satisfied by Venezeula or abandoned by England.

I am, Sir, your obedient servant,
GEORGE TAUBMAN GOLDIE.

Caracas, Jan. 24.

28. 16 September, 1913. Page 7 Column 5

PHYSICAL AND MILITARY EDUCATION

TO THE EDITOR OF THE TIMES

Sir,—Admiral Sir N. Bowden-Smith (28) asks for a home army of at least 400,000 men ready for instant mobilization.

Since the unfortunate beginning of this century many of us have urged that the recruiting difficulty, both for the Regular Army and for a home army, would entirely disappear, within a few years, if the nation began at the right end by giving a sound physical and military education to its boys, just as, under Mr. Forster's Act, it gives them a sound elementary education in other ways.

Ten valuable years have been lost since this proposal was first made officially in the volume issued by the Royal Commission (29) on the South African War—a delay partly due to the fear of each political party of unfair treatment in the constituencies—but there are many signs of our approaching this solution of our difficulties. There is reason to believe that some of our leading Ministers would be favourably disposed, if they could be assured of the question being removed from the political arena. On the other hand, Lord Lansdowne has taken every recent opportunity in the House of Lords of advocating the proposal. The committee of the National Defence Association, a very influential and non-party body, strongly urged the proposal a few months ago on Mr. Asquith, as Chairman of the Imperial Defence Committee.

I will not encroach on your kindness by a repetition of arguments to which you have so often afforded the hospitality of your columns. My desire now is only to express the belief that the time has come when the Press can do an incalculable service to the country and Empire by keeping this important subject before the public.

I am, Sir, your obedient servant,
GEORGE TAUBMAN GOLDIE. (30)

September 15.

(1) The seventh Earl of Hopetoun and the first Marquess of Linlithgow, 1860-1908. Lord Hopetoun was the first Governor-General of Australia, 1900-1902.

(2) Perham *op cit.,* p. 67.

(3) It is not easy, in these days of International Aid Programmes, to understand the extreme controversy which the decision to construct a railway from Mombasa to the shores of Lake Victoria sparked off when it was first announced.

Very quickly, as the work went ahead, the project was nicknamed *"The Lunatic Line"* after a doggerell verse which appeared in a London newspaper.

"What it will cost, no words can express,
What is its object, no brain can suppose.
Where it will start from, no one can guess,
Where it is going to, nobody knows.
What is the use of it, none can conjecture,
What it will carry, no one can define,
and in spite of George Curzon's superior lecture,
it clearly is naught but a lunatic line."

(Attributed to Heny Labouchere.)

George Curzon, of course, became both Viceroy of India and later Foreign Secretary. At the time, he was Under Secretary for Foreign Affairs.

In actual fact, the line set many records, but cost was not one of them. A great deal of trouble was caused to the construction gangs by lions, elephants and rhino: some of the supervisory staff were killed by the Kikuyu. The final spike was driven in by Mrs. R. O. Preston, wife of one of the Works Foremen, who had come with him from India and had

191

remained throughout the whole construction. The date was 19 December, 1901. Goldie must therefore almost certainly have been on the inaugural train. For a somewhat different account of this railway from that which Goldie gives, see J. Mannix, *African Bush Adventure,* Hamilton, London, 1954.

(4) Mr. (later Sir) George Whitehouse, 1857-1938. Railway Engineer who worked in Natal, Mexico, India, Peru, Argentine and Uganda. He was Manager and Chief Engineer of the Uganda Railway from 1895-1903.

(5) "No caparisons, miss, if you please. Caparisons don't become a young woman. No!" R. B. Sheridan, *The Rivals,* Act IV, Scene II, Line 6.

(6) The area that later came to be called "The White Highlands" of Kenya.

(7) Goldie was always insistent that he had never held office under the Crown, but his insistence was open to possible challenge, since he was a Privy Councillor.

(8) French proverbial saying, "One does not constitute an act of usage" i.e. "One swallow doesn't make a summer" etc.

(9) This letter represents the only example of Goldie's involvement in the affairs of a domestic governing body (in this case, the L.C.C.) that has come to light. At this time, Goldie was not yet a member of the L.C.C.

His reference to the possible "conflict of interest" resulting from his financial commitment has an extraordinarily modern ring.

(10) The reference is to John Elliot Burns, 1858-1943. Labour leader, Trade Unionist, Socialist Politician and Radical. In 1880-81, Burns was employed by the United African Company as a foreman engineer on dockyard construction at Akassa. Later his career turned to politics. L.C.C. Representative for Battersea, 1889-1907; Member of Parliament, 1892-1918; the "first artisan" (D.N.B.) to attain Cabinet rank, he was successively Pres. Local Govt. Board, 1905-12; Minister of Health, 1912-14; President of the Board of Trade, 1914. Burns opposed the 1914-18 War and resigned his post in protest. See also page 52.

(11) Goldie was a member of the London County Council, as an Alderman, from 1908 to 1921, becoming Chairman of the Finance Committee in 1919. No doubt his stand on this issue was one which commended him to the Council in due course.

(12) See pages 206-208.

(13) Sir Clement Hill was a member of the Selborne Committee. On retirement from the Civil Service he entered Parliament. He also succeeded Goldie as President of the African Society and they appear to have become friendly, though their earlier encounters, especially in 1897, had not been marked by either trust or cordiality.

(14) For both the addresses referred to in the extract, see pages 238 and 247.

(15) Although disappointed on this occasion, Bruce (1866-1939) led both the 1922 and 1924 expeditions to attempt Mount Everest.

(16) Thomas George Longstaff, b.1875; Alpinist. Contributed a chapter in C. A. Sherring's book *Western Tibet and the British Border-land etc.,* Arnold, London, 1906.

(17) Sherring, Charles Atmore, led expedition into Tibet in 1905.

(18) But see page 22. Goldie was certainly advocating being "furtive" then. Perhaps he regarded the Company's relations with France as being tantamount to a state of war!

(19) Goldie's letter of 25 December, 1899 was not in fact perceived by the Editor of the *Times* to be primarily a protest against the then proposed day of national humiliation and prayer. Its chief concern was that the public preoccupation with the misfortunes of the time might damage its appreciation and support of the Livingstone Exhibition. That letter, the last Goldie wrote whilst Governor of the R.N.C., is reproduced on page 174.

(20) This refers to the formation of the "Territorial Army," originally conceived as an exclusively Home Defence Force. This was, of course, immediately modified on the outbreak of the 1914-18 War, by whole units "volunteering" for service overseas. The idea of exclusive home-service was eminently unsound from the start, and Goldie naturally spotted this.

(21) Goldie's interest in matters of National Defence had always been acute. It will be recalled that he dwelt on this subject at some length in his introduction to Vandeleur, and that there are several other references to the same subject in his other writings or speeches and in particular there is the minority report which he attached to the South African War Commission. See page 206 ff.

(22) Castro, Cipriano, 1858-1924. Dictator of Venezuela from 1899-1908, when he went to Paris for medical treatment and was deposed by Gomez. In 1902, a combined

British, German and Italian fleet had blockaded Carraccas to enforce the payment of international debts.

(23) Gomez, Gen. Juan Vincente, 1864-1935. Dictator of Venezuela, 1908-1935. Castro's righthand man in his own push for power, Gomez overthrew him when he left the country. Though considerably better than the Castro regime, Gomez's was equally absolute, and to its opponents, equally objectionable. On Gomez's death there was no structured mechanism of succession. He did not build beyond his own personal rule. Goldie was entirely correct in his assessment of the "absolutism" of the regime.

(24) Bolivar, Simon, 1783-1830. A Venezuelan aristocrat who became the prime-mover in the Latin American independence movement as "el Libertador."

(25) Guzman Blanco, Antonio, 1829-1899. Venezuelan President, 1870-89. An out and out dictator, his regime was marked by a period of brutality and oppression. He died in Paris after ten years of exile.

(26) Goldie's low opinion of "Mediterranean types" is a constant! See page 181.

(27) Captain Sir Vincent Corbett, 1861-1936. Foreign Service. British Minister-Resident, Venezuela, 1907-10.

(28) Admiral Sir Nathaniel Bowden-Smith, 1838-1921. C. in C. Australia, 1892-95; of the Nore, 1895-1900. Attended International Maritime Conference, Washington, 1889.

(29) See pages 204 ff.

(30) This is the last letter that Goldie wrote to the *Times* (or that the paper published). The cut-off is abrupt and the reason for it is obscure.

IX. INTERVIEWS WITH REUTERS' CORRESPONDENTS AND EXPRESSIONS OF OPINION

FIRST INTERVIEW WITH REUTERS' CORRESPONDENT

The interview took place on 6 April, 1897 and was reported in the *Times* the following day, April 7th, page 12, column 2.

RETURN OF SIR GEORGE GOLDIE

Sir George Goldie, the Governor of the Niger Company, arrived at Calais last night from the Niger Territories, having travelled *via* Lisbon and Paris. He left Senegal by the French mail steamer on February 25. Lord Scarbrough accompanied Sir George Goldie from Paris.

A representative of Reuter's Agency met Sir George Goldie on his arrival and travelled with him to London. In the course of conversation and in reply to questions Sir George Goldie said:—

"The political situation in the region of the recent operations is thoroughly satisfactory. The new Emir of Bida has stated that his authority is recognized by the native Fulah princes in Northern Nupé, and that he is thoroughly determined to carry out his engagements with the company.(1) He feels quite capable of holding his own, and there is no fear that he will try to throw off the yoke of the company. This precludes any possibility of a renewal of the practices of slave-raiding which principally brought about the recent war. The three mile strip on the north-east bank of the Niger, reserved by the company, is now organized under native rulers, who feel secure of the company's support against any possible invasion from the north.(2) In the region south-west of the Niger no possibility exists of any further trouble, Ilorin Lafiaci *(sic)* and Shonga feeling themselves isolated from the rest of the Fulah Empire, while South Nupé is locally administered by the numerous tribes as in the days before the Fulah conquest.(3) Autonomous rule is now established as in all the pagan regions administered by the company during the past ten years. The relations with Sokoto and the Fulah Emirs are excellent, and I have no reason to anticipate any trouble in that direction."

Asked whether there was no possibility of an infraction of the treaties entered into with the company, Sir George Goldie replied:—

"It must be remembered that we have not been conquering the natives of the country, but their taskmasters, who must not be regarded as ignorant savages. The present Emir of Bida knows full well that if he were to lose the support of the company he would not retain his throne for a day. Moreover, the company has, in order to enforce its treaties if necessary, the same force with which it compelled the conclusion of those treaties. The position of the troops of the company is now almost exactly as before the campaign commenced. The main body still has its headquarters at Lokoja."

In reply to questions regarding the position at Boussa, Sir George Goldie remarked:—

"I have not the slightest anxiety on that point. The rights involved are not those of the company but of Great Britain. After the issue of the charter her Majesty's Government declared a protectorate over all the territories of the company, and at a later period notified France and Germany of the political treaty of 1890 between the company and Boussa. It is therefore impossible to suppose that the Government of the Republic is responsible directly for the invasion of a region about the value of which opinions may differ, but which undoubtedly falls within the British protectorate as notified by the Powers. I have little doubt that the occupation in question, although undoubtedly official, is the act only of the French colony of Dahomey, and that the Government of Paris will not hesitate, when the facts are put fully before them, to withdraw from an untenable position." (4)

"As you have touched upon this question," continued Sir George Goldie, "I should like to correct an entirely erroneous statement which is reproduced in the French Press as to my occupation last year of a position opposite to Bajibo. It is asserted that the French Government withdrew their troops from Fort d' Arenberg in view of a conference being held at Paris to discuss French and British rights in these regions, and that thereupon I occupied that post. This is quite inexact; the withdrawal of the French from Fort d' Arenberg, which was due to the representations of her Majesty's Government, took place three months before the appointment of the Paris Commission, it being recognized that the region opposite Bajibo was really a portion of Boussa and therefore within the British protectorate. In placing the company's troops in that post I had no idea whatever of providing against any return of the French there. My action was due entirely to a rumour which reached me on my way to Boussa, but which afterwards proved untrue, that a German expedition from Togoland was crossing the Niger with a view to establishing itself opposite to Bajibo. The new name given to the post of Fort Goldie (5) was not given by myself but by Captain Turner after I had left. As a matter of fact I was on the Niger when the Commission met and was unaware of their proceedings. I never contemplated the possibility of a French return to Bajibo."

SECOND INTERVIEW WITH REUTERS' CORRESPONDENT

The interview took place on 23 October, 1897. The following report of it appeared in the *Times* the following Monday, October 25th. Page 6 Column 6.

SIR GEORGE GOLDIE ON WEST AFRICA

A representative of Reuter's Agency called upon Sir George Goldie, Governor of the Royal Niger Company, on Saturday, for the purpose of eliciting some information with regard to the situation created by the conflicting claims of Great Britain and France in West Africa. In reply to questions put to him, Sir George Goldie said:—

"As regards the immense region known as the bend of the Niger, stretching from the west bank of the Middle Niger to the east bank of the Upper Niger, I am not at liberty to discuss the respective rights of Great Britain and France, for this question is now being dealt with by the Joint Commission sitting in Paris. I may, however, correct some important errors of fact, which, if not contradicted, would reflect on the Niger Company. One of these errors has been repeated almost daily for the last six months in one organ or another of the French Press. It is the effect that the Niger Company has never had troops in Boussa, and has, therefore, shown no signs of occupying the country. I think that this error has arisen from a very natural confusion of the extensive territory known as Boussa, which covers nearly the whole west branch of the Middle Niger from Say down to the Ilorin frontier, with its capital, Boussa Town. Now, in February, 1896—that is to say, nearly 13 months before the recent French invasion—I myself established two military posts in Boussa. One of these is at Leaba, about 30 miles south of Boussa Town. The company had for years had a political and commercial station at Leaba. The other military post was about 60 miles south of Boussa Town, and was named Fort Goldie by Captain Turner, whom I placed in command there. At that time, February, 1896, there was not a single French soldier, traveller, missionary, or trader anywhere either in Boussa territory, or in the *Hinterland* of Lagos, as the French expeditions which had previously traversed those regions had been withdrawn to Dahomey on the representations of Lord Rosebery that those districts were within the British Empire. In fact, an official intimation of a British protectorate had been sent to Paris on January 1, 1895, by her Majesty's Government, and had been received without any protest."

"Why did you not put troops into the capital, Boussa Town, instead of Leaba and Fort Goldie?"

"Well, I did casually throw out that suggestion to the late King Dagba(6) when I visited him at Boussa Town in February, 1896."

"And I suppose he objected?"

"No, he said very little about it, but his favourite wife, a very able and voluble lady, who monopolised most of the conversation, said that so long as the Niger Company afforded, when wanted, the assistance promised in the treaty made by Mr. Lister in 1890, placing the country under the protection of the Great Queen, there was no need to have troops in Boussa town; that the company already had troops in two places—this reference being to Leaba and Fort Goldie—that every one knew how troublesome 'women palavers' were in Lokoja and other towns where troops were stationed; and that Boussa town having a large population, and being the King's residence, they did not want to have those troubles there. I entirely agreed with her view, being myself stongly opposed to stationing coloured troops amongst large populations, unless absolutely necessary."

"Then, as a matter of fact, the company's troops have never entered Boussa town?"

"Oh, yes. Our Agent-General, Mr. Wallace, had an escort of Hausa troops with him when he visited Boussa town in 1894, on his return from his mission to Gandu and Wurnu, the capital of the Sokoto Empire. I took a small escort of Hausa troops there in February, 1896, and Lieutenant Carroll (Norfolk Regiment) took a considerable body of our troops there in December, 1896, only a month before the recent French invasion."

"How was it that you did not forestall the French in their occupation last January?"

"You may remember that during the whole of January and February last I was engaged with the entire available force of the company in the wars with Nupe and Ilorin, on the very hazardous issue of which depended the existence of British influence over the half million square miles which constitute Nigeria."

"Then you imply that the French took an unfair advantage of your critical position?"

"I imply nothing. I only state facts."

"You referred just now to other errors of fact?"

"The most important is the constantly-repeated statement that the King of Boussa did not recognize the protectorate of Great Britain. On this I need only say that the late King Dagba, after reading a letter from her Majesty[7] that I was commissioned to deliver to him, received publicly from my hands a British flag, and said that he would show it, as a proof of the British Protectorate, to any of the 'wandering people' who might come there. That reference was to the French expeditions which had traversed Boussa territory the previous year. He laid great stress on the unbroken and advantageous relations he had had with the Niger Company for years, and his firm intention of upholding the 1890 treaty with Great Britain. It is well to point out that the present King, Ikki,[8] carried out the intention of his brother and predecessor, King Dagba, by at once producing the British flag on the arrival last January of the French force under Lieutenant Bretonnet; but, according to a message that King Ikki sent to me, the French officer replied by threatening to destroy his town. King Ikki sent repeated messages between January and July last asking the Niger Company to come and drive the French out, which would have been an easy matter, but, its steadfast refusal to do so has now undoubtedly driven the King into the arms of France."

"What force has the company at its disposal?"

"Without counting irregular levies, it has a thoroughly disciplined force of 1,000 troops, chiefly Hausas, well trained in musketry and machine gun drill. Its armament consists of Whitworth field guns, Nordenfelt shell guns, seven-pounder mountain guns, Maxim machine guns, and Gardner machine guns."[9]

"Is it not a fact that at the Berlin conference of 1884 France induced the 14 nations represented not to extend to the interior of Africa the new principle of effective occupation which the conference was then imposing on the coast possessions of the African continent, and that in the recent convention between France and Germany regarding Togoland the basis of settlement was priority of treaties with native rulers? Have you seen the telegram published to-day, quoting a letter to the *Temps* from 'A Colonist' on the subject of your agent Mr. Macaulay?"

"Yes, it is very amusing, but altogether inaccurate. I do not see how the company can seriously reply to anonymous inventions of that character. The company have already stated that Mr. Macaulay is no Nigerian savage. He is an educated native of Sierra Leone, a British subject, and he has for many years borne so excellent a character that he need not concern himself with the attacks of Captain Toutée. I may add that, in the matter of clothes, he is usually as well dressed as any one on the Boulevard des Italians, but in the climate of West Africa even Europeans appear sometimes in light costume. But the question is not whether Captain Toutée surprised Mr. Macaulay in his pyjamas or without them. Captain Toutée made a definite accusation that Mr. Macaulay stole his sugar. It does not seem fair to further political objects by destroying the private character of an honourable man even though he has a black skin. Yet in spite of the industrious manner in which this calumny has been repeated in the French Press during the last year, the company would not have taken the trouble to deny it if it had not been reproduced in an editorial article of so influential a newspaper as the *Temps,* which takes the opportunity to scoff at British stations directed by such an agent.[10] I notice that while the anonymous 'Colonist' is at pains to prove that Captain Toutée did not pass himself off as a private individual when in Boussa territory, a fact which the company never asserted, he does not meet the real point—namely, that before he started for Africa the friends of Captain Toutée in France both wrote to and interviewed the company in London asking it to help Captain Toutée up as far as Boussa, from which place he wished to proceed to the French possession at Timbukto, and definitely stating that he had no political object but was going solely as a private individual.''

THIRD INTERVIEW WITH REUTERS' CORRESPONDENT

According to Stephen Gwynn (who might, in fact, have been the correspondent concerned) this interview took place on 5 July, 1899. There is some supporting evidence for this date in the text, but if so, the *Times* did not carry the interview, nor can Messers. Reuters, who have been helpful in making a search, trace any record of the original draft. [11] Gwynn, however is quite specific as to the date and the source, and he quotes extensively from it in his historical preface to Lady Wellesley's book. Since Messers. Reuters can not authenticate the text, however, there is no assurance that what follows, in a form that has been reconstructed from the separate though often lengthy quotations which Gwynn employed, contains all of what passed between Goldie and his interviewer or that it has not been edited in the process. Of course, exactly the same thing could be said in respect to any other published interview and only if the original text is available is this qualification negated.

Thus both the following and the previous texts are really all "second hand":—

Question:—"Have you carried out all that you originally intended?"

Answer:—"By no means! At thirty, one's dreams are in excess of the capacity of execution.

At the close of 1877, when the idea of making Nigeria British was first conceived, there was no foreigner, whether trader, soldier, missionary or traveller, in the entire basins of the Niger and Lake Chad, between the French colony of Senegal on the extreme west of Africa and the valley of the Nile on the extreme east, or between the seaboard factories on the Gulf of Guinea to the south and the Algerian and Tunisian frontiers on the north. But it took until July, 1879 to amalgamate British Nigerian interests, and then two years had to be allowed to prove the value of Niger commerce before attempting to float a public company with a capital of a million sterling, with the object of obtaining a charter of government.

For I must tell you that I made the first application for a charter in 1881, when I found that a large capital would be an essential preliminary to obtaining it. When in consequence the National African Company was launched in July 1882, we had already completed the negotiations with the Paris Society for amalgamating with us under the British flag, another essential preliminary to the issue of a charter; but meanwhile M. Gambetta pushed into the Lower Niger a Marseilles Society with a large capital, so that when I went over to Paris with the deeds for signature, I was met by a refusal at the last moment; as the Paris people pointed out that they would be sacrificing their flag to no purpose, seeing that another French Society was in the field. This made the issue of a charter impossible for the time.

198

When some two years later, we had at last cleared the way for a charter by taking over both the French Societies, Germany, to the surprise of the world, suddenly launched out as a colonising Power, and summoned the West African Conference in Berlin, thus commencing the real scramble for Africa. We were then told that a charter could not be granted, and we had to wait a year for it.

The only stroke of fortune that we have had throughout was the reaction in France in 1884 against colonial enterprises, in consequence of those disasters in Tonking, to which M. Jules Ferry, the great Colonial Minister, owed his downfall, and the nickname of 'Le Tonkinois.' But for this reaction in France, which lasted until the Paris Exhibition of 1889, and which she has long and rightly deplored, we might have been pushed out of Nigeria. If, apart from this, we had had a little less ill luck throughout, we should have extended British influence over double our present area, and should, in extent of territory, have rivalled British India.

Not that the loss is very greatly to be regretted, for England has, in Nigeria, even as now limited, the most populous and valuable area of tropical Africa. She may well rest and be thankful. On the ratification last month of the Anglo-French Convention, her work of political expansion in those regions terminated, and the ground became clear for the coming work of commercial and industrial development.

I attribute the success of the Company chiefly to our following a definite plan from the commencement instead of growing up by accident. I do not mean that we have not modified the details of that plan under stress of circumstances; but in the main the policy conceded on the Niger in 1877 has been maintained to this day and has been played out like a game of chess.''

Question:—''Is the transfer satisfactory from an Imperial standpoint?''

Answer:—''Very much so, as a pecuniary transaction; for the empire is buying for a mess of pottage a great province, which has cost twenty years of arduous labour to build up, and for which either Germany, or France, or both, would have paid a very different sum. Yet I would rather have seen the transfer deferred, if practicable, for ten or fifteen years, with some modification of the charter such as I have advocated, not only since its issue, but in earlier days, especially in 1884 and 1885. However I fully recognise that the recent international crisis precipitated matters, for the company has always aroused a good deal of animosity abroad. This could not possibly be otherwise, since the colonial parties of two foreign nations considered Nigeria to be the most valuable part of tropical Africa and were annoyed at being forestalled. Before July 1890 we were not popular in Germany, where efforts were made to get our charter withdrawn. This, happily, is long ago forgotten; but from November 1890 we have been unfortunately quite disliked in France, where—as in Germany—our work is much better known than it is in England, whose Colonial Empire is too wide for public opinion to pay much attention to Nigeria. I can only conceive that as our political work of foundation is completed, it may now be in the wider interests of the Empire to replace us by a direct Imperial administration.''

Question:—''How do you regard the terms, as considered from the shareholders' standpoint?''

Answer:—''In the early seventies, during some Carlist troubles, I met at a *fonda* in the Spanish Pyrenees a commercial traveller, of course a Liberal, who was complaining bitterly of a Carlist band having stopped the Gerona diligence and appropriated his boxes. A priest asked whether his clothes were left on him, and being told they were, said, 'Then you ought to think yourself well treated; for, a short time ago a band of Liberals stopped the diligence and sent the passengers away in newspapers.' ''

Question:—"What are your personal feelings about the transfer?"

Answer:—"I suppose that no man could lay down without some slight wrench the almost uncontrolled powers which the confidence both of my colleagues and also of the Secretaries of State has left in my hands during the thirteen years of our existence as a Chartered Government. Yet I am glad to be released from almost crushing work, always at full speed and high pressure. Until I went to the Andes last autumn to get away from dispatches and telegrams, I had not had a rest for over twenty years. There is also some pleasure at having realised what, in 1877, was only a conception, subject to risks of failure. To-day Great Britain is about to take up and carry on our work, which, while giving peace and freedom to the millions of Nigeria, will add not inconsiderably to the well-being of the millions of our own island."

Question:—"Why as has been already announced, do you propose to sever your connection with the Company, and what is your future to be?"

Answer:—"There are two personal reasons for my ceasing to belong to the Company when it ceases to govern Nigeria. The only one that I choose to make public is one of pride.

When I first took up this Niger question I had no personal pecuniary interest in it whatever, nor did I intend ever to have such an interest. My investment in it came later. I have given to the work what no pecuniary reward, however great, could have induced me to give. Probably my name will soon be forgotten in connection with Nigeria, and to this I am indifferent; but, if it is remembered, it shall not be as chairman of a Nigerian financial company, which, however useful and however important, will necessarily exist for purposes of profit alone."

Question:—"Is there any truth in the statement that you are to obtain some responsible Government appointment?"

Answer:—"None whatever, these persistent remarks have caused me a good deal of annoyance and correspondence, and I shall be obliged if you will contradict them emphatically. Up to last Friday I had been battling with a cautious and economical Treasury on behalf of shareholders whose risks had made success possible. I had been in the position of a trustee negotiating for those whose interests I was bound to put before all others. I could not possibly have mixed up with these negotiations any discussion as to my own occupations for the future. If later on the Government consider that I could be of service to the Empire in any capacity I should, of course, be proud to serve it."

(1) In the event, Goldie's hopes proved too sanguine. The Markum Muhammadu, whom Goldie had installed as Emir was not able to hold on to his post even till the end of 1897. That this was a result of the French incursion "hamstringing" the Company by precluding the military action Goldie here envisages, cannot be doubted.
(2) Note the immediate application of the basic principle of Indirect Rule.
(3) Note, also, the application of that same principle to "Pagan" political systems, a thing which Lugard never effectively attempted. It was left to Sir Donald Cameron (1931-1935) to initiate this policy fully.
(4) As in fact they eventually did, though not without side-effects which ultimately destroyed Goldie's system of Company rule.
(5) It is interesting to see Goldie disclaiming having any part in the naming of Fort Goldie. Turner probably knew his man!

(6) The ruling Chief of Bussa when Goldie visited him in 1896 was the tenth Chief in P. R. Diggle's table of geneology as reproduced in the *Kontagora Provincial Gazeteer*, Waterlow & Son, London, 1920. His name was Kissan Dogo and he ruled from 1895 to 1902. His predecessor was Dan Tauro, 1862-1895. By Bussa reckoning, Dan Tauro was the 706th Chief.

(7) See also page 149.

(8) Actually Kissan Dogo, 1895-1902. The only explanation that can be offered for these extraordinary names that Goldie uses is that he was *"ad libbing"* them and had little fear of contradiction!

(9) Goldie is clearly indulging in a little "sabre rattling," no doubt for the edification of his French readers.

(10) The R.N.C.'s policy in respect to the promotion of its black employees to positions of responsibilty has been noted elsewhere, but see also pages 142, 163 and p. 147 footnote 11.

(11) Exhaustive searches were made, but the negative results were reported in two letters dated 17 October and 22 November, 1974.

X. "SIR GEORGE GOLDIE ON . . ."

During the active years, in addition to the correspondence from him, the *Times* published three expressions of Goldie's opinion. One of them, in effect constitutes a minority report constituting a part of the Report of the Royal Commission on the Conduct of the South African War, is of major importance. The other two are minor, but nonetheless not without their specialised interest. The first of them appeared in the *Times* on 17 January, 1898 (page 10, column 3). It contains an eloquent expression of hope for Anglo-American co-operation during the twentieth century.

SIR GEORGE GOLDIE ON NIGERIA

The monthly dinner of the Anglo-African Writers' Club was held last night at the Grand Hotel. Mr. H. Rider Haggard(1) occupied the chair, and among those present were Sir George Goldie (the guest of the evening), Sir Walter Peace, Mr. J. Hays Hammond, Mr. Silva White, Captain E.A. Haggard, Mr. C. Kiralfy, the Hon. Howard Spensley, Lieutenant-Colonel Forrester, Mr. H. A. Bryden, Captain Beville, Captain Dyke Acland, Mr. Lionel Decle, and Mr. Greville E. Matheson (hon. secretary).

The CHAIRMAN, in proposing "The Guest of the Evening," said that the club had on previous occasions entertained many distinguished men, among them Mr. Rudyard Kipling, Mr. Justice Koetze, and Mr. Bryce. (2) To-night they entertained a man of action in the person of Sir George Goldie, one of those who had aided to build up the Empire of which they were all so proud, and which was now the wonder of the world. (Cheers.)This Empire had been largely raised, not by Governments at home, but by individuals. Individuals had done the work, and afterwards, frequently with reluctance, the Governments had approved that work. Their guest, who began life as a good soldier, had shown his ability in many ways. He had, for example, learned eight languages, a by no means easy feat (laughter), and he was the moving spirit of the Royal Niger Company. The campaign against the Mohammedan power in Nigeria had been organized by Sir George Goldie, and had been carried by him to a successful end. By his aid there had been added a vast territory to the British Empire, and Sir George had been doing in West Africa what Mr. Rhodes had been striving to secure in South Africa. (Cheers.) At the end of the campaign Sir George was able to write to his company:—"I have this day issued on behalf of the Council of Administration a decree abolishing the legal *status* of slavery in the Niger territories." (Cheers.) As the keynote of society in this region had been slavery of a peculiarly cruel kind, those were very proud words for any man to be able to write, knowing them to be true. (Cheers.)

SIR GEORGE GOLDIE, in response, said that the whole of his working life had been absorbed in watching and helping the most exciting drama that this century had offered to their contemplation—the regeneration of Africa, (Cheers.) In this great drama our country could not have taken the leading part which it had taken if it had not been for the ideas, the influence, and the co-operation of Anglo-African writers. He did not refer solely to what was generally known as serious literature. If he were asked to say to what class of writing South Africa owed so much he should give the palm to fiction.(Laughter.) (3) It was a commonplace to say that the policy of this country was directed by "the man in the street," but even commonplaces were sometimes true. One had only to glance at the lists of our public libraries to know that out of the books which the general public read there were nine of fiction to one of other literature. Works of imagination appealed especially to the young, and it was by the young that new Africa was to be made; and he feared that Mr. Rider Haggard and others must bear the responsibility of sending a large number of stalwart young Britons to seek their fortunes in South Africa. (Laughter and cheers.) Equatorial Africa had not been made the happy hunting ground of the newspaper correspondent, except when a large campaign had been organized, and Equatorial Africa had not hitherto been prolific of fiction. (Laughter.) He defined Equatorial Africa as those tropical regions where in the present state of our medical knowledge the northern races could not settle from generation to generation. He expressly excluded from the term anything which meant those tropical regions, if there were any—and he did not assert that there were—where at present such colonizing was possible. It would be a great service if Anglo-African writers could devise a term which the public could accept for Equatorial Africa such as he had defined it. It would simplify discussions on African questions. He made an effort in that direction himself, but he had been discouraged by an unkind criticism, which said that his term was at once too long and too brief, whereas another critic went on to say that the description was both brief and Anglo-Saxon. (Laughter.) In 1892-93 an eminent Frenchman wrote an admirable brochure entitled "Les Indes Noires." This, name went straight to the root of the question of Equatorial Africa, because it put the question—"Can or cannot new Indies be carved out of Equatorial Africa?" That was a question which was constantly reviving in this country. Twenty-two years ago he began to preach the doctrine that there was only one thing needed to create a new India out of one portion of Equatorial Africa, and, though the public were indifferent to the question, it enabled the preliminary steps to be taken for carrying that theory into effect. In 1884 Germany came into the field as a colonizing Power, and the belief in Equatorial Africa as a colonizing field went up to fever heat. For the last two years the temperature had been decidedly high, and the feeling has been crowned by the great success of Omdurman; but he already saw signs that the opposite party were trying to work in the contrary direction. The other day Mr. Courtney (4) delivered an admirable and powerful address, but he differed *in toto* from the inferences which the right hon. gentleman indicated rather than drew from his illustration. From 22 years' experience and study he said that provided, the proper methods were followed, there was only one possible solution of the question of Equatorial Africa, or at any rate of the portion he was considering, and that solution was success. (Cheers.) It was a complex problem, but that was the very reason why he thought that Great Britain could best solve it, and perhaps alone solve it, among all the nations of the world. We had an ever-growing surplus of educated and athletic young men fond of outdoor life, which for Equatorial Africa was a good thing. Then we had a long and exceptional colonial experience, which enabled us to know how to deal with native races; and, lastly, we had inherited from our forefathers a happy combination of persistence and individuality which, together with a touch of audacity, had made the Empire such as it was at the end of the 19th century, and which would, by the 20th century, joined by similar qualities possessed by another nation over the water, carry peace, justice, and commerce over the globe. (Cheers.) Mr. Courtney took as his example the Congo Free State, but, considering the enormous difficulties of the Belgians and the extent of the territory, he thought that they had done remarkably well. He further pointed out that in Nigeria they had a good deal of civilization and an enormous population capable of high organization. They had their own laws, history, and religion; and out of this territory they could make as great an Empire in time as they had already achieved by their efforts out of India. (Cheers.)

THE SOUTH AFRICAN WAR

Goldie's participation in the two Royal Commissions concerned with enquiring into the conduct of the South African War has already been considered in some detail from the standpoint of the leverage that would accrue to him thereby. [5] The following excerpts from the *Times* gives a good general impression of the *impact* of his contribution

As far as the second Royal Commission, that on "War Stores in South Africa," under the chairmanship of Lord Justice Farwell [6] and consisting of himself, Goldie, Sir Francis Mowatt, [7] Sir George White, [8] and Mr. Samuel Morley [9] there is little to be said. The *Times* described the group as "a strong combination of financial and military experience." It's findings were not the whitewash that some commentators have suggested [10] and in its condemnation of the bureaucracy, both Civil and Military, for "a want of intelligence that is deplorable" and "inexcusable carelessness and extraordinary ineptitude," to say nothing of "irresponsibility and indifference to the public interest," [11] the Commission can hardly be said to have been pulling punches.

The findings and the Report were unanimous, and Goldie does not emerge as an individual throughout it. That he agreed with it can be taken for granted, and even its language may owe something to his forthrightness.

The first Commission, however, the Royal Commission of Inquiry into the Conduct of the War in South Africa was a different matter entirely. To begin with, two extra members were added, Lord Strathcona and Mountroyal to secure and represent Canadian interests, and Sir Frederick Darley those of Australia. Lord Strathcona was the Canadian High Commissioner, and Sir Frederick a distinguished Australian judge.

The Commission began its hearings on 11 October, 1902, examined 114 witnesses, posed 22,000 questions which were answered and submitted its Report, signed by all members, which was published on 25 August, 1903.

Two subordinate "Memoranda," authored by Lord Esher and by Goldie, attracted almost as much comment as the Report itself.

Lord Esher's Memorandum, reported in the *Times* of 1 September, 1903, dealt with the need for the re-organisation of the War Office. Its recommendations were summarised as follows:—

First, to reorganize the War Office Council, and to define more clearly their functions, as an advisory and executive Board, presided over by the Secretary of State, in whom, however, final responsibility to Parliament must be reserved.

Secondly, to decentralize internally the War Department, by a rearrangement of duties, under the respective members of the Board, abolishing the cross jurisdiction now existing.

Thirdly, to abolish the Commandership-in-Chief and to appoint a General Officer Commanding the Army, responsible to the Secretary of State for the efficiency of the military forces of the Crown.

The *Times* then published Goldie's views on Esher's Memorandum:—

VIEWS OF SIR GEORGE GOLDIE

In this matter I agree generally with the Note of Lord Esher. I feel, with the Hartington Commission, (12) that the retention of that office, as an administrative post, is incompatible with an effective system of administration of the Army by a permanent War Office Board or Council, such as the Report recommends, or as exists at the Admiralty. To adopt Lord Wolseley's simile (in his Memorandum to Lord Salisbury of 12th November, 1900) the Commander-in-Chief becomes "a fifth wheel to a coach." So large a fifth wheel is either rigid and follows its own course, which the other wheels have to follow, or is loose and obstructs the other wheels. On the other hand, I doubt if public opinion is ripe for the alternative system, advocated by Lord Wolseley and recently suggested by Lord Rosebery, of selecting the most capable soldier as a War Minister sitting in the Cabinet but holding aloof from general politics. Yet it is only fair to point out that in other countries under Parliamentary institutions expert Ministers, whether of Marine, Foreign Affairs, or War, have held office (without apparent friction) in successive Cabinets of very diverse political views. The attempt in 1895 to combine the two opposing principles of centralization in an individual soldier and devolution to a Board of soldiers, under the general control of a civilian Secretary of State, did not work satisfactorily; and, in 1900, an attempt was made to readjust the machinery. But I submit that the present system could not work well under normal conditions. Any success it has attained has been due to the exceptional position of Lord Roberts in the estimation of the Nation, the Army, and the Secretary of State. I look forward with anxiety to the time following his retirement; and although I heartily concur in the hope (expressed in paragraphs 270 and 272 of the Report) "that the state of affairs in 1899 cannot recur," this hope, on my part, is a wish and not an expectation. I desire to disclaim expressly any suggestion of attaching blame to the Cabinet or the Secretary of State in 1895. Public opinion at that time was strongly opposed to the continuance of centralization in the Commander-in-Chief. Yet the Cabinet could hardly resist the special pressure then put upon them to retain the office, and compromise is a favourite panacea. But I submit that while in legislation, where the objective is generally statical equilibrium, compromise is both necessary and valuable, it can only produce inertia in an administrative system—especially for our fighting services—where the main objective is dynamic force.

Sir John Jackson also records in a minute his agreement with the views of Lord Esher and Sir George Goldie.

Two days later, the *Times* carried a report on the substance of Goldie's own proposals. It is self explanatory, and comment on it would be superfluous, except to say that reaction to it was generally favourable and that one letter, published under the superscription X (an unusual practice for the *Times*, possibly signifying a Royal author), described it as "By far the most pregnant of the suggestions contained in the Report ... This proposal is an excellent one ..." (13)

September 3, 1903. Page 9 Column 1

THE WAR COMMISSION

SIR GEORGE GOLDIE ON UNIVERSAL MILITARY TRAINING

In addition to his recommendations for the reorganization of the War Office on the lines of the Hartington Commission which we reproduced in *The Times* of Tuesday, Sir G. Goldie put forward, in his note appended to the report of the Commissioners, a very strong note urging the necessity of some system of national military education in order to provide the country with men capable of serving as soldiers whether for home defence or for any great national emergency abroad which, like the South African War, might require an enormous temporary increase of our forces. The plan Sir. G. Goldie favours is a system of national cadet schools in which every physically sound boy of 17 would have to be trained for a term of six or eight months, unless he has already received a certificate of efficiency as a Volunteer. The advantages of the system over any system of a short service militia like the Swiss are that it would interfere less with civil employment, and that the physical, educational, and moral development would be greater at the age of 17 than later. The training of these schools would be conducted by Regular officers, and the scheme would thus incidentally help to meet the present very serious deficiency of officers for war purposes. The whole subject is one of the utmost national importance, and the proposal is one of the most practical that has yet been brought forward. It may be worth noting that the question of national defence is being approached on similar lines, by the organization of a cadet system, in Australia. Sir G. Goldie's scheme has the support of Lord Esher, Sir F. Darley, and Sir J. Edge.

THE LACK OF TRAINED MEN

"The second and far more serious defect in our military preparations for the war was in not having a sufficient number of trained men to furnish (by voluntary effort in a national emergency) the large reinforcements demanded both by the wastage of war and by the vast area of the operations. In close relation with this defect was the lamentable insufficiency of trained officers. Our Report deals with the facts and results of these defects. It does not pronounce definitely how they might have been remedied. I believe these questions to be still vital to the security of the United Kingdom and of the British dependencies, and the remedy which I submit is National Military Education. Although prepared to furnish a detailed scheme, it is not possible in this brief Note to do more than roughly sketch a general outline, as follows.

NATIONAL CADET SCHOOLS

After two or three years' interval to allow of the perfecting of existing Volunteer Cadet Corps and the general creation of others throughout the country, every physically sound boy of 17 years of age, not serving in the Navy or the Merchant Service and unprovided with a certificate (from the appointed military authority) that he is an efficient member of a Volunteer Cadet Corps, would have to serve for a term in National Cadet Schools—officered, as are Woolwich and Sandhurst, by officers of the Regular Army. The length of the

206

term—whether six, eight, or ten months—is a question for expert inquiry; but our evidence shows that, for boys of the age of the junior Gentlemen Cadets of Woolwich, it might be far shorter than the time now needed to convert an infantry recruit into a trained soldier. For instance, Sir Evelyn Wood (Q. 4355) says: Although I advocate great attention being paid to the training of our men, it is not possible to add a great deal to it with our men whom you have to coax into the service, as they would not come at all; they would say, 'Oh, no, if this is military training, I would sooner be a civilian,' and our desires with regard to the training of men are strictly limited by what the recruiting officer tells us is the character of training which would be agreeable to the population, which we hope will come into the Army." But assuming the *maximum* term to be eight months, probably a very large proportion, consisting of the most intelligent and of those who had only just failed to secure previous certificates of efficiency, could be discharged as efficient after three or four months, thus diminishing the amount of tent, hut, or barrack accommodation required, which is the first material difficulty arising in any scheme of general military training. Much may be done to meet this difficulty by billeting and similar methods; just as undergraduates, for whom there is no room in college, are boarded out. But it may be confidently anticipated that the system of exemption certificates for efficiency would vastly reduce the numbers annually presenting themselves at the National Cadet Schools; for, with such an inducement, Volunteer Cadet Corps would spread throughout the country and bring the efficiency of their members up to the standard. Assuming that a balance of 100,000 uncertificated boys would annually join the National Cadet Schools, it is clear that a large number of trained regular officers would be required for the work, who would be available for active service in a national emergency at home or abroad. This would meet Lord Robert's objection to an increase in the present number of officers with each regiment, on the ground that they would not have enough to do. My suggestion is that officers should not be permanently attached to the National Cadet Schools, but that each regiment should furnish a quota of majors, captains, and subalterns in annual rotation.

THE SWISS SYSTEM

In proposing this plan of National Military Education, I do not wish to depreciate an alternative scheme—the Swiss system—which has received considerable public support. But it seems to me that the former would be as effective and not open to many of the objections which, rightly or wrongly, have been raised to the Swiss system. For instance, it has been said that military service, even for short periods, extending between the ages of 18 and 23, would seriously interfere with the avocations of young men during the most decisive period of their lives. Again, at that more advanced age, it would be difficult to prevent any tendency to acquire alcoholic habits; while stringent regulations, as at Woolwich and Sandhurst, would be practicable with boys of 17. Again, at this younger age, it would be easier to trace identity and residence through the School Board lists. Again, boys of 17 are far better fitted for instruction and discipline than at a later age. Finally, there has appeared a natural prejudice against the Swiss system on the part of many who take a warm personal interest in the Militia and Volunteers, on the ground that its introduction would lead to the abolition of these valuable forces.

THE POSITION OF THE AUXILIARY FORCES

The scheme of National Military Education would not tend to supplant the Militia or Volunteers, but, on the contrary, would make them both more popular and less costly, as the man joining them would not have to undergo the tedious drudgery of training as recruits, and these branches of the service having only a very limited period for training would thereby gain greatly in efficiency. This advantage would be equally felt in the Yeomanry, in which too much of the limited time of recruits has to be occupied in learning to shoot and in preliminary drill. The same consideration applies to the existing difficulty of obtaining suitable recruits for the Regular Army, and would also obviate the necessity for a substantial increase in the rate of pay.

OBJECTIONS REFUTED

I cannot deal here with a score of minor obvious objections to the scheme beyond saying that most of them can be overcome, and that the few which prove insuperable must be accepted as the less of two evils; but I wish to meet two leading objections which will certainly be raised. The first is that it would add to the national expenditure. If it were so I should still urge it, because the true measure of our military and naval expenditure should be our national security. I am convinced, however, that the system would result in a great diminution of expenditure by permitting a large reduction of the number of men serving with the colours in the Regular Army, as well as in many other ways. I regret that space will not allow of my entering into details on these points, or urging collateral advantages, or dealing with the complicated question of providing drafts for India and the Colonies. The second leading objection is that the nation will not submit to any such scheme. It seems a sufficient reply to recall that, prior to 1870, the same objection was raised, with the same confidence, to the proposals for a system of National Civil Education. I have said nothing of the moral, social, mental, and physical advantages of the scheme, because the business of the Commission is confined to our military preparations. Moreover, these immense indirect gains to the country have been abundantly expounded by the advocates of all plans of general military service. But such gains are nevertheless germane to this Note, inasmuch as their prospect will tend to overcome any prejudice against the adoption of National Military Education, if not in the form that I have suggested, then in some other form.

OUR EXISTENCE AT STAKE

Indeed, I regret deeply being compelled to put forward any definite plan, which may savour of presumption, especially in the didactic form necessitated by extreme conciseness. But no other course was open to a member of the Commission convinced, as I am, that this particular defect in our military organization has cost the country no less than a hundred millions sterling, that it was a principal indirect cause of the outbreak of war, that for some months it left the United Kingdom practically denuded of trained soldiers, and that it produced the most perilous international situation in which the Empire has found itself since the days of Napoleon. Only an extraordinary combination of fortunate circumstances, external and internal, saved the Empire during the early months of 1900, and there is no reason to expect a repetition of such fortune if, as appears probable, the next national emergency finds us still discussing our preparations. (14)"

ADVANCES IN AGRICULTURAL TECHNOLOGY

11 December, 1906. Page 13 Column 3

SIR G. GOLDIE ON IRRIGATION IN SOUTH AFRICA

Sir George Goldie presided last night at a meeting of the Royal Geographical Society, when Major J. H. Beacom, United States Army, read a paper on "Irrigation in the United States: Its Geographical and Economical Results." After introducing the lecturer, Sir George Goldie said that this question of extensive irrigation was of untold importance to large portions of our own Empire. Much had already been effected in India, which fortunately possessed its own Government, and in Australia, where the colonists were not fettered by medieval modes of thought, while vast extensions of irrigation had been carried out in Egypt under the wise autocracy of Lord Cromer. But there was one part of the British Empire where not only the economical future, but even the political future was dependent on the thoroughness with which a system of irrigation was applied. He meant, of course, the two new colonies in South Africa, together with a considerable portion of Cape Colony. Our rulers at home had not hitherto shown any consistent or lasting appreciation of this position; nor was this surprising in view of the disdain with which so many otherwise cultured persons regarded geography; for he need hardly point out that a system of irrigation covering large regions was essentially a geographical question, dependent, as it was, on their morphological conditions, on their climatic conditions, and on the nature of their soil. It would be interesting to listen to a paper by a citizen of a rapidly progressing country, where—as, indeed, was also the case in Germany—geography was regarded as an essential branch of education. (15)

(1) H. Rider Haggard, later Sir Henry, 1856-1925. In 1875, went to South Africa as Secretary to the Governor of Natal. Registrar of the High Court, 1878. Retired 1879 and devoted himself to the production of novels with an African theme, the best known of which are *King Solomon's Mines* (1884), *She* (1887) and *Ayesha* (1905). Has sometimes been compared with Fennimore Cooper.

(2) James Bryce (later Viscount Bryce (1914)), 1838-1922. A Scottish Liberal who was widely travelled. Distinguished as a scholar, especially for his justly celebrated *History of the American Commonwealth*, Bryce was British Ambassador to Washington during the 1914-18 War.

(3) Goldie here ascribes to "Anglo-African" writers a role not unlike that fulfilled in the middle and later twentieth century by "science fiction" writers, i.e. the conditioning of the public towards the acceptance of hitherto incomprehensible actuality! See also page 263.

(4) Courtney, Leonard Henry, first Baron Penworth, 1832-1918. An obstinate opponent of Imperialism in any form, including British policy in South Africa, especially the Jameson Raid, and in Egypt and the Sudan. The "Mr. Justice Koetze" referred to the Chairman's opening speech is undoubtedly John Gilbert Kotzé, 1849-1940, Chief Justice of the South African Republic, dismissed by President Krueger in 1898 on a disagreement over a Constitutional interpretation. He had opposed Krueger in the 1893 presidential election and lost.

(5) See page 50 *et seq.*

(6) Mr. Justice (later Lord Justice) Farwell, 1845-1915. Judge in the Chancery Division, 1899. Lord Justice of Appeal, 1906-1913.

(7) Sir Francis Mowatt, 1837-1903; A most eminent Civil Servant who from 1894-1903 was Permanent Secretary to the Treasury, and thus Head of the Civil Service.

(8) Field Marshal Sir George Stuart White, 1835-1912, Q.M.G. at the War Office, 1897. Commanded in Natal, 1898-1901.

(9) Goldie was the only person to serve on both Commissions, a testimonial to his capability first as a statesman and then as an administrator, (and, perhaps as a soldier too!).

(10) For example, Frank Harris, one time Editor of the *Fortnightly Review*. In his

209

book *My Life and Loves* (Grove Press, New York, 1963), he praises General Sir William Butler (1838-1910) for raising the issue, but implies that his was the only serious investigation of the charges.

(11) See the *Times*, 10 August, 1906. The Commission sat from 1905-1906. It did not visit South Africa, but enjoyed the services of a travelling assistant, armed with statutory powers, to gather and record evidence there. He was "Mr. Roope Reeve, a barrister [who showed] exceptional skill and determination in dealing with a particularly reluctant and short-memoried set of witnesses." Roope Reeve still holds the world record for a trout caught on a dry fly.

(12) The Hartington Commission had considered this very issue in 1888. Nothing came of its recommendations, even though the Committee had consisted of men like Randolph Churchill, W. H. Smith, Lord Revelstoke, Campell-Bannerman, Sir Richard Temple (C. L. Temple's father), Sir F. Richards, Sir H. Brackenbury and T. S. Ismay. Hartington later became Duke of Devonshire. Lord Esher had close ties to him and once was his Private Secretary.

(13) Letter to the Times from "X", dated 2 September, 1903, and published on 3 September, page 9, columns 2 & 3. The possibility that it was this letter which spurred the *Times* to take notice of Goldie's Memorandum can not be discounted. The *Times* has confirmed the possibility of Royal authorship but has, regrettably, been unable to establish who it was.

(14) The *Times* report is all but verbatim. The only difference between it and the official text is that the *Times* omits the following opening preamble:

"I have signed the Report, as I accept and concur with it generally; but, with the approval of my colleagues, I desire to attach a note on two matters with which the Report deals, but on which it does not pronounce definite conclusions.

The first relates to the office of Commander-in-Chief . . ." See *Report* of the Royal Commission into the conduct of the War in South Africa, pp. 147-149.

(15) This brief excerpt is of tremendous interest because it underlines vividly the recurrent theme in Goldie's philosophy, namely that the development of the Empire could not be effected by what he called "Colonial Office methods", but that what was required was a new system employing new men and new methods. Only a Cromer-like "autocracy" or a free rein for the Colonists, as in Australia, could neutralise the constrictions imposed by "medieval modes of thought."

There is a hint here of both anger and frustration, but then, Goldie never did suffer fools gladly! But, see also page 220, and 259-263.

IV

Obituaries

Clerks at Burutu. *Courtesy U.A.C. International.*

I. LORD ABERDARE (1895)

The relationship which Goldie perceived to exist between himself and Lord Aberdare has already been noted. It was both personal and professional. No doubt, in the first instance, Lord Aberdare had been invited to serve as, first, Chairman of the National African Company, and then as Governor of the Chartered Company, because Goldie felt that the presence of such a man would facilitate the still intricate negotiations as to matters of detail as well as, possibly, generating a somewhat higher level of receptivity than would be the case if he himself held the titular power. In fact, Goldie stated quite bluntly in this obituary itself that Aberdare[1] had been invited specifically because he was President of the Royal Geographical Society.

But there is equally no doubt that over the years, deep bonds of friendship and affection added strength and meaning to their association. Goldie felt the loss as a personal one[2] and, it may be, never completely overcame it:—

Henry Austin Bruce was born in 1815, at the commencement of the long peace; and, although the latter half of his life witnessed repeated outbreaks of the international jealousies of Europe, he remained to the end unshaken in the hopes prevalent during his earlier manhood. If fears were expressed before him that France would force a war upon this country, he would say that he had heard that prophecy for seventy years, and if he were spared till it were verified, he believed he might attain double that age. Yet he approved of preserving peace by preparing for war. His strong affection for France dated from his boyhood, when he resided there for six years. It was the period when the Napoleonic legend was at its height; and, encyclopaedic as was Lord Aberdare's literary knowledge, I doubt whether, to the last, any publications yielded him more interest than those which threw fresh light on the life of Bonaparte. Biography was, indeed, the favourite mental recreation of his later years.

Mr. Bruce's career in Parliament and the Cabinet is rather a matter for history than for this brief notice. But the loss of his seat for Merthyr, which he had represented from 1852 to 1868, deserves remark. It was mainly due to his uncompromising opposition to the principle of the ballot.[3] His frank and courageous nature was averse from concealment of any kind; and, in common with many of the highest minds of that time, he feared lest a spirit of deception might be encouraged amongst the electors. In the days of restricted suffrage, the use of a vote was generally regarded more as a trust for the community and less as an individual right, than at present. It is characteristic of the rare openness of mind which distinguished Lord Aberdare throughout his life that, at a later date, he became convinced of the necessity—as a protection from popular violence—of the very measure which had cost him his seat. From 1862 to 1868 he had filled in turn the posts of Under-Secretary of State at the Home Office, and Vice-President of the Council. Soon after his defeat at Merthyr he was returned for Renfrewshire, and became Home Secretary until 1873, when he was raised to the peerage and exchanged his office for that of President of the Council, which he held till the close of his political career in 1874. His only serious mishap, during his long tenure of the unthankful office of Home Secretary, was the failure to pass his Licensing Bill, which not a few political opponents have since regretted. Seventeen years later, an elaborate and remarkable tribute to the merits of that measure was paid by the late Lord Randolph Churchill [4] in the House of Commons, on April 29, 1890, and was received with general cheers. I can only quote the following short passage: "The right hon. gentleman, the present Lord Aberdare, when he was Home Secretary as Mr. Bruce, introduced a Bill for the comprehensive reform of the licensing laws, which, I greatly regret to say, led to no result. It was produced by him in a speech of great power, and, curiously enough, it was received by the House with great approval. I am not old enough to recollect, and I have not been able to ascertain, the precise causes which led to the precipitate abandonment of that Bill. But it was abandoned owing to the party feeling of the time, and considerable unpopularity accrued to the Government, very unjustly I think, for having introduced the Bill."

Lord Aberdare became a Fellow of the Geographical Society in 1859. At the Anniversary Meeting of 1880, the jubilee year of the Society, he was elected President for the first time, and, with the exception of one year, continued to hold that office until 1887. Although he was then compelled to retire by the multiplicity of public claims on his energies, which advancing age made it every year more difficult for him to meet, his close connection with the Society, as a joint trustee with Sir John Lubbock, [5] did not cease until his death, on February 25 last, a few weeks before completing his eightieth year. His successor in the President's chair, General Strachey, [6] only expressed the general feeling of the Fellows when he said, in the annual address of 1887, that, with the exception of Sir Roderick Murchison, [7] there was no one of the presidents to whom the Society had been so much indebted.

During his second year of office, Lord Aberdare consented to represent the Society, conjointly with the late Sir Henry Layard [8] and Mr. John Ball, [9] at the International Geographical Congress at Venice [10] a congenial duty, apart from the service to geography; as Sir Henry Layard, who had taken up his residence in Venice since 1880, was a close friend of more than forty years' standing. It will be remembered that Lord Aberdare's latest literary work was a delightful "Introductory Notice" to the new edition published last Christmas of Sir Henry Layard's 'Early Adventures in Persia, Susiana, and Babylonia.' [11] Lord Aberdare's remarks on the International Congress, made at the opening meeting of the session of the Royal Geographical Society in November, 1881, are especially interesting at the present moment, when the hopes which he then expressed that the Congress would before long meet in London, are on the point of being realized. The weighty reasons he gave for this desire would suffer from abridgement, and I must therefore refer those interested to the *Proceedings* of the Society.

Lord Aberdare considered himself fortunate in having, during the whole term of his office, two active coadjutors as hon. secretaries—the present President [12] and Mr. Freshfield. [13] His tenure of the chair covered the interesting period of the incubation and outbreak of the European occupation of the Dark Continent, which, as the least-known quarter of the globe, has perhaps furnished the most extensive and interesting field for exploration during this century; while the international struggles involved in the "scramble for Africa" aroused a degree of public attention which purely scientific research does not always command. His first evening in the chair (November, 1880) was on the occasion of Mr. Joseph Thomson's paper on the Society's East African Expedition, [14] and during the following seven years Africa was continually in the foreground. As a geographer, he always insisted that knowledge has no nationality, and he terminated his annual address of May, 1882, with some striking remarks on this point, concluding with the characteristic sentence, "Long may there be Rohlfs, Serpa Pintos, and Nachtigals to dispute the highest honours we can confer with the Gills, Leigh Smiths, and Kirks of our native land." [15]

But outside the walls of the Society, he was not willing that his native land should be outstripped in the work of civilizing a new continent; and, on this ground, he accepted the chair of the Niger Company, which was expressly offered to him as the President of the Geographical Society. His interest in the Niger enterprise did not slacken with advancing years, but grew with his strengthening conviction of the field of usefulness that it opened up. The point of view from which he always regarded it was expressed in a letter written on November 3 last, in which, after speaking of "the truth of Burke's pathetic saying, 'What shadows we are, and what shadows we pursue!' " he added, "and yet not wholly so, if no small part of our pursuit is the good of millions of our fellow-creatures, as I know ours to be." [16]

Lord Aberdare's life-long work in connection with questions of education, other than geographical, was too extensive for detailed notice here, but a brief reference must be made to the foundation of a university for Wales. [17] To his excessive exertions in completing this work, of which he had been the moving spirit, and to his anxious labours as Chairman of the Royal Commission on the Aged Poor, may be attributed the sudden breakdown of his health. He was elected unanimously as the first chancellor of the new university, and his investiture was fixed for the present month. Probably no statesman of this century has taken a leading part in so many and diverse public movements for the advantage and elevation of the human race. Nor was his detestation of injustice and needless suffering displayed only within this limit; for he was, during fifteen years, President of the Society for the Prevention of Cruelty to Animals, and only advancing age compelled him, in 1893, to resign in favour of H.R.H. the Duke of York.

Great intellectual power and moral excellencies command respect, but do not necessarily invite affection. Lord Aberdare's sympathetic and genial nature was irresistible to those with whom he was in frequent contact. He knew not only how to elicit the confidence and affection of the humblest neighbours of his Welsh home, but how to bridge over the wider gulf between age and youth; for his own heart always remained young, and though this is not the place to touch on the subject of his family relations, I may, perhaps, say that he had in perfection *l'art d'être grand père*. [18] With such a rare combination of gifts, it was only natural that his noble life should be crowned with—
> "That which should accompany old age,
> As honour, love, obedience, troops of friends." [19]

II. DR. WILLIAM HENRY CROSSE (1903)

It was not only upon Goldie that Dr. Crosse, the first Chief Medical Officer of the Royal Niger Company, impressed his personality.

Lugard met him on his way to Nikki and in his own words took "a very great liking" to him. He had "ideas and thoughts on great subjects."[20] Later, he was to record his praise of him as a medical man as well.

It is one of the more revealing traits of Goldie's character that he should compose a note on the death of a Company official even though he had left the service of the R.N.C. five years before it ceased its operations. That they met frequently is sure, and Crosse often participated in the shareholders meetings of the R.N.C., as well as being an active member of the R.G.S., but that only makes it doubly perplexing as to why, when Wallace died in 1916, Goldie did not pay him a similar tribute. [21]

William Henry Crosse, M.D., F.R.G.S., died in London on February 24, at the comparatively early age of forty-four, through illness resulting from his residence in Africa. He was probably best known to Fellows of the Society generally by the Medical Hints published in the 'Hints to Travellers.' This chapter (VII.), elaborated by Dr. Crosse with characteristic care, is of special value to residents and travellers in tropical countries, owing to Dr. Crosse's long personal experience of Equatorial Africa and his subsequent practice in London as a consulting physician in cases connected with tropical diseases.

He was the son of the present Vicar of Terrington St. Clement. He was born at Lucan, Dublin, and educated at St. John's Foundation School, Leatherhead. At the age of seventeen he entered Guy's Hospital. After leaving the hospital, a small practice in Cubitt Town was bought by him. Such was his skill and energy that in five years his income rose from £300[22] to about £1,500, a fine result for a young man who was too modest and retiring to be an adept in the art of self-advertisement.[23] Illness, through overwork, compelled him to relinquish his practice; but after voyages to China and other parts of the world, he recovered his health.

At that time (1886) the Royal Niger Company had just received its charter, and was seeking for an able and energetic head of its medical staff. This post his exceptional testimonials secured for him, and he passed most of the following nine years in what is now known as Southern Nigeria. He paid two or three brief visits to England, and travelled extensively in Northern Nigeria when his duties

216

required it; but, as principal medical officer, his official residence was at Asaba, the seat of the company's civil administration. There he was able to employ his scanty leisure in the interesting study of the pagan tribes of that region, and in compiling more than one useful treatise on malarial fever and other tropical diseases. His surgical skill was also of great value, as there was scarcely one of the company's numerous military expeditions, from 1886 to 1895, in Southern Nigeria in which he did not take part. These were to him the most interesting years of his life. Although, after his return to London in 1895, he gradually built up a good practice, he more than once contemplated a return to Nigeria, where his sympathetic nature and his unwearying care for his patients will be remembered with affection and regret by all who knew him.

Dr. Crosse was also much interested in natural history, and made collections whenever the chance was offered, insects being his particular favourites. The first series from his collections was presented by him to the British Museum, and the second set he gave to the Hope Museum at Oxford. One of the most beautiful of West African butterflies has been named after him, *Euphaedra crossei,* by Miss E. M. Bowdler-Sharpe (24)

GEORGE TAUBMAN GOLDIE.

III. SIR MOUNTSTUART GRANT DUFF (1906)

This obituary appeared in the Geographical Journal, Vol. XXVII, 1906. Grant Duff was one of the most highly respected and even revered figures of his day. His most famous memory is probably that of the tradition he established as Member of Parliament for Elgin, under which, each year, he gave an account of his role in Parliament as he saw it with the changing times. These "Elgin Addresses" became famous and were in direct contrast to John Stuart Mill's refusal to have more than the most casual contact with either his constituents or his constituency.

Like Goldie, he was an educational reformer, advocating the placing of less emphasis on the Classics and more on the Sciences. His Presidential Address to the R.G.S., in May of 1892 was a landmark in the movement in this direction. Goldie followed in his footsteps.

If the available space in our Society's *Journal* permitted any approach to an adequate account of the life of Sir Mountstuart Grant Duff, (25) that task could not, without presumption be undertaken by one of almost a generation younger who had not the advantage of knowing him during his parliamentary career. But it can hardly be doubted that before long the memoir of so widely known a personality will be written by some competent hand, and I am unable to resist the view that this brief obituary of one of the most intellectual and cultured of our former Presidents should be undertaken by the present occupant of his chair.

Mountstuart Elphinstone Grant Duff, who died on January 12, at the age of nearly seventy-seven, was born in February, 1829. The son of an active and well-known Indian official, who had been Resident at Sattara, he may be said to have inherited an interest in the great dependency with which he was afterwards so closely connected. He was educated at Balliol College, Oxford, where he graduated in 1850, and he was called to the Bar at the Inner Temple in 1854, having obtained a certificate of honour and a studentship in the previous year. Unfortunately, while at Balliol his eyes went seriously wrong, and for the rest of his life he had to work largely with the eyes of others.

With his vivid and alert nature, it was inevitable that he should enter political life, where he could give the fullest satisfaction to his craving to be always in close touch with the social and international problems of his time, as well as with the individuals, in various departments of art and science, who were making history. For he practised to the utmost the Poet's dictum, (26) that the proper study of mankind is man; although this did not preclude him from other interests, of which perhaps the keenest and most enduring was his love of botany. For nearly a quarter of a century, without a break, he represented the Elgin Burghs in Parliament. He served as Under-Secretary of State for India—the country of his predilection—from 1868 to 1874, when the Gladstone ministry fell. He also served as Under-Secretary of State for the Colonies from 1880 until, in 1881, he accepted the governorship of the Madras Presidency.

His knowledge of foreign affairs was probably unsurpassed by any of our countrymen of that period. He not only brought to their study the philosophic mind, the keen perception, and the patient industry which remained unimpaired to his last days, but he devoted the recesses of Parliament to travels on the continent, where he could utilize his social tastes and his remarkable capacity for noting and remembering the opinions of men and women who exercised any material influence on the course of European progress. His annual addresses to his constituents, known as the "Elgin Addresses," were always reproduced by the Press and were regarded throughout the country as valuable contributions to the knowledge of continental politics. They have still a living interest for those whose inevitable gap between school history and personal knowledge extends from the Crimean war to the Franco-German war. Of the same period and of equal value were two of his works, entitled 'Studies in European Politics,'[27] and 'A Political Survey.'[28] The latter, treating largely of outlying countries, of which, in the sixties, our knowledge was very different from that of to-day, has a strange old-world interest to the reader in the twentieth century.

During the period 1874-80, Mr. Grant Duff produced several works. One of the best known is his 'Miscellanies, Political and Literary' (1878),[29] which includes a specially fine and just estimate of Castelar,[30] beyond question the greatest orator of our time. But Mr. Grant Duff's most delightful book of that period was his 'Notes of an Indian Journey'[31] a voyage of several months which he undertook immediately on his quitting the India Office in 1874. His pleasure in freedom from the trammels of office and in visiting the country to which his mind had so often turned, breaks out on every page of these 'Notes,' which testify to a joie de vivre in the gorgeous East that must have played a considerable part, six years later, in determining him to abandon parliamentary life to become "a providence" for the teeming millions of the Madras Presidency.

The five years (1881-1886) that he spent there as governor were probably the happiest in his life. They were certainly the fullest, as he was untiring in travelling over his Presidency, making himself acquainted with the needs of the people. His administration has always been admitted to have been most successful, and his official minutes are excellent reading, as he issued full reviews of everything done by him for the information of his successors. Yet he found time for much private enjoyment, as he showed in an address delivered before the Society of Arts in February, 1898, entitled 'Recreations of an Indian Official.' In this he characteristically quotes Geothe's saying, "Time is endlessly long, and every day is a vat into which a great deal may be poured if you will only fill it up."[32] Much of the 'Recreations' is occupied with observations on the fauna and flora of his Presidency.

After his return home, he divided his energies between literature and the care of various learned societies. His most attractive book of this period was 'Ernest Renan' (1893),[33] in which the charm of the great Frenchman seems to have fallen as a mantle on his biographer. Other Memoirs were those of Sir H. S. Maine[34] and Lord de Tabley.[35] The editing of a very full Victorian Anthology[36] occupied considerable time, but was a labour of love. Probably however to the general public of today Sir Mountstuart Grant Duff is most intimately known through his 'Out of the Past' (37) and his *Notes from a Diary,* '(38) the former of which he described "as supplementary to" the latter.

His diary covers a period of half a century, from 1851 up to an including the first meeting of the Privy Council on the morning after the decease of Queen Victoria. With the exception of this historic gathering on the accession of His Majesty, the author carefully excludes from these volumes the official and graver side of his life, and they consequently form an admirable mirror to the opinions and *obiter dicta* of a mass of celebrities during their hours of relaxation. Sir Mountstuart's accuracy of memory and care of detail have given a value to this *olla podrida*(39) of personal reminiscences, which is heightened by the wit and subtlety of the author himself. Accuracy was, indeed, the very breath of his nostrils. In the 'Notes,' he quotes the following passage from Mr. J. A. Froude's *Legend of St. Neots:*(40) "We all write legends. This does not arise from any wish to leave a false impression—scarcely from carelessness—but only because facts refuse to remain bare and isolated in our memory. Facts are thus perpetually, so to say, becoming unfixed and rearranged in a more conceptional order;" to which Sir Mountstuart adds, "It would be difficult to put more distinctly the way in which we should *not* deal with facts." This absolute accuracy of statement added incalculably to the charm of Sir Mountstuart's conversation. His apt references to some bygone facts or saying were always clearcut and convincing, while they sparkled with wit and delicate humour.

To deal briefly with his connection with learned bodies— he had been in his earlier days Lord Rector of the Aberdeen University; he became a member of the Senate of the University of London in 1891; he was President of the Royal Historical Society from 1892 to 1899; he was the King's trustee of the British Museum from 1903; and, finally, he was President of our Society from 1889 to 1893. He retired owing to a difference of opinion amongst our Fellows as to the advisability of admitting lady travellers to Fellowship in the Society.(41) His presidency was marked by great energy and ability, while his public addresses were always of deep interest. At the conclusion of one of these, his predecessor—the late Lord Aberdare, himself a man of high culture and intellect—struck the keynote of Sir Mountstuart's power. He said, "To those who can read between the lines, almost every paragraph of the address shows a man who has spent his life in the constant acquisition of various knowledge." Sir Mountstuart was keenly alive to the necessity of more time being given in schools to the study of history and geography, "those twin brethren, Castor and Pollux." In one of his addresses to us (June, 1892), he said, "Put composition in the ancient tongues, (42) as a piece of regular school business, behind the fire," and he added that there would then be "time to read a great deal more of the classics than there is now, and to teach as much history and geography as any one wishes to teach a boy under eighteen or nineteen." He continued to the last to watch with interest the growth of geographical knowledge. On his death, he had been a Fellow of our Society for forty-five years.

Following the practice of our *Journal,* this obituary must be confined to Sir Mountstuart Grant Duff's public life; but his large circle of friends know that, well filled as that public life was, he displayed his greatness of soul and his personal charm no less consistently in his private life, to which it was an honour to be admitted. Although he was not one of those who "suffer fools gladly," his essentially kind nature displayed itself both in personal intercourse and in his writings, and perhaps his most appropriate epitaph would be the quotation from Renan which he selected as a preface to his *Notes from a Diary:* "On ne doit jamais écrire que de ce qu'on aime. L'oubli et le silence sont la punition qu'on inflige à ce qu'on a trouvé laid ou commun dans le promenade à travers la vie." (43)

GEORGE TAUBMAN GOLDIE. (44)

(1) See pages 214-215.

(2) See page 12.

(3) The 1867 Reform Act introduced the concept of "Household Franchise," by which the vote was extended to skilled urban artisans, while still excluding both town and country labourers. The leader of the Reform movement was John Bright, of Birmingham (1811-1889).

(4) Lord Randolph Henry Spencer Churchill, 1841-1894, 3rd son of the 6th Duke of Marlborough. First elected to Parliament for Woodstock in 1874, he held the India Office in 1885-86, and became Chancellor of the Exchequer in 1886, resigning in order, as he thought, to force acceptance of his own position. The Prime Minister did not respond, and Churchill never held office again. In 1894, Lord Randolph died from G.P.I.

(5) Sir John Lubbock, later Baron Avebury, 1834-1913. Banker, scientist, author of numerous ethical and scientific works, and politician.

(6) General Sir Richard Strachey, 1817-1908. Engineer and meteorologist; explored Kumaon, the Himalayas and Tibet, 1847-48. A Vice-President of the R.G.S.

(7) Murchison, Sir Roderick Impey, 1792-1871. Probably the greatest President of the R.G.S., from 1843-1871. A geologist.

(8) Sir (Austen) Henry Layard, 1818-94. Geographer and archeologist; Excavated Nineveh and Babylon, c. 1850-53. Travelled extensively in Persia, Armenia and the Middle East. M.P., 1852-57; Ambassador to Spain, 1869-80.

(9) Ball, John, 1818-89. Geologist and alpinist.Author of *Guides* to both western and eastern Alps (1863 and 1868) and other authoritative works on geology and alpine formation.

(10) The Third International Congress, 1881.

(11) First published in 1887.

(12) Sir Clements Markham, 1830-1916. President of the R.G.S. from 1887-05.

(13) D. W. Freshfield, 1845-1934. Author of *Round Kangchenjunga* (1903) and other works.

(14) That of 1878. Thomson took charge when the expedition's leader Alexander Keith Johnston died.

(15) Rohlf, Freidrich Gerhard, 1831-96. See page 96.

Serpa Pinto, Alexandre Alberto da Rocha de, 1846-1900. Portuguese explorer and administrator of Mozambique and Angola. Governor-General of Mozambique, 1889.

Nachtigal, Gustav, 1834-1885. German explorer of the inner Sahara and Bornu, 1868. Returned via Cairo, 1874. German Consul, Tunis, 1882-84.

Gill, Sir David, 1843-1914. Geographer and astronomer. Royal Astronomer at the Cape of Good Hope, 1879-1907.

Leigh Smith, explored the Arctic Ocean and Franz-Joseph Land, 1872-81.

Kirk, Sir John. See page 103.

(16) Speech to the electors of Bristol, on declining election, 9th September, 1780. "The worthy gentleman [Mr. Coombe] . . . has feelingly told us what shadows we are etc." Mr. Coombe died suddenly during the campaign.

(17) Founded in 1893.

(18) Literally, "the knack of being a grandfather," i.e. "How to grow old gracefully." The title of a book of poetry by Victor Hugo, published in 1877.

(19) W. Shakespeare, *Macbeth,* Act V Sc. 3. This obituary appeared in the *Geographical Journal* Vol. V., April, 1895.

(20) See Perham and Bull, *op cit.,* p. 88.

(21) Wallace's obituary in the *Geographical Journal* is brief and unsigned.

(22) It would appear a trifle incongrous, nowadays, to see professional competence measured in such mundane yardsticks as relative income! Certainly, such would be out of place in an obituary. But these were the days of "philanthropy plus five percent" and status was often in direct relationship to affluence.

(23) Goldie would find it easy to praise self-effacement.

221

(24) This notice appeared in the *Geographical Journal* Vol. XXI of 1903.

(25) Grant Duff was President of the R.G.S. at the time (1891) that Goldie became a member of the Council. He was a statesman, administrator, and an author. Scottish Liberal M.P. for Elgin, 1857-81, he was also President of the Royal Historical Society from 1892-99. F.R.S., 1901.

(26) From *Essay on Man,* Epistle II, 1. 2.

(27) Published by Edmonston & Douglas, Edinburgh, 1866.

(28) Same publisher, 1868.

(29) Published by Macmillan, London, 1878.

(30) Castelar y Ripoll, Emilio, 1832-99. Spanish statesman and author and champion of the Republican movement in Spain. President of the first Spanish Republic, 1873-74.

(31) Published by Macmillan, 1876.

(32) "Die Zeit ist unendlich lang und jeder Tag ein Geräss, in das sich sehr viel eingiessen Lässt, wenn man es wirklich ausfüllen will." (Dichtung und Wahrheit, Book 8.)

(33) Published by Macmillan & Co.

(34) Henry James Sumner Maine, 1822-88. Jurist, author of *Early History of Institutions* (1875) and *Village Communities* (1871). In many respects he was the "father" of modern anthropology and sociology. Grant Duff's book *H. S. Maine* was first published by Holt & Co., New York, in 1892.

(35) Published in *The Flora of Cheshire* by J. B. L. Warren, 3rd Baron Tabley, 1899. Also as *Memoir of Lord de Tabley, 1889.*

(36) Published in London in 1892.

(37) Published by Murray, London, 1903.

(38) Published by Murray, London, in 1897.

(39) *"Olla podrida"* a dish composed of different sorts of meat and vegetables, boiled together = "Hotch-potch."

(40) James Anthony Froude, 1818-94, wrote a *Life of St. Neot* for J. H. Newman's, *Lives of the English Saints* (1844). Then, breaking with orthodoxy, he wrote *A legend of St. Neot* (1844) and *Nemesis of Faith* (1849).

(41) One might assume, in light of Goldie's views on Women's Suffrage, that he would not have favoured this move. Grant Duff, it appears, was favourably inclined, but was over-ruled, and Goldie always showed the highest regard for Mary Kingsley.

(42) i.e. Greek and Latin.

(43) "No-one ought ever to write, except about what he loves. Oblivion and silence are the punishments inflicted on that which is perceived to be either coarse or vulgar in the journey through life." Ernest Renan, French author and man of letters, was born in 1823 and died in 1892. The quotation comes from the preface to *Souvenirs d'Enfance et de Jeunesse* published in Paris in 1883.

(44) This Obituary appeared in the *Geographical Journal,* Vol. XXVII, 1906.

V

Scholarly Presentations

The Niger Company's Station at Atani. *Courtesy U.A.C. International.*

The Station at Jebba in 1900. *Courtesy U.A.C. International.*

I. THE AFRICA OF PRINCE HENRY THE NAVIGATOR (1894)

On the fifth of March, 1894, a special meeting of the Royal Geographic Society was held at the University of London to commemorate the five hundredth anniversary of the birth of Prince Henry the Navigator.

Among those present were H.R.H. The Duke of York, later King George V, and the Portuguese Ambassador Senhor da Soveral. The speakers at the symposium were Markham, the President, Goldie, Captain W. J. L. Wharton, the Admiralty Hydrographer, Mr. Raymond Beazley and a Mr. Yule Oldham.

Telegrams were exchanged between the Duke of York and the King of Portugal and Da Soveral, who had been back to Portugal prior to the meeting had broken his journey in Paris to have an audience of King Edward VII, who, as Sovereign Patron of the Society, had sent his expressions of interest and support for the event through the Ambassador. Altogether, it was a rather splendid occasion!

I have been asked to-night to give a short description of the African regions discovered by Prince Henry. (1) Our President (2) has given a most able address, I am sure we shall all agree, covering the general career of Prince Henry, and I understand that we have here to-night two gentlemen (3) who have made a special study of the subject, and who will, no doubt, give us many interesting details of the expeditions sent out by that Prince. I propose, therefore, not to deal directly with Prince Henry's work, because to do so would be to weary you with repetitions, but there is one feature of his character to which I must refer, because it is intimately allied with the subject allotted me this evening. It is that Prince Henry was content to work, not for his own generation, but for posterity. It was only with the eye of faith that he could see the extraordinary greatness to which the small country of Portugal rose during the 120 years after his death. To-day there are five or six European nations all engaged in working for posterity in the equatorial regions of the same great continent of Africa to which Prince Henry devoted his attentions, regions which cannot be expected in a single generation to yield those brilliant material results which alone command popular admiration. As you know, from time immemorial the inhabitants of these regions have lived under conditions of insecurity to property and liberty and life, absolutely incompatible with the growth of industry or the accumulation of capital. I have never wavered in my belief that the introduction of better political social conditions will gradually make equatorial Africa wealthy as well as free, (4) but the workers of our time—and I have no doubt there are many of them here to-night—must be content, like Prince Henry the Navigator, to look at a promised land into which they themselves will never enter, and in which, with perhaps one or two exceptions, like the King of the Belgians and H. M. Stanley, their very names will be forgotten. (5)

The unknown Africa of Prince Henry's time may be taken as commencing with Cape Juby, opposite the Canary Islands, the regions to the north lying within the Mediterranean State of Morocco, which two thousand years ago was a province of Rome. The southernmost point reached by Prince Henry's emissaries was Cape Mesurado, in Liberia. In taking this limit, I am assuming as one of his expeditions that which actually left Portugal (after his death) in 1461, but there is no doubt that Prince Henry planned it and probably organized it. The distance between Cape Juby and Cape Mesurado, following the coast, is about 1,800 miles, and my difficulty is how, in the course of five minutes, I am to give you an adequate description of that immense region without laying myself open to the charge of inaccuracy. I am rather cautious on this point, as I have just had a lesson. About a fortnight ago I was asked about the wandering tribes of the Tuaregs by an interviewer, and in order to get rid of him, for the sake of brevity, I described them as the Arabs of the Central Sahara, just as people talk of the Gallegos (6) as the Auvergnats (7) of Spain. A few days afterwards, I saw a short leader in one of our great London journals, which not only stated the undeniable fact that the Tuaregs are not Arabs, but indulged in some gentle sarcasm either about the inaccuracy of the reporter or my ignorance, I could not quite make out which. But you will understand that, speaking very briefly, I must speak generally. That region is divided into two nearly equal but very dissimilar parts. From Cape Juby down to the Senegal river is the western limit of the Great Sahara, so I need hardly tell you it possesses what Lord Salisbury on a notable occasion a "light soil," that it is deficient in water, healthy in climate for those who don't mind heat, and very sparsely populated. Its inhabitants are wandering and pastoral tribes, varying in colour from light brown to dark brown. In the southern half, namely, from the Senegal river to Cape Mesurado, every one of these conditions is different. Here you have again, speaking broadly, a fertile soil, a decidedly unhealthy climate—there are many here who can vouch for that—very plentiful waterways, and a population comparatively dense, and consisting of more or less pure negro races, who are sedentary and agricultural in habit. I shall not weary you with a long catalogue of the races and tribes scattered over this immense maritime region. Such a catalogue would be useless to those acquainted with the subject, and could not possibly be remembered by those who are not. But I will say a few words about the existing political divisions.

From Cape Juby to Cape Bojador in the only part of the coast of Western Africa not yet appropriated by some recognized state. Certain claims are raised to it by Morocco, and certain others by Spain, (8) while at Cape Juby itself there has been, since 1880, an important British station, which has not been recognized as a British possession, but of which I hope our countrymen will not lose sight. From Cape Bojador to Cape Blanco, nearly 500 miles, is held by Spain, which also claims about the same distance into the interior; but I have noticed in the Paris papers, since the taking of Timbuctoo, an inclination to draw a line from Cape Blanco at a sharp angle with the coast, cutting Spain off with a very small section indeed.

At Cape Blanco begins the great West African possession of France known under the different names, for administrative purposes, of Senegal, Sudan Français, and Rivieres du Sud, which form, however, one great possession, of which the French are very naturally proud, and on which they are spending a great deal of money. It extends inland 900 miles from the Atlantic as far as Timbuctoo. With the exception of two very interesting small wedges belonging to other nations, France extends on the seaboard right down to the frontier of Sierra Leone. This British possession has a coast-line of about 200 miles, and extends about the same distance into the interior, but can go no further. I may remind you that about fourteen years ago France, then firmly established on the Senegal, commenced a policy of what is called *lateral expansion,* and has gradually cut off the coast colonies of England and Portugal from the interior. As this is a Geographical Society, and not a Colonial meeting, I merely state facts without any comment. I mentioned two small wedges in the French coast-line. The northernmost is the British possession of the Gambia, which is of special interest to us at present, on account of the late disaster there. (9) I dare say we shall hear something to-night, from those going to tell us of Prince Henry's work, of the interesting fact that the first expedition that discovered the Gambia, was almost annihilated by coming in conflict with the natives. One cannot help thinking of the enormous stride made, during the last three or four centuries, by the public conscience of Europe. In those days, our conflicts with the natives generally arose from our trying to capture them as slaves. To-day our conflicts in Africa are due to our trying to prevent the capture of the natives as slaves by marauding chiefs like Fode Silah (10) or their extermination by savage potentates like Lobengula. (11) Not far south of British Gambia comes the small Portuguese colony of Guinea on the Rio Grande. This is doubly interesting to us to-night—firstly, because this was the last discovery of which Prince Henry heard before his death, in 1460; and, secondly, because, although Portugal still holds great African possessions south of the equator, this little territory of Guinea is all that remains north of the equator of the vast regions gained for her by Prince Henry and his successors. It is not for me to dwell on the causes of this decline before this audience—the disastrous union with Spain in 1580, (12) and the "sixty years' captivity" which gradually destroyed the spirit of Portuguese enterprise created by Prince Henry—but I may perhaps venture to say this, that although the power of Portugal has waned in that northwestern region as in the far East, nothing can rob her of the glory of having led the van of modern exploration, a work without which, I venture to say, Columbus would not have discovered America, while Prince Henry the Navigator, whose genius and patient industry conceived and organized this great work, has built himself an everlasting name.

(1) Prince Henry the Navigator, third son of King John I, 1394-1460. Sponsored the exploration of the coasts of Africa which began in 1420.

(2) Sir Clements Markham, 1830-1916. President of the R.G.S. from 1893 to 1905.

(3) Capt. (later Sir William) Wharton, 1843-1905, died of fever in Cape Town, and Mr. (later Sir Charles) Raymond Beazley, a noted geographer and authority on early explorations (1868-1955).

(4) Goldie has this as a constant under current of his thinking. See page 232 in regard to Australia.

(5) Again, Goldie is apparently dazzled in his perception of the Congo, unless, that is, his views have changed diametrically.

(6) The inhabitants of Galicia, descendants of the Celtic Gallaeci and the later Visigoths. Gallegos, strictly speaking is a language closely related to Portuguese, and not a people.

(7) Auvergnats, inhabitants of the Auvergne and the descendants of Vercingetorix's Arveni.

(8) The Spanish Sahara, as the area became called, extended from Cape Juby to Cape Bojador. C. Juby was occupied on behalf of Spain in 1916. The occupation of the rest was

effected in stages up to 1934. The territory was incorporated into metropolitan Spain in 1958 but has since been divided between Morocco and Mauritania, this division still being opposed by some factions. Prince Henry's sea captains penetrated south of Cape Bojador in 1434.

(9) On 22 Feb., 1894, a combined Royal Navy, Royal Marine & Royal West India Regt. column of 14 Officers and 206 men was ambushed near Dansoiama by Fode Silla. 15 were killed, 47 wounded and 47 rifles, 6,000 rounds and a field-gun were lost.

(10) Fode Silla, a Marabout, opposed the British penetration along the Gambia River which was begun in 1891. He was finally defeated, after stiff opposition, in 1894. Another Marabout, Fode Kabba, continued resistance until 1900.

(11) See page 288 and footnote 7 on page 289.

(12) Subsequent, that is, to the Battle of Al Kasr al Kabr, fought in 1578 between the Portuguese and the Moroccans. King Sebastian of Portugal, grandson of King John III, fired by a crusading zeal, landed an army of some 25,000 men on the coast near Tangiers. He was engaged by the followers of the Sherrif of Morocco, Abd el Malek, at Al Qasr al Kabr (Alcazar) situated on the road junction to Tangier, Rabat and Fez. 24,500 Portuguese were killed or captured, their King being killed. As a result, two years later, Phillip II of Spain, a nephew of John III, usurped the Crown, and Spanish domination of Portugal continued until the appearance of the House of Braganza in 1641. The Sherrif was also killed at the battle and was succeeded by his younger brother, Mulai Ahmed, who took the title "el Mansur," (The Victorious). In 1590/91, his forces under Judar Pasha invaded the Niger Bend, taking over the Songhai Empire. Moroccan rule there was sporadic until 1628, when the venture finally collapsed. The Battle of Alcazar ranks with Lepanto as a major landmark in Christian-Islam relations—though for different reasons!

II. THE PROGRESS OF EXPLORATION AND THE SPREAD AND CONSOLIDATION OF EMPIRE IN AMERICA, AUSTRALIA AND AFRICA (1901)

On 11 February, 1901, the Royal Geographical Society held a special meeting devoted to "the commemoration of Her Majesty's reign from the point of view of our science," and which was designed also to acknowledge "the deep and reverential grief of . . . her subjects when the news of her death cast a shadow of gloom on her vast empire." [1]

There were three speakers, Markham, Goldie and Sir Thomas Holdich, an expert on frontier problems, who had been Superintendant of Frontier Surveys in India from 1892-1898. His topic was "Advances in Asia and Imperial Consolidation in India." Markham spoke "In Commeration of her late Majesty" to open the proceedings, and "On the Accession of King Edward VII" to close them. In this last address, he alluded to King Edward's statement to him when attending a dinner in honour of H. M. Stanley, "I have taken the greatest interest in the grand project of the exploration of Equitorial Africa."

Goldie said:—

The part allotted to me this evening calls for the utmost exercise of your indulgence, for it is the survey, in thirty minutes or thereabout, of the work effected during the last sixty-four years in the exploration, spread, and consolidation of the British Empire in the area of about ten million square miles, or about eighty times the area of the British Isles—a work to which I could only do justice in a long course of lectures. To-night a rough sketch, indicating salient features, is alone possible; and if what artists call "the distribution of values" appears faulty, you will bear in mind that our special concern here is to regard matters from the geographical point of view.

In this survey the Dominion of Canada takes precedence, and the subject is peculiarly appropriate at this Commemorative Meeting, because the modern political history of "Our Lady of the Snows" dates from the first year of the Victorian age. It was within twelve months of Her Majesty's accession that Lord Durham [2] landed at Quebec, as "Governor-General of all British provinces within and adjacent to the continent of North America." His famous mission resulted in the adoption (in 1840) of a rational principle of colonial policy—that principle of self-government which, a century earlier, might have saved to the

Empire the great regions lying between Canada and the Gulf of Mexico. Lord Durham was a man of remarkable prescience. At a time when most other English great landowners still looked askance at railways, he recommended an intercolonial railway, as a means of bringing the Canadian provinces into line. With what pleasure would he have seen the great results already realized by the completion of that splendid enterprise, the Canadian-Pacific railway!

But Lord Durham also foresaw the development that would result from the granting of free institutions. Referring to this question of expansion in his report of 1839, he said, "The constitution of the form of government, the regulation of foreign relations and of trade with the mother country and foreign nations, are the only points on which the mother country requires a control. The privileges, carried to their logical conclusion of representative government will do the rest."(3) Certainly, under the old *regime* the two main instruments of the exploration and settlement of the vast area of the Dominion would have been wanting. The first of these was the creation of the Geological Survey of Canada, which under that modest title has carried its work over immense regions, and covered much more than the field of geology. Geography, botany, zoology, ethnology, and other branches of knowledge have alike shared in the benefits of this fine organization. Proposals for such a survey for Upper Canada had been pressed from 1832 onwards; but it was not until the concession of self-government that the project was carried into effect, in 1842, by the Provincial Government of the two Canadas, and Sir William Logan(4) was appointed to organize and direct it. Logan resigned in 1869, and was succeeded by Dr. G. M. Dawson,(5) whose earlier personal explorations in the Rocky mountains had made his name familiar to us on this side of the Atlantic. After the Federation of 1867, the Geological Survey extended its operations gradually across the continent to the shores of the Pacific. Although the scientific exploration of the Dominion, during the late reign, has been largely the work of the Geological Survey, we must not lose sight of the important and independent work of the Topographical Survey, while it would be unjust to overlook the valuable part played by the Hudson Bay Company(6) in its huge territory between 1837 and 1870, when it handed over its power as a government. Nor must I omit to mention Captain Palliser's important expedition of 1857-58 (in and about the Rocky mountains), undertaken at the instance of this Society, which also awarded him its Gold Medal. (7)

But scientific exploration could not have been consistently maintained, nor could it have served much practical purpose, if there had not been an army of hardy and energetic settlers behind it—and, at a later date, a mining population ready to press into the newly opened regions; and it is beyond doubt that this development would not have taken place but for the combination of free local institutions with unity of central government which the Dominion of Canada enjoys.

At the commencement of the last reign the white population was 1,335,000. Last year it was estimated at five and a quarter millions. I shall not give statistics of trade in 1837-38, because of the extraordinary discrepancies that exist between the two highest authorities of those days, Montgomery Martin(8) and Herman Merivale,(9) and there is no time to-night to try and reconcile their differences. But, in any case, the volume of trade then was insignificant compared with the 33 million pounds of exports and 28 million pounds of imports which the Dominion now shows.

There is no occasion to refer to our other possessions in the Western world, beyond mentioning the valuable geographical work of Sir Robert

Schomburgh [10] in British Guiana early in the last reign, and that of Mr. Im Thurn and others more recently.

The expansion of Australia during the Victorian period demands more detailed notice than that of Canada, because the southern continent had not a long antecedent history of exploration and settlement. It is very difficult to realize that the foundation of Melbourne was contemporaneous with the accession of Her Majesty, the earliest settlements in Victoria having only been formed in 1835; that the first settlers of the famous Wakefield Company [11] only sailed from England in 1836 for South Australia, where Governor Hindmarsh, [12] under a tree near the beach, read his commission to a small audience of emigrants and officials, that the then recently established Swan River Settlement (which afterwards became the colony of West Australia) was, in 1837, little superior to the settlement of Eden, as described by Dickens in 'Martin Chuzzlewit:' that Queensland was known only by its penal establishment at Moreton bay; that Tasmania, though somewhat better known and populated, owing to its insular formation, was in its infancy; and, finally, that New South Wales, our premier Australian colony, was, in 1837, still practically confined to the narrow strip lying between the ocean and the watershed of that mountain range which follows the whole eastern coast and part of the southern coast of the continent. To compare the condition of Australia in 1900 with that in 1837, brings forcibly home to our minds both the unprecedented duration of the last reign and the rapidity with which our race can develop the resources of a new country when in possession of their greatest heritage—free institutions. But this advance of settlement had to be preceded by exploration; and the story of this in Australia derives a special interest for the terrible hardships often endured owing to the nature of the interior of the continent. During the eighteen years before Her Majesty's accession, some valuable expeditions—but all confined to the south-east corner of the continent—had been made by Oxley, [13] Mitchell, [14] Hume, [15] Cunningham, [16] and Sturt, [17] the last of whom, through his later and greater work, earned the name of "the father of Australian exploration." But about the commencement of the Victorian age, a new impulse was given to the opening up of the continent by the fact that the southern and western coasts at last possessed settlements, so that the interior was attacked from three sides instead of from the east coast alone. Time permits only a brief reference to a few leading names out of a great number of explorers. In 1837 and 1839, Captain Grey, [18] afterwards Governor of South Australia, explored a portion of West Australia and claimed the discovery of ten rivers. E. J. Eyre, [19] after preliminary inland travels in 1838 and 1839, made his famous march round the Great Bight, suffering terrible privations. In 1844-45, Sturt led the first Great Central Desert expedition to the very heart of the continent. At the same time, Mitchell completed his fame as an explorer by his Barcoo expedition; and Leichhardt [20] travelled from the Darling Downs to the Gulf of Carpentaria. His subsequent journey in 1848, in which his entire party, including five other white men, disappeared for ever, is notable for the valuable search expeditions to which it gave rise. So it is that, whether in the polar seas, or in the heart of Australia, or in the deepest recesses of Africa, the disappearance of an explorer has often found its compensation in the progress of mankind by the energies called forth in solving the mystery. A. C. Gregory, [21] who had explored the interior of Western Australia in 1846, and the Gascoyne in 1848, commenced in 1855 the series of travels in search of the Leichhardt party, which produced such valuable geographical results.

We now come to the efforts to cross the continent from south to north. I need not deal with all of these, nor with any at length, as they are within the memories of many of us in this hall. J. MacDowall Stuart's (22) successful journey from Adelaide across the Van Diemen Gulf, Burke and Wills' (23) journey from Melbourne to the Gulf of Carpentaria, and the terrible fate of this expedition on its way back, aroused much interest at home, as did also the work done by M. Kinley, as leader of one of the many expeditions sent out in search of the Burke and Wills party. (23) The name of Forest (24) (from 1869 to 1874) and Giles (25) (1872 to 1875) must be added to this list of the leading explorers. It is important to note that exploration in Australia was quickly followed by settlement, whenever the nature of the country permitted it. An Australian writer has observed of the squatters, "these men and their subordinates were close on the footsteps of the explorers, and should the adventurers remain some months absent from civilization, he found, on his return, settlement far across what had been the frontier line when he departed." Here is again displayed the same spirit of individual effort in colonization which we noticed in the Dominion of Canada, and which differentiates our race from other races in modern days. Passing from exploration and settlement to the question of consolidation, it is unnecessary to make more than a passing reference to the Federation, which came into effect on New Year's day, only three weeks before the close of the Victorian age; (26) for all that could be said on this subject has been quite recently said in the Home and Colonial Parliaments and press. Although the general review of the geographical and hydrographical work of the Royal Navy is, fortunately, outside the sphere marked out for me this evening, no story of Australian exploration would be complete without some reference to the celebrated survey of the entire coasts of the continent during seven years by H.M.S. *Beagle,* first under Captain Wickham, and after him Captain Stokes. She sailed from England only a few weeks after the accession of Queen Victoria. This voyage should not be confounded (as it often is) with the earlier voyage of the *Beagle* round the world, including a visit to Australia—a voyage to which we owe the delightful journal of Darwin. A few lines at the close of that journal seem appropriate to-night. Darwin wrote as follows: "In the same quarter of the globe, Australia is rising into a grand centre of civilization, which, at some not very remote period, will rule as empress over the southern hemisphere. It is impossible for an Englishman to behold our distant colonies without a high pride and satisfaction. To hoist the British flag seems to draw with it, as a certain consequence, wealth, prosperity, and civilization." (27)

The following figures will show the extent to which this prophecy has been already fulfilled: The white population in 1837 was about 131,000, the export and import trade with the United Kingdom was about two million pounds sterling; the entire exports and imports amounted to less than three millions; and the revenue collected in the colonies was under half a million. The white population is now estimated at over four millions; the combined export and import trade with the United Kingdom is nearly 45 millions sterling; the entire export and import trade of the six colonies before federation was about 130 millions sterling; and the aggregate of their revenues was about 27 millions.

With such a record, our brethren under the Southern Cross may well be proud of that watchword which finds a heartfelt echo throughout the British Empire—"Advance, Australia."

The settlement of New Zealand, though no less remarkable than that of Australia, did not call for exploration on a large scale, inasmuch as no point in its islands is 100 miles distant from the seaboard; so that it does not offer the same material for geographical notice. It was not until after Her Majesty's accession that the occupation of New Zealand was commenced by the New Zealand Company, another creation of the indefatigable Wakefield. (28) It is wonderful to note how, within a single reign, New Zealand has been made into a country almost as settled as England. The main cause has been, of course, the energy of the settlers; but a great debt of gratitude is due to Wakefield's Company, which carried on its valuable work until its dissolution in 1851. The existing Colonial Government was established by the Act of Parliament of 1852. Since that time exploration has been mainly carried out by the Colonial Survey under Sir James Hector [29] and Sir Julian von Hoast. Here are a few figures showing the growth of the colony. In 1896, the population, exclusive of aborigines, was 703,000. The revenue in 1899 was nearly five million sterling. The export and import trade with the United Kingdom aggregate about 13½ million pounds, and the total exports and imports are about 20 millions.

Before leaving Australasia, British New Guinea, which was founded by an Act of Parliament in 1887, calls for notice at a geographical gathering, owing to the excellent work done by its late Governor, Sir William MacGregor. [30]

I have decided to treat the subject of Africa very briefly. This is certainly not from want of material, either from the point of view of geography or from that of expansion of the Empire. Three or four years ago, our President, speaking in this hall on geographical exploration, said, "The continent of Africa was a vast blank on the map of the world in the year of the Queen's accession, and its subsequent exploration has been in great part due to the energy and liberality of this Society, of which Her Majesty is the Patron." Then again, as regards political expansion, it is certain that immense areas have been added to the Empire in that continent. Nor, again, can it be said that the progress of exploration and expansion in Africa has been steady and almost mechanical as in Canada, and therefore not presenting many salient points of interest. Just the contrary is the case. Owing to the vastness of the continent, to the immense native populations massed in some parts, to the climatic conditions, and finally to international and political causes, the story of British expansion in Africa is a long series of thrilling adventures, terrible hardships, sanguinary wars, and keen diplomatic struggles. It might seem, therefore, to call for treatment at considerable length. Nevertheless, there are valid reasons to justify a more concise method. In the first place, our political expansion there is the recent outcome of a continuous and extremely heated international scramble, which—during the last sixteen years—has more than once brought Great Britain to the verge of a European war, and which wrung from Lord Salisbury the cry that Africa had been created to be the plague of Foreign Offices. It seems to me that one cannot now deal in any adequate way with that controversial history before a Society which, though never forgetting that it is a British Society, invites geographers of all nationalities to its meetings, and pursues the even tenor of its scientific and therefore cosmopolitan way in the acquisition, encouragement, and diffusion of geographical knowledge. In the second place, passing from political expansion to statistics, another result of the neogenesis of British Empire in Africa is that, for much of the territory acquired, statistics of revenue or commerce would be altogether misleading as a criterion of the potential values of these new possessions, while exact statistics of population do not exist, and mere estimates are very untrustworthy. For instance, in one province, Nigeria, some experienced travellers and geographers have estimated the population as high as 40 millions, and others as low as 20 millions. Even statistics of the area of British possessions are wanting in exactness, that area varying between 2½ million square miles and 3½ million square miles, according to the political points of view from which you choose to regard it.

Lastly, in regard to the geographical work of British explorers during the sixteen years since the scramble for Africa began—a work of immense detail performed by a great number of still living men—it would require more judgment (and certainly more courage) than I possess to draw a line between those who must be mentioned and those who must be excluded for want of time, while a long catalogue of names would be wearisome and serve no useful purpose. I propose, then, to deal only with the great preparatory explorations during the first forty-seven and a half years of the late reign, and to terminate with the momentous meeting of fourteen nations at the Berlin Conference towards the close of 1884. This story of exploration falls naturally into three sections, that relating to Western and Nigerian Africa, that relating to Southern and Zambezian Africa, and that relating to Eastern and Nilotic Africa, though the two last are, in a few cases, difficult to separate. I have put these three spheres in the chronological order in which they engaged public interest and support.

The discoveries of Mungo Park and Lander, the travels of Denham and Clapperton, and the enterprise of MacGregor, Laird, and Beecroft, had attracted much attention to Western Africa at the time of Her Majesty's accession. It was largely due to the Prince Consort that Parliament took up the question. The first effort was the Government expedition up the Niger in 1841-42, in the hopes of opening up relations with the populous and semi-civilized States in the region now known as Northern Nigeria. In 1849 the Government proposed to attain the same object from the Mediterranean, and they dispatched Richardson with Overweg and Barth to Bornu, where the two former died. Barth then took command, and in the four following years made his celebrated journeys in the Central and Western Sudan. The Government next ordered the *Pleiad* to ascend the Niger and Benue, in command of Dr. Baikie, R.N., who, in 1854, reached a point not far short of Yola. In 1858, Lieut. Glover, R.N., afterwards Sir John Glover, (31) ascended the main Niger in the *Dayspring* to Rabba, travelled thence to Boussa, and finally overland to Lagos. This was the last Government effort to open up those regions, and over twenty years passed before that work (to be coupled this time with the acquisition of political power, without which no advance can be permanently maintained) was again taken up and successfully carried out by private enterprise. But it must never be forgotten that this private enterprise would not have been conceived but for the information given to the world by the explorers of a previous generation. As the blood of the martyrs is the seed of the Church, so the expansion of the British Empire has, to a large extent, been the natural sequel to the lives and deaths of explorers whose labours may have appeared at that time to be unfruitful.

The exploration of Southern and Zambezian Africa during the Victorian age will always be associated with the name of Livingstone. His earliest visit to the Zambezi was in 1851; and the following year he started on the first great journey which made him widely known at home. It included the discovery of the Victoria falls, and the crossing of the continent from Loanda to the mouth of the Zambezi. So brilliant a success secured to Livingstone the support of the British Government and of this Society. In 1858 he started for his second great exploration, which lasted until 1864. He was accompanied by a young traveller, who was later to make the name of Sir John Kirk so familiar both as an explorer and as British Political Agent in regions much of which have since come within the circle of the Empire. The discovery of Nyasa Land, important as it has proved, was only one out of many results of these five years of constant effort. The subsequent labours of Livingstone, under the auspices of this Society, from 1865 until his death at Bangweolo in 1873, gain additional interest from the expeditions sent out to his relief, mainly under the auspices of this Society. The most important was that under Cameron, who, after he had convinced himself of Livingstone's death, crossed the continent from Zanzibar to Benguela. Two years before this, however, Livingstone had been relieved by Stanley, who thus laid the foundation for his subsequent work in the Dark Continent.

Of other explorers in Southern Africa, I will only mention Erskine and Elton(32) (in the Limpopo and other regions) between 1868 and 1877, and Joseph Thomson, who, on the death of Keith Johnston,(33) directly after his landing in Africa in May, 1879, took command of his expedition, which had been sent out by this Society, and, after exploring Lake Nyasa and part of Tanganyika, discovered Lake Rukwa. But, apart from what we may call professional explorers, there have been a host of big-game hunters, to whom we owe much geographical knowledge of South Africa. Of these, the most famous is Mr. Selous,(34) whose earliest thirteen years of wanderings, from 1871 to 1884, fall within the limit of time that I have set myself.

The exploration of Eastern and Nilotic Africa have attracted more sustained attention than that of either Western or Southern Africa, and they have been, for the most part, connected with this Society. Burton and Speke were despatched in 1856 to discover the great lakes reported to exist. Burton mapped out the northern half of Tanganyika, and Speke discovered the south shores of the Victoria Nyanza. In 1860 Speke was again sent, with Captain Grant,(35) to discover the sources of the Nile. They reached the western shores of the Victoria Nyanza, found the outlet of the great river, and followed it down to Gondokoro, where they met Baker ascending the White Nile, after he had explored the regions of the Atbara and the Blue Nile. Baker, proceeding southward, discovered the Albert Nyanza, which had been missed by Speke and Grant. It is impossible to do justice here to the multitude of explorers who have contributed valuable information on the Egyptian Sudan and neighbouring regions; but a passing reference must be made to the first opening up of Somaliland in 1883, by Messrs. James,(36) Alymer,(37) and Lort-Phillips(38) a work which has since been so ably extended by Dr. Donaldson-Smith and other notable explorers.

I must now pass to the new era opened up by the great journey of H. M. Stanley from Zanzibar to the mouth of the Congo in the years 1875 to 1877. Only the earlier portion of that memorable journey falls within what is now a part of the British empire; but Stanley's great discoveries were the torch that fired the dormant idea of developing and settling equatorial Africa. Although some years elapsed before that smouldering fire burst into flame, there were a few minds in Europe who saw that the partition of Africa was approaching, and who set to work to prepare for it, so that when the moment came, in 1884,(39) they were ready to act instead of losing years in deliberating and creating the necessary organization. During that period of incubation, the Royal Geographical Society displayed great activity in sending out expeditions entirely at its own expense. The most important was that led by Joseph Thomson through the Masai country in 1883-84, in which he succeeded in reaching the north-east coast of the Victoria Nyanza, and also visited Mounts Kenia *(sic)* and Kilimanjaro. About the same time, the latter of these was explored and ascended by Mr. H. H. Johnston, who had previously visited other parts of Africa. I specially introduce his name because, as Sir Harry Johnston,(40) he has proved himself a brilliant administrator in British Central Africa, and is at present engaged in organizing a system of government for that great province of Uganda, which Captain Lugard (now General Sir Frederick Lugard) won for the Empire under the auspices of the Imperial British East Africa Company.

This ends my sketch; but I would add a few words on a question which the future historian will assuredly ask:—In what spirit has this vast expansion of the Empire been conducted?

Now, looking only at British America, Australasia, and Africa, because

British India is outside my province to-night, these fall roughly into two sections, one which is mainly peopled by white races capable of self-government, while the other is peopled by coloured races, which (when unprotected) fall a prey to cruel tyranny and inhuman fetish practices, or are devastated by unceasing inter-tribal war, or are swept away by the incursion of slave-raiding hordes.

Throughout the Victorian age, Great Britain has dealt with the white races on the principle of constitutional liberty, when assured of loyalty to the Crown and flag; and the chief aim in dealing with coloured races had undoubtedly been beneficence, though this aim, like other human ideals, has too often been marred by imperfect knowledge or faulty judgment. But perhaps the dominant note throughout this period of expansion has been the devotion to duty of those concerned in it, whether soldiers, sailors, or civilians; whether in the United Kingdom or in the Colonies; whether explorers of unknown regions or their supporters living within the bounds of civilization.

And it was that triple watchword of Liberty, Beneficence, and Duty which made our late Sovereign the perfect symbol of the cohesive forces that bound this vast Empire together; her respect for the constitutional liberty of her subjects was only equalled by her deep human sympathy with all kind of suffering, and by that extraordinary devotion to duty, which was carried to the very verge of the grave. So it was that Her Majesty stood as the type and example of all that is best and truly greatest in our race; and as long as English history shall endure and wherever the English language shall be spoken, the last Sovereign of the Hanoverian line will be revered by our descendants as Victoria the Beloved.

(1) From the President's opening remarks. The whole proceedings are reported in the *Geographical Journal,* Vol. XVII, No. 3 of March, 1901.

(2) John George Lambton, Earl of Durham, 1792-1840. Governor General of Canada, 1838. Challenged on his policy towards French Canada, he returned to Britain a year later, relinquishing his post but not resigning.

(3) An attitude extraordinarily close to that of C. L. Temple in *loc sit.*

(4) 1798-1875. Appointed Director of Canadian Surveys, 1842.

(5) 1849-1901. Dawson City in the Yukon was named after him.

(6) Goldie would be the last person on earth to omit paying a well deserved tribute to the work of a Chartered Company!

(7) Captain John Palliser, 1807-1887.

(8) Montgomery Martin, 1811-1882.

(9) Herman Merivale, 1806-1874.

(10) Sir Robert Schomburgh (—burgk, —boork), 1831-1835 explored British Guiana and discovered the magnificent *Victoria Regia* lily.

(11) See page 232.

(12) Rear Adml. Sir John Hindmarsh, (d. 1860), Gov. of South Aust., 1836-7.

(13) John Oxley, 1781-1828.

(14) Sir Thomas Livingstone Mitchell, 1792-1855.

(15) Alexander Hamilton Hume, 1797-1869.

(16) Alan Cunningham (D. 1839), a botanist from Kew Gardens, went out in 1816.

(17) Charles Sturt, 1795-1869.

(18) Sir George Grey, 1812-1898. Gov. of S.Aust., 1841; of N.Z., 1845; of Cape Colony, 1861-68; then again N.Z., etc.

(19) Edward John Eyre, 1815-1901.

(20) Frederich Wilhem Ludwig, 1813-1848.

(21) Sir Augustus Charles Gregory, 1819-1905.

(22) John C. MacDowell Stuart, 1815-1866.

(23) Robert O'Hara Burke (1820-61) and William John Wills (1834-61).

(24) John Forest.

(25) Ernest Giles.

(26) See pages 178-179.

(27) See Charles Darwin, *Journal of Researches,* Collier & Sons, N.Y., 1890, page 569. It is not clear why Goldie did not quote in full " . . . Australia is rising, or indeed may be said to have risen, into a grand center etc."

(28) Edward Gibbon Wakefield, 1796-1862. In 1827 was sentenced to transportation for abduction. Whilst still a prisoner wrote *A letter from Sydney* (1829) followed by *A View of the Art of Colonization* (1833). In 1836, Wakefield founded the South Australia Association.

(29) 1834-1907.

(30) Sir William MacGregor, 1847-1919, was Governor of New Guinea, then of Lagos, Newfoundland, and, from 1909-1914, of Queensland.

(31) Glover, Sir John Hawley. See page 91 and footnote.

(32) James Frederick Elton, 1840-1877.

(33) See also page 253.

(34) Frederick Courteney Selous, 1851-1917, the greatest hunter of them all and the man on whom John Buchan modelled "Peter Pineaar."

(35) James Augustus Grant, 1827-1892.

(36) Frank Linsly James, 1851-1890.

(37) Possibly a misprint for General Sir Fenton Aylmer, 1862-1935.

(38) Lieut.-Col. Frederick, 1845-1926.

(39) Amongst these surely, even prime amongst these, is Goldie himself.

(40) See also page 253.

III. TWENTY-FIVE YEARS GEOGRAPHICAL PROGRESS (1906)

The following address was delivered by Sir George Goldie to the Annual Meeting of the British Association for the Advancement of Science in York, on Thursday, 2 August, 1906. Sir George, then President of the R.G.S., presided also over this division of the Association's meeting— Section E, Geography. [1]

It is just a quarter of a century since the British Association held its last meeting in this ancient city of York and celebrated the Jubilee of its foundation, so that from the moment of accepting the invitation to preside over this Section it was clear to my mind that the most appropriate subject for my Address would be the progress of geography between that Jubilee and what I believe would be called in other spheres our Diamond Jubilee. For although the immediate concern of geographers is with the earth's surface, yet we cannot avoid sharing with the rest of our race the religious observance of astronomical periods and the tendency to regard certain numbers of such periods as having a peculiar value. Geographers, indeed, might be excused some tendency to this human weakness, as they are entirely dependent on astronomical methods and on an elaborate use of numbers for the primary necessity of ascertaining where they are on that surface which it is their business to examine and describe.

I do not propose in this Address to deal only, or even chiefly, with the progress of exploration since our Jubilee Meeting in York, for although that progress has been remarkable, its effects are probably less far-reaching than the growth during the same period of the scientific treatment of geography; while both of these advances, taken together, are, to my mind, of less importance to our country—and we are, after all, a "British" Association—than the spread of the geographical spirit amongst our people, on the main cause of which I shall say a few words. Let me deal, then, with these matters in turn, bearing in mind, however, that the two latter subjects—the growth of scientific method and what I may term the democratisation of geography—are so interwoven as to make it impossible to separate them altogether.

First, then, as to the advance of exploration since 1881. In that section of the Arctic regions in which the Nares [2] and the Greely [3] expeditions had done their work considerable progress has been made, mainly by Lieutenant Peary, [4] who carried the investigation of the coast of Greenland further north and east than had been the case before, while his contributions to our knowledge of the inland ice are of much value. The explorations of Captain Sverdrup [5] among the lands lying north of America, and the not less important expeditions of Nordenskjöld(6) and Nansen(7) across the centre of Greenland, have added much to our knowledge, not only of the physical geography, but also of the geology, biology, and ice conditions of a land which, though lying to a large extent outside the Arctic circle, is essentially Arctic in character. Another expedition, under Captain Amundsen, (8) is now completing its work, which has extended over about three years, around the North Magnetic Pole. Both English and Swedish expeditions have greatly improved our knowledge of the islands of Spitzbergen, while Jackson, (9) Nansen, and others (10) have enabled us to lay down with something approaching to accuracy the archipelago of Franz-Josef Land. (11) But perhaps the largest addition to our information about the North Polar region during these twenty-five years have been through the ever-memorable expedition of Dr. Nansen, during which he reached within four degrees of the Pole, obtained soundings down to two thousand fathoms, and collected a vast amount of meteorological, physical, and biological information, which has enabled him to work out, to a large extent, the probable conditions which prevail around the Pole itself.

Let us pass now to the other end of the earth—to the great continent which, it now appears beyond doubt, surrounds the Southern Pole. Here also very considerable progress has been made during the last twenty-five years. For a long period after the time of Ross, (12) over sixty years ago, only spasmodic efforts had been made to continue the work of South Polar exploration. But in recent years numerous national expeditions—Belgian, German, Swedish, and British—have pursued this work, producing a mass of data in geology, physics, meteorology, and biology which should throw a flood of light on both the present conditions and on the history of this dead continent. Perhaps, as the successor in the Presidential Chair of the Royal Geographical Society to that great geographer, Sir Clements Markham, (13) a Yorkshireman, I may be allowed to dwell specially on the splendid and varied work of the National Antarctic Expedition under Captain Scott, (14) which not only carried our knowledge of the Antarctic continent about five degrees further south than the limits of exploration previously reached, but also collected a vast amount of scientific information.

And now, leaving the Polar regions, let me try to recall the position of exploration of the African continent in 1881. Stanley had only recently completed that history-making journey across Africa, by which he traced on the map the last great line in the framework of the continent, the river Congo; and so accurate were his observations that, notwithstanding the vast number of later explorers, the course of the river laid down by him has practically remained unaltered. But a glance at a map of Africa of 1881 reminds us that enormous blanks existed, almost from the tropic of Capricorn to the upper bend of the Niger, in the centre and west of the continent; that the region between the equator and the Gulf of Aden was almost unknown; that our knowledge of the great lake region of Central Africa, as also of the eastern and western tributaries of the Upper Nile, was most imperfect. Little had been done for the Central Sudan States since the days of Barth, (15) and only very vague notions existed as to the real character of the Sahara. Since 1881, through the efforts of Stanley himself and a host of Belgian, French, and British explorers, the map of the whole Congo Basin has been crowded with rivers, defined with a fair approach to accuracy, while the hypothetical lakes of the past have evaporated. In the southern quarter of the continent, all the region from the northern limit of Cape Colony up to the Congo watershed and Lake Tanganyika has been to a large extent mapped in a provisional way and all the main features laid down. The work of exploration in the eastern regions of Africa has been no less complete. Stanley, on his expedition for the relief of Emin Pasha, (16) discovered the important range of Ruwenzori, and laid down with some precision the outlines of Lake Albert Edward; while British and German explorers have made very fully known those remote feeders of the Nile which supply the Victoria Nyanza, and have contributed largely to our knowledge of the great Rift valleys and the lakes which occupy them. Joseph Thomson, (17) the original pioneer from the East Coast through Masailand towards Uganda, has been followed by many others, so that the map of this region is thickly studded with new features; while the Anglo-German Boundary Surveys have been able to lay down a trigonometrical basis for a complete and trustworthy map of the whole region. Somaliland, the outlying parts of Abyssinina, Lake Rudolf, the rivers that run into it, and the rivers that run from the south-east into the Sobat and the Nile—all these have been explored and laid down with wonderful fullness since the Association last met in York; while, after the breaking down of the barrier of Mahdism, the advance in our knowledge of the Egyptian Sudan became almost too rapid for record. Nor has the progress of exploration in Western Africa been less remarkable. Through the energy of the officials of the Chartered Royal Niger Company, of Sir Frederick Lugard and his staff, (18) of Binger, Monteil, and a host of other French as well as German explorers, great blanks have been filled in, and mapping of the most detailed character in many districts has been rendered possible. Our knowledge of Lake Chad and of its present and its probable past has been greatly extended, and many problems have been suggested which will provide ample work for the geographer and the geologist. The Sahara has been crossed and recrossed in many directions during recent years, especially by French explorers, with the result that we have been compelled to revise the prevailing impression of the great desert, which is by no means the featureless waste it used to be considered. Taking the continent of Africa as a whole, its map has been thickly covered with a network of features, and, so far as cartography is concerned, all that remains to be done is to fill in the meshes of that network with local details and to give precision to our maps by careful triangulation.

I have dealt at some length with exploratory work in Africa, because it is the continent of which we knew least in 1881, and our knowledge of which has made the greatest strides since then; but the contemporaneous advance of our acquaintance with the topographical and physical conditions of other portions of the lithosphere has been very remarkable. A host of explorers, of whom I will only mention Younghusband, Littledale, Bower, Sven Hedin, and Huntington, (19) have crossed the centre of Asia in various directions. During the same period the topographical survey of India has been brought to completion, while Indian officers and others have carried geographical investigations far beyond the limits of our great Dependency, and have made much progress in the mapping of Baluchistan and Persia. The recent Tibet expedition practically settled the question of the sources of the Brahmaputra, and laid down its central and upper course. I do not know whether we should regret that they were not able to fill in the long gap in the lower course of that river, for we still enjoy the pleasures of hope of solving this interesting problem, which, with some equally unsolved problems in other parts of the globe, reminds us that explorers need not yet sigh, like Alexander, for other worlds to conquer. Numerous travellers have crossed China in all directions, and have done much for its accurate mapping, as have also the French in their Indo-China possessions. Even in Turkey in Asia, where serious difficulties are encountered by explorers, such men as Ramsay and Maunsell have done much valuable work. (20)

Turning to America, the very efficient surveys of Canada and of the United States have made an immense advance in the accurate mapping of their respective countries, while much has also been done in Mexico and in Central America. The Argentine Republic and Chile have made great progress in the exploration and mapping of their territories, and Peru and Bolivia have within recent years shown creditable diligence in this respect; but there remain in the southern continent areas covering from two or three million square miles still practically unexplored, so that to-day, as far as preliminary exploration is concerned, there is more to be done in South America than in Africa.

I have perhaps, sufficiently indicated the marvellous progress of exploration of the lithosphere. I have naturally less to say of the advance of oceanography, for the 'Challenger' (21) expedition had completed its voyages before the Jubilee meeting of the Association in 1881, although the results were not then worked out. It is, indeed, only within the last few years that Sir John Murray (22) has been able to complete this immense work, which occupies no less than fifty volumes. Since the voyages of the 'Challenger' there has been no equally extensive expedition for oceanographic work, but the study of the oceans has been carried on steadily, if slowly. The German expedition in the 'Valdivia' (23) added much to what the 'Challenger' had achieved, especially in the Indian Ocean; where also, only within the last year, Mr. Stanley Gardiner has carried out an enterprise which promises to yield results of the first importance. (24) Further east in the seas around the Malay Archipelago, the Dutch 'Siboga' (25) expedition added something to our knowledge of the ocean bed; and not less important than any of these later expeditions was the enterprise carried out over a series of years in the Pacific and in the Gulf of Mexico by Mr. Alexander Agassiz, (26) entirely at his own expense. The cable-laying companies have also done a good deal on behalf of oceanography, and some of the results of their investigations have been published by the Royal Geographical Society, under the superintendence of Sir John Murray. The immensely valuable work constantly carried on by His Majesty's surveying vessels, under the direction of the Hydrographic Department of the Admiralty, is so generally known as to make it unnecessary for me to dwell upon it.

Long before the close of the nineteenth century, however, oceanic navigation had ceased to be of a pioneer or exploratory character, except in the Polar regions, and had devoted itself to the no less important tasks of filling in details and of undertaking scientific research, while the comparatively new subject of limnology, which deals with those other portions of the hydrosphere known as lakes or inland seas, and which has had such immense and valuable labour devoted to it in this country by Sir John Murray, falls strictly within the limits of scientific research. To this end all geographical travel and all geographical study must come; and I am thus led to the second branch of my address, dealing with the growth of the scientific side of our subject and the concurrent spread of interest in its study. On these points I propose to deal mainly with our own country; but I shall be compelled to draw certain comparisons, however unwillingly, with the more advanced conditions, in this respect, of other countries, and notably of Germany. No one, indeed, could assert that the importance of problems relating to the geomorphology of the lithosphere, to the distribution of land and water, and to the influence of these (combined with climatic conditions) upon the distribution of life and on human interests, were not recognised amongst us long before the last meeting of the British Association at York. The underlying principles of scientific geography have been perceived in all ages and in all countries by a few thinkers; but so late as twenty-five years ago a true conception of the functions and scope of geography was confined to a very limited circle of specialists. In confirmation of this, I may remind you of an inquiry which the Royal Geographical Society undertook about that time into the position of geography at home and abroad.

For many years previously the Society had been endeavouring to awaken the public mind as to the high capabilities of geography when dealt with on scientific lines, and to encourage the teaching of the subject on a higher plane by the award of medals on the results of examinations. The failure of these attempts induced the Society to make the investigation to which I refer, and its report (published only a few years after the York meeting) may be regarded as the starting-point of the revolution that has since occurred. It was found that Germany even then had professors of geography in nearly all its universities, and a number of thoroughly trained and earnest students who devoted themselves to investigation of the subject in all directions; and that in Austria, as well as in Germany, geography had attained a position, both in universities and in schools of all grades, practically on a level with other subjects of education; while in this country it was generally regarded with apathy, and even contempt. It had no place in our universities; it was barely tolerated in our secondary and higher schools;while in the simple geography of our elementary schools there was great room for improvement. Practical work in geographical research scarcely existed, except in so far as it was an outcome of geology. There was no encouragement for students, there was no high-class geographical literature, such as existed in Germany, and for standard works we had to resort either to that country or France. The great treasure-house for geographers was Elisée Reclus's 'Géographie Universelle,' (27) which, fortunately, was translated into English. There existed, indeed, a few popular works in this country, but these were more or less of a purely descriptive and unscientific character, excluding altogether the fundamental data of the subject. In the Society's report to which I have referred were also given very interesting quotations from the opinions of headmasters of English public schools as to the value of geography and the educational position which it ought to have. It was melancholy reading. Only a few of them took a favourable view of the subject, while the majority treated it with little respect. The remarks of those who favoured its study are to-day chiefly interesting as showing the entire inadequacy of the methods of geographical tuition in those days and the little importance attached to it in educational circles. I must, however, quote with approbation the words of one master, who said: 'I feel strongly the great importance of the subject, not only as a mental discipline, an essential part of a liberal education, but as more especially necessary for Englishmen, many of whom will be called upon in after-life to turn their geographical knowledge to practical and serious account'; and he added: 'One of the difficulties in doing justice to the claims of the subject is the somewhat absurd prejudice in teaching geography, as if it were less worthy of first-rate men than Latin prose, or essay writing, or criticism.' On the other hand, most of the headmasters threw cold water on any attempt to give geography a substantial place in our great public schools. They considered it not sufficiently important as an educational instrument; it was hardly a discipline; it was little more than an effort of memory; it was quite worthless educationally till it became a branch of history; problems in it could not be set. These masters were supported by the opinion of a distinguished geologist that geography was not suitable as a university subject because it was a 'graphy,' and not a 'logy.' Nor, indeed, can it be contended that these depreciatory views of geography, as it was then generally taught, were unreasonable. The text-books of that time were, as a whole, worthy of the position which the subject held in the education of the country, and on a par with its reputation among the educated public. The use of maps in the daily newspapers was almost unknown; while as regards military geography, the late Lord Napier of Magdala, (28) at the opening of the Education

Exhibition of the Society, forcibly contrasted the position at home with the importance attached to the subject in the German Army, where at the manoeuvres every third soldier has a map of the ground, and where in the Franco-German war maps formed part of the equipment of every company. If the position of geography in this country was so unsatisfactory a quarter of a century ago, it was not because its raw material was wanting in our language. On the contrary, few countries then possessed a literature of travel and exploration so wide and of so high a class as ours. The source of our weakness was the paucity of men qualified to apply scientific method to this raw material, and there was no institution where it was possible to obtain a thorough training in geography, such as could be obtained at a score of universities in Germany, Austria, and France. This was the position which had to be faced before placing the subject on a more satisfactory footing.

It is unnecessary for me to describe in detail the methods adopted by the Royal Geographical Society—so far as its resources and influence permitted—in carrying out the work of reformation. I need only bring before you the general results. No one will now doubt that the active minds in this great movement were right in believing that the surest means of influencing our schools of all grades, and also of obtaining in the country generally a recognition of the subject as a department of science, as a field for research, and as a subject of practical importance in various spheres of national activity, was to obtain, in the first place, proper recognition at our great universities. Attempts had, indeed, been made in the same direction as far back as 1871 and 1874, but without effect. I need hardly remind you that the later efforts of the Society had a very different result. For many years now there has been a school of geography at Oxford, while a readership established at Cambridge several years ago has also developed into a fairly well-equipped school. At Oxford there is a reader with a staff of three lecturers, and a diploma in geography is granted which practically amounts to honours in the subject. The field covered may be seen from the subjects of examination for this diploma. They are: (1) Regional Geography, (2) Climatology and Oceanography, (3) Geomorphology, (4) Ancient Historical Geography, (5) Modern Historical Geography, (6) History of Geography, and (7) Surveying. It may give a more complete idea of what English students regard as included in their subject if I mention the principal topics in the examination on regional geography—the cartographical analysis of the physical regions of the world—an elementary knowledge of the chief generalisations regarding the surface forms of the land; the movements of air and water, and the distribution of plant associations, animals, and man;the chief facts of modern political and economic geography, considered in relation to the influence of physical features. Candidates are also required to be familiar with the principles of map-making by plane table, prismatic compass, and clinometer, with the representation of relief, and with the orientation, reading, and measurement of maps. Equally thorough and exhaustive are the various topics included under the other heads of examination. Both in ancient and modern historical geography the subject has to be considered in relation to the influence of physical features. The standard adopted at Oxford is as high as that which exists at any university in Germany. The establishment of a school at Cambridge being recent, one cannot yet speak as positively of its success as in the case of Oxford. But Cambridge has gone a step further than Oxford in placing geography as a subject in the examination for its B.A. degree; and while that may be regarded as a simple pass, the student may also enter for the examination for the diploma in geography, the standard of which is no less high than that at Oxford, while the ground covered is essentially the same. In both universities the training in cartography and surveying is thorough, and it is to be hoped that such students as propose to follow either a military or a colonial career will take advantage of the opportunity thus presented. The example of Oxford and Cambridge has been followed elsewhere, though to a lesser extent. In the University of London there is a board of geographical studies, and the subject holds a substantial place in the University examination, and is a compulsory subject for a degree in economics. There are chairs or lectureships of geography at Victoria University, Manchester, at the University of Liverpool, and at the University of Birmingham. Steps are being taken to establish a chair at the University of Edinburgh; while other institutions of a similar kind would be glad to follow the example of the great universities if only their funds permitted. In the elementary schools the programme is nearly all that can be desired, the one thing needed here, as elsewhere, being a sufficiency of teachers who have been thoroughly trained in the subject. In the secondary schools progress has been somewhat more slow; but there has been a steady advance in recent years, and a step recently taken by the Board of Education, in issuing 'a very satisfactory syllabus for the teaching of geography, is certain to give a strong impetus to the subject. In the London School of Economics, under the directorship of Mr. Mackinder, [29] which is attended annually by over a thousand students, geographical teaching holds a place of the first rank. The publishers have kept pace with this great revolution in the schools, so that today there is no difficulty whatever for anyone, from the elementary school up to the university, in obtaining a text-book, or an atlas, or special maps suitable for his requirements. The country has been, indeed, almost flooded with cheap atlases issued in parts, some of them of a highly creditable quality, while the slides of photographs taken by explorers are sold by the thousand for educational and lecture purposes.

The main cause of this remarkable growth of interest in geography amongst our educated classes dates back to about three years after the last Meeting of the Association at York. In 1884, Germany, which in the middle of the century had been still said to rule the air (while France ruled the land and Britain the sea), and which in later years had been absorbed in the process of unification by blood and iron, [30] suddenly launched out as a world Power and gave the signal for the partition of Africa. England and France, in both of which countries a few men had been carefully preparing, during several years, for this inevitable partition, hastened to join in the international race, and the spirit of colonial expansion, long-dormant, reawakened, and reached out to all parts of the earth where settled government did not forbid advance. We, who have lived through the last quarter of a century, are apt to underestimate the revolution through which we have passed, for a true analogy to which we must go back to the Elizabethan age. The impulse given by this movement to the study of geography can hardly be overestimated. War has been called the best teacher of geography, and certainly Napoleon, the highest exponent of the art of war, was as ardent a student of geography as he was of mathematics; but it now appears that empire-building is an even greater factor than war in advancing and popularising geographical knowledge. Amongst the educated classes of England, France, and Germany, and, in a lesser degree, of Italy and Belgium, there are few persons who have not had relatives or friends engaged as explorers, or missionaries, or officials, or soldiers, or traders in previously little known parts of the world, while countless numbers have been concerned in the new movement through vast shipping and other interests that shared in it. The Press, which prior to 1884 had paid little attention to the outlying lands in question, gradually devoted more and more space to everything connected with them, and continually produced most useful maps, showing not only their physical features, but also their economical conditions. It is not my business here to attempt to forecast the judgment of the

244

future historian on the more general results of this colonial expansion, but he will assuredly recognise its enormous effect on popular attention to geographical subjects, as well as, or even more than, on exploration.

It must not be inferred that the popularity of a subject is taken by me as a test of its place in the ranks of science; but, owing to the widening of the area from which students can be drawn and men of genius evolved, this democratisation of geographical ideas is, to my mind, a very hopeful feature as regards the future of the scientific treatment of the subject.

I should have to extend my address to undue length if I attempted to demonstrate the recent growth of the scientific method at home by giving you even an imperfect catalogue of the geographical books and papers of a scientific nature published during the period under consideration, and especially in later years. I can only select for mention a few typical books, such as Dr. Mill's 'International Geography', [31] Mr. Mackinder's 'Britain and the British Seas', [32] Mr. Hogarth's 'Nearer East', [33] and Sir Thomas Holdich's work on 'India', [34] and other works in Mr. Mackinder's series entitled 'The Regions of the World', [35]. As to papers dealing with this kind of work, I will mention those of Messrs. Buckman and Strahan giving the results of their investigations on the river systems of the west of England; by Mr. Cooper Read on the river system of East Yorkshire; by Dr. Herbertson on the major natural regions of the world, and on the distribution of rainfall over the earth's surface; by Mr. Chisholm on the distribution of towns and villages, and on the geographical conditions affecting British trade; by Messrs. Smith, Lewis and Moss on the geographical distribution of vegetation in England and Scotland; by Mr. Marr on the waterways of English Lakeland; and last, but not least, by Dr. Mill on the Clyde Sea Area, on a fragment of the geography of England, and on England and Wales viewed geographically. It must, indeed, be confessed that in this respect we are still behind Germany, which has been pouring forth a mass of geographical literature of the highest scientific value. But this backwardness is the result of past neglect of the subject, and not of present apathy. There was a current saying a quarter of a century ago that the schoolmaster was abroad. I have shown you that, in a different sense, the geographer was then abroad; but I believe that we can now say that the geographer is at home and has come to stay. There is a whole school of young geographers—not yet very large, it is true, but zealous and active—full of the new ideas, the new methods, the new hopes of our rising science, and I do not think it too sanguine to expect that when the British Association holds its centenary meeting, twenty-five years hence, perhaps in this very city of York, our countrymen will be found to occupy the same position in the front rank of scientific geography that their forefathers held in pioneer exploration.

(1) I am grateful to the Secretary, British Association for the Advancement of Science, for providing me with the text of this address.

(2) Sir George Nares, 1831-1915.

(3) A. W. Greely, 1844-1935, U.S. Polar explorer.

(4) Robert Edwin Peary, USA. 1856-1920. Credited with being the first man to reach the North Pole, though this is sometimes disputed.

(5) Harald Ulrik Sverdrup, 1868-1957.

(6) Nordenskjöld, Nils Otto Gustav, 1869-1928.

(7) Nansen, Dr. Fridtjof, 1861-1930.

(8) Amundsen, Raold, 1872-1928.

(9) Jackson, F. G. Explorer, b.1860.

(10) Notably Weyprecht and Payer, who discovered it and named it in 1873!

(11) An archepelago of some 187 Islands in the North Barents Sea. The area is part of the Russian Province of Archangel.

(12) Sir John Ross, 1777-1856. Polar explorer whose name is for ever associated with the search for the North-West Passage. Located Magnetic North Pole in 1831. Later explored South Polar regions.

(13) See page 271.

(14) Robert Falcon Scott, 1868-1912.

(15) See page 95.

(16) Emin Pasha (Eduard Schnitzer), 1840-92. Born in Oppeln in Polish Silesia. Governor of Equitoria in the Sudan under Gordon, 1878. He resented Stanley's "rescue".

(17) See page 67.

(18) See page 78. Goldie does not hesitate to use the opportunity to press a claim for "collective credit" on behalf of "the officials of the Chartered Royal Niger Company".

(19) (a) Sir Francis Edward Younghusband, 1863-1942.

    (b) Littledale, St. G.R.: Explored the Pamirs and Central Asia, 1891-92.

    (c) Bower, Capt. H. A., explored Tibet, crossing it in 1891-92.

    (d) Hedin, Sven Anders, 1865-1952.

    (e) Huntington, Ellsworth, 1876-1943, U.S. explorer of Cent. Asia, 1903-06.

(20) (a) Ramsay, W. M. author of *An Historical Geography of Asia Minor,* 1890.

    (b) Maunsell, J. R., *The Geography of Eastern Turkey in Asia,* 1894.

(21) H.M.S. *Challenger,* a corvette of 2306 tons was fitted out as a survey vessel in 1872, and undertook a circumnavigation of the world lasting four years, during which she sailed 68,890 nautical miles. Her Captain was Nares and her Scientific Director, Sir Charles Wyville Thomson (1830-82), whilst the Naturalist in Charge was John Murray, (later Sir).

(22) Published between 1880 and 1895.

(23) In 1898-99.

(24) On the *Sealark,* 1905-06, in the area of the Seychelles and Maldives.

(25) In 1899-1900.

(26) Alexander Emmanuel Rodolphe Agassiz, 1835-1910. Swiss born American copper magnate who was an amateur (and highly regarded) Marine Zoologist and Oceanographer, who was generous in his provision of funds for such work.

(27) Actually, *Nouvelle Géographie Universelle,* published in nineteen volumes between 1876 and 1894. See also page 249.

(28) Robert Cornelis Napier, Royal Engineers, First Baron Napier of Magdala. A revered and well loved military figure in both Britain and India. Born 1810, died 1890.

(29) See page 255.

(30) The Bismarckian philosophy of *"Blut und Eisen",* as expounded by him on 22 March, 1849, before the 14th Meeting of the 2nd Chamber of the Prussian *Landtag.* Actually, it is surprising that Goldie does not note the fact that Bismark borrowed the concept from Quintilian (Marcus Fabius Quintilianus), c.350 A.D. "Caedes videtur significare sanguinem et ferrum." (Slaughter means to signify blood and iron). Bismarck was merely substituting "Unity" for "Slaughter."

(31) Published by Newnes, London, 1899.

(32) Published in 1902.

(33) David George Hogarth, 1862-1927. Published by Heinemann, London, 1902.

(34) Sir Thomas Hungerford Holdich, 1843-1929. Published by Frowde, London, 1904. See also page 229.

(35) Published by Heinemann, London, 1902.

IV. GEOGRAPHICAL IDEALS (1906)

An address delivered to the Royal Scottish Geographical Society by Sir George Goldie on 22 November, 1906, on the occasion of the award to him by the Society of its Livingstone Medal. (1) He was the sixth person to receive the award.

Geography is an eminently practical branch of knowledge, and it may, perhaps, be contended that it has no place for ideals. There is, indeed, a general aspect of the subject which appeals to the imagination with almost overwhelming force. To explain my meaning, let me first ask and answer the question, What is the *locus* or field of Geography? It is the surface of our globe, in which term we also include the atmosphere and such depths of the lithosphere and hydrosphere as are or have been penetrated or examined by man; so that, to a large extent, it coincides with the *locus* or field of biology, although the contents of the two sciences are, of course, very different. The exactness of my definition may be disputed, but it is sufficiently accurate for my purpose. The entire field of geography is, in any case, only a thin film of air, earth and water rotating and advancing amongst the immensities of the stellar system. But this exiguous film, insignificant in dimensions as compared even with the volume of our small planet, contains all that we know of thought and sensation existing in the universe. Speculate as we may, hope as we may, believe as we may, this minute and whirling field of geography is to us the only place in which, so far as our present knowledge goes, those phenomena exist which differentiate life from inert matter, the only field where the mysteries of reproduction, volition, reason and imagination have their home. (2)

But apart from this general aspect of an awe-inspiring and yet fantastic position, the science of geography is essentially utilitarian. Why then should it need ideals? The answer, to my mind, is that in order to produce the most effective practical work in any department of life, it is necessary to have ideals; even though we can no more hope to attain them absolutely than the asymptote can actually reach the curve which it is ever approaching. Counsels of perfection are, indeed, so often employed as a reason for ill-considered action, or as an excuse for inaction, that it is easy to understand the impatience with which they are generally brushed aside by the practical but not highly imaginative Englishman; but when they are set up only as goals towards which we should struggle, by paths however devious, by successions of compromises, with well timed haste and with well timed rest, their value cannot be overestimated. I can think of no finer example of this truth than is to be found in the life of David Livingstone, who was

247

at once an idealist and practical worker in the highest degree, and who may also be held to have approached as nearly as human nature permits to our conception of an ideal explorer.

I propose to deal, in the first place, with the ideal explorer, partly because of the occasion which brings me here tonight, the award of the Livingstone medal, but mainly because exploration in the present or in the past is the very foundation on which all geography rests. Whether the term exploration be applied to travel amongst barbarous tribes in the heart of an unknown continent, or to the peripatetic examination of some geographical problem in one's own country, the category of the most effective qualities of character and method remains much the same, however different may be the degree in which those qualities are called upon to be displayed.

With an almost unprecedented store of the more passive qualities of physical courage, tact, patience and endurance, which a long life of dangers, obstacles, privations and sickness could not exhaust, Livingstone[3] possessed an equally remarkable store of those more active qualities—which many men have shown for shorter periods, but which few have been able to maintain, as he did, during decade after decade—the power of initiative, the almost unerring perception of the most effective ways of attaining his objects with the very limited resources at his disposal, the unwearying persistence in pursuing those objects, and perhaps, above all, the moral courage with which he continually risked one of the most depressing of human calamities, failure. With the exception of physical courage and endurance, the need for which in geographical exploration is rapidly disappearing, these passive and active qualities of character will always remain essential, though in a lesser degree, to the investigator of nature abroad or- at home.

As regards Livingstone's qualities of method, I would specially deal with his adaptation and cultivation of his mental acquirements for service in every branch of the work which he set himself to perform. Geographers are, perhaps, apt to forget, and missionary societies, at one[4] period of his life, certainly forgot that although Livingstone ranks as the most notable explorer of modern days, taking into account the great number of years over which his services extended, he was (one may say) born a missionary, he lived a missionary, he died a missionary. He foresaw, when still a youth, that for his work a medical education would be invaluable, a truth which was not so widely appreciated in those days as it is now. The story of his extreme privations and difficulties in obtaining the desired education in surgery and medicine, while barely earning his living in a factory, is at once pathetic and bracing, but my business is only to note that if he had not acquired that knowledge it would not have been a question of his succeeding less completely as an explorer; it would have meant his entire failure at an early stage of his explorations. Of similar character was his thorough acquaintance with the use of tools, which he foresaw would be of some value when he became a missionary, and which proved of incalculable value when he, at a later period, superimposed on that calling the career of an explorer. Fortunately also, for general science, Livingstone had, as a boy, taken great interest in botany, geology and zoology, and had devoted his leisure to searches for specimens in the country surrounding his home. At a later period, he cultivated to his utmost power his acquaintance with these branches of knowledge, with the result that the great value of his contributions from Africa was recognized by the most competent authorities. I need only refer to the testimony of no less a person than Professor Owen[5] as regards Livingstone's contributions to zoology and paleontology, to the repeated tribute which Sir Roderick Murchison paid to his services to geology and physical geography, and to the following remark made by the then astronomer-royal at the Cape. "I never knew a man" said Sir Thomas Maclear, (6) "who, knowing scarcely anything of the method of making geographical observations or laying down positions, became so soon adept, that he could take the complete lunar observation and altitudes for time within fifteen minutes." I quote this verbatim because it shows the intensity and whole-heartedness with which Livingstone threw himself into any new study which his new career demanded, but the need of which he could not forsee until he determined to abandon his South African mission station for exploration in unknown lands.

The special branches of knowledge in which Livingstone trained and perfected himself are not, of course, all needed for explorers in every part of the world, or in every branch of exploration in its widest and truest sense. The explorer who travels round the shores of Britain to examine the conditions of coast erosion will not need for this purpose the particular mental equipment with which Livingstone armed himself, such as medical knowledge, skill in the use of tools, acquaintance with botany and zoology, ability to take accurate astonomical observations; but he will need, as fully as Livingstone needed, whatever special acquirements his object demands, and he will approach the ideal explorer in exact proportion to his previous cultivation of the necessary technical knowledge and powers of scientific observation, and to the character which he displays in the pursuit of his labours. Tact, persistence and moral courage are hardly less essential to genuine success in civilized lands than they are in barbarous regions, and it is indeed an open question whether African chiefs, in the days of their independence, were not, as a rule, less unsatisfactory to deal with than the governments of our own and neighbouring countries.

Upon the foundation of exploration, in its wider meaning, geography constructs its basement of cartography on which must rest the entire super-structure of the science, so that our next question concerns the ideals towards which cartographers should advance. Many years ago the late Elisée Reclus, (7) perhaps the greatest geographer of the generation now passing away, strongly advocated before the Royal Geographical Society a method which must, I fear, long remain only an ideal, namely the use of relief globes, or sections of globes, of such dimensions—say on the scale of 1 to 100,000—that even heights of 150 feet would be distinctly shown, without adopting the usual method in relief maps of exaggerating the proportional height of hills and mountains. On globes of such dimensions the geological and ecological features of the surface could also be displayed in considerable detail. After quoting the view urged many years ago by a scientist, whom he justly termed "one of our eminent geographers, Dr. H. R. Mill," (8) that "accurate cartographic representation is the very essence of geography," Elisée Reclus proceeded to point out that "there is only one way to represent truly the surface of the Earth. Curves are to be translated in curves . . . Therefore are we really astonished that public attention and the special care of geographers are so little attracted towards this logical mode of geographical work." He noted that globes of considerable dimensions—up to the scale of one millionth—had indeed been made for exhibition purposes, but that these had "made no pretence to accuracy in geography proper." He might have added that on so small a scale, such globes would have been useless for effective hypsometrical representation as regards regions where the elevation were generally less than 3,000 feet, so that while Scotland would display some of her beautiful hypsometrical features, England would show a somewhat plain face. It will not be denied that there is immense force in Elisée Reclus's proposals. Under the existing system of education boys are taught to think of the Earth's surface only in terms of plane trigonometry; and although this method is approximately accurate over small areas, it is absolutely misleading when the areas are large, the globes in ordinary use being so small as to make it difficult for a boy to co-ordinate them in thought with the flat maps presented to him of individual countries. Moreover, it is one of the important advantages of real geographical study, as it is of the study of astronomy, that the mind is trained to think in terms of both spherical and plane trigonometry; and this double standpoint gives the student that stereoscopic view of nature which is essential in every department of thought, if existence is to be appreciated as a solid reality instead of as a flat and unsubstantial picture. The more effective qualities of the average officer of the navy or the mercantile marine (as compared with the average landsman of equal general education) are everywhere recognized, and are, doubtless, due to several concurrent causes; but it does not seem to me far-fetched to attribute them in some part to his studies in navigation which necessitate his acquisition of the habit of viewing space from a double standpoint. In elucidation of my meaning I would recall a remark made to me many years ago by a great philologist that when a man for the first time studies another language than his own, he acquires ideas on language generally which would otherwise have always remained unknown, and even inconceivable to him. One of our leading statesmen invented the happy phrase "Learn to think imperially." (9) I would say to the young geographer, learn to think spherically.

Before leaving Elisée Reclus's proposals for exhibiting the Earth's surface on curves and in relief with the same scale for plan and elevations, I feel compelled to protest, of course with the greatest deference, against the unmitigated scorn and condemnation which he and some other eminent geographers have heaped upon the usual system of relief maps or globes which exaggerate the proportional height of hills. Until we reach Reclus's ideal of globes or sections of sufficient dimensions to depict the true hypsometrical proportions, and until such globes or sections can be so multiplied as to be within reach of every school throughout the civilized world, it is difficult to see how an average boy is to acquire, without the aid of the ordinary relief map, an initial grasp of the morphology of an extensive region. No doubt the use of the ordinary relief map must be accompanied by careful explanation of the difference of the vertical and horizontal scales; but it does not require much imagination in the student to make the necessary mental adjustments. Those of you who have, when bicycling or motoring, used a guide book giving profiles of the roads with a vertical scale several times as large as the horizontal scale, will, I feel sure, confirm this view. My protest arises from personal experience. It was not until, at the age of nineteen, I visited Switzerland and Germany, which, even at that date, possessed excellent relief maps, with of course exaggerated heights, that morphology became a reality to me; and there must be millions who, like myself, have not been gifted with an innate initial power of full realization from representation by projection, where perspective cannot be called in to assist. Once the sentiment of reality is fully established by the aid of relief representations of a region over which one moves, flat projections become for ever as communicative as they are to those more fortunate persons who are born cartographers.

For the present, Reclus's gigantic globes or sections of globes are not available and we must do the best that we can to improve our flat maps. The ideal flat map would include every datum with which the science of Geography in its most advanced state would deal. It would represent all the great physical features of the Earth's surface, land and water in all their various forms, mountains and hills, valleys, plains, plateaus and depressions, oceans, inland seas, lakes and rivers. It would show both the hypsometrical features of the lithosphere and the bathymetrical features of the hydrosphere. It would indicate in a general way the surface geology. It would mark the average rainfall and prevailing temperature. It would show the main economic or ecological characteristics of regions represented on a small scale, and would deal in detail, on a large scale, with regions calling for special attention; while in wholly undeveloped parts of the world, the characteristics of the surface would be exhibited, such as forest, prairie or other grass lands, desert and swamp. It would indicate the distribution of life in its various forms, showing the leading features of vegetable life, and the principal types of wild animals, where such existed. So far, however, the ideal map would exhibit only the frame-work in which humanity is set, the theatre on which man has to play his part. To make it complete, it must show the distribution of various types of mankind over the face of the Earth, the boundaries of states, the density of population, and to some extent the general results of man's interference with natural conditions, or what is generally regarded as political and economic geography. I do not pretend to have exhausted all that it should exhibit. I have only pointed out leading features that it should not omit; and I may sum up by saying that the ideal map of a region should contain in cartographical symbols all the information which would be necessary to a student who wished to write a complete geographical memoir of the region; for cartography is the basis of all sound geography. Such a map is at present only an ideal which should be striven after by all conscientious and competent cartographers, as far as is now practicable. The question of the best methods and symbols to be employed must be left for discussion by cartographical experts, who appear, however, to have widely differing views on the subject; but criticism is permissible to those who have not constructive or creative genius, and I may point out one method which is clearly unscientific. One has seen maps issued from time to time under the title of commercial maps, and professing to show the distribution of products and industries, in which the names of these seemed as if they had been distributed over the sheet by means of a pepper box. Horses, silk, cattle, iron, sheep, grass, pigs, wheat, wine, and scores of other names were scattered in a haphazard fashion, which not only failed to inform, but actually misled anyone unacquainted with the regions represented.

One of the most difficult tasks for the cartographer seems to be an adequate representation of the hypsometrical features of the Earth's surface. For certain purposes the contour map is very useful, especially if, as in the Swedish Official Survey map, each contour is shaded with a gradually intensified tint of brown from the sea-level upwards. A very effective method of contouring is that which Japan adopted some twenty years ago, and which is now used in the United States Geological and Geographical Survey. This consists of lines in a tint of brown so arranged that at a slight distance it produces the effect of excellent hill shading: while, on close inspection, one is able to read the contours. Perhaps, however, the best result is produced when really good hill shading is used in combination with contours, as is the case with the Swiss Survey maps. This method shows very clearly the lie of the land, while one can also read the contours from the lowest level to the highest. Another very good example of this method is the map of Tunis, on a scale of 1 to 50,000, which has been recently published by the French Intelligence Department. I feel that it might be invidious to mention by name any particular cartographical establishment in these islands, or even on the continent of Europe, but I have little doubt that most of you have already made up your minds as to which, on the whole, are the most useful as well as the most artistic Atlases available in the United Kingdom. My chief fear is that the majority of the general public who have not yet been reached by the geographical training so rapidly spreading on improved lines all over the country, may form their estimate of atlases on their cheapness or on their quantity and not their quality, or on the number of names which are to be found in their indexes. Other things being equal and subject to there being no sacrifice of clearness, a large number of names is an advantage, but if they are divorced from their natural physical and economic setting they convey very little real information. I hope that the time has passed when it was thought that any production was good enough for a school map or a school atlas, and that we are alive to the obvious fact that the maps on which children are trained have no less importance than those which are for the use of adults. It may not perhaps be practicable to produce an atlas in which all the maps are on the same scale, but some confusion in juvenile minds might perhaps be avoided if the maps were all on a multiple or a measure of a standard scale. It will, I think, be generally agreed that there is room today for even a better atlas than any now existing, and we can only hope that with the spread of geographical education the necessary encouragement may be given to publishers to expend the large amounts which the production of a first class atlas would undoubtedly require.

To whatever point of excellence cartography may be brought,however, it can never be more than a means to an end, excepting to a small number of artistic minds to whom a really fine map is a thing of beauty and a joy for ever. The same principle applies to geographical knowledge generally, which may be its own reward to a few detached minds, but which will be estimated by most men at its practical value to mankind. A few words must therefore be said as to their most important uses in war and peace, and we may possibly find some ideals at which we should aim in these directions. I put war first as the primitive state of mankind and not yet entirely out of date. It is a moot question whether war is more useful to geography or geography to war. The proposition that war has been one of the greatest geographers has been so frequently expounded at length and is so obvious to the student of history that I need not dwell upon it in this brief address, only remarking that it is interesting to find the conviction of its truth existing even in the United States where, more than in any other great country, the development of geographical knowledge and peaceful expansion have gone hand in hand.

During the Spanish-American war a well-known scientific authority, Prof. Chamberlin of Chicago, (10) pointed out that the war might be expected to produce a great revival of interest in geography throughout the United States. He concluded: "It was observed at the close of the Civil War that those who returned from its campaigns possessed an appreciation of the elements of position and physical relationship quite beyond that realized by the preceding generation educated under the benign influences of peace." We now know that Prof. Chamberlin's forecast was correct, the Spanish-American War having given an undoubted acceleration to the progress of the geographical spirit in the United States similar to that which he tells us was observed after the Civil War.

The value of geography in war, on the other hand, may perhaps be best brought home to our own countrymen by recalling the enormous expenditure in which the want both of maps and of geographical training of our officers indirectly involved us during the Boer War. I can speak confidently on these points from having served (for nearly a year) on the Royal Commission on the South African War. (11) It is a matter of deep regret that, during the many years of peace and colonial expansion at the close of the last century, Great Britain did not expend a moderate sum annually in mapping the unsurveyed portions of the Empire. We should not then have found ourselves attempting to relieve Lady-smith or advancing to the Modder river without maps of the country. It is only fair to add that the lesson of the war, in this respect, has not been altogether forgotten. During the last four years a certain amount of money has been expended in imperial mapping of hitherto unsurveyed regions; and if this process

252

is not altogether arrested by a spirit of false economy, we may possibly at some distant date possess fairly adequate maps of all British possessions. That is at any rate an ideal which we should strive to attain. As regards the want of geographical training of our officers, I have not time to cite the mass of evidence given before our Commission by the most competent authorities as to the general deficiency in knowledge of ground, than which, as Lord Roberts (12) and others pointed out, nothing could be more important in war. Even as regards staff officers, who have considerably more training in this subject than the ordinary regimental officers, Lord Roberts was often struck with their inability to read maps well or to explain quickly and intelligently about the contours and elevations. In this respect our ideal should be to reach the level attained by Japanese and German officers.

Geographical ignorance is a costly luxury in times of war, but it is perhaps still more costly in times of peace. No estimate, even of the roughest kind, can be formed of the vast sums that have been wasted in modern days through States collectively, on the one hand, and individual settlers, on the other hand, attempting to produce grapes from thorns and figs from thistles.

This subject of the practical uses of ecology, or economic geography, is far too large to be treated here incidentally; it would require an address or rather a series of addresses to itself. A mass of literature on the subject already exists; but this will probably be read only by specialists, or by those who can give a good deal of their time to scientific geography. For others, the best short manual on the general question is still, to my mind, that entitled 'Applied Geography,' by Dr. Scott Keltie, who is recognized, both at home and abroad, as one of the most capable and best informed geographers of this or any other country. I understand that he is a Scotchman; and as I am speaking to a Scottish audience, I may briefly refer to the splendid ecological work that Scotland has done in the exploration, settling and development of those vast regions known as the Dominion of Canada, which have before them so assured and so great a future. The part that Scotland has played in that work up to 1882 is, I think, best told in Mr. Rattray's (13) 'The Scot in British North America,' which many of you will have read. I may say that it was lent to me by a very distinguished Scot, whom the rising generation probably know chiefly as the Lord Strathcona, (14) who raised and equipped Strathcona's horse during the Boer War, but whom older geographers remember as the Donald Smith who played so important a part in the development of the North-West regions. I need hardly remind you that from Canada comes another Scot—Sir John Murray (15) —who is, admittedly, the greatest oceanographer and limnologist that the world has produced; that the most successful settlement in South Africa was the Scottish settlement in Cape Colony; that Natal is a second Scotland; that the acquisition of British rights in East Africa, which promises to show important ecological results, was due to the efforts of the late Sir William Mackinnon, (16) and was largely the result of the explorations of Joseph Thomson; that the province known by the misleading name of British Central Africa was opened up to commerce by the Scottish African Lakes Company, and was made into a peaceful British possession by the first recipient of your Livingstone Medal, Sir Harry Johnston, (17) or that, a century ago, the marvellous travels of Mungo Park were the genesis of the entire movement which has opened up Africa to civilization. It must, I think, be admitted that Scotland was in the forefront of the great geographical and imperial movement of the nineteenth century. Nor has she neglected the more purely scientific sides of geography, as was evidenced by the recent successful national expedition to the Antarctic Regions; while her cartography, as represented by Keith Johnston (18) and Bartholomew, (19) has undoubtedly led the way in these islands. I trust that this vigorous and practical geographical spirit may long endure and, if possible, increase. Although the era of exploration, in the conventional sense, is drawing to a close, there is an unlimited field open for scientific exploration and economic treatment. Mankind has hitherto dealt with the surface of Mother Earth in a haphazard, a hand to mouth fashion, without much scientific study of the varying ecological conditions in different localities, due to the various combinations of slightly differing climates, soils and other geographical data. Is it an unattainable ideal that scientific changes in the distribution and methods of production may some day raise humanity, so far as material comfort is concerned, as much above its existing standard as this is above the material condition of the ill-clothed, ill-sheltered, ill-fed denizens of these islands at the commencement of our present era?

Whatever may be the proper aims of geography as a science of the utmost value, both in war and in peace, sound and extensive geographical education is an essential condition of advance towards those aims, and the question at once confronts us as to what should be our educational ideals. You will remember that, after the Household Suffrage Act, Robert Lowe (20) gave the celebrated advice, often attributed to Lord Beaconsfield, (21) "Let us educate our masters." By our masters Mr. Lowe meant of course the masses, and the nation have *(sic)* had the question of the education of the masses with them for a whole generation; while—at any rate south of the Tweed—they seem likely to have it with them for some generations to come; but I venture to repeat here, what I have often urged elsewhere, that on many subjects, of which geography is one, we need in the first place to educate the classes. This may not be an unattainable ideal, though it is still distant.

In an address which I delivered at York last August before the British Association I pointed out the advance during the last quarter of a century in the interest in and appreciation of geography displayed by the governing classes. A case of atavism, recently brought to my notice, makes me fear that I was too sanguine as to the permanence of that advance, at any rate in one important quarter.

In November 1899, regulations were laid down for the examinations for the Foreign Office and Diplomatic Service, which naturally (and I believe merely in repetition of earlier regulations) made geography an obligatory subject. A notice has lately been issued, to come into effect after July 1 next, under which geography will not only not be obligatory, but will altogether cease to be one of the subjects of examination. I have not time to give you a list of the many other subjects for which marks will be given to candidates, and which do not seem to be as important as geography to a Foreign Office clerk or to a Secretary of an Embassy. I will only select six rather striking examples: Animal Physiology, Physics, Chemistry, Moral and Metaphysical Philosophy, Sanskrit Language and Literature, and Zoology, which, of course, may be useful if the official spends his leave in a country where big game is plentiful. In these six subjects the candidate might make 3600 marks out of the maximum of 6,000, which he is not allowed to exceed; while not a single mark is given for Geography. One is reminded of Mr. W. S. Gilbert's (22) "Pattern of a modern Major General," in 'The Pirates of Penzance,' who was an adept in every branch of human knowledge, excepting tactics and strategy.

The urgency of the case impels me to narrate an interesting incident not yet published, especially as the principal actors in the scene are dead, so that no one's feelings will be hurt by the narration. A good many years ago a territorial arrangement with France was in discussion, and I was invited to consider it. The French proposals appeared to the Foreign Office satisfactory; but I found that they were expressed, as might have been expected, in longitudes reckoned from the meridian of Paris, while the map with which our Foreign Office had considered these proposals was made in Germany and reckoned its longitudes from the meridian of Greenwich. The arrangement in question was never completed.(23)

This was an instance which came under my personal observation, but it is a matter of notoriety that some of our most serious international disputes of recent years have arisen from the faulty geographical knowledge of the negotiators of treaties in the darker ages. I believe that our Foreign Office and Diplomatic Service for years past have been filled with men of considerable geographical knowledge; but this improved condition will not last if geography is to be eliminated from their examinations, and Great Britain will see its future diplomatists contending with bows and arrows against foreign diplomatists armed with the best weapons of the twentieth century. The most serious feature of the case, however, is that such an official denial of the national importance of geographical education is today possible. It shows the immense obstacles that still confront our Geographical Societies before they can make great and lasting advance in what seems to me one of their most urgent duties, that of educating the classes of Britain.

Turning from this fundamental postulate to the general principles underlying a sound geographical education, I should like to put before you the substance of a most interesting letter on the subject which I have recently received from Mr. H. J. Mackinder,(24) Director of the London School of Economics, and whom you know to be one of the highest authorities in Britain on Geographical Education. I have only time to read extracts; so that you will not hold the writer too closely to passages given without their context. He says, "Geography must not be thought of as a mass of information merely, or indeed chiefly. Its distinguishing characteristic, giving it peculiar value as a discipline, is that it has its own special point of view and mode of thought and of memory. The geographer thinks in spaces and shapes. So far from names being material to the subject, even words are not essential to geographical thought. . . . In the elementary stage the teaching of geography should not adhere pedantically to any method. The main point is that a few things should be vividly and rationally taught. Such precision as is involved in the use of latitudes and longitudes should be eschewed, unless in the highest standards. No doubt nature-study should come first, but it must not be substituted for geography, for which it only prepares . . . In secondary education the teaching of geography should, I think, be more methodical and precise, but what is chiefly important is that it should be progressive in method. Geography may well serve in this stage for the purpose of correlating subjects, both scientific and historical, but the more that such a function is assigned to it the more necessary does it become to have a clearly defined and strictly geographical argument running through the whole of the teaching. In other words, the geographical point of view must be dominant, and not the view points of this or that auxiliary science. . . . In the University stage, geography should be studied both from a specialist and from a general standpoint; that is to say, that while it is a condition of progress in our knowledge that we forsake the whole field and concentrate on some part of it, yet it is only in the university stage that what I may describe as the philosophy of the subject can be fully appreciated. It is essential, however, that the specialist should already have firmly acquired the geographical method and the geographical point of view. Until secondary education in geography is more generally thorough, I fear that the University teacher of the subject will have to teach much which in a future generation will have been learned by his pupils before they come to him. To my mind, by far the most important function of the University teacher of geography in the present and immediate future must be to produce a considerable number of good secondary teachers of the subject, and to establish a tradition of geographical school teaching. The danger of the moment is that in view of the sudden demand for school teachers of geography which has recently sprung up, we shall be tempted to equip and employ persons of inferior general education and mental power. Geography requires in the teacher both a firm grasp of principle and a broad out-look. With these qualities, I believe that it can be made a discipline of the highest order, but no subject is so easily reduced by an inferior teacher to a low pedagogic value, worthy of all the contempt that has been poured upon it.''

Although Mr. Mackinder's remarks in this letter proceed from elementary teaching upward to the university, we know that he is in full accord with the policy followed by the Royal Geographical Society during the last twenty years, of regarding recognition of geography at our great universities as the first and most important step in impregnating the country with a geographical spirit, and of working downward from there into the masses of the nation. As I dwelt on this question at length in my York address, I will only add that it now seems certain that the Welsh University will shortly have a Reader in Geography, and that I cannot doubt that Scotland will succeed in her present efforts to endow a Chair of Geography at the University of Edinburgh, which has, I understand, done all in its power to facilitate such a measure. It would, indeed, be extraordinary if this country, which, as I have just shown, has been in the forefront of the great geographical movement of the last century, should allow herself to be permanently distanced *(sic)* in this one direction—admittedly of the highest importance—not only by Oxford, Cambridge and London, but also by Manchester, Birmingham and gallant little Wales.

Amongst the minor methods of arousing interest and imparting information in geographical matters, perhaps the most effective is the comparitively modern use of photographic lantern slides. For either purpose the value of accurate and artistic visual representation accompanying aural explanations can hardly be over-estimated, whether the spectators and audience are trained geographers or elementary school children. Even so lately as thirty years ago geographical lectures were generally dreary affairs— except for the enthusiastic few—unrelieved, as they were, by pictorial representations. I feel very keenly the disadvantage I am under, or rather that you are under to-night, through my having no slides; but there was no remedy; for although photographs have, I am told, been taken of ghosts, no one has yet attempted to photograph an ideal. When we consider the instruction of children the necessity becomes still more evident of interesting the eye as well as the ear; and I hope that this principle will be more and more understood in our schools, in many of which the study of geography still consists of learning strings of names. The method of visual representation has, indeed, spread greatly during the last decade; but it does not yet cover a tenth of the field that it might usefully occupy. I believe this is partly due to the cost and difficulty of getting good slides, and I may be doing a service to some who wish to interest and instruct their fellow-parishioners in the country by drawing their attention to the series of the Diagram Company, whose address is West Barnes Lane, New Malden, Surrey. I could not, of course, mention this Company if they had been formed for purposes of profit. I am told, however, that their objects were scientific, and that they do not at present cover their expenses. Many of you, doubtless, know their excellent slides. We have a complete series in Saville Row, and I understood that one was kept at the Outlook Tower in this city; but Prof. Geddes [25] tells me that this is not now the case.

Another minor educational ideal is that all books involving movement from one geographical locality to another should have sketch maps attached to them.

This principle applies especially to works of fiction, which reach a far wider public than is the case with serious books. When we re-read the Waverley Novels(26) after reaching maturity, and with a knowledge of the positions and surroundings of the localities dealt with, we cannot avoid regret that our childish interest in each of them was not quickened and our knowledge insensibly increased by a simple sketch map on the frontispiece. This stimulating power of pictorial representation is perhaps most clearly demonstrated by a case in which the map was as imaginary as the text. How much of the interest of Treasure Island would have been lost but for the immortal map with which Robert Louis Stevenson(27) enriched it! Stevenson, indeed, was deeply imbued with the geographical spirit, and in several books—I can particularly recall 'Kidnapped'—produced real maps which greatly assist the young reader. Half a century ago, even history—ancient, mediaeval and modern—was read in the best schools without any reference to maps, with the result that most of us had to endure the loss of time in re-reading, when grown up, a mass of works which we had literally, but not geographically, mastered in our youth.

I have reserved to the last the few words I need say on the most vital and far-reaching of all instruments of geographical education—I mean societies such as this. They have afforded means of higher and ever-extending knowledge even to the most instructed of their Fellows; they have encouraged the geographical spirit amongst their less zealous members; they have been the chief authors or supporters of all other modern means of improvement in geographical education; while the role that lies before them is even more important than that which they have hitherto filled. That is why I am here tonight; and if I might add one more ideal to my list of geographical ideals, it is that every educated man in Scotland should join your Society, and, by his contributions to your funds, enable you to extend and intensify your work in promoting a branch of knowledge which is one of the most important, if not the most important, of the material sciences to the future welfare and progress of mankind.

(1) The Livingstone Medal is awarded for "Outstanding Public Service in which Geography has played an important part, either by exploration, by administration, or in other directions where its principles have been applied to the benefit of the human race."

(2) The whole of the philosophy expressed in this sentiment is highly reminiscent of the concept of the *Space-ship Earth* of Barbara Ward (Lady Jackson) as enunciated during the George B. Pegram Lectures at Columbia University, 1965, and published under that title by Columbia University Press, 1966.

(3) Livingstone, David, 1813-73. Livingstone worked as a "piecer" in a cotton mill from the age of ten and financed an education in the process.

(4) In 1857 Livingstone quietly disassociated himself from the work of the London Missionary Society. In 1858 he was appointed H.M. Consul at Quilimane.

(5) Professor (Sir) Richard Owen, 1804-1892, a distinguished comparative anatomist, zoologist and paleontologist, author of many definitive works in that field.

(6) Maclear, Sir Thomas, 1794-1879. Astronomer at the Royal Observatory, Cape of Good Hope.

(7) Elisée Reclus, 1830-1905. French geographer who because of his Republican ideas was obliged to leave France in 1851 and travelled widely in Europe and America before his return in 1857. He collaborated with his brother in many geographical texts.

(8) H. R. Mill, a Vice-President of the R.G.S., 1861-1950. Geographer and meteorologist, who for many years was in charge of R.G.S. publications. He wrote Goldie's own obituary nótice for the *Geographical Journal* in 1925, and was the author of the *Record of the Royal Geographical Society, 1830-1930,* its centenary project, published in 1930.

(9) Joseph Chamberlain, the Colonial Secretary, in a speech at the Guildhall, London, 19 January, 1904. Goldie's views on language training have an extraordinary pertinence for the debate currently raging in American educational circles.

(10) Chamberlin, Thomas Chrowder, 1843-1928. American geologist, who after a most distinguished career as an academic administrator, in 1892 relinquished the post of President of Wisconsin University to become Head of the Department of Geology at Chicago University, where he remained until 1919. He is the author of the planetesimal hypothesis of the origin of the solar system. In the light of geography's place in *modern* Higher Education in America, Chamberlin's remarks (and Goldie's hopes) have proven too sanguine.

(11) See page 204 ff.

(12) Lord Roberts of Kandahar, 1832-1914.

(13) Rattray, William Jordan, 1835-1883. Published by Maclean & Co., Toronto.

(14) Donald Alexander Smith. Lord Strathcona and Mount Royal, 1820-1914. See pages 204 ff.

(15) Sir John Murray, a Canadian, 1841-1914. Marine naturalist and oceanographer, who was Naturalist in charge of Collections during the *Challenger* expedition, 1872-76. See page 241.

(16) Sir William Mackinnon, 1823-93. Patron and friend of Stanley, he was, in a sense, the Goldie of East Africa—though not so successful!

(17) See page 235.

(18) See page 234.

(19) Bartholomew, John George, cartographer, 1860-1920.

(20) Lowe, Robert, 1st Viscount Sherbrooke, 1811-1892. M.P. for Calne, 1859-67 (and for other constituencies at other times). Noted for his speeches during the Reform Debates.

(21) Benjamin Disraeli, 1st Earl of Beaconsfield, 1804-1881.

(22) Gilbert, Sir William Schwenk, 1836-1911. *The Pirates of Penzance* was first produced, for the general public, in New York in 1879. The model for the "modern Major-General" was General Sir Garnet Wolesley, later Field Marshal Lord Wolesley, Goldie's friend and colleague on the Board of the Hausa Association. He was also the commander in the first Ashanti campaign, and in the attempt to relieve Gordon in Khartoum. An "intellectual soldier" in days when these were rare (he was born in 1833 and died in 1913), Wolesley wrote the *Field Service Pocketbook,* still issued virtually unchanged to all officers as late as 1938, and designed the "Wolesley Pith Helmet and Spinepad" for use in the tropics. These were issued (and promptly discarded by the troops!) throughout the Second World War. "All Sir Garnett"—British Army slang for "in perfect order etc."

(23) This probably refers to French attempts to have the Say-Barrua line of 1891 revised shortly after it was agreed. See also page 80, of which this passage is an almost verbatim quote!

(24) 1861-1947. Sir Halford John Mackinder was the first Reader in Geography at Oxford under the R.G.S. assisted programme, 1887-1905. He liked to say that Richard Hakluyt (1574-1655) was Oxford's first "Reader in Geography" and that he was the second! See also pages 279 and 283.

(25) Professor Sir Patrick Geddes, 1854-1932. Established "the world's first sociological laboratory" in Outlook Tower, Castlehill, Edinburgh, in 1892.

(26) By Sir Walter Scott, 1771-1832. Published between 1814 and 1832.

(27) But Goldie does not relate that Stevenson (1850-94) records that the publishers lost the first map of *Treasure Island* which he produced and that the makeshift that he provided in its place never satisfied him to the same degree.

V. GEOGRAPHY AND THE CIVIL SERVICE (1907)

This address, which was presented at the Anniversary Meeting of the Royal Geographical Society on 27 May, 1907, is reprinted from the Geographical Journal, Volume XXX, No. 1 of July, 1907.

It is an interesting and lucid exposition of Goldie's determination to mobilise public opinion in support of one of his pet projects, namely the elevation of geography to its proper position as a true science worthy of intensive study in British schools and universities. It has already been noted that H. R. Mill, in the *Record* of the Society which was published in its centenary year, credited Goldie with an almost single handed victory in this respect. [1]

This apart, the address is also of interest in that Goldie makes, during the course of it, a fleeting reference to his own all too little known boyhood and schooldays.

I shall not follow to-day the frequent practice at these annual meetings of summarizing the geographical history of the preceding twelve months, as I desire to concentrate your attention on one question of unusual importance, which has suddenly come into prominent notice since our last meeting. For the same reason, I shall be as brief as is consistent with an intelligible exposition of the case; for the urgency of a satisfactory solution of the question with which I propose to deal calls for public attention, and this would be distracted rather than aroused by burying the matter under a cloud of words or by allowing it to overflow into side issues.

The question is whether Geography shall be accorded a place alongside of other sciences amongst the subjects eligible by candidates for the examinations which admit to the Civil Services of this country and its dependencies. As some of you may not have noticed, or may have forgotten, how this question first came to the front, I will briefly re-capitulate the main facts. For a good many years, the Foreign Office has stood in an exceptional position amongst the Civil Services of the Crown by including Geography amongst the subjects for the entrance examinations of candidates. The Foreign Office, indeed, went further by making a pass in this subject compulsory. I may say, in passing, that it is reasonable to attribute partly to this attitude of the Foreign Office the noticeable fact that, of late years, so many valuable additions to our geographical knowledge have been due to members of the diplomatic and (especially) the consular services; for Geography, with its unceasing contact with an immense range of allied sciences, has an ever-growing attraction for those who have once venturerd to penetrate into its sphere. It was a reasonable matter of hope that, with the advance of education and the widening of public opinion, the enlightened example of the Foreign Office would be gradually followed by some of our other public departments. The most important of these is the Colonial Office, which administers or controls vast regions contiguous to the possessions of foreign powers, which has to initiate or supervise frequent treaties with these powers of immense future importance, and which habitually supports or rejects proposals by its local administrators for the development of their colonies or dependencies, without necessarily possessing any knowledge whatever of the economic conditions of the regions with which it is dealing. In the Indian Civil Service, the Board of Trade, and the Post Office, some elementary knowledge of geography amongst even their subordinate members would surely be of value. I am inclined to add to this list our Education Department itself, from which—not so very long ago—was despatched that often-quoted letter addressed to "Ottawa, Ontario, United States of America."

It may safely be asserted that in no country but our own would the policy have been followed of securing uniformity in the system of examinations for all the Public Services, not by levelling up to the standard of the Foreign Office, but by the opposite process of levelling down. That, however, has been our characteristically British method. After next month, Geography will cease to be a subject which candidates for the Foreign Office may even voluntarily select. It was inevitable that this remarkable decision should arouse a great deal of public attention, mainly, of course, on the ground of the maintenance of our national and imperial interests which come into touch with those of foreign nations in so many parts of the world.

This is, no doubt, a consideration worthy of much attention, but I am concerned to make it clear that the question is one of far wider importance than as merely affecting the efficiency of certain of our public services. That this fact has been so little recognized is, I think, due to a natural and even commendable repugnance on the part of cultured minds to admit that our educational systems, based nominally and to a large extent really on intrinsically sound educational principles—such as developing the thinking powers of the student, strengthening his judgment, quickening his perceptive faculties, and cultivating his memory—have also necessarily rested largely on what, for want of a better phrase, I must describe as financial considerations. These fall into two divisions. The first of them affects directly only the universities, but it affects indirectly the educational systems of all the non-State-aided schools in this country, as these for various reasons base their systems entirely on those adopted by the universities. It is a serious misfortune that but few of the latter have been in a position to set apart sufficient funds for the endowment of a Chair in Geography or a School of Geography. Yet I do not know a single instance of a university in the United Kingdom which is indifferent on this question of geographical education. So far as I can gather—and I have taken considerable trouble to ascertain the general trend of feeling—nothing but the want of money prevents any of the universities from following the examples of Oxford, Cambridge and London. But in most cases the too scanty funds are already appropriated to older established branches of study which no thinking man would wish to see starved. Unfortunately, the Royal Geographical Society has no extensive resources of its own with which to come to the assistance in this matter of the universities generally. It has for years shared in the maintenance of the Schools of Geography of Oxford and Cambridge; but it would not be justified in advancing much further in this direction, in view of the heavy and urgent calls made upon its resources in entirely different directions. If, however, amongst its Fellows, or its sympathizers, there are any who are able and disposed to aid the advance of human knowledge by endowment, I do not think that they could better serve their purpose than by contributing to the founding of a Chair of Geography at any one of the universities as yet unprovided with a Geography School. (2)

The other division of financial considerations to which I alluded just now is of a less simple nature, but it is not less effective in blocking the progress of geographical education and the introduction of this subject into the list of those eligible by candidates for the public services. To avoid misapprehension on this point, let me premise that I am not dealing at present with the educational systems of our State—or rate-aided schools which are not dependent on the favour of parents nor subject to competition with other schools. It will suffice to confine our attention for the moment to private schools, public schools, and, to some extent, universities, that is to say, to institutions where the sons of the leisured classes, or the well-to-do classes, are brought up, and from which strata our educational ideas and systems have invariably filtered down to the less-favoured classes which are waging a daily struggle for bare existence. With rare exceptions, every educational institution, not supported by public funds, has to some degree—though a varying degree—to strike a tacit bargain with the parents of its students; the parents paying the money on which the prosperity or, most frequently, the existence of the institution depends; and requiring in return, in the vast majority of cases, that their boys shall receive such instruction as shall best enable them to compete on equal terms with their fellow-students. The proprietors of private schools, the governing bodies of public schools, and even, though to a lesser extent, the universities themselves, cannot therefore afford to give the same prominence to a subject which carries no marks in the civil and military examinations that they give to subjects which carry such marks. On the other hand, the Civil Service Commissioners naturally hesitate to demand proficiency in a subject which holds only a secondary position, or sometimes no position at all, in the educational institutions of the country; and the question thus moves in a vicious circle.

I do not, of course, imagine that all the sons of the well-to-do classes of this country compete in examinations controlled by the Civil Service Commissioners; but the proportion of them so competing is sufficiently large to affect very seriously the standing in the whole educational sphere of any subject, according as it is or is not a means of gaining marks in the civil and military examinations; and it may, I think, be confidently asserted that if geography received the recognition which we desire, it would very shortly take its place in Great Britain, as it has long since done in the United States, Germany, and other countries, as one of the fundamental and indispensable elements in the education of childhood and youth. That this has not been the case up to now is probably due to the unintelligent and unmethodical manner in which the subject was taught until some twenty years ago, with the result that the majority of those who are to-day in a position to speak with authority, retain an entirely false impression of its scope and objects. Certainly, during my own school life, the hour in the week devoted to geography was universally anticipated with strong aversion as a dreary exercise of the memory in acquiring names entirely divorced from the realities of life, so that one of the most human and interesting of all branches of knowledge, intimately connected as it is with the history of mankind, with our present occupations and with our future development, was presented to us as an arid and flowerless waste. The new methods and conceptions of geography have been so frequently and fully placed before you by the most competent experts in our

261

science that I must not attempt to summarize them in this brief address. I would recommend those who are not yet informed on this point to procure and study the questions in the examination papers of the University of Oxford. They will gather from them an idea of the true scope and value of the science, and they will probably find opening out before them new and unexpected lines of thought which will add materially to the interests of their own lives. It is, indeed, to the University of Oxford, supported, as I cannot doubt that it will be, by the Universities of Cambridge, London, Edinburgh, and other great centres of education, that geographers must look for a satisfactory solution of this important question; for, so far as can be gathered in the columns of the *Times*(3) some months ago, the Civil Service Commissioners are willing to consider the admission of geography as one of the voluntary subjects for examinations, provided the great universities will give a lead. In taking such a step, both the universities and the commissioners will have behind them an immense pressure of public opinion, owing to the sudden awakening both of interest in the empire as a whole, and of recognition of our widespread ignorance of its geographical conditions. The mass of cheap and, on the whole, useful literature that has recently been published on this subject, (4) the new leagues that have been formed with the object of disseminating widely every kind of information on the features and potentialities of the various provinces of the empire, the important public meetings that have recently been held for the same purpose, and even such indications as the issue and ready sale of several new atlases containing far more detailed ecological and other information than had previously been shown—all combine to support the conviction that the educated classes of this country are awakening to the necessity of more thorough acquaintance with the various branches of our science. It is not to be denied that this new public feeling is to-day directed mainly towards knowledge of the empire. Only those who have travelled widely can fully realize the disadvantage under which British enterprise of every kind now lies, as compared with German and American enterprise, in maintaining and increasing its hold in foreign lands; but we may rest assured that if geographical interest and modes of thought are developed and established amongst us in regard to our widely scattered empire, we shall not fail to extend that interest and these modes of thought to the rest of the globe.

It may be thought by some of you that I have dealt with this subject on a too material or, at any rate, a too narrow basis; that I have dwelt exclusively on the disadvantages to our country of not emerging, as other nations have done, from geographical twilight into the brightness of knowledge; that I have said nothing of the highest of all pleasures, the love of science for its own sake. My justification is that the problem of the moment is how to diffuse over an entire nation an interest in geography, no matter on what grounds; that with every increase in the number of geographical students there will be found an increasing number of truly scientific geographers. The love of one's country and the desire for material prosperity are powerful human motives that no practical philosopher can afford to despise; while the rivalry between nations in extending the bounds of knowledge deserves his warmest commendation. Great Britain has exceptional duties to humanity in this direction. With her unrivalled history of exploration, with her predominance on the ocean, both as regards her navy and her mercantile marine, with her immense and widely scattered colonies and dependencies, with her great wealth and free institutions, she is the trustee of many talents, which she must not bury in the ground; and instead of lagging behind as she has, for many years, been content to do, in bringing up her children with some knowledge of the world they live on, it is her duty, as it will be her interest, to take her rightful place in the van of geographical science.

(1) See page 21. For Goldie's letters to the *Times* on this same subject, see also page 184 ff.

(2) As "that liberal citizen [of Sheffield], Mr. Allen" was to do in respect to the University of Sheffield, almost immediately afterwards. See page 283.

(3) See page 184 for Goldie's letter, from whence ensuing correspondence can be followed up if desired.

(4) For Goldie's views on "Travel Fiction", see pages 202-204.

Company employees on the Lower Niger. *Courtesy U.A.C. International.*

A village street scene. *Courtesy U.A.C. International.*

VI

Addresses to Learned and Philanthropic Societies

At Kabba: Sir George Goldie proclaiming the freedom of Southern Nupé from Foulah oppression, January, 1897. *From The Illustrated London News, courtesy Professor A. H. M. Kirk-Greene, Oxford.*

"The Guns" at Jebba. *Courtesy U.A.C. International.* This photograph has been ascribed to the West African Frontier Force detachment, but if, as seems possible, the fifth figure from the left on the back row is Goldie (whom it remarkably resembles) the picture must be of the Royal Niger Constabulary Gun Detachment and must date from about February, 1897.

I. NATIVE RACES AND THE LIQUOR TRADE (1901)

This is not a very profound address. It was delivered at the Annual meeting of the Native Races and the Liquor Traffic United Committee at Grosvenor House, London, on May 22, 1901. Goldie is by now the chairman of the meeting—a far cry from his previously expressed reservations. The address also has a certain interest of its own, because of his firm refusal to talk about West Africa and because of the reference which it contains to Lugard, with whom Goldie's relationship still appears quite cordial. Lugard spoke immediately following the opening remarks by Goldie, the Chairman, who said:—

The main business of this Annual Meeting is to consider, discuss and adopt the report, of which a summary has just been read to you; and as we have a number of speakers and time is short, I propose very briefly to touch on two or three points in that report, and then to conclude my few remarks with some observations on the general work and procedure of this Society. Now, the first thing that every Society requires is a head, so that it is very natural that the report should commence with an expression of great satisfaction at His Grace the Duke of Westminister having consented to fill the position which was filled from the very foundation of the Society by his lamented grandfather. It is now four or five years since I had the honour of speaking [1] at a meeting of this Society from this platform, and my mind is carried back to the figure which then occupied this chair and which was that of a public-spirited, high-minded and noble man. I saw this morning in a newspaper, with reference to a memorial that has just been erected to the Duke of Westminster, that the tablet bears this inscription—"To the friend and benefactor of his poorer brethren." No more noble inscription could be placed on anyone's monument. I think that we who are addressing ourselves to the interests of the native races of the Empire must be fully aware that the sympathy which he showed to the poorer and needier brethren in this country was also extended to those poorer and needier races of the Empire who demand our sympathies whether as statesmen or philanthropists. Now, passing to the practical working part of the report, I think, we must all note with satisfaction that it puts in the foremost place the question of liquor legislation in those two new Colonies of South Africa which have attracted so much attention of late. On this subject there are quite a number of experienced gentlemen present to address you— Sir Godfrey Lagden, [2] Mr. Rose Innes, [3] The Hon. A. Wilmot, [4] Mr. Lionel Phillips, [5] and others— so that I do not propose to say a single word on the subject. But, I must just remark, as Sir Godfrey Lagden is about to address you, that it has always seemed to me that the remarkable work performed by him in the administration of Basutoland during a period of great crisis, did not receive at first as much recognition as it should have received. No doubt, it was because at that time the nation was entirely absorbed in the military operations that were being carried on in that part of the country. But during the past twelve months the public have awakened to the fact that he rendered splendid service. He displayed good sound judgment and knowledge in the management of those races. I allude to this, not by way of compliment to Sir Godfrey Lagden, but simply because I think it is a guarantee that we may rely implicitly on all that he may have to tell us this afternoon.

The report then passes on to the question of West Africa, and it is possible, that those of you who happen to be aware of my earlier connection with that region, may expect that I should say something upon this special subject. But I do not intend to, and for two reasons. The first is a personal one—that I have made it a rule since the transfer of Nigeria to His Majesty's Government fifteen months ago not to discuss, publicly or privately, the question of West Africa. (6) The second reason, is because we have here today, ready to speak on this subject, Sir Frederick Lugard, the High Commissioner of Northern Nigeria, which occupies as you know more than five-sixths of the entire province of Nigeria, and contains also the vast bulk of its teeming population. It would be an impertinence on my part to try and lay before you Sir Frederick Lugard's claim to speak to you with authority, either on that or any other part of Africa. He is far too well known to us all as an explorer and traveller to need any assurance from me, that whatever he says will be valued as the opinion of a man of wide experience and sound judgment. (7)

I will pass now to a point upon which I wish to congratulate your Committee—I refer to their efforts to promote international legislation in this matter. I allude chiefly to what they have done in France and in the United States. As you probably know, your indefatigable Honorary Secretary, Dr. Harford-Battersby, (8) visited the United States and did most useful work there. Some of you may remember, that when I addressed you four or five years ago, I urged upon you the importance of rousing public opinion in France on the subject. It was partly on political grounds, because France had possessions in all parts of the world, interlaced with British possessions, which raised enormous difficulties in dealing with the liquor legislation. As regards the United States, I have no doubt that public opinion there will more and more support the views of this Committee. Our brethren on that side of the water are extremely wide-awake in matters of business, and I do not see how any man of business can doubt the conviction which forced itself upon me twenty years ago—and which I have never forsaken since—that unrestricted traffic in intoxicating liquors amongst the races of mankind is a serious prejudice, and in some cases an absolute barrier to Imperial progress. I feel that that view will impress itself more and more upon the people of the United States, and therefore you are certain of strong support from that side.

I will now leave the report and hastily sum up some of the reasons why I think this Society is worthy of strong support, and why it should receive generous support, not only from yourselves, but from such of your friends outside as you can induce to hear you on the subject. This Society is a very exceptional Society. I have watched its proceedings with great interest ever since its foundation and I have noted a number of good points in it which other Societies do not possess. I am not alluding to its objects alone, because good intentions, when ill-directed, are often very much worse than apathy itself. This Society has no political or denominational bias, and that is really an enormous advantage. It is that rock which many societies have not been able to avoid. All sorts and conditions of men and women are invited to take part in its proceedings, and share in the work done. Secondly, while steadfastly aiming at its main object—the diminution of the liquor traffic amongst the native races—it has not been bound by any rigid and narrow theories—what are very fitly described as "fads." I cannot say how much I value, and I think most of you will value this freedom. The result is that the Society has been able to assimilate the work of numbers of men who differ very much in the reasons for which they have taken up the work—as to why it should be diminished or abolished altogether. And on the procedure to be adopted there are all sorts of opinions. You may say, *tot homines tot sententiae.* (9) Now this Society has enabled all such men to work together simply from the fact that it has been liberal and catholic in its methods. Then there is a third point and one with which I am very much concerned, as I am sure you will be also. Since its foundation, this Society has taken enormous trouble in sifting evidence, and making certain that any statements put forward can be supported; and at the same time it has carefully avoided all extravagance of language. Some of us who have known philanthropic societies throughout the world, know that some of them have failed in that respect. It is a great weakness, not only to the societies themselves, but because it diminishes the influence they might otherwise exercise, and thus there is a gap in the work of the world which they alone, as the only organised bodies, can properly fill. I think, you are to be congratulated on the fact that you have never been, so to speak, "caught out" in any false statement, and that you have never been convicted of exaggerated language. There are two minor points also which I should like to mention. One is the extreme unostentation with which this Society does its work. It does not agitate violently and attack individuals, or governments, or ministers; it works quietly by means of circulars, interviews and deputations. It does its work in an unostentatious manner, and work of that character, I believe, is the best work in the world. (10) In dealing with foreign countries and self-governing colonies, it is very important not to attempt to exercise pressure from without. This Society does not try to get the British Government to put pressure upon foreign or colonial governments; it prefers to go to those governments direct, and to work from within. In the course of this report, and in previous reports, I have noticed it said again and again, that the great statesmen of to-day in this country, are all in favour of the objects of this Society. Lord Salisbury has expressed his sympathies again and again, and as for Mr. Chamberlain, he has done perhaps more than any statesman of our generation. And I can quite imagine that those who do not wish to give, or to listen to those who urge them to give, may say. "What is the use of the Society now? Its objects are practically achieved. You have converted the statesmen, and what is more to be done?" To imagine that that is the only aim of this Society is an entire delusion. Governments are like individuals. They are harassed by all sorts of pressure from various directions. Demands are made upon them to rectify this abuse or that abuse, and it is useless to expect governments to consider and work upon the lines you want them to work upon unless you are always at hand to give them that gentle urging and pressure which you do. Governments not only need to be reminded of what ought to be done, but they need the pressure of public opinion behind them to enable them to do it. No Government can act unless it is assured that it has behind it a large body of public opinion. In conclusion, let me say that I have watched your career since the formation of the Society, and I know the influence you have exerted, and its great value, and I strongly urge you to continue your work in the same spirit which has animated you in the past.

(1) Actually in May, 1895. See page 86.

(2) Lagden, Sir Godfrey Yeatman, 1851-1934. Chairman, South African Native Affairs Commission, 1903-1905.

(3) Rose-Innes, Sir James, 1855-1942. Chief Justice, Transvaal, 1902-10; S.A. Supreme Court, 1910-14; Chief Justice, 1914-27. A zealous champion of native rights.

(4) Wilmot, Hon. Alexander, 1836-1923. 1854 entered the Cape Colony Civil Service. Retired as Civil Commissioner 1886. President, Temperance Alliance; author of *Monomatopa—its Monuments and History,* Unwin, 1896 and other historical works of note.

(5) Phillips, Sir Lionel (Bart), 1855-1936. Mining magnate and friend of Cecil Rhodes. Sentenced to death for his part in the Jameson Raid, but sentence was commuted to a fine of £25,000.

(6) This is an extremely interesting remark, since it reveals how totally Goldie perceived himself to have severed any connection with his former sphere of action. He did, however depart from it once, in 1912 and it is doubtful if it ever fully operated in the way that Goldie perceived it to do so.

(7) Could Goldie have had his tongue in his cheek when making this somewhat fulsome allusion? He did so again in 1912. See page 294.

(8) Charles Forbes Harford-Battersby (d. 1925). Formerly a Medical Missionary of the C.M.S. along with Wilmot-Brooke at Lokoja in 1890-1892. In 1893, with others, founded the Livingstone College. Hon. Sec. 1896-1904.

(9) A slight mis-quotation from Terence, who bids fair to being Goldie's favourite Latin poet. The full quotation, which appears at line 454 of *Phormio,* is "Quot homines tot sententiae: suos quoique mos" There are as many opinions as men: each has his own character. For Goldie's views on Terence, see page 287.

(10) Goldie has clearly abandoned any of the reservations which he previously may have had about the work of this Society. His praise of it gives an interesting insight into the vehemence with which he unceasingly pursued his own personal creed as examplified by the motto he had adopted.

II. SIR CLEMENTS MARKHAM (1901)

In this after dinner speech, at a banquet held on 22 May, 1905, in honour of the retiring President of the Royal Geographical Society, Goldie is at his scintillating best, witty, humorous, light-hearted, but none the less, with an occasional flash of fire.

The occasion was an important one, marked as it was by the receipt of telegrams from both the King and the Prince of Wales. As the new, incoming, President it fell to Goldie to "stage-manage" the whole proceedings and this he did with a consummate skill and one which may in no small measure due to the recipe which he himself gives as alone being capable of ensuring excellence in administration—a painstaking attention to detail.

In proposing the toast to the guest of honour, Goldie said:-

My lords and gentlemen, it has been the unbroken custom of the Royal Geographical Society for more years than I can remember, and I believe, on good authority, from time immemorial, to commemorate its foundation by an anniversary Dinner held on the day, which is today, of the Anniversary Meeting. For once that commemoration is in abeyance. We have met here tonight to do honour, not to an institution, but to a man—our guest of the evening, Sir Clements Markham. And as it is my privilege, my sad privilege, because I—but you will understand—have to propose his health, it also devolves upon me to place on record the reasons that have impelled us to this exceptional, this unique, departure from our time-honoured custom. I cannot do this without reviewing to some extent the long and varied career of our distinguished guest, and yet I feel that I must not overstep too far, even on this special occasion, the limits which the progress of civilization has imposed on after-dinner speeches. My only resource is to follow the methods of those who I understand are known in other halls as "lightning artists." I must also, to my great regret, but after careful consideration, exclude from any notice whatever the numerous distinguished and well-known persons—some of them are dining with us tonight—with whom Sir Clements Markham has served, or who have served under his instructions, or who have collaborated with him in any of his undertakings. My sketch, however meagre, must be a personal portrait and not a panopticon of celebrities. Every Yorkshireman in this room, and I have seen some here, knows that Sir Clements Markham comes of a good old family of that county which has given us a champion cricket team and a champion geographer. Every old Westminster (1) here will have fresh in his mind the references to Sir Clements Markham in the Epilogue of last December; but he must be a really old Westminster if he remembers, what I discovered in a book, that so far back as 1867 Sir Clements Markham—or, as he was then, Mr. Markham—was already so famous that he received similar humorous notice in the prologue of the Westminster play of that year. And every naval officer here—there are a good many—will remember that it was as a midshipman in the Royal Navy that our guest took part in the Arctic Expedition of 1850-51. (2) He has just told me with a genuine air of regret that, owing to his being a junior officer—I think he called himself the "Boots" of the expedition—he was only allowed to go for forty-five days' sledge travelling. I should imagine that forty-five days' sledge travelling would be enough to nip in the bud the affections of most people for Arctic travelling. But we know that his were not affected, because we find that twenty-three years later he actually applied for and obtained special leave from the Secretary of State for India in order that he might accompany as far as Greenland—they could not allow him to go further—the Arctic Expedition of 1875. (3) For the last few days I have been taking special interest in Sir Clements Markham, and on Saturday morning I read through his contribution to the *Proceedings,* or what we now call the *Journal,* of the Royal Geographical Society some thirty years ago, describing that most interesting voyage to Greenland and back in the *Alert* and the *Valorous.* I can recommend it to your notice. It is extremely interesting, and I took the trouble to note down the reference; it is p.55, vol. 20 of the *Proceedings.* There can be no doubt that to the very early affection acquired by Sir Clements Markham for polar exploration we are in part indebted for his having, between forty and fifty years later, initiated and carried through that National Antarctic Expedition to which I must refer presently. After some eight years' service he passed for his lieutenancy, and then left the navy. He has not told me why. I know why, by experience. He had a passion for exploration. Having left the service, he went off to South America and explored there for two or three years, chiefly in the forests east of the Andes. (4) After that he entered the India Office, where he remained for twenty-three years; but when I say he remained there, that is only a figure of speech. His soul was not fettered to an office stool, and he appears to have entirely disregarded the advice of Sir Joseph Porter in H.M.S. *Pinafore*; for instead of sticking close to his desk and never going to sea, (5) Sir Clements Markham seems to have been constantly going to sea and exploring distant lands in the service of his country. I cannot closely follow him in his extensive travels; but as he had, for the moment, turned his back on "Greenland's icy mountains," we are not surprised to find him on "India's coral strand," while the breadth of his survey of mankind is perhaps best expressed by the title of one of his many publications, 'From China to Peru.' (6) But perhaps I ought to mention that this particular work of his, 'From China to Peru,' did not describe his own travels. I have been talking to him about it during dinner. It was a question of introducing Chinese coolies into Peru, so that it is quite clear that Sir Clements Markham was the forerunner of Lord Milner. (7) As I have mentioned his publications, let me diverge for a moment, lest I should forget, and let me draw your attention to one of the leading characteristics of our guest tonight—I mean his remarkable and perennial literary activity. I take it for granted that every Fellow of the Royal Geographical Society knows about (one could not expect him to be conversant with) the stream of publications that has come from Sir Clements Markham's pen on geography and cognate subjects, during the forty-three consecutive years he has been a member of our Council, or the fifty and more years he has been a Fellow of our Society. (8) Books, pamphlets, articles, essays, reviews; their name is legion. But the literary world knows that he has not confined himself to these geographical subjects, but that he has dealt, equally effectively although less extensively, with many other matters. I may mention history, biography, memoirs, grammars and dictionaries of little-known languages; but the bibliography of Sir Clements Markham might occupy an evening to itself. I am not sure whether I ought to remind a learned Society that he has written a romance.(9) But I may say in extenuation that it is a quasi-historical romance, and a patriotic romance, because it deals with the supposed adventures of those slaves, *non angli, sed angeli,* whom Pope Gregory the Great saw in Rome.(10) I may add that Sir Clements Markham was careful not to publish this novel until after he had been elected President; but in making this remark, I do not wish to discourage any distinguished novelist who may be present, and who may think that he carries in his pocket the baton of the presidency of a learned society. Well, gentlemen, I have dwelt on his literary activity, partly, of course, on account of the intrinsic excellence of Sir Clements Markham's writings, but also because it is the most tangible, the most visible outward sign that I can present to you of that inward fire, that restless energy, that untiring industry, which only those who have worked with him can fully appreciate. But all this is by way of parenthesis, and I must go back to his foreign travels. His greatest achievement at that time was the introduction from South America into India of the quinine-yielding cinchona tree. That work is so widely known that I need not dwell upon it beyond remarking that it occupied several years and a great deal of energy, and that it produced incalculable beneficial results to large sections of the Indian population. But, to my mind, his most interesting journey must have been when he went as geographer with the British army to Magdala, at the storming of which place he was present—I do not know whether he took an active part or not (I understand Sir Clements to say that he did not kill anybody) during the Abyssinian war of 1867-68.(11) Deeply interesting from the geographical standpoint, because Abyssinia was in those days a very little-known country, but also interesting, I think, on account of the expedition itself, which to my mind has always appeared one of the best conceived, one of the best engineered, and therefore one of the least costly in blood and money, of all the British expeditions of the nineteenth century of the same magnitude and the same military success, although, unfortunately, from a political standpoint, one of the most fruitless, owing to the deplorably low ebb to which the imperial spirit had fallen during the apathetic sixties.(12) Partly on account of the Abyssinian expedition, no doubt, but I suppose mainly for his general valuable service under the India Office, Mr. Markham received a C.B. in 1871; and this may be a convenient moment to remind you that he received his K.C.B. in 1896, that he has been the recipient of various foreign orders of distinction, and that the Congress of Peru voted him a gold medal; and, leaving these State decorations aside, that he is a Fellow of the Royal Society, that he has been the President of the Hakluyt Society for some fifteen years, and that he has received innumerable marks of approbation from many societies both at home and abroad. Yet I am confident that of all the honours that have been showered upon him, and which are not one-half of what he deserves, there is not one that he values more highly, that he cherished more deeply than the Founder's Medal of the Royal Geographical Society. My confidence, is based on the conviction that, although circumstances have led Sir Clements Markham into various occupations, he was really born a geographer. I do not think that he will deny the soft impeachment that geography has been the ruling passion of his life. And if a man is so fortunate, so happily balanced as to be able to live and move and have his being in the realms of science, I ask you what more attractive, what more valuable province could he choose to explore than the science dealing with this outer film of our globe, this thin film of land and air and sea where not only our own race, but where every sentient organism of whose existence we have any knowledge whatever, must dree its weird? Born a geographer, Sir Clements Markham became a Fellow of this Society at the early age of twenty-four. Eight years afterwards he was elected a member of the Council, one of the youngest who has ever sat upon it. and the following year he was elected also to the position of Honorary Secretary, and he filled that post with great distinction for no less than a quarter of a century. In 1888, for some reason, he preferred to be re-elected only as an ordinary member of the Council. That lasted until 1893, by which time he had been for over thirty years a Member of the Council in one capacity or another, and for nearly forty years a Fellow of the Society. If at the end of that period Sir Clements Markham had abandoned the Society, an almost unthinkable hypothesis, he would even then have been handed down in its annals as a shining light; but those forty years were only a prelude to his taking possession of the promised land, for in 1893 he was elected unanimously to the chair, and he has been so re-elected to it year after year, as a mattter of course, until this fatal afternoon, when to our inexpressible regret he retired on the unanswerable, the irresistible plea of the need of rest. I am afraid that my remarks have a tendency to fall into the minor key of an obituary notice; but it is difficult to avoid a pathetic note in lamenting the official decease of an ideal President, especially when the speaker is an ephemeral successor to the office which he has seen raised to a standard that he cannot hope even to approach.(13) Fortunately, the decease in question is only official, as we can see tonight. Unlike Mark Antony, I come to praise Caesar—not to bury him; and as Sir Clements Markham, with true geographical spirit, has accepted a Vice-Presidency, he will be in a position, after a period of rest, to give to his successors the benefit, the immense benefit, of his experience and his advice. I shall not attempt this evening—I have spoken at great length already—to put before you any connected account of the services of our twelve years' President during the time that he was in the chair. In the first place, all that is modern history, and I assume that most of the Fellows of the Society are conversant with it. In the second place, Sir Clements Markham himself gave a brief account of his stewardship this afternoon at the Anniversary Meeting, which I hope a good many of you attended, while those who could not attend will find a report in the *Journal* of our Society; and I would especially draw their attention to that portion referring to the progress of education in this country, to the work which our Society has done in that direction, and to the fact that the two universities of Oxford and Cambridge have established schools of geography, each of which is partly subsidized and partly controlled by the Royal Geographical Society. But I have a third and better reason for not dealing with his Presidentship, and that is I could not possibly condense into a few sentences any intelligible idea of the value of the services that he has rendered to geography in general, and to this Society in particular. It would serve no useful purpose if I read out a list, a sort of index, of the salient acts of his administration. You know as well as I do that administrative work whether it is ruling an empire or a brigade or a battleship or a business, consists in the main, not of striking actions, but of innumerable details, and that success depends on the initiative, the knowledge, the care, and the persistence—I dwell especially on the persistence—with which those details are managed.(14) Now, these are exactly the qualities that have so deeply impressed me in watching the work of Sir Clements Markham during his twelve years' Presidency. But there is one matter to which I must refer, because without it any sketch of Sir Clements Markham's life would really be like the play of *Hamlet* with the Prince of Denmark left out. I refer, of course, to the National Antarctic Expedition.(15) I think that it is generally understood now throughout the country, not only that

Sir Clements Markham initiated the expedition, but that he had, in the first place, to create that public opinion without which progress was impossible. From the day that he became President he took up the matter actively. For some years I used to watch, with admiration mixed with a good deal of scepticism as to the result, his efforts to procure the sinews of war. At last he got the money, thanks to one generous donor,(16) to a large subscription of the Geographical Society, to a great number of smaller subscribers, and to a much-abused Treasury; and having got it, he threw himself heart and soul into the organization of the expedition, and neglected no detail, however minute, that could contribute to its success from the point of view of either geographical exploration or of scientific research, and no detail tending to minimize the risks to the health or lives of those concerned; and I think that his arduous work and anxiety must be also almost compensated by the magnificent results achieved. But as the expedition is to form the subject of the next item on our toast list, I must not further pursue the topic beyond expressing the opinion that it has added to the laurels of the navy, to whose officers and men was entrusted the carrying out of the work; that it has been a genuine satisfaction to the nation, whose maritime primacy, whether naval or commercial, made it almost a duty, or, as Sir Clements Markham has often said, quite a duty, to establish its primacy or exploration in the Antarctic Regions; that it has been a source of legitimate pride to the Royal Geographical Society; and, finally, that it has been the crowning triumph of Sir Clements Markham's career. I think, perhaps, I have said enough to justify our setting aside an Anniversary Dinner on his behalf. There used to be a tacit convention in our Society that it would be little less than treason to suggest that any President could surpass, or even equal, Sir Roderick Murchison.(17) I shall not attempt to weigh these two great geographers nicely in the balance. In the word of Dryden, "Let both divide the crown;"(18) and I venture to prophesy that when the story of the first century of our Society's work comes to be written, the names of Murchison and Markham will be bracketed together as stars of the first magnitude. My lords and gentlemen, I fully decided before coming here tonight that I would speak only of Sir Clements Markham in his public capacities, because it seemed to me that in his presence and before so very large a gathering, most of whom cannot have had the advantage of working with him, and many of whom probably do not know him very intimately, it would be impossible for me to speak of him as a friend and as a colleague in the only way in which I could so speak of him. But it struck me that perhaps one short sentence might at any rate suggest the feelings in this direction of his co-workers, whether on successive councils of the Royal Geographical Society or among that admirable, that highly efficient permanent staff in Saville Row, who have so ably seconded his efforts, and that brief sentence is, that in quitting the Presidential chair he carries with him, not only our respect and admiration, but also our affection and our esteem. And I am confident that the Fellows of this Society scattered over the world will join in our fervent hope that a period of rest will speedily restore his strength, and that he may be spared for many, many years to watch the satisfactory progress of that great Society on whose behalf he has so long, so ably, so strenuously laboured. I venture, then, on behalf of the whole body of the Fellows, those absent as well as those present, to call upon you now to receive with all honours the toast of the evening, "Sir Clements Markham."

(1) Markham had attended Westminster School in 1842-1844, (and had remained an active and enthusiastic "Old Boy" throughout his life), before joining the Royal Navy as a Midshipman. He was then aged fourteen.
(2) This was "The Franklin Search Expedition" in H.M.S. *Assistance,* with Captain Horatio Austin in command.

(3) This was the expedition to Greenland, under Captain (later Sir) George Nares. Markham's cousin, Albert Hastings Markham, was second in command. Nares later commanded H.M.S. *Challenger.*

(4) From this resulted *Cuzio: A journey to the ancient capital of Peru; etc.,* Chapman Hall & Co., London, 1856.

(5) Again Goldie reveals himself as a Gilbert and Sullivan fan. *Pinafore* was written in 1878.

(6) "Immigration to Peru from China", *Geographical Magazine,* Vol. 1, 1874.

(7) Alfred Milner, 1st Viscount, 1854-1925. High Commissioner, South Africa, 1897-1905. In 1904 was responsible for a large injection of Chinese labour.

(8) Markham became the youngest ever Fellow of the R.G.S. in 1854.

(9) Amongst his published works are 18 Biographies, 20 Historical or Ethnographic studies, several works on Polar Exploration and 3 Historical Romances.

(10) This reference to "Not Angles, but Angels", attributed to Pope Gregory the Great (c. 540-604) on seeing a group of Anglo-Saxon children on sale in the Roman slave market, forms the theme of Markham's *Paladins of Edwin the Great [A Tale],* written by Markham and published in London by A. & C. Black, 1896, with a second edition in 1908. Gregory was Pope from A.D. 590-604.

(11) From which resulted *A History of the Abyssinian Expedition,* Macmillan, London, 1869.

(12) Goldie is of course referring primarily to the Parliamentary Declaration of 1865, which deprecated further acquisition of territory by Britain in West Africa, a policy which he was successful in thwarting almost single handedly!

(13) Goldie held the office from 1905 to 1908. Notice again his references to a finite earth, an attitude in considerable contrast to that which generally prevailed at that time.

(14) Comparable to Disraeli's axiom "Nothing is the product of genius unless it is first the product of enthusiasm."

(15) This was Scott's first expedition in 1901. Markham was a driving force, but as is shown by Mill (see page 21) Goldie also played no small part in the arrangements.

(16) This benefactor was Lieut-Colonel Llewellyn Wood Longstaff, 1841-1918.

(17) President from 1843-1871.

(18) "Let old Timotheus yield the prize or both divide the crown." John Dryden, *Alexander's Feast,* 1.167.

III. PRESIDENTIAL ADDRESS TO THE R.G.S. (1906)

This address constitutes the review of the Society's activities throughout the year 1905/6. As such, it was Goldie's first address covering a year of achievement, since he had only assumed the Presidency at the corresponding Anniversary Meeting the year before, when Sir Clements Markham had retired.

Goldie spoke on 21 May, 1906. His speech was workmanlike and comprehensive, and the extract which is reproduced below serves well to indicate the very considerable command which he had over all aspects of the Society's multifarious operations. The address is printed in full in Volume XXVIII, No. 1, July, 1906, of the Geographical Journal.

You are aware that the increasingly scientific character of our geographical work led to the establishment some three of four years ago, of a Research Department, mainly devoted to discussions on subjects of too technical a character to be suitable for our fortnightly meetings. These discussions are, of course, open to all Fellows of the Society, but not to visitors, except by invitation of the Research Committee. This department has been active during the past year. One interesting discussion was that on Mr. Randall MacIver's[1] views as to the date and origin of the Zimbabwe ruins in South Africa, a subject intimately connected with the early history of African exploration. Another valuable discussion was that raised by Mr. Scott Elliot's advocacy of an inquiry into the resources of the Empire.[2] Dr. Nansen's paper on ''The Oscillation of Shore-lines'' also led to a lively discussion by specialists, and I understand that the Research Department may soon expect another paper from Dr. Nansen on the same subject. Certain points connected with the Seistan lake-basin involving technical scientific considerations were also brought before this department by Sir Henry McMahon.[3] A discussion on a paper by Sir Clements Markham dealt with the problems still to be solved in the north polar area, and it is in the attempt to solve these problems that Mr. Einar Mikkelsen[4] is now making his way through Behring straits to Prince Patrick Land. Part of the funds required for the work has been furnished by our Society. Captain Lyons[5] of the Egyptian Survey brought before the Research Department the subject of the Nile flood, which he has now expanded into a book (entitled 'The Physiography of the River Nile and its Basin'), published by the Egyptian Government. This elaborate work contains a mass of valuable information on a most interesting and important subject. Through the Research Department we are initiating an investigation into the changes which have taken place in the North Sea coast region of England during the historical period. The inquiry is a complicated one, and will require the assistance of many workers, but it is worth carrying out, as the results can hardly fail to be of value both to pure geography and to history. In the same way we have arranged for a special investigation of a limited river area in the Thames basin, with a view to discover the rate at which the land is being worn away through influences of rainfall and other causes. We have every reason to hope that in the near future, as trained geographical students become more and more numerous, practical work of various kinds will go on increasing under the auspices of the Society.

I will say a few words on geographical work already completed, or in the course of completion, which has not yet been brought fully to the notice of our Society. Mr. Ellsworth Huntington,(6) a young American explorer of a thorough scientific training, has just returned to this country from Central Asia with his companion, Mr. Barrett. I believe that Mr. Huntington has done much to solve some of the problems connected with the geography, the desiccation, and the archaeology of Central Asia; but a full account from his pen will be published in the *Journal* very shortly. You all know that Dr. Sven Hedin(7) has started on another of his great expeditions. He has already traversed Persia, and he believes that he has solved some of the more important geographical problems of the eastern provinces of that country. We understand that his next field will be Tibet. To us, as British geographers, it is somewhat tantalizing that the British Government has declined to grant permission to experienced British officers(8) to enter Tibet or to explore the unknown reaches of its great rivers; but this is not the place for either approval or condemnation of the policy on which this decision is based. In the continent of Africa, the expedition under Captain Gosling and Lieut. Boyd Alexander(9) has been at work in Nigeria, on Lake Chad, on the Shari, on the Mobangi, and in other regions for about two years. It is making its way to Lado, and may probably before long return down the Nile. Valuable results are expected from this expedition. Some of them have, indeed, already appeared in the *Journal*, including an excellent map of part of Nigeria by Mr. Talbot, one of the surveyors of the expedition. During the past year our Gold Medalist, Commander Peary,(10) has made a fresh start for the purpose of reaching the pole. We wish him every success. Captain Amundsen, who, some three years ago, went out with two or three companions to carry out a series of observations around the north magnetic pole, has accomplished the North-West Passage. He has since returned to his companions, and will probably carry on the projected work for another year. Another interesting matter connected with the north pole region is the establishment of a Danish scientific station at Disco, on the west coast of Greenland, for the purpose of making continuous scientific observations. During the year Captain Scott's magnificent narrative of the National Antarctic Expedition has been given to the world,(11) and we are now awaiting publication of the detailed scientific results. Meanwhile, the scientific results of the Swedish Antarctic Expedition have appeared in several large volumes, some of which are published in English. Strenuous efforts are being made by Lieut. Barne, R.N., to obtain funds for a small Antarctic expedition to supplement that in which he bore so admirable a part. In view of the heavy expenditure recently incurred by the Society in the National Antarctic Expedition, your Council do not at present feel justified even in considering the question of a contribution to the new fund; but they fully recognize the importance of continuity in Antarctic exploration, and they have learned with satisfaction Captain Scott's emphatic opinion as to the qualifications of Lieut. Barne for conducting the proposed enterprise.

With regard to the ever-important subject of geographical education, we have every reason to be satisfied with the progress that has been made during the past year. We have excellent reports from Oxford, where, under the new reader, Dr. Herbertson,(12) the school continues to flourish. The number of students during the present term has increased very largely over the past term, and not a few of them propose to devote themselves specially to obtain the full diploma of the school, which implies a very thorough mastery of the subject in all its departments. A special course of lectures by men of high standing in the different branches of the subject has been instituted there, and these promise to be completely successful. At Cambridge, also, we have reason to believe that steady progress is being made. There, also, a series of lectures has been initiated during the past year. Sir Clements Markham opened the series with a lecture on the Field of Geography. This has been followed by others by Sir Archibald Geikie,(13) Mr. Hogarth,(14) and Major Hills.(15) Perhaps one of the most encouraging steps taken during the year was the issue by the Education Department of a syllabus for geographical teaching in secondary schools. It was hardly to be expected that, at the outset, this syllabus would be all that exacting geographers might wish; but on the whole it is satisfactory, and the mere fact that such a syllabus has been issued by the Education Department is highly significant of the important position which geography has assumed in education in this country, compared to what it was a generation ago. But this spread of geography in recent years, not only in secondary schools and in the universities, but in military and in other circles, is one which would demand an address by itself, and I have only been able to touch upon it here. I need not dwell on the increasingly important position which geography has been allotted in the examination of the University of London, largely due to the energy of Mr. Mackinder,(16) who, as director of the London School of Economics, gives the subject a place of the first importance there.

(1) David Randall-MacIver, 1873-1945; author of *Mediaeval Rhodesia*, Macmillan, London, 1906.

(2) George Francis Scott Elliot, 1862-1934. A botanist.

(3) Sir (Arthur) Henry McMahon, 1862-1949.

(4) Eniar Mikkelsen, 1880-1971.

(5) Lyons, Sir Henry George, 1864-1944; his book was published by the National Print Dept., Cairo, in 1906.

(6) Ellsworth Huntington, see page 240.

(7) Sven Hedin, see page 240.

(8) See page 186 ff., for Goldie's reaction to the refusal of the British Government to support a British expedition through Tibet to attempt an assault on Mount Everest.

(9) Boyd Alexander, author of *From the Niger to the Nile*, Arnold, London, 1907. The expedition began in 1904.

(10) See page 238.

(11) *The Voyage of the Discovery*, by Robert Falcon Scott, Smith, Elder and Co., London, 1905.

(12) Herbertson, Andrew John, died 1914.

(13) Sir Archibald Geikie, 1835-1924.

(14) Hogarth, David George, 1862-1927.

(15) Major E. H. Hills, an expert on topography.

(16) See page 255.

IV. THE EARL OF ONSLOW (1907)

A dinner was given by the African Society at the Criterion on November 29th, 1907. The guest of honour was the President of the Society, the Earl of Onslow. Goldie, who was to succeed him the following year, was in the chair.

The impression can hardly be avoided that the two were not on the best of terms. If Goldie could have said less than he did in introducing the Society's guest, without causing offence, it would have been a miracle. The proceedings were noteworthy, however, for the waspish response which a somewhat vague and ill-considered observation by the speaker induced in Goldie.[1]

I shall say very little, as we have met only to hear Lord Onslow[2] deliver the address which he would have delivered in July, but for a passing indisposition. I have a second reason for brevity. There are two classes of people about whom it is very difficult to speak at length. One class contains men who have done nothing in life: the other contains men who have done a great deal, and have been constantly before the public. To attempt to speak about the latter is like reciting history. What I propose to do is to give you a summary of Lord Onslow's public offices so far as I can remember them. I will only go back twenty years. In 1887, one remembers him as Under-Secretary of State for the Colonies, and if I am not mistaken, with that office, he also held the post of Vice-President of the Colonial Conference. That was a very important matter, because that Colonial Conference was the first of all these Colonial Conferences, and the ancestor of the Imperial Conference which is going to meet in the future, and which is going to draw the Empire into closer bonds. After that, Lord Onslow was Parliamentary Secretary to the Board of Trade. That he gave up only to take the Governorship of New Zealand, where he passed the usual term of four years. On returning home, he found his Party going out of power, but after the General Election of 1895, he became Under-Secretary of State for India until 1900. There, again, was another entirely different order of experience, and of an entirely different character. In 1900, there were Ministerial changes made, and Lord Onslow went back to his old office, the Colonial Office, for another three years. It is owing to his two terms at the Colonial Office that he has been brought so much into contact with Africa. In 1903 he became President of the Board of Agriculture, and that office he held until the General Election of 1905, when, of course, his work came to an end. But then, Lord Onslow, in the House of Lords, was made Chairman of Committees;

280

those who have studied our Constitution know that this is one of the most important offices in the country, involving a great amount of work, and requiring a very high degree of tact, firmness, and courage.

This short summary of his services, I think, sufficient justification for the great gratification which the Society feel in his accepting the office of President.

On the conclusion of Lord Onslow's Presidential Address, Professor Wyndham Dunstan, F.R.S., [3] in proposing the health of the Chairman, said:—

Sir George Goldie is in the category of people of whom it is difficult to speak because they have done so much, and it is unnecessary for me at a meeting of the African Society to speak of the services which the founder of Nigeria has rendered. They are known wherever the history of our Empire is known. But I would like to allude to the additional claims which Sir George Goldie has upon our gratitude as members of the African Society, in connection with recent developments in the Society itself. As a member of the Council, I can testify to the great skill and resources he has shown in dealing with its affairs.

The Chairman, in acknowledging, said: My first duty is to express the feeling which we all have of the valuable nature of the address to which we have listened with so much interest. It was full of matter, and admirable for its quality and tone. Lord Onslow has referred to the fact that a time always arrives when the duty of a company to its shareholders must be incompatible with the interests of the State. I recognised that before I founded the Niger Company, and I put it in a memorandum before Lord Salisbury. I took care to let Lord Salisbury know, and also Lord Rosebery, that I should see that the shareholders, with whose money the Company was built up, were fairly treated. The phrase was that "the pioneer was always ruined," and I said that in this case the pioneer should not be ruined, and he was not. I had gone into the street, and induced people to give me a million to begin with. I was bound to see that they got a fair return for their money. If I had not done so, I should have been committing a breach of trust. My work was an international struggle to obtain British possession of that territory, and I may remind you that this work was brought to a successful conclusion before the Niger charter came to an end. I think you will agree with me that I was absolutely bound to protect the shareholders' interests in the first place, but I may add that during the fifteen years the Charter lasted, we never once had a sustained remonstrance from the Foreign Office. I think that is a record for any Government. My whole interests were Imperial interests, and on the day of the transfer to the Crown, my work was done.

The proceedings then terminated.

(1) See page 56. The report of both Onslow's and Goldie's remarks is contained in Volume VII, No. XXVI, January, 1908, *Journal* of the African Society.

(2) See page 56.

(3) Sir Wyndham Rowland Dunstan, 1861-1949. A noted pharmaceutical chemist and from 1903-1924, Director of the Imperial Institute. In this position, he recast and greatly developed the work of the organisation particularly in the expansion of its research and development interest, which he directed especially towards an investigation of the economic resources of the empire.

V. PRESIDENTIAL ADDRESS TO THE R.G.S. (1908)

This address, Goldie's last as President, was delivered to the 1908 Anniversary Meeting which was held on 25 May, 1908.

In it will be found reference to several items which have by now received the stamp of being of particular interest to him, and other aspects of which are dealt with elsewhere in this work.

The speech has been cut by a very small amount indeed, and it has been reproduced from Volume XXXII, No. 1, July, 1908, of the *Geographical Journal*, where the full text can be found.

. . . Let me first deal briefly with certain questions connected with the growth, both in quantity and quality, of geographical education in this country. Our older Fellows know that the successive Councils of the Society have, especially during the last quarter of a century, made strenuous and unceasing efforts to revolutionize the general position of geography in our national scheme of education. If the Royal Geographical Society had done no other work, it would have amply justified its existence by the success of its labours in this single direction. No one will misunderstand me as endeavouring to conceal or lessen the credit due to our great universities, to other institutions or associations, or to individual geographers not directly connected with our Society, for the important part that they have played in the remarkable movement of the last twenty-five years, which has gradually transformed geography from the Cinderella of the sciences into a respected and sought-after branch of human knowledge; but I fear no contradiction when I assert that the Royal Geographical Society was the initiator, and has been the constant mainspring of that great movement. In my address a year ago, I brought to your notice the efforts we were then making to secure for our subject its proper place (which it had never before had) in the Civil Service examinations, and I indicated the reasons for attaching very high importance to this question. Since then, as you know from the Press, our efforts have been completely successful, thanks to the cordial co-operation of certain of our great universities, and to the wide views taken on this matter both by ministers of the Crown and by the Civil Service commissioners. The effect of this change on the attitude of educational institutions towards our subject is already considerable. It cannot fail to be both widespread and deep unless the instinct of self-preservation should lose its force, which I see no reason to anticipate. Before I leave the subject of education I would remind you that quite recently the University of Edinburgh has established a readership in geography, and that the first occupant of that chair will be our distinguished Fellow, Mr. Chisholm,[1] whose absence from London will be constantly regretted by our Society, and that the University of Sheffield, under the care of its vice-chancellor, Sir Charles Eliot,[2] and with the aid of that liberal citizen, Mr. Allen,[3] has established a lectureship in geography, the first selection for which has not yet been made public. Lectureships in Glasgow University and other parts of the country are, I believe, likely to be established before long. I must also refer briefly to an effort now being made by that strenuous and able geographer, Mr. Mackinder, to establish an effective London School of Geography, mainly for teachers, within his highly successful School of Economics. This effort has the most cordial moral support of our Society, and though the many and varied calls made upon its limited means prevent the Society offering to Mr. Mackinder's scheme direct pecuniary support, yet we feel that the relatively small capital sum which is required to equip the proposed geographical department will be obtained without difficulty.

I will now deal concisely with the main features of exploration during the last twelve months.

Perhaps the most notable event has been the departure of the expedition, under Lieut. Shackleton, [4] for the resumption of work in the Antarctic Regions. He has safely landed, with all his staff and equipment, at a point near the old headquarters of the *Discovery* Expedition. There is reason to believe that Mr. Shackleton will soon be followed by other expeditions. Dr. Charcot[5] will take his departure in August, his main object being to explore the region between King Edward VII Land and Graham Land. Dr. Bruce[6] is endeavouring to obtain funds for a fresh effort, and there is reason to believe that other expeditions are in contemplation; so that, within the next three or four years, we ought to have made very solid progress towards the solution of the remaining unsolved problems of Antarctic geography. During the last twelve months the Natural History Museum has issued a volume of the scientific reports of the National Antarctic Expedition, and other volumes may be expected very shortly. Our Society has just issued the admirable charts of the expedition which have been prepared by Lieut. Mulock

Turning to the North Polar Region, we have to note the return of Mr. Harrison[7] from his attempt to penetrate into the Arctic Ocean, with the expectation of discovering a great extent of land. He was unable to carry out his scheme completely; but he has contributed considerably to our knowledge of the oceanic conditions between the mainland and Banks' Land, and has also done valuable survey and other work along the Arctic coast of America. Mr. Mikkelsen, who had the same end in view, has met with various disasters, which have unfortunately prevented him from accomplishing his designs. Dr. Bruce has given to the Society an address on his work in Spitsbergen, under the auspices of the Prince of Monaco. On the other hand, the Duke of Orleans has been unable to favour us with his promised lecture on the important researches which he accomplished in the Novaya Zemlya region.

Asia is so overrun with expeditions of all nationalities that only very brief reference can be made to them. Dr. Sven Hedin is pursuing his successful career as an explorer of the unknown and less known regions of Tibet and Central Asia. He will have a rich harvest to lay before the world on his return, which, it is hoped, will be this year. There is every likelihood also, that our accomplished Fellow, Dr. Stein,[8] will return this year, to tell us the story of the remarkable discoveries which he has been making in Eastern Turkestan and the borders of China. As Dr. Stein's work is always of the most thorough character, and as he has the assistance of that able surveyor, Ram Singh, his contributions to geography are likely to be of the highest value. I would draw your attention to the publication, during the past year, of Mr. Ellsworth Huntington's remarkable book, entitled "The Pulse of Asia," (9) a work of great interest to those who wish to realize the important bearing which geographical conditions have had on human history and human enterprise in Central Asia. Our knowledge of the Himalayan regions has been considerably extended during the year by the explorations of Dr. and Mrs. Workman, (10) of Dr. Longstaff, (11) and of Messrs. Rubenson and Monrad Aas, and we may expect further important additions to our knowledge of Central Asia from the expedition on which Captain Kozloff (12) has recently set out, while we shall be interested to see the detailed results of Dr. Tafel's (13) work in Eastern Tibet. You may be interested to know that the Society has now in hand, with the assistance of Colonel Maunsell, a new map of the whole of Turkey in Asia.

Africa is still flooded with explorers; but, as might be expected, these explorations are becoming of a more and more special character, seeing that the pioneer work has been practically accomplished. The French, especially, are showing praiseworthy zeal in the exploration of the Sahara, and one of the most interesting expeditions of the past year was that of M. Felix Dubois, (14) across the Sahara to the Niger. Not less important was that of Captain Arnaud, (15) from Algeria to the coast of Dahomey. Captain Lenfant (16) has been doing excellent work between the French Congo and Lake Chad. Dr. Leo Frobenius (17) has entered upon an expedition likely to be fruitful in results from Senegal (by the upper Niger) to the Lower Niger and the Kameruns. In East Africa, Dr. Jaeger has been doing careful work between Mount Kilimanjaro and the Victoria Nyanza. Further south, the elaborate expedition under the Duke of Mecklenburg is covering the ground about Lake Kivu. Our own Society has given substantial support to an interesting piece of work in connection with the Anglo-Belgian Survey in the Ruwenzori region. By the sanction of the authorities, the British members of that expedition have been allowed to undertake the geodetic measurement of a section of the arc, which it is hoped will ultimately be included in a complete geodetic network from the Cape to Cairo. Finally, so far as Africa is concerned, I will draw attention to the remarkably able paper contributed to the *Journal* by Mr. Lamplugh (18) on the Gorge of the Zambezi river.

In South America, Major Fawcett has been re-engaged by the Bolivian Government to carry out the work of delimitation along the frontiers of that country. From the original maps which he has placed at our disposal, it is evident that he will carry out this delimitation with complete competency, and that when his operations are completed, he will have added substantially to our knowledge of the geography of that particular region. Major Fawcett's (19) map will be of great service in the preparation of a new map which the Society has undertaken of a section of South America, embracing part of Bolivia. So far as Central America is concerned, Dr. Tempest Anderson's (20) interesting paper on Guatemala must have been to many of us a revelation as to the real character of the physical geography of that Central American country. At the southern end of the continent, we learn, from communications which have just been received from Dr. Carl Skottsberg, (21) that as commander of the Swedish Magellanian expedition, he has been doing excellent work, both in Tierra del Fuego and in the Falkland Islands. I may, perhaps, remind you that the Surveys of Canada and of the United States are rapidly mapping the whole of those regions, while excellent work of the same nature continues to be done by Argentina and by Chile, and, we have reason to believe, by Brazil.

The same may be said of Australia, the various states of which have competent Surveys, although there still remains a considerable amount of pioneer work to be done in the interior, and in this respect the journey of Mr. Cumming across Western Australia deserves to be mentioned. The Society during the past year has contributed to an expedition which is at work, under Mr. Rivers,[22] on the island of Guadalcanar *(sic),* in the Solomn group, from which we expect interesting results in anthropography. No less interesting results maybe expected from Mr. Louis Becke,[23] whom the Society has also subsidized, and who intends to take up his residence for a considerable period in Bougainville island, one of the same group. Mr. Becke will have with him a competent New Zealand surveyor.

I have not time for more than a cursory reference to the subject of geographical research. At our ordinary meetings we had Dr. Nansen's lecture on North Polar Problems, Mr. Mackinder's on the Geographical Conditions affecting the Development of the British Empire, Mr. Chisholm's on Inland Waterways, and Mr. Gomme's on the Story of London Maps. Nor must I omit to mention Dr. Mill's six lectures on the "Geographical Distribution of Rainfall in the British Islands," which were so highly appreciated and so well attended that they had to be given in the usual hall instead of in the map-room, as was originally intended. Our Research Department has had before it such subjects as Dr. Woolacott's investigation of the "Origin and Influence of the Physical Features of Northumberland and Durham," Dr. Owen's paper on Sea Currents, Lieut. Vivian Thompson's account of the very successful method of Stereo-photo Surveying, Mr. Reeve's account of his New Distance Finder, and the report by Dr. Strahan and his colleagues of their Rivers Investigation . . .

(1) George Goudie Chisholm, 1850-1830.

(2) Sir Alfred Charles Eliot, 1835-1911.

(3) See also page 261. Sheffield, one of the "Red Bricks" was founded in 1905.

(4) Sir Ernest Henry Shackleton, 1874-1922.

(5) Charcot, Jean-Baptiste, 1867-1936. Drowned when sunk off Iceland in 1936, when the French Polar Exploration Vessel *Pourquoi Pas* foundered.

(6) William Spiers Bruce, 1867-1921.

(7) The attempt of 1905-07 aboard the *Jeanette.*

(8) Later Sir Aurel Stein, 1862-1943.

(9) Published by Houghton Mifflin, Boston, 1907.

(10) Dr. W. H. Workman, 1847-1937, and his wife Fanny Bullock Workman, (d. 1925), were both Anglo-American Asian scholars.

(11) See page 186 ff.

(12) Kozloff, Piotr, 1863-1935; Russian explorer of Central Asia.

(13) Dr. Albrecht Tafel.

(14) In 1907, Felix Dubois travelled without escort from Algeria to Timbuktu.

(15) In 1907, also, Arnaud left In Salah and met up with two platoons of Camel Corps out of the French Sudan at Timiaouine Oasis.

(16) In 1900-01, Captain Lenfant navigated a string of twenty laden barges up the Niger from the Delta to Say. In 1902 a barge fleet for the lower Niger was formed, but without much success.

(17) Frobenius, Dr. Leo Victor, 1873-1930.

(18) Lamplugh, Augustus Osborne, 1877-1925.

(19) Major, later Colonel, Percy Fawcett, 1867-1925.

(20) Dr. Tempest Anderson, an authority on volcanoes, 1846-1913.

(21) The expedition lasted from 1907-1909.

(22) William Halse Rivers, 1864-1922.

(23) (George) Louis Becke, 1855-1913. Best known for his "Travel Fiction" adventure stories of the Pacific and South Seas, such as *By Reef and Palm,* etc.

VI. BRITAIN IN AFRICA (1911)

On 22 February, 1911, the African Society gave a dinner in honour of Field Marshal H.R.H. the Duke of Connaught[1] who had just returned from a visit to Africa, including the inauguration of the new Dominion of South Africa, which he had attended as the special representative of his nephew the new King George V.

Just as Goldie's tenure of the Royal Geographical Society Presidency had been marked by the meeting attended by the King and the Prince of Wales when the Duke of Abruzzi had delivered a paper, so this Royal recognition of the African Society marks Goldie's culminating achievement also, for on 28 July of that year, he relinquished the Presidency to Sir Clement Hill. The Duke was not to remain in Britian long, however, and almost immediately afterwards left to take up the post of Governor General of Canada.

Goldie said:—

The toast I have now to propose is, of course, the toast of the evening. It is that of his Royal Highness the Duke of Connaught. In any circumstances, the African Society would deeply value the privilege of receiving his Royal Highness here to-night, but this is a special occasion, because he has quite recently returned from a momentous and historical event in South Africa, where, on behalf of his Majesty the King, he has inaugurated the union into an indivisible nation of races which, during the previous century, had too often been in conflict, and had too often been the victims of philanthropic theories. (2) We, the African Society, like the rest of his Majesty's subjects, followed with the deepest interest the progress of his Royal Highness through the sub-continent, and we give a respectful and cordial welcome to one who has paid many visits to various parts of Africa.

But before I speak to the African Society of its illustrious guest, who is known to all the world, it may not be amiss if I address a few words to His Royal Highness about the African Society, which is not yet known to all the world. For, although its list of members contains many notable names—notable in science, administration, literature, politics, industry, commerce, and in a number of other branches of human activity—it is still young, having been founded only ten years ago. It started originally as the "Mary Kingsley Society," its inception being due to a lady who is here to-night—the historian, Mrs. J. R. Green, who desired to perpetuate the memory of Mary Kingsley and her most valuable work in West Africa. But it was quickly found that, in order to secure effective and wide co-operation, it would be necessary to extend the area and scope of our action; and, accordingly, the society became "The African Society," with the object of diffusing knowledge of all kinds connected with all parts of the continent, but especially British Africa. With a slight variation of the hackneyed phrase of Terence, our society might say:— "Africanus sum, Africani nihil a me alienum puto"; (3) and the misquotation would be the more excusable because Terence was himself an African, and if he had lived twenty centuries or so later would undoubtedly have been dining here to-night and discussing "regions Caesar never knew." (4)

In our early days we were constantly met by the inquiry, "There are so many scientific societies; why start another?" The inquirers had not realised the effect of the change of the relations between Europe and Africa during the last twenty years of the Victorian Era—a transformation which, for suddenness, has probably no parallel in history.

Let us go back to 1879. In North Africa, Western civilisation controlled only maritime Algeria. In East and West Africa, Portugal held a certain amount of coast line; France had not begun her great advance inland from her little colony of Senegal, and Britain still held her small posts on the West Coast, in spite of the recommendation of the celebrated committee of the House of Commons in 1865 that we should withdraw as soon as possible from our scattered settlements on the sea board. But our successful campaigns in Abyssinia and Ashanti—the former in 1868 and the latter in 1873-4—had been followed by the evacuation of both countries. In the extreme south of the continent, two races of European stock (there is, happily, no need now to distinguish between them) held a great area from Cape Agulhas to the Limpopo, but the vast expanses of Southern Africa from the Limpopo to the Equator were only known to the general public at home as mysterious regions where explorers, such as Livingstone and Stanley, periodically vanished and reappeared. I think it will seem incredible to history that twenty years before the close of the nineteenth century nine-tenths of a continent three times the size of Europe, and lying almost in contact with it, was untouched by Western civilisation. This is not the occasion to detail at length the extraordinary change during the following twenty years, but it is absolutely necessary for my argument to say a few words on the part played and the responsibilities—to adopt a phrase of the late President Kruger, "moral and intellectual responsibilities"—assumed by Britain.

The first British move was in the west. In 1879 a company (5) was formed with the express object of obtaining a reversal of the decision of the House of Commons Committee of 1865, for it held, as an axiom, that in uncivilised countries there can be no permanence of commerce or industry without political power. The silent progress of that company during twenty years was marked by the issue of the first African charter in 1886 and by numerous international agreements based on the company's treaties from 1884 onwards, until the Anglo-French agreement of 1899 set the final seal to the rights of Britain in West Africa.

It is not necessary for me to say anything of the second British advance—that in the north-east of Africa. Everyone is familiar with the occupation of Egypt in 1882, then believed to be temporary, in which his Royal Highness took a distinguished part as a Major-General. The splendid subsequent history of Britian in Egypt is known to all the world, as also how it was crowned in 1898 by the occupation of the Anglo-Egyptian Sudan, which put an end to a rule of unspeakable cruelty and oppression.

The third great British advance, in East Africa, began in 1885, when the late Sir William Mackinnon and others were able at last to commence their plans and to initiate schemes which had previously been urged on our Government. His company's charter, issued in 1888, was taken over seven years later, but its great and patriotic work of foundation resulted in Great Britain being, before the close of the century, recognised, by agreements with all the Powers concerned, as possessor of British East Africa and Uganda. (6)

I have reserved for the last the fourth and, to my mind, the most interesting advance, namely, that from South Africa into the regions north of the Limpopo, in which the first practical step was the acquisition of the Lobengula (7) concessions in 1888 and the next the creation of a third chartered company in 1889. The career of that great company (8) has been so public, and the personality of its founder, Mr. Cecil Rhodes, so striking, that even those who have not stood, as His Royal Highness has stood, by Mr. Rhodes's lonely grave on the Matoppos, cannot but be impressed by the romantic side to that great chapter of African history.

Meanwhile, Belgium, France, Germany, Italy, and Portugal were engaged in similar work, and had obtained similar recognitions from the Powers interested, with the result that before the close of the nineteenth century and of the Victorian Era, Western civilisation had—one might say suddenly—assumed responsibility for the whole of that vast continent, with the exception of Abyssinia and Morocco. A new and incalculable importance had thus been given to the scientific study of all African matters. Native laws and customs, native ideas and wants, native languages and religions, the vegetable and mineral resources and potentialities of the continent, its existing trade routes, its future railway systems, the causes, prevention, and treatment of tropical diseases both in man and beast—these and many more subjects became of urgent importance to the colonising nations and to all who are moved by scientific or humanitarian motives.

Now I ask you, is it surprising that a large body of private individuals in this public-spirited country should have felt impelled to unite for the collection and diffusion of so much needed knowledge and to form themselves into an African society specifically directed to this object? And is it not natural that they should desire to give a special welcome to His Royal Highness on his return from that continent?

We have not, of course, the presumption to claim the Duke of Connaught for Africa alone. If we did so, no doubt India, for instance, might raise a stronger claim. I had the advantage of visiting that country eight years ago, (9) when His Royal Highness, on behalf of his late Majesty, opened the Coronation Durbar, and I was immensely impressed by the unanimous feelings of deep respect, admiration, and attachment expressed by all the Anglo-Indians one met, whether soldiers or civilians, who had been in India during his command in Bengal from 1883 to 1886, or as Commander-in-Chief of the Bombay Presidency from 1886 to 1890.

Or, passing from the Far East to the Far West, I am not sure that Canada might not make a claim upon her coming Governor-General, and might remind us that his earliest active service was during the Fenian raid into Canada more than forty years ago. (10) Nevertheless, Africa still claims him, for he has given a great deal of time and attention to Africa. Besides his share in the Egyptian campaign of 1882, His Royal Highness has been many times up the Nile, and has travelled in the Sudan as far as Fashoda. We remember his opening that colossal work the Assouan Dam. He has travelled extensively in East Africa. Some four or five years ago, when Inspector-General of the Forces, he made a tour in South Africa, and his quite recent journey into the Equatorial region north of the Zambesi is fresh in our minds. By some of us special satisfaction is felt at His Royal Highness having, on his homeward voyage, visited Sierra Leone, which, formerly known as the "white man's grave," seems likely, owing to the progress of bacteriology, to become a winter resort for invalids.

I have now put before you, as briefly as I could, some of the grounds which emboldened your Council to ask that the African Society might have the honour of receiving His Royal Highness, and I invite you to drink to his health and to wish him God-speed in the Imperial mission that lies before him in the West.

(1) Arthur William Patrick Albert, Duke of Connaught and Strathearn, 1850-1942; third (and favourite) son of Queen Victoria. Served in Egypt on the Staff of the G.O.C., in 1882; Inspector General of the Forces, 1904-19. Governor General of Canada, 1913-17. H.R.H. commanded the Guards Brigade at the battle of Tel el Kebir.

(2) Goldie is referring, of course, to the formal inauguration of the Union of South Africa 1911-61, after which it became a Republic and was forced out of the Commonwealth.

(3) Terence (Publius Terentius Afer, c. 185-159 B.C.). *Homo sum: humani nil a me alienum puto (Heauton Timorumenos,* 77). "I am a man; I hold that nothing human is alien to me." Terence was a "Libyan"—probably Berber—slave who was given a liberal education and then his freedom by his master Terentius Lucanus, the Senator.

(4) "Regions Caesar never knew, thy posterity shall sway . . ."; from *Boadicea* by William Cowper, *v.* 8.
      " . . . Where his eagles never flew
           None invincible as they."

(5) His Royal guest notwithstanding, Goldie is now advancing a claim for the United African Company to be considered as the pioneer in the acquisition of British West Africa's most valuable and populous area—or, indeed in the acquisition of any British Protectorate at all on that Continent. Note the specificity of his claim, "with the express purpose etc." This is not the only time that Goldie makes such a claim.

(6) The Imperial British East Africa Company.

(7) Lobengula, 2nd and last King of the Matabele. Ascended the throne in 1870, two years after the death of his father and after a bitter civil war. In 1816 he granted farming "concessions" and in 1888, mineral "concessions" to Cecil Rhodes' Company, but after the discovery of gold near Bulawayo in 1893 the Company embarked upon the Matabele War, and the Kingdom was destroyed.

(8) The British South Africa Company.

(9) In 1903.

(10) "Fenian Raids" were mounted on Canada from the United States in 1866, 1870 and in 1871. They were all ineffectual and abortive. The Fenian Society was founded jointly in the U.S. and Ireland by John O'Mahony and James Stephens respectively. In 1865, the Fenian Society split into two wings, the one under W. R. Roberts being especially active against Canada.

VII. SIR FREDERICK LUGARD (1912)

ADDRESS DELIVERED BY SIR GEORGE GOLDIE AT A DINNER OF THE AFRICAN SOCIETY IN HONOUR OF SIR FREDERICK LUGARD AND OF THE RT. HON. JOHN BURNS, M.P., SIR HESKETH BELL, SIR WALTER EGERTON AND SIR PERCY GIROUARD, 16 MAY, 1912.

At this dinner, at which Sir Clement Hill, as President of the Society presided, Goldie was the principal speaker. Lugard, who had handed over to Sir Percy Girouard in Northern Nigeria in 1907, after Wallace—late of the Company—had held the fort for a while, had then been posted to Hong Kong. In 1912, however, he was on his way back from the Far East to take up his appointment as Governor of both Northern and Southern Nigeria. Later, of course, on the occasion of the formal amalgamation of the two territories into one Nigeria—in 1914—he became Governor-General.

Lugard [1] was the principal guest of honour. But it can not be denied that the inclusion, on an occasion such as this, of four others as well to share in the glory—and especially when three of them were themselves pro-consuls of such distinction as Egerton, [2] Hesketh Bell [3] and Girouard [4] made this particular dinner more than merely run-of-the-mill. The inclusion of Burns, [5] moreover, even though he was Minister of Health, was a little unusual.

As has been noted, John Elliot Burns had briefly been employed by the United African Company at Akassa as a foreman engineer. He had remained on the Coast exactly one year, a fact which hardly qualified him for expert status and, though he was now a respected and distinguished Minister of the Crown, his interests and activities during the interim had not maintained him in any sort of active relationship with African affairs. But he was a man whom Goldie had taken to, most probably during their encounters on the London County Council, and the two could now be said to be almost cronies—though they often had had their differences. It is hard to believe that there would have been a relationship of this sort growing out of Burns' African experience alone. Why therefore is Goldie, who is clearly the person responsible for Burns'

290

presence at all, so fulsome in his praise of what Burns had done for Africa? Why indeed, had Goldie decided in this instance to break his self-imposed and self-proclaimed rule of silence in respect of matters concerning West Africa? [6]

Nicolson [7] maintains that the dinner was a carefully designed endeavour to impress on Lugard that there were others who had been involved in the development of British West Africa and that it was not the "one man show" that he and Flora Shaw (Lady Lugard) so often seemed to be trying to make out. Today, we should say that tendencies towards a cult of personality were being discouraged!

The open breach which occurred between Goldie and Lugard has been discussed at some length, but it is difficult to believe that it had reached anything like implacability at the time that Goldie is speaking. His insistence, towards the end of the address which follows, that his very first "official" acquaintance with Lugard "developed in the course of a very few weeks into an intimate friendship *which has lasted ever since*" belies such an interpretation. There was no need for Goldie to say that if it was not true. Certainly, in saying what he does in his address, he might be seen to be "needling" Lugard somewhat. He is bantering and playful in joshing Lugard, as he does, about his "excessive modesty." But Goldie was prone to do this sort of thing and even, on occasions, took a similar tilt at a target as remote and austere as the Marquess of Salisbury, who was very touchy indeed on matters of protocol. [8] This was not the first time that he had made references of this nature either. [9] Goldie therefore meant what he said, or else was "mending his fences," which means that he was both willing and anxious that the breach, if it had occurred, should be closed. [10] Clearly, either the rift came later, or Lugard rejected the olive branch if it had occurred already. By 1925, it had become a chasm.

On 21 May of that year, the African Society, of which Goldie had been both a Founder Member and a most distinguished Past President, gave another dinner in honour of "General Rt. Hon. Sir Frederick Lugard, P.C., G.C.M.G., D.S.O., at which he was to be presented with the third Gold Medal that the Society had ever awarded. Goldie was then dying of emphysema.

The best that Lugard could find to say about the man who had once been his patron, who had given him his first real grip on fame as opposed to notoriety was this:—" . . . the Tropical part of Africa lacked the driving force of any great personality. It is true that Sir George Goldie had the foresight to acquire Nigeria for the Empire, but he did not live and work in Africa . . ." [11] Such a comment did little credit to the man who made it!

To return to the dinner of the African Society, held at the Trocadero Restaurant on 16th May, 1912, Sir Clement Hill [12] introduced Goldie as the principal speaker. He said:—

"You must allow me to say that the dinner which is taking place tonight in reference to Nigeria could not possibly have taken place had it not been for the existence of Sir George Goldie. Sir George Goldie was the founder of Nigeria. To him we, as the African Society—far above the African Society, the British Empire—owe the acquisition of these great territories now known as Nigeria. And I feel certain that this Society will be glad to think that the toast of the evening is to be proposed tonight in the presence of so many governors by the founder of Nigeria and a gentleman who has been for two years President of this Society."(13)

Goldie replied:—

When last I vacated the chair, which you, Mr. President, so much more worthily fill, I little thought that I should so soon be again addressing the African Society, but this evening held for me an attraction which I could not resist. It is not Nigeria that has mainly drawn me here to-night, though, of course, it has a permanent interest for a British society founded for the express purpose of collecting and diffusing knowledge on African questions, and there are reasons why it should have a special interest for us at the present moment. Nigeria for a very long time has been a source of monetary benefit to the wage-earning classes of this country, as well as to the consumers and users of African products, and I am told by those who ought to know that we are likely to see great further development. Remember also that this means not merely an advantage to the wage-earning classes of Great Britain, but also a corresponding advantage to what I may call the wage-earning classes of Nigeria. I make no apology for putting in the forefront this purely material or monetary aspect. It was said, nineteen centuries ago, that man cannot live by bread alone, and that great truth applies equally to those aggregations of individuals that we call nations. But the very form of the aphorism, "by bread *alone*," implies that physical well-being is the necessary basis of all higher social development, and we, in the twentieth century, are at last beginning to recognise that fact in relation to the children of our own land.

But I venture to think that it will be in the direction of the higher social development of Nigeria that our Society will take more interest. It is always the complex and difficult problems that are most attractive, and I can imagine no position in which there are more difficult and complex problems to solve than that in which an administrator of a United Nigeria will find himself. Just consider what it is. In these days in which science is taking such extraordinary strides, it would be presumptuous to assert that Nigeria can never become a white man's land. Any man who says that convicts himself of an unscientific mind; but for present practical purposes we are justified in assuming Nigeria is not a white man's land. It contains already a vast native population, and under the climatic and social conditions of equatorial Africa that population must increase rapidly to immense proportions now that slave raiding and intertribal wars have ceased. But it is not the numbers of the population of Nigeria that will make the difficulty of the administrator; it is the heterogeneous nature of their characters and training. Whoever administers Nigeria—an United Nigeria—in the near future will have to deal with almost every stage of humanity since the dawn of history. In the material and political sphere he will have to deal with people ranging from the almost autonomous families who earn their living on their solitary platforms fishing in the swamps of the delta, up to highly organised communities having a large acquaintance with the decorative and useful arts. In the sphere of emotions he will have to deal with people ranging from the lowest form of fetishism up to those who hold the pure tenets of Islam; and in the intellectual sphere he will have to deal with those ranging from ignorant savagery up to a race of whom a high authority, Henry M. Stanley, once said that they were the only African people who loved a book.

292

Let me give a third reason why Nigeria is interesting at the present moment. That young brunette has come out at last and attracted the notice of the general public. During her infancy she enjoyed only the affection of her fond parents, and later on she engaged the spasmodic attentions of statesmen, who sometimes played the part of foster mother, and sometimes that of step-mother. But a great change has taken place. During the last few months the man in the street, and especially the man in Throgmorton Street, has paid attention to Nigeria. All that missionaries and explorers and geographers and administrators and merchants had striven to do for a whole generation, viz., to bring Nigeria home to the British public, has been achieved in the course of a few months by a base metal—tin. When, last December, I went abroad, there was probably not one man in ten out of those who are styled by courtesy the educated classes who could have at once laid his finger on the spot where Nigeria was on a terrestrial globe. I have come back in May, and I find that everybody not only knows that Nigeria is in West Africa, but is familiar with geographical details which I, a past President of the Royal Geographical Society, am unacquainted with. One can hardly open a newspaper now without seeing the name of Nigeria. All that to my mind is very healthy. I do not mean that any region, any nation, can prosper permanently on mineral products. But there is no question that the influx of capital due to the discovery of mineral products, will have its effect in giving an impulse to more lasting forms of development. (14)

We have another attraction to-night in the presence of a galaxy of eminent Nigerians. I will name three of four in order of seniority—that is, seniority of acquaintence with Nigeria. The first is the Rt. Hon. John Burns. That carries us back a whole generation. Mr. Burns went out to fill a post of very considerable responsibility; his business was to create what was then much wanted, the first dockyard in tropical Africa. He was then a very young man, and you may ask why he was accepted. Well! I have always believed in youth, so he went out, and most fully justified our choice, and left a record there that no Nigerian will ever forget.

I must pass from him to Sir Walter Egerton, who has, as we all know, most admirably carried on the government of Southern Nigeria for a great number of years, and to Sir Percy Girouard, who has introduced railways into Northern Nigeria with the same skill, knowledge, and energy that he showed in managing the railways of South Africa during the war, and to Sir Hesketh Bell, (15) who has faithfully carried on the principles laid down by his predecessors; but I am unable to do justice to them, because I must now come to the real reason why I am here to-night. You, Mr. President, were good enough to have it intimated to me that, if I proposed this toast of Nigeria, I should have the great privilege of coupling with it the name of Sir Frederick Lugard. It is a great many years since I first made the official acquaintance of Captain Lugard, as he was then, and that official acquaintance developed in the course of a very few weeks into an intimate friendship which has lasted ever since, and it was not many months before I discovered that he possessed an extraordinary combination of qualities. I cannot enumerate them all. I will mention only that infinite capacity for taking pains which is one of the definitions of genius and a habit (which he has never lost) of putting his work in the foreground and keeping himself in the background. (16)

But there is a particular reason why we are entertaining Sir Frederick Lugard to-night, and that is the union of the two Nigerias. Now, Mr. President, in 1899 you were the permanent official who represented the Foreign Office as regards the vast African possessions which the Foreign Office in those days supervised, and it will be in your memory a very careful inquiry by a committee of which I was a member as to whether Nigeria should be one province or two (17). I think to-day that the decision then arrived at of establishing two Nigerias was a sound one. I also think to-day that the decision to have a single Nigeria is a sound one. The fact is that circumstances have altered, but some of you may have been struck by the very odd coincidence that it was a Unionist Government that went in for decentralisation in 1899, and it was the Government of which the Rt. Hon. John Burns is a distinguished member that is going for centralisation in 1912. That is one of the ironies of fate. The moral is that every case must be decided according to its merits. Whatever may be the opinion as to the policy of union, there can be only one opinion as to the right man to govern the united province. On that not only those in Africa, but every individual in this country who follows up affairs, will agree that Sir Frederick Lugard is the one man who ought to take up this great work. I shall not presume to dilate on Sir Frederick's great record, which is as well known to you and to the world at large as it is to me. But I know him to be as modest as he is great, and that any prolongation of these remarks must be painful to him, so I will at once propose the toast of "Nigeria," coupled with the name of General Sir Frederick Lugard.

(1) Lugard, Frederick Dealtry (Sir, later Lord Lugard of Abinger), 1858-1945. Served in Afghanistan and Burma, then employed by the Imperial Br. East Africa Co., the Royal Niger Co., and the British South Africa Company. Selected to raise and command the West African Frontier Force, 1898. High Commissioner Northern Nigeria, 1900-1906. Governor of Hong Kong, 1907-1912. Governor General of Nigeria, 1912-1919.

(2) Egerton, Sir Walter, 1858-1947. 1880-1903, Strait Settlements; 1903, High Commissioner, Southern Nigeria; 1904-06, Governor of Lagos; 1906-12, Governor of Southern Nigeria; 1912-17, Governor of British Guyana.

(3) See page 45.

(4) Girouard, Sir Percy, 1867-1932. A Colonel in the Canadian Royal Engineers, Girouard, who was of French-Canadian origin, was a "railwayman." He was the Director of Railways in both Egypt and South Africa during military campaigns and became Governor of Northern Nigeria in 1907-08 to push railway construction. He became Governor of the East African Protectorate in 1909-12.

(5) See page 184.

(6) See page 268.

(7) Nicolson, *op cit.*, p. 191.

(8) Richard Burton once told Frank Harris that he believed he had been denied preferment because he had once addressed the Marquis as "Salisbury" instead of as "My Lord." Frank Harris, *My Life and Loves,* Grove Press, N.Y., 1963, p.618.

(9) See page 72.

(10) See page 40.

(11) See the speech by Lugard as recorded in the *Journal* of the African Society, Vol. XXIV, pp. 354 *et seq.*, 1924/25.

(12) See page 297.

(13) *Journal* of the African Society, Vol XI, 1911-12; pp. 459-460.

(14) Goldie holds to the same conviction that he expressed nearly two decades earlier. See pages 66 ff., 105 and 107.

(15) In view of the Burdon-Bell correspondence from the National Archives, Nigeria, this remark now raises echoes that are almost uncanny. Hesketh Bell had two "predecessors" in the strict heirarchy of Colonial Office protocol—Lugard and Girouard. But, as he made clear to Burdon, *the policy he was executing was Goldie's* NOT Lugard's. The existence of the Hesketh Bell minute to Burdon destroys the premises behind Perham's suggestion that both Bell and Girouard treated Lugard's work "with almost reverent acceptance," *for they did not regard it as being his.* See Perham *op cit.,* page 471. See also page 45 *et seq.*

(16) *L'oeuvre c'est tout: L'homme c'est rien!* Also, see page 274 fn. 14.

(17) The Selborne Committee, see page 297 surely this is incontrovertible proof of the weight which Goldie attached to his role therein?

VII

Extracts from the Draft Report of the Selborne Committee (1898)

A group of District Police with the Royal Niger Constabulary on the Lower Niger. *Courtesy U.A.C. International.*

Officers of the West African Frontier Force with Colonel Willcocks (Commandant) and Sir F. D. Lugard (High Commissioner) at Jebba. *Courtesy U.A.C. International.*

THE DRAFT REPORT OF THE SELBORNE COMMITTEE

(C.O. 446/3.)

THE SELBORNE COMMITTEE

The following extract from the interdepartmental "Selborne Committee"—the Committee of experts set up under the Chairmanship of the Under-Secretary of State, the Earl of Selborne in 1898—reproduces all the relevant information as to the recommendations arrived at and the views expressed by Goldie.

The Committee consisted of:—

The Earl of Selborne [1]
The Right Honourable Sir George Goldie, P.C., K.C.M.G.
Sir Clement Hill, K.C.M.G. [2]
Sir Ralph Moor, K.C.M.G. [3]
R. L. Antrobus, Esq., C.B., and [4]
Sir H. McCallum, K.C.M.G. [5]

It reported to the Secretary of State for the Colonies, Mr. Joseph Chamberlain.

The Committee's terms of reference were:—

I. Should the future administration of the three territories of Lagos, Niger Coast Protectorate and Niger Company's Territories be united under one head or, if not, into how many administrations and with what limits and with what seats of Government? What would be the arrangement of Military Forces? What Customs duties? On the basis of a Customs Union, what Customs Union? What other, if any, taxation is possible? What Estimate can be furnished of the cost of administration and of the probable revenue?

II. As regards Sokoto, what is to be the future policy as to a Resident, as to Railways and as to Bornu and Rabah? (sic) [6]

The Committee did not understand that they were required to present an elaborate and formal report which could be submitted to Parliament, but rather that they should without delay furnish such concise and specific answers to the questions asked as would furnish a convenient basis for the interdepartmental consideration of the matters referred to. Accordingly I present the following report as expressing the general view of the Committee. Where any of its members differ from these conclusions, I make mention of the fact.

Its recommendations—in synopsis—were:—

(1) On the question of the future administration of the 3 territories, Lagos, Niger Coast Protectorate and Niger Company's Territories—whether they should be united under one head—we are of opinion that the object to be aimed at is the eventual establishment of a Governor General for the whole of the territories, resident in the territories.

But we feel that the appointment of a Governor General is inadvisable at present.

(a) For climatic reasons: it would be impossible under present circumstances to get any but a young man to do efficient work in West Africa—and even a young man would require to be away to recruit his health one third or more of the time, so that continuity of policy would be lost.

Sir G. Goldie said that, this difficulty would be removed in time—by the establishment of a "Simla" in the Bautshi Highlands. (7)

(b) Because of the absence of telegraphs and roads which render it really more difficult to communicate with all the parts of the territory from any possible point within it than from Downing Street.

This difficulty will, of course, also be removed in time.

For the present we are of opinion that the administration of these territories must be conducted through the medium of provincial Governors under the direct superintendence of the Colonial Office.

The Public Record Office copy of the Report then shows a significant deletion of some lines—a dozen approximately—on page 386, where the text has been completely excised, after which the opening lines of page 387 are out of context. It then continues:—

We are of opinion that the Niger cannot form the dividing line; both banks of the Niger must be under one jurisdiction on account of the international questions which will probably arise in connection with the use of the river; and also because if there are different jurisdictions on opposite banks the administration of the criminal and civil law will be more difficult. (8)

The division we think should be into a Maritime Province and a Sudan Province, between the Sudan regions governed by Mohammedans and the Pagan regions of the Niger Delta, including however with the latter the Mohammedan Yorubas . . . The seat of Government of the Sudan Province we think should for the present be Lokoja. (9)

The question then arises whether the Maritime Province should be further divided.

If it is divided, we are agreed that the division should be into a western province with its capital at Lagos, and with an area similar to that of the existing Colony of Lagos, and an eastern province with its capital at Asaba including the rest of the Niger Delta. (10)

There then occurs the following passage which has been struck out by four vertical lines in ink and which concern the continuation of the Company's main headquarters at Asaba:—

On the whole, however, we are of opinion that the entire Maritime Province can be administered as one. On this point Mr. Antrobus does not differ but prefers to reserve his judgment. The question whether the best seat of Government will be Asaba or Lagos must be left to be settled by experience.

The report then continues:—

The Provinces, whether two or three in number, will have to be divided into Divisions and Districts.

Sir H. McCallum recommends that the native chiefs, subsidised as hereinafter suggested by him, should in all cases be organised as Village and District Councils.

We recommend that the Military Force should be one for both or all three of the Provinces and that its units should be strictly interchangeable between them. Such interchangeability is recommended with reference to emergencies arising in any particular province in ordinary times and in default of such emergencies the interchangeability should not be used more than is absolutely necessary, because it is highly desirable that the officers of the Force should acquire fluency in the language spoken by their men and whereas the *lingua franca* of the Sudan Province will be beyond all question Hausa, Yoruba will be the more important language in the Maritime Province or Provinces.

The division therefore of the Military Force in each province should be retained under the command of a separate Commandant.

We have reason to believe that a project is under the consideration of Her Majesty's Government by which the Colonial Military Forces in all the West African Colonies and territories are to be brought into combination. Regarding this proposal from the point of view of Nigeria we venture to consider it of the highest importance and practicability.

We hope that a General will be appointed as Inspecting Officer for a term of years for the whole of the Colonial Military Forces in West Africa and we think that this Officer, if appointed should be resident in England, should make annual tours of inspection to the West Coast of Africa, and should assume the command of all expeditions of importance in West Africa during his term of office. (11) The great advantage of this arrangement will be that, if an expedition were necessary, say against Rabah, and the division of the Colonial Military Force in the Sudan province was augmented for the occasion by contingents of the Colonial Military Forces in the Maritime province, Gold Coast and Sierra Leone, these various contingents would all find themselves equally serving under their own General Officer in command. (12)

After considering the financial prospects of the new Administrations—admittedly in the broadest and most tentative terms, the Report then goes on to examine the effect on Revenue of the revocation of the Company's Charter.

. . . . We recommend that there should be a customs union for both the provinces or all three provinces of Nigeria and that in the first instance the existing Lagos tariff should be universally adopted . . .

It must be observed that the result of the approaching Brussels Liquor Conference may not improbably be to diminish the estimated revenue by checking the importation of spirits in Lagos and the Niger Coast Protectorate by international agreement.

Sir George Goldie on the other hand expresses as his opinion that the effect of the abolition of the Royal Niger Company's trade regulations will be a large increase in the trade in spirits and a proportional rise in the revenue.

We are unanimously of opinion that it would not be prudent at the present time to attempt to impose any form of direct taxation on the natives, but with the exception of Sir George Goldie we think that a village tax in some form or other may be gradually imposed in the future. (13)

Sir H. McCallum however suggests that some form of internal taxation may be devised from which payments can be made to the chiefs who in consequence of British intervention have been or will be deprived of their former sources of income, the principal one of which was slave-raiding. Such internal taxation might he thinks take the form in the maritime province of lekin (14) duties on such articles as spirits and salt and might be farmed out to the chiefs themselves.

It then proceeds:—

In respect of Sokoto and as to Bornu and Rabah the Commitee have naturally felt themselves bound to be guided by the advice of Sir George Goldie, who almost alone had knowledge on the subject.

He is of opinion that the Sultan of Sokoto would not voluntarily receive a Resident accompanied by a sufficient guard. It would therefore he thinks be useless to send one until the Fulah power is crushed.

No attempt should be made to do this by a general *coup de main.* It should be done gradually, each Emir being taken in turn. The necessity for a forward policy is not so urgent now that Her Majesty's Government have come to an agreement with the French Government and Her Majesty's Government may well wait until the new Governor of the Sudan province can advise them as to the time for making an advance. (15)

Sir George Goldie does not think that the Sultan of Sokoto, if pressed, would refuse to accept a Resident with a small escort, but he would deprecate in the strongest possible manner a Resident being sent to Sokoto under such conditions. He thinks that the fate of Major Cavagnari would probably await him. (16)

On the subject of the proposed railway line—the sure hallmark, within the context of the time, of Colonial incorporation—the Committee was clearly greatly divided.

With reference to railway construction the Committee are unanimously of opinion that the great trunk line must be one from Kano down the valley of the Kaduna to its junction with the Niger. Thence goods would at first have to be conveyed by water to meet the ocean-going steamers on the coast, but in future the line should be continued to some port where ocean-going steamers can come alongside.

Such a port might either be Lagos or Warri or Sapele on the Benin River or some spot on the Niger itself such as Asaba.

At present the port of Lagos can only accommodate steamers of not more than nine feet draught. Merchandize has therefore to be shipped from the railway into branch steamers and carried to Forcados and there transhipped into ocean-going steamers. An estimate has been prepared by Messrs. Shelford and Co. for making the harbour of Lagos practicable for ocean-going steamers by the removal of the bar at a cost of £800,000. (17)

Sir H. McCallum is of opinion that the line now being constructed from Lagos to Abeokuta should be continued to the Niger to meet the line from Kano, as he is of opinion that Lagos harbour when improved at the estimated cost will in every respect form the most suitable port.

Sir Ralph Moor and Sir George Goldie on the contrary think that the natural point, to which the line from Kano should be eventually extended, is either Warri or Sapele on the Benin River, both of which are, they assert, already available as ports for ocean-going steamers of the largest size. I understand that Sir H. McCallum does not admit this last assertion.

So far as the very limited information at our disposal enables us to form an opinion, which must however be considered as purely provisional and subject to further knowledge and experience; Sir Clement Hill and I are inclined to agree with Sir Ralph Moor and Sir George Goldie.

Mr. Antrobus holds his opinion on this subject in suspense. [18]

If the view of Sir Ralph Moor and Sir George Goldie should eventually be adopted, the future course of the Lagos line would have to be decided with a view to developing the Colony of Lagos and the district of Bornu [19] rather than with a view to meeting the line from Kano.

As regards the possibility of making a port in the Niger itself whether at Asaba or at some other spot, a much more careful survey of the Niger must be made before any opinion can be formed. It appears that extensive works would certainly be necessary for deepening the bed of the Niger in certain places and for removing obstacles. [20]

and finally concludes:—

The earliest possible date for the change of administration is January the first, 1899, and we recommend that it should take place then. [21]

(1) William Waldegrave Palmer, 2nd Earl of Selborne, 1859-1942. Under Secretary of State for the Colonies, 1895-1900; First Lord, 1900-05; Governor of the Transvaal and High Commissioner for South Africa, 1905-10; etc. Married a daughter of the 3rd Marquis of Salisbury.

(2) Hill, Sir Clement H. Foreign Office; Ass. Clerk of African Dept. 1886; Knighted, 1897; Head of the African Dept., 1894; Could not be considered amongst Goldie's warmest supporters, although he appears to mellow later.

(3) See page 103.

(4) Antrobus, Sir Reginald A., 1853-1942. Colonial Office, 1877; 1889-90, Governor of St. Helena; 1898-1909 Assistant Under Secretary; 1908-18, Sen. Crown Agent for the Colonies.

(5) McCallum, Sir Henry E., 1852-1919. Royal Engineers 1871; held various colonial posts until appointed Governor of Lagos, 1897-99; Newfoundland, 1899-1901; Natal, 1901-07; Ceylon, 1907-13.

(6) Rabeh Zobeir, c. 1844-1900. Sudanese-Arab adventurer. Reputedly a son by concubinage of Zobeir Pasha, Rabeh is said to have formed part of the escort provided for Miss Alexandrine Tinné (1839-69) on her journey to Bahr el Gazal, 1862-4. In July, 1879 he fled west from a force under Gessi Pasha which had been sent by Gordon to subdue him and his co-commander Suleiman, Zobeir's son, who was captured and executed on Gordon's orders. Rabeh was invited by the Madhi to join him in 1884, but declined, refusing to go to Omdurman. In 1891, he marched against Wadai and conquered it, then, in 1893, he overcame Bornu, putting the Shehu to death. Avoiding confrontation with the Company, he was killed by the French under Major François-Joseph Lamy at the battle of Kusseri on 20 April, 1900. Rabeh's headquarters were latterly at Dikwa. The last of the Sudanic conquerors.

(7) Echoing his previous position, see page 109.

(8) This question of split jurisdiction bedevilled the relationship between the Company and the Oil Rivers Protectorate (etc.) throughout the whole of its existence.

(9) A decision which Lugard immediately negated on assuming office, on grounds which were somewhat specious.

(10) The two "provinces" were amalgamated in 1906. Eventually, the Western Provinces' Headquarters were at Ibadan and the Eastern Provinces' at Enugu, but this was not until the full amalgamation had been effected and the modern Nigeria had almost fully emerged.

(11) This provision was eventually written into the Standing Orders of the West African Frontier Force and was invoked by the Colonial Office in 1903. See Muffett, D.J.M. *Concerning Brave Captains,* André Deutsch, London, 1964. Cap. 7.

(12) The grounds cited in 1903 in the decision referred to in fn. (11).

(13) Such a proposal for direct taxation would, of course run absolutely counter to and be utterly destructive of any policy of "Indirect Rule." Goldie had no option but to oppose such a step if he was to be true to his principles—as he was! In fact, the Government *never* levied direct taxes in the Northern Region, save under the very restricted provisions of the Income Tax Ordinance. Such taxes were levied by the Native Authorities, which then paid Government a proportion for central services etc.

(14) Lekin Duties: Excise Duties on staples.

(15) This is just what did not happen, Lugard taking pains to conceal his intentions from the Colonial Office until the last moment. See Muffett *op cit.*

(16) Cavagnari, Sir Pierre Louis Napoleon, 1841-1879. French-born British Military Administrator; Naturalised and entered the service of the East India Co., 1858; Indian Mutiny, 1858-59; 1861 Punjab; 1877, Deputy Commissioner, Peshawar; 1879, Kabul. Negotiated the Treaty of Gandamak in 1879, apparently putting Afghanistan under British protection. Appointed British Resident, Kabul, 1879; took up appointment in July but in September he and his whole Staff as well as a small escort were massacred in a sudden rising. Actually Goldie was remarkably prescient. This is exactly what happened to Captain G. W. Moloney at Keffi in 1902.

(17) The bar was never "removed" but a ship channel was dredged.

(18) Antrobus was always a very cautious man!

(19) The railway was extended to Bornu in the 1960's!

(20) Undertaken by the Dutch engineering firm NEDECO between 1950 and 1958, in part only, in connection with the Niger Dam at Kanji.

(21) Actually not effected until 1 January, 1900. These extracts are reproduced with the permission of the Keeper of the Public Records Office, which is acknowledged with gratitude.

Epilogue

The Empire landing Sir F. Lugard at Jebba at the end of January, 1900, on moving his headquarters there. *Courtesy U.A.C. International.*

Gun practice at Lokoja. *Courtesy U.A.C. International.*

On the ninth of January, 1935, the following letter appeared in the *Times* from Goldie's old friend and colleague, Leonard Darwin, the son of the great scientist.

SIR GEORGE GOLDIE

THE MAKING OF NIGERIA

TO THE EDITOR OF THE TIMES

Sir,—Next spring it will be just 50 years since all the territories which came under the rule of the Royal Niger Company in 1886 were secured by treaty rights to Great Britain, some 300,000 square miles being thus added to the Empire as the result of the almost single-handed efforts of Sir George Taubman Goldie.

Ever since I began to watch his career when at the Intelligence Department of the War Office I have wondered why his name is so little known to the public, for in fact he was connected with an "achievement only to be paralleled" at that date by that previously accomplished by the East India Company in the course of two centuries *(The Times,* January 1, 1900).

Why no full life of Goldie has yet appeared has been partly explained by the fact that before his death he burnt every record about himself in his possession. Something has now been done to fill this gap by the recent publication of Mr. Stephen Gwynn's excellent account of the making of Nigeria, which is combined with Lady Gerald Wellesley's vivid sketch of this very strange but very great man. May I therefore now appeal to *The Times* to use its great influence to ensure recognition of this significant date in colonial expansion and of the man responsible for it? Goldie should always be reckoned among the three or four of our greatest Empire builders, and as one who did his work without thought of any gain for himself.

Yours faithfully,

LEONARD DARWIN.
Cripps's Corner, Forest Row, Jan. 7.

Nothing came of the plea for recognition which this letter contained. Already, the myth of Lugardian omniscience had taken too firm a hold on the public imagination—in so far indeed that it was in the slightest degree concerned with Nigerian affairs at all!

Later, that myth was to be further institutionalised. Only recently has it come to be questioned, and it is to be hoped that this questioning will not be abated by the sometimes rather strident cries of his defenders. It is not lèse-majesty to apply the basic principles of critical analysis to an examination of Lugard's role in the formative days of Nigeria's incorporation under the Crown. His achievements are big enough in themselves, without any need to endow him with infallibility or to ascribe to him the authorship of concepts which he was presented with by others.

Above all, it should never be forgotten that, but for Sir George Goldie, Nigeria, as it stands today, the giant of Africa, and the political system on that continent most widely regarded as being the first (if not the only one) likely to emerge as a major World Power, would never have existed.

Had it not been for him, the most probable effect of the European scramble into West Africa would have been the creation of a mere couple of tiny British-oriented enclaves bedded in an enormous French dominated amporphism which, given an inevitable emergence into independence which such a hegemony would by no means have assured, would almost certainly have produced a group of relatively minor polities, some land-locked, many poverty stricken, most scarcely viable and none with the multi-potentiality that Nigeria so patently displays.

As Lord Scarbrough attested, Nigeria was founded by one man—George Taubman Goldie.

Index

View of Lokoja town. *Courtesy U.A.C. International.*

Loko market. *Courtesy U.A.C. International.*

Index

313

314

315

316

Indirect Rule (I.R.) (cont.)

Maclean in formulating doctrine, 43 ff.; Sir Hesketh Bell on, 45 ff.; 47; G.'s views on, 53 ff.; G. develops opposition to L.'s policy of, after 1912, 54; L.'s perversion of, 54 ff.; Allows for "civilized" as opposed to "alien" govt., 57; G.'s speeches foreshadow enunciation of doctrine of, 109; 135.

Jackson, Sir John
50; and fn.

Joffre, Marshal of France J. J. C.
Capture of Timbuktu, 79; and fn. 14.

Johnston, Sir Harry
33; 67; and fn.; 108; and fn.; 116; 167; Views of on Hausas, 167; 235.

Keith-Johnston, Alexander
215 fn. 14.

Keltie, (Sir) J. Scott
Secretary of R.G.S., 39; Draws G.'s attention to Lugard's proposed attack on him, 39; Book by, 67; and fn.; 253.

Kingsley, Mary
View of on G., 43; Discussion of I.R. by, 43-44; Shared G.'s dream of Empire, 83 fn.; Her view of Fashoda incident, 83; 114; G.'s tribute to, 105; Her plan for Nigeria, 102; 109 fn. 21; Book, *West African Studies,* 137; Letter to Edward Clodd, 139; African Society founded in honour of, 30 fn. 7; 286.

Kimberly, Lord; see Wodehouse, John

Kirk, Sir John
103; 104; Report on activities of R.N.C., 103; and fn.; Joins R.N.C., 103; On the Hausa Association, 169; In Africa, 215; and fn.

Koetze, Mr. Justice J. G.
202; 203 fn.

Kona, Pagan town of
Attacked by Mizon, 154 ff.; 170.

L'Affaire Mizon, see Mizon, L.A.A.

Laing, Alexander Gordon
94; and fn.

Laird, Macgregor
95; and fn.

Lagden, Sir Godfrey
267; and fn.

Lambermont, Charles-Auguste, Baron
Arbitrator in the case of the *Sergent Malamine,* 171; and fn.; Finds in favour of R.N.C. as to legality of its action, 171.

Lambton, John George (Earl of Durham)
229; and fn.

Lander, John
95 fn.

Lander, Richard
95.

Landeshoheit, The concept of
Fundamentally rejected by African Tribal Societies, 118.

Las Casas, Bishop Bartolomé de
Initiated Slave Trade, 116; and fn.

320

322

324

Rhodes, Cecil (cont.) with Flora Shaw, 29 fn. 28; In Africa, 171; Death of, 176; Mentioned, 288.

Richardson, James 95.

Robinson, Canon C. H. 116; and fn.; And the Hausa Ass., 166 ff.

Robinson, J. A., Rev. Missionary, 165; Death of, 165. Hausa Ass. founded in memory of, 165 ff.

Roche Abbey Poem by G., 25.

Rochefort, Henry Denounces Mizon in *L'Intransigeant,* 172.

Rohlf, Friedrich Gerhard 96; 215.

Roope Reeve, Mr. Raymond (Q.C.) 204 fn. 11.

Rose—Innes, Sir James 267; and fn.

Rosmersholm 19; and fn.

Royal Niger Company, Chartered and Limited 20; Undertaking to limit use of its troops, 28; and fn.; 37 fn.; Its Administrative hand over to the Crown, 29-30; Staff made available to Crown, 30 fn. Its Administration impugned by Flora Shaw, 40 ff.; Inaccurate references to it by the Earl of Onslow, 56; G's. care for the shareholders of, 56; 57; 176; 194; 280 ff.; G. claims territory on behalf of as far north as Air or Asben, 70; Employment of Africans by, 73 fn.; 82; 142; 160; 197; Its leadership in supression of the Liquor Trade, 86-88; Campaign by against Bida and Ilorin, 91; 107; 194 ff.; Dogged pursuit of objective of, 96; Challenged on Middle Niger by French, 91; Treaty making by, 91; Proposed continuation of Administration but abandonment of trading by, 102; 113; Method of Administration explained, 109 ff.; Refutation of Flora Shaw's assumptions of the inadequacy of, 137; Council of, 151; Role of in the partition of Africa, 171; 240; 287; G. on the revocation of the Charter of, 198 ff.

Royal Niger Constabulary, The Attendance in the Diamond Jubilee Procession, 91.

Royal Yacht Squadron, The G. a member of, 171; 172;

Sadi-Carnot, François Marie, President of France Publicly embraces Mizon's concubine, 171; and fn.

Salisbury, Lord G's. anger at, 21; Supports G. in the Somerset incident, 35; G's. jibe

Wilberforce, Bishop Samuel

Authored doggerel verse quoted by G., 70; and fn.; Debated Huxley, 76.

Willcocks, Colonel James (later Gen. Sir)

L's Deputy Commandant, 34; and fn.; involved in clash with Ilorin, 34; ff.; Despatches Somerset with a patrol, 34; Learned his lesson, 44 fn.

Wilmot, Hon. Alexander
267; and fn.

Wodehouse, John, 1st Earl of Kimberly
103; and fn.

Wolesley, Field Marshal Sir Garnet
On Board of Hausa Association, 165; ff.; Referred to, 254 fn.

World, The
123; 126 fn. 23.

Zainabu
Mizon's concubine, 171 fn.

Zanzibar, Island of
26.

Zentgraff, Dr. Eugen
146.

Zoubeir (Zubairu) Emir of Yola
Relations with Mizon, 152.

Zweifel Case, The
136; and fn.

Zweifel, Joshué
136 fn.

Selected Bibliography

Selected Bibliography

In addition to *THE TIMES,* without whose contribution this book could not have appeared in its present form and the courteous, and even enthusiastic response of whose archivists to innumerable and tedious enquiries is most gratefully acknowledged, the *JOURNALS* or the *PROCEEDINGS* of the following learned Societies were heavily drawn upon:

The African Society
The British Association for the Advancement of Science
The Royal Geographical Society
The Royal Scottish Geographical Society
To all of them a full measure of appreciation is due!

The following works published as books were also consulted for either background or data.

Clodd, Edward	*Memories;* London, 1916.
Crowder, Michael	*West African Resistance;* London, 1971.
Flint, J. E.	*Sir George Goldie and the making of Nigeria;* Oxford, 1960.
Harris, Frank	*My Life and Loves;* New York, 1963.
Kingsley, Mary	*Travels in West Africa;* London, 1897.
	West African Studies; London, 1899.
Leslie, Anita	*The Marlborough House Set;* New York, 1972.
Lugard, Lord	*Political Memoranda;* London, 1906.
	The Dual Mandate; London, 1922.
Mannix, J.	*African Bush Adventure;* London, 1954.
Mill, H. R.	*The Record of the Royal Geographical Society, 1830-1930;* London, 1930.
Moberly Bell, E.	*Flora Shaw, (Lady Lugard, D.B.E.);* London, 1947.
Muffett, D. J. M.	*Concerning Brave Captains;* London, 1964.
Nicolson, I. F.	*The Administration of Nigeria, 1900-1960;* Oxford, 1969.
Perham, Dame M.	*Lugard, The Years of Adventure;* London, 1956.
	Lugard, The Years of Authority; London, 1960.
(with Bull, M.)	*The Diaries of Lord Lugard, 1889-1898;* London, 1970.
Ponsonby, Sir F.	*Recollections of Three Reigns;* London, 1951.
Robinson, C.	*Hausaland, or Fifteen Hundred Miles Through the Central Sudan;* London, 1896.
Temple, Charles L.	*Native Races and Their Rulers;* Cape Town, 1918.

Vandeleur, C. F. S.   *Campaigning on the Upper Nile and Niger;* London, 1898.

Wellesley, Lady G.   *Sir George Goldie: Founder of Nigeria;* London, (with historical essay   1934.
by Stephen Gwynn)

The following Government publications were also utilised.

Draft *Report* of the Selborne Committee, 1898 (C.O.446/3).
Report, Royal Commission into the Conduct of the War in South Africa, 1906.
Colonial *Annual Reports* (Nigeria), 1900-1911.

Gazetteers of the following Provinces of Northern Nigeria:—

Kontagora Province
Muri Province
Nassarawa Province
Nupe Province

Other works consulted are referred to in the appropriate footnotes.